Narrative in Culture

Narrative
in Culture

Edited by
Astrid Erll and Roy Sommer

DE GRUYTER

ISBN 978-3-11-076344-7
e-ISBN (PDF) 978-3-11-065437-0
e-ISBN (EPUB) 978-3-11-065230-7

Library of Congress Control Number: 2019938703

Bibliographic information published by the Deutsche Nationalbibliothek
The Deutsche Nationalbibliothek lists this publication in the Deutsche Nationalbibliografie;
detailed bibliographic data are available on the Internet at http://dnb.dnb.de.

© 2021 Walter de Gruyter GmbH, Berlin/Boston
This volume is text- and page-identical with the hardback published in 2019.
Typesetting: Integra Software Services Pvt. Ltd.
Printing and binding: CPI books GmbH, Leck
Cover image: Using images by
Juliia Tochilina/iStock/Getty Images Plus (forest) and
luchioly/iStock/Getty Images Plus (raven)

www.degruyter.com

Contents

Astrid Erll and Roy Sommer
A Tale of Two Concepts: Ansgar Nünning at Sixty —— 1

Michael Basseler
Stories of Dangerous Life in the Post-Trauma Age: Toward a Cultural Narratology of Resilience —— 15

Sibylle Baumbach
Mind the Narratives: Towards a Cultural Narratology of Attention —— 37

Marion Gymnich
The End of the World (as We Know It)? – Cultural Ways of Worldmaking in Contemporary Post-Apocalyptic Narratives —— 57

Jan Rupp
Plumbing Distant Spatiotemporal Scales: Towards an Econarratology of Planetary Memory in Narratives of the Global South —— 75

Birgit Neumann
Narrative Forms in the Age of the Anthropocene: Negotiating Human-Nonhuman Relations in Global South Novels —— 91

Sandra Heinen
Fact, Fiction, and Everything in-between: Strategies of Reader Activation in Postcolonial Graphic Narratives —— 109

Carola Surkamp
'It's Not Our Opinion, It's the Opinion of Our roles' – *Fremdverstehen* Revisited or: Where Foreign Language Education and Narratology Can Meet —— 129

Hanne Birk
Narrative and Visual Resources of Culture in Contemporary Indigenous Children's Books from Australia —— 149

Stella Butter
Troubling Justice: Narratives of Revenge —— 165

Guido Isekenmeier
Erin Burnett in Mali: Bardic Television and the Genealogy of Cultural Narratology —— 185

Dorothee Birke
New Media Narratives: Olivia Sudjic's *Sympathy* and Identity in the Digital Age —— 199

Bruno Zerweck
The 'Death' of the Unreliable Narrator: Toward a Functional History of Narrative Unreliability —— 215

Astrid Erll
Odyssean Travels: The Migration of Narrative Form (Homer – Lamb – Joyce) —— 241

Janine Hauthal
A European Storyteller? Collective Narration in John Berger's *Into Their Labours* —— 269

Roy Sommer
Brexit as Cultural Performance: Towards a Narratology of Social Drama —— 293

Contributors —— 321

Astrid Erll and Roy Sommer
A Tale of Two Concepts:
Ansgar Nünning at Sixty

One of the nicest rituals in academic life is celebrating the achievements of esteemed colleagues by honoring them with a collection of articles dedicated to their work. What is the point of such a retrospective enterprise, one might wonder, if its addressee, the narratee of the story it is about to tell, shows no signs of slowing down? This volume seeks to redefine the generic template of the academic Festschrift, reinventing it as a prospective narrative of encouragement that not only dwells on past achievements but also outlines – through a series of original essays on core issues and emergent fields of cultural and historical narratology – the shape of things to come.

There is hardly anyone who has devoted more time, energy, and enthusiasm to furthering our discipline, English and American Studies, or, more generally, to the study of literature and culture than Ansgar Nünning. Chair of English and American Literature at Giessen University since 1995, Ansgar Nünning is the author and co-author of 16 books and more than 250 scholarly articles on a wide variety of topics, ranging from the forms and functions of literature, through the concepts needed for a systematic study of culture, to the principles of education. His oeuvre, partly translated into French, Portuguese, Korean, Chinese, Albanian, Hungarian, and Polish, is completed by an impressive amount of editorial work. In recognition of his outstanding achievements in the fields of narratology, literary studies, and cultural theory, Ansgar Nünning was awarded an honorary doctorate by the University of Stockholm in 2017.

As if this were not enough, Ansgar Nünning is also a pioneer in the field of postgraduate education. He is the founding director of both the Giessen Graduate School for the Humanities (GGK, established in 2000) and the International Graduate Centre for the Study of Culture (GCSC), a flagship institution funded since 2006 by the German 'Excellence Initiative', which aims at providing the best research conditions for PhD students and postdoctoral fellows. He established Giessen University's International PhD program "Literary and Cultural Studies", launched in 2002, and has been a member of the core faculty of the European PhD network for literary and cultural studies, with partner institutions at the University of Helsinki, the University of Bergamo, the Catholic University of Lisbon, the University of Graz, and the University of Stockholm, for more than fifteen years. In 2007 he was awarded the "Excellence in Teaching"

https://doi.org/10.1515/9783110654370-001

prize by the Hessian Ministry of Higher Education, Research and the Arts together with the Hertie Foundation.

Given the broad range of his research, any attempt to do justice to Ansgar Nünning's work, short of an in-depth scholarly biography, must be too reductionist to warrant the effort. In order to appreciate his staggering versatility, we will approach Ansgar Nünning from four closely related angles, portraying him as an avid reader, a prolific scholar, a relentless editor, and a pioneering builder of institutions. These four perspectives – or, narratologically speaking, subplots – coalesce into a single coherent narrative, a tale of two concepts that link Ansgar Nünning's earliest interests to his most recent efforts: narrative and culture. As every narratologist knows, however, a plot presupposes some sort of meaningful connection between its basic elements; hence our focus is on one specific trajectory: narrative *in* culture. This inconspicuous preposition best expresses what Ansgar Nünning's work stands for: the conviction that the study of culture and the study of narrative are neither unrelated nor competing endeavors, but complementary perspectives: ways of investigating the processes, manifestations, and effects of human worldmaking that have emerged from different scholarly traditions but work best in unison.

Narrative in Culture, the title of this volume, thus serves as a motto that allows us to track and trace Ansgar Nünning's development as a literary scholar. Three recurring themes have guided his thinking for the last thirty years, namely the semantics of narrative form, the performative power of narrative as a cultural way of worldmaking, and the value of literature as an art form and cognitive resource. If narrative is a dominant way of worldmaking, as Ansgar Nünning (2013a) has consistently and convincingly argued, the study of culture has to take into account how stories emerge, circulate, and allow – or fail to allow – narrative communities to develop a sense of coherence and belonging. A narrative take on culture not only foregrounds the worldmaking qualities of fictional narration and factual storytelling, but also investigates their disruptive potential. Cultural theory, a truly cross-disciplinary endeavor, and narratology, the systematic study of the forms and functions of narrative, are not conceptual alternatives but complementary frameworks that provide us with new "ways of seeing" (John Berger), helping us to come to terms with diverse histories and possible worlds, both past and future.

Thirty years ago, Ansgar Nünning's PhD dissertation on the forms and functions of narrative mediation in the novels of George Eliot (Nünning 1989) marked the beginning of a lifelong engagement with literature that has taken him from what is today called classical narratology, rooted in the structuralist paradigm of the 1970s and 1980s, to the realms of culture, cognition, and memory that have redefined literary studies since the 1990s. If we look at this itinerary in more detail, one thing becomes immediately clear: Ansgar Nünning's journey through histories and worlds, ideas and discourses was never a one-directional trip from A (narrative) to B (culture), but rather a series of excursions and forays into the unknown – excursions from which he, the avid reader, always returned to base. And base meant literature, and narrative fiction in particular.

When engaging with the difficult task of charting Ansgar Nünning's encounters with the novel, his preferred genre, one might imagine him as a reader who keeps returning to his favorites, but is equally fascinated by new developments. His recent interview with *DIEGESIS* is a case in point. When asked which narrative he would like to take with him to a lonely island, he replied with atypical indecision that he would be tempted to consider Eliot's *Middlemarch* (the subject of his dissertation), James Joyce's *Ulysses*, Thomas Mann's *The Magic Mountain*, Gabriel García Marquez's *Cien años de soledad*, Marcel Proust's *À la recherche du temps perdu*, Laurence Sterne's *Tristram Shandy*, or Virginia Woolf's novels – in fact, all of them (his second book, with Vera Nünning, was an introduction to the great modernist writer; Nünning and Nünning 1991). Finally he admitted that "rather than re-read a novel that I greatly enjoyed on previous occasions, I would probably end up with a pile of narratives that I have wanted to read for a long time, but have not yet got round to" (Nünning 2015b, 104).

His wide reading, helped by an astounding memory that never fails to amaze those who have the pleasure of working with him, has always informed his theoretical contributions. Following his awe-inspiring two-volume history and theory of the historical novel since 1945, accepted as a *Habilitationsschrift* (postdoctoral thesis) at the University of Cologne in 1993 (Nünning 1995a, 1995b), he turned to unreliable narration, publishing a collection of articles that continued his transition from a predominantly formalist to a contextualist and cognitivist framework (Nünning et al. 1998). This framework is based on a foundational insight that has shaped his work ever since, the conviction that in semiotic objects – across genres, modes, media, and periods – form not only matters, but actually *is* content, in the sense that linguistic, visual, or auditive signs construct what we regard as the meaning of a given narrative. Likewise, form and function cannot be separated, although for heuristic reasons they sometimes need to be viewed in isolation.

Ansgar Nünning's early work on unreliability and his reconceptualization of the implied author, his contributions to the theory and history of literary perspectives and multiperspectivity (Nünning and Nünning 2000), and his explorations of mediality, intermediality, metaization, and generic hybridity as a driving force behind the development of the novel (Nünning and Nünning 2002a; 2002b; Nünning and Schwanecke 2013) are all attempts to come to terms with the semantic potential of narrative techniques. To this he soon added a second line of investigation, namely the performative power of narrative. Exploring the uses of storytelling in drama (Nünning and Sommer 2011), he continued to outline his transgeneric take on narrative as a performative mode of expression that is tied neither to a specific corpus of texts or set of genres nor to the medium of verbal literature. Later, he once again widened his horizons, exploring the performative power of narrative as a cultural way of worldmaking in a series of articles and collections.

While Ansgar Nünning's work was initially dedicated to the complex relationships between narrative forms and aesthetic experience, as well as to an understanding of literary history as a key aspect of cultural history, he soon adopted an even wider lens on narrative and culture. As the editor of an immensely successful dictionary of literary and cultural theory (*Metzler Lexikon Literatur- und Kulturtheorie*, first published in 1998 and meanwhile in its fifth edition) he not only helped a whole generation of aspiring graduate students to get their heads around the explosion of new and rediscovered theories since the 1990s, but also contributed to shaping the academic field of (English) literary studies. He was a driving force behind the reinvention of an erstwhile philological discipline as a modern field that integrates, and contributes to, developments in neighboring disciplines in the humanities, the social sciences, and even beyond (Nünning and Schlaeger 2007).

Ansgar Nünning's preoccupation with the nexus of narrative and culture ultimately led to the foundation of the GCSC, fully dedicated to the interdisciplinary study of culture at Giessen University, in 2006. Around this time, Ansgar Nünning had already ventured into the emergent field of interdisciplinary memory studies (Nünning 2003; Erll and Nünning 2008). From there he proceeded to explore more systematically the concepts of metanarrative and metafiction (Nünning 2004; 2005c), the confluences of metaphor, narrative, and cultural memory (Nünning 2005a), hybrid genres like meta(auto)biographies (Nünning 2005b; 2013b), the fact-fiction divide (e.g. Nünning 2004; 2005b) as well as the notions of traveling concepts and cultural transfers (Nünning et al. 2014; Neumann and Nünning 2012).

Since the early 2010s, Ansgar Nünning has directed his attention more specifically at the ways and purposes of cultural worldmaking (see Nünning et al. 2010) and the study of culture (Nünning 2014). His work on the nature of events (Nünning 2010) and turning points (Nünning and Sicks 2012), the intersection of cognitive metaphor theory and the transnational study of culture (Nünning 2014), narratives of crisis and catastrophes (Nünning 2011; 2013c), the metaphorical framing of financial crises (2015a), the narrativity of rituals (Nünning and Nünning 2013), the epistemological relevance of literary studies as a life science (Nünning and Basseler 2013), and his analysis of the narrative rhetoric of George W. Bush (Nünning and Nünning 2017a) demonstrate time and again that narrative self-fashioning and community-building are really two sides of the same coin. In his interview with *DIEGESIS*, he outlines a research program that will not only keep cultural narratologists busy for years to come, but also paves the way for new forms of ideology critique that focus not only on political messages but also on the functioning of rhetoric in a way that appeals to our storied minds, the core of any narrative community:

> The worldmaking capacity of stories and storytelling has not received the degree of attention that it arguably deserves. The same holds true for the performative power of narratives to create or make not only worlds, but also communities, nations, and selves, as well as conflicts, enemies, and wars. Moreover, narratives can also be abused as ideological and propagandistic devices, as means of fostering collective delusions, and as 'weapons of mass destruction'. Narratology is thus not just indispensable for literary and cultural studies. On the contrary, anyone interested in what has been, and is, going on in the realms of finance, law and politics just cannot afford to ignore the study and theory of factual and fictional narratives. (Nünning 2015b, 105)

This visionary proposal also lends weight to Ansgar Nünning's argument that literary and cultural studies should be considered as a form of life science (Nünning 2015c), for more often than not, a story reveals as much about life as a microscope. This is also true in a more literal sense, as his latest work on the capacity of narratives to foster wellbeing shows (Nünning and Nünning 2017b). The emergent fields of narrative medicine and happiness studies have caught Ansgar Nünning's most recent attention, and it will be interesting to see where his narratological journey through Anglophone literatures and cultures will take him – and us – in the future.

Of course, this story of the development of an avid reader and eminent scholar is a retrospective construction. As Ansgar Nünning (2012) reminds us in a highly original interpretation of Kazuo Ishiguro's novel *The Remains of the Day*, it always seems easy to identify turning points and interpret the meaning of events with the benefit of hindsight. This is also true of our struggling attempt to summarize his multi-faceted work, an endeavor that also operates with chronology and closure – the domain of narrative. Ansgar Nünning never considers anything done, but will resume the concerns of his earlier work whenever a different theoretical or methodological angle allows him to shed new light on old issues. Thus, he recently revisited unreliable narration and the narratology of drama (Nünning and Schwanecke 2015), concepts he had worked on in the late 1990s and early 2000s.

Likewise, his recent engagement with standards, norms, and evaluations in literary studies (see Nünning et al. 2015), as well as epistemological issues (Nünning 2016), takes up again his earlier interest in methodology.

Let us now turn to his work as a curator and disseminator of knowledge, which completes his staggering oeuvre. One can only marvel, in a slight variation on the subtitle of Sir Walter Scott's novel *Waverley* (1814), at the fact that 'tis indeed sixty books since Ansgar Nünning started fostering and promoting cutting-edge research as an editor and co-editor. Ansgar Nünning has conceived and launched twelve book series to date that have flourished under his aegis. These include the immensely popular ELCH (Studies in English Literary and Cultural History) series with Wissenschaftlicher Verlag Trier, which, at the time of writing, comprises 75 volumes, the renowned Media and Cultural Memory (MCM, De Gruyter) series he has co-edited with Astrid Erll since 2004, and Concepts for the Study of Culture (CSC, De Gruyter), which he co-edits with his GCSC colleagues Doris Bachmann-Medick, Horst Carl, and Wolfgang Hallet.

The Klett Uni-Wissen series, aimed at introducing students to the field of English and American studies, is evidence of the fact that Ansgar Nünning's research interests have always been accompanied by a strong focus on teaching at all levels, from undergraduate to postgraduate studies (see also Surkamp and Nünning 2006). Both as a scholar and university teacher, Ansgar Nünning has, indeed, always been an 'influencer' in the best (or rather, the only acceptable) sense of the word: someone who is at the cutting edge of research and still readily shares his knowledge with newcomers to the field, always eager to help the next generation join the community.

Our tale of two concepts would not be complete without a fourth subplot. If the versatility of its protagonist, a truly round character, defies any attempt at pinpointing one specific academic profile that 'formats' him once and for all as a narratologist, Anglicist, cultural theorist, structuralist, or something else along these lines, we need to be more creative. Should we not rather approach Ansgar Nünning, the self-confessed Humboldtian constructivist, via his own ideas in "Bildung durch Wissenschaft als die Idee der Universität", as the title of his latest programmatic reflection on the value of scholarship in the tradition of Humboldt has it (see Nünning 2018): that the *raison d'être* of the university is education through scholarship? A working life built on humanist notions of *Bildung* as well as a deep interest in literature as an artistic – and often artful – expression of human consciousness implies not a classical success story as we know it from the worlds of money and power, but a narrative of values and ideals that have inspired, and continue to inspire, others; a story of institution building as team building; and a story of academic leadership built on mutual trust, shared ideas, collaborative research, and joint publications.

This is a story of the university in the original meaning of *universitas*: community. The foundational idea of the university can be traced back to medieval colleges that imagined and described themselves as a specific kind of community, the *universitas scholarium et magistrorum*. Later the word *universitas* was used without a specifier and then, somewhere along the way, its original meaning changed, so that university today designates not a community but an institution. Yet university should not be reduced to a community of professionals, a scholarly guild, as it were. It is a community of learners, whether they be students or teachers – a community united by the will to knowledge and education in the spirit of the Enlightenment and along the lines laid out by Wilhelm von Humboldt.

Ansgar Nünning not only believes in community but knows how to create university in the best sense of the word. Establishing a study group (Cultural and Historical Narratology) on his arrival in Giessen as a newly appointed, tenured professor, he revealed an extraordinary talent for creating stimulating conditions for collaborative research and encouraging young scholars to pursue their own interests. The study group was followed by the graduate school, among the first of its kind in Germany, and finally the GCSC. Meanwhile, 76 PhD students have completed their dissertations under his supervision, 63 at Giessen and 13 at international universities, and many more are currently working toward their degrees. In addition to this, he has helped six postdoctoral researchers to complete and defend their *Habilitation* theses.

Complementing the traditional model of one-to-one supervision with innovative forms of peer-to-peer coaching and early access to publication, he has always embodied the idea that joint projects involving graduate students, postdoctoral researchers, and professors are the best way to foster a scholarly community. This is, by any standard, an amazing track record. The profiler trying to sum up the values Ansgar Nünning stands for could do far worse than calling him an inspired, and inspirational, *primus inter pares*. His vision of mutual support in the pursuit of knowledge and *Bildung* revives the ancient idea of *communitas* and reinvents university for the 21st century, not as a neoliberal enterprise built on planning, controlling, and monitoring, but as a space for creative thinking and open debate. That space now exists, thanks to Ansgar Nünning, at Alter Steinbacher Weg 38 on the campus of Giessen University.

We should also mention that, by freely sharing his visions, ideas, and ways of thinking, Ansgar Nünning has expanded horizons and brought people together, not just metaphorically but also very literally. Several marriages among former PhD students who have found not just professional fulfillment, but also private happiness at Giessen are strong evidence of the particular appeal of narrative and culture. This extended family of scholars would have filled not just one Festschrift, but a whole series of books. For this reason, the contributors to this volume only represent the first and second generations of scholars who have on countless occasions benefitted from his generous help and advice.

This volume contains 15 essays we happily dedicate to Ansgar Nünning on the occasion of his 60th birthday. We all started our careers at Giessen, way back when the GCSC was still a strip of grass between the cafeteria and the parking lot. Many things have changed since then, but narrative and culture have stayed with us. Ansgar Nünning provided us with concepts and tools that we have further developed, refined, and supplemented, applying them in other places and contexts to meet different, but ultimately related challenges. The essays collected here offer a wide range of case studies and theoretical approaches that give an overview of the state of the art in cultural narratology and aim at boosting the narrative study of culture in the 21st century.

Michael Basseler and Sibylle Baumbach explore new horizons for a *cultural narratology* that responds to Ansgar Nünning's vision. Drawing on current psychological, cultural, and literary discourses of trauma, Basseler outlines a cultural narratology of resilience. Proceeding from the observation that in a world of risk and crisis we need new ways of coping, he explores how narration functions as a healing mechanism and resource that helps individuals, communities, and whole societies to come to terms with change in the age of post-trauma. In a similarly cross-disciplinary project, Baumbach develops a cultural narratology of attention and argues that (lack of) attention is often brought about by technological change. Investigating the ways in which narratives of attention create moments of 'inattentional blindness', she suggests an approach that bridges cognitive psychology and cultural as well as literary studies.

The essays by Marion Gymnich, Jan Rupp, and Birgit Neumann critically engage with what Ansgar Nünning has defined as *narratives of catastrophe*. Gymnich's essay approaches post-apocalyptic narratives from a historical and functional perspective. In contrast to earlier 'last man' stories, she argues, more recent examples can be read as stories of survival, as the dystopian worlds envisaged do not necessarily lead to the extinction of the human species. Gymnich engages critically with the ethical questions raised by such stories and readings, which seem to downplay the ultimate consequences of global warming and other man-made catastrophes. Rupp is more specifically concerned with postcolonial responses to climate change. From an ecocritical point of view, his essay traces environmental memory in narratives from the Global South that work against collective amnesia and call for an increased awareness of the impact of anthropogenic change. Neumann continues the discussion of narratives from the Global South and literary responses to the challenges of sustainability and multiple ecologies. Her reading of Yvonne Owuor's novel

Dust (2013) focuses on narrative forms that engage with the changed political, economic, and ecological demands of the Anthropocene. It also paves the way for a systematic discussion of the narratological implications of novel representations of time, events, and space.

Sandra Heinen, Carola Surkamp, and Hanne Birk focus on various aspects of *postcolonial and cross-cultural storytelling*. Heinen shows how postcolonial comics and graphic novels blur the boundaries between fact and fiction in order to give urgency to their political goals, raising awareness and appealing to readers to join the fight against different forms of discrimination and violence based on gender, ethnicity and caste, and the horrors of genocide and war. Surkamp discusses didactic uses of storytelling in foreign language teaching. Her evaluation of a classroom experiment with stories designed to foster empathy and perspective-taking in students shows that the framework of cultural narratology can also help explain how intercultural learning may work in practice. Directing attention to the ways in which illustrations provide 'semanticized' visualizations of culture-specific knowledge, Birk proposes a new concept of 'visual resources' as a complement to existing narratological terminology. Her analysis of three Indigenous picturebooks from Australia highlights the tension between culture-specific knowledge and transcultural worldmaking.

The essays by Stella Butter, Guido Isekenmeier, and Dorothee Birke deal with *generic and transmedial takes on narrative* in culture. Butter explores the genre of the revenge tale as actualizing cultural templates of retribution. Analyzing Giorgos Lanthimos's film *The Killing of a Sacred Deer* (2017), she investigates the complex relations between revenge, vengeance, and violence, and shows how popular storytelling as a cultural way of worldmaking negotiates the meaning of justice. Isekenmeier approaches cultural narratology from the points of view of British cultural and media studies. His essay revisits the concept of bardic television proposed by John Hartley and John Fiske in 1983 and uses a case study of CNN news coverage to explore the nexus between storytelling and reporting. Birke pays attention to an emergent subgenre of the Bildungsroman, the Instagram novel. Her reading of Olivia Sudjic's *Sympathy* (2017) not only shows how digital media afford new possibilities and techniques for the staging of identity, but also demonstrates how – from a historical perspective – they help to reinvent the novel as a mind-reading genre.

The focus of Bruno Zerweck's and Astrid Erll's essays is on the emergent field of *historical narratology*. Zerweck revisits unreliable narration, a concept that continues to haunt narratological debates. He outlines a functional-historical approach to narrative unreliability that grounds the phenomenon in modern and postmodern stagings of narrative ambiguity. Proclaiming the death of the unreliable narrator, he then argues that in a post-truth age semantic disruption, the original function of 'unreliable' narrative literature, is replaced by new forms of ambiguity – a rebirth of unreliability – in other genres. Erll studies the migration of narrative forms across long stretches of time. Using the example of the *Odyssey*, she shows how the forms and functions of unreliable narration, multiperspectivity, and narrative coping have traveled from Greek antiquity to modern English and Irish literature. In a comparison of the Odysseys of Homer, Charles Lamb, and James Joyce, she brings cultural and historical narratology into a conversation with memory studies and classical reception studies.

Janine Hauthal and Roy Sommer tackle competing *narratives of Europe*: Hauthal's essay deals with fictions of Europe in John Berger's *Into Their Labours* (1979–1990), a trilogy set mostly in the French Alps. Hauthal demonstrates how Berger uses generic hybridity, multiperspectivity, and collective narration to represent, and pay homage to, peasant culture as a narrative community. She argues that Berger's transnational perspective and refusal to employ national stereotypes render him a truly 'European' storyteller who radically challenges British Euroskepticism. In stark contrast, moving from fictional to non-fictional and from productive to destructive narratives of Europe, Sommer addresses the logic of Brexit narratives. He shows how a narratology of drama, traditionally concerned with the uses of narrative on the stage, can be extended to account for social and political upheavals. Redefining Victor Turner's anthropological notion of social drama as narratives in conflict, he makes the case for a narratological approach to current events, opening up the horizons of cultural narratology both as a critique of politics and as a dialogue with political science.

In sum, the essays collected here demonstrate the scope of narrative in culture. There is no worldmaking without storytelling and no storytelling without worldmaking, from the earliest European narrative, Homer's *Odyssey*, to the most recent European drama, Brexit. Narratives of crisis and revenge, climate change novels and the literature of the Global South, postcolonial comics and Australian picturebooks, the uses of narrative in teaching and on television – the range of narrative responses to culture and the variety of cultural contexts in which narratives are embedded emphasize the relevance of mixed methodologies. One can hardly imagine any cultural phenomena that are not negotiated in narrative genres, media, or contexts, from resilience to attention deficits.

Narrative theory thus provides an invaluable resource for the study of culture, a toolbox that Ansgar Nünning has helped to fill and to refine. More than that, he has taught us how to use the cognitive tools it supplies and has always encouraged us to join him in further developing these resources, devising ever new concepts, adopting new perspectives, and asking new questions. At this point, our retrospective tale of two concepts turns into a prospective story of collaborative research, a narrative of open-ended inquiry that resists closure on principle. Ansgar Nünning has already embarked on his next big project at the intersection of reading, theory, history, and *Bildung*, a project dedicated to nothing less than the value of literature. We are curious to see where it will take him, and us.

Our heartfelt thanks go to Joseph Swann, who did a tremendous job of English language editing for this collection, to Roxane Dänner, who has been a great help in the formal editing process, to Alexander Scherr and Marie-Theres Stickel for conducting valuable research, and to Manuela Gerlof, who agreed instantaneously with us that *Narrative in Culture*, a Festschrift on the occasion of Ansgar Nünning's 60th birthday, is a book that should appear with De Gruyter.

References

Nünning, Ansgar. *Grundzüge eines kommunikationstheoretischen Modells der erzählerischen Vermittlung. Die Funktionen der Erzählinstanz in den Romanen George Eliots*. Trier: Wissenschaftlicher Verlag Trier, 1989.

Nünning, Vera, and Ansgar Nünning. *Virginia Woolf zur Einführung*. Hamburg: Junius, 1991.

Nünning, Ansgar. *Von historischer Fiktion zu historiographischer Metafiktion. Bd. 1.: Theorie, Typologie und Poetik des historischen Romans*. Trier: Wissenschaftlicher Verlag Trier, 1995a.

Nünning, Ansgar. *Von historischer Fiktion zu historiographischer Metafiktion. Bd. 2.: Erscheinungsformen und Entwicklungstendenzen des historischen Romans in England seit 1950*. Trier: Wissenschaftlicher Verlag Trier, 1995b.

Nünning, Ansgar (ed.). *Metzler Lexikon Literatur- und Kulturtheorie: Ansätze – Personen – Grundbegriffe*. Fifth ed. Stuttgart: J.B. Metzler Verlag, 2013 [1998].

Nünning, Ansgar, Carola Surkamp, and Bruno Zerweck (eds.). *Unreliable Narration: Studien zur Theorie und Praxis unglaubwürdigen Erzählens in der englischsprachigen Erzählliteratur*. Trier: Wissenschaftlicher Verlag Trier, 1998.

Nünning, Vera, and Ansgar Nünning (eds.). *Multiperspektivisches Erzählen: Zur Theorie und Geschichte der Perspektivenstruktur im englischen Roman des 18. bis 20. Jahrhunderts*. Trier: Wissenschaftlicher Verlag Trier, 2000.

Nünning, Ansgar, and Vera Nünning (eds.). *Neue Ansätze in der Erzähltheorie*. Trier: Wissenschaftlicher Verlag Trier, 2002a.

Nünning, Vera, and Ansgar Nünning (eds.). *Erzähltheorie transgenerisch, intermedial, interdisziplinär*. Trier: Wissenschaftlicher Verlag Trier, 2002b.

Nünning, Ansgar (ed.). *Fictions of Memory*. *Journal for the Study of British Cultures* 10.1 (2003).

Nünning, Ansgar. "Where Historiographic Metafiction and Narratology Meet: Towards an Applied Cultural Narratology." *Style* 38.3 (2004): 352–375.

Nünning, Ansgar. "On the Emergence of an Empire of the Mind: Metaphorical Re-Membering as a Means of Narrativizing and Naturalizing Cultural Transformations." *Metamorphoses. Structures of Cultural Transformations*. Ed. Jürgen Schlaeger. Tübingen: Narr 2005a. 59–97.

Nünning, Ansgar. "Metabiographies and Metaautobiographies: Towards a Definition, Typology, and Analysis of Self-Reflexive Hybrid Meta-Genres." *Self-Reflexivity in Literature*. Eds. Werner Huber, Martin Middeke, and Hubert Zapf. Würzburg: Königshausen and Neumann, 2005b. 195–209.

Nünning, Ansgar. "On Metanarrative: Towards a Definition, a Typology, and an Outline of the Functions of Metanarrative Commentary." *The Dynamics of Narrative Form. Studies in Anglo-American Narratology*. Ed. John Pier. Berlin: de Gruyter, 2005c. 11–57.

Surkamp, Carola, and Ansgar Nünning. *Englische Literatur unterrichten 1: Grundlagen und Methoden*. Fourth ed. Seelze-Velber: Klett-Kallmeyer, 2016 [2006].

Nünning, Ansgar, and Jürgen Schlaeger (eds.). *English Studies Today: Recent Developments and New Directions*. Trier: Wissenschaftlicher Verlag Trier, 2007.

Erll, Astrid, and Ansgar Nünning (eds.). *Cultural Memory Studies: An International and Interdisciplinary Handbook*. Berlin: de Gruyter, 2008.

Nünning, Ansgar. "Making Events – Making Stories – Making Worlds: Ways of Worldmaking from a Narratological Point of View." *Cultural Ways of Worldmaking: Media and Narratives*. Eds. Vera Nünning, Ansgar Nünning, and Birgit Neumann. New York: de Gruyter, 2010. 191–214.

Nünning, Vera, Ansgar Nünning, and Birgit Neumann (eds.). *Cultural Ways of Worldmaking: Media and Narratives*. Berlin: de Gruyter, 2010.

Nünning, Ansgar. "Towards a Metaphorology of Crises, or: The Uses of Cognitive Metaphor Theory for the Study of Culture." *Cognition and Culture*. Eds. Ana Margarida Abrantes and Peter Hanenberg. Frankfurt a. M.: Peter Lang, 2011. 71–98.

Nünning, Ansgar, and Roy Sommer. "The Performative Power of Narrative in Drama: On the Forms and Functions of Dramatic Storytelling in Shakespeare's Plays." *Current Trends in Narratology*. Ed. Greta Olson. Berlin: de Gruyter, 2011. 200–231.

Nünning, Ansgar. "'With the Benefit of Hindsight': Features and Functions of Turning-Points as a Narratological Concept and as a Way of Self-Making." *Turning Points. Concepts and Narratives of Change in Literature and Other Media*. Eds. Ansgar Nünning and Kai Sicks. Berlin: de Gruyter, 2012. 31–58.

Neumann, Birgit, and Ansgar Nünning (eds.). *Travelling Concepts for the Study of Culture*. Berlin: de Gruyter, 2012.

Nünning, Ansgar, and Kai Sicks. "Turning Points as Metaphors and Mininarrations: Analysing Concepts of Change in Literature and Other Media." *Turning Points. Concepts and Narratives of Change in Literature and Other Media*. Eds. Ansgar Nünning and Kai Sicks. Berlin: de Gruyter, 2012. 1–28.

Nünning, Ansgar. "Wie Erzählungen Kulturen erzeugen: Prämissen, Konzepte und Perspektiven für eine kulturwissenschaftliche Narratologie." *Kultur – Wissen – Narration: Perspektiven transdisziplinärer Erzählforschung für die Kulturwissenschaften*. Ed. Alexandra Strohmaier. Bielefeld: transcript, 2013a. 15–53.

Nünning, Ansgar. "Meta-Autobiographien: Gattungstypologische, narratologische und funktionsgeschichtliche Überlegungen zur Poetik und zum Wissen innovativer Autobiographien." *Autobiographie: Eine interdisziplinäre Gattung zwischen klassischer Tradition und (post-)moderner Variation*. Eds. Uwe Baumann and Karl August Neuhausen. Göttingen: V&R unipress, 2013b. 27–81.

Nünning, Ansgar. "Krise als Erzählung und Metapher: Literaturwissenschaftliche Bausteine für eine Metaphorologie und Narratologie von Krisen." *Krisengeschichte(n): 'Krise' als Leitbegriff und Erzählmuster in kulturwissenschaftlicher Perspektive*. Eds. Gerrit Schenk, Carla Meyer, and Katja Patzel-Mattern. Stuttgart: Franz Steiner, 2013c. 117–144.

Nünning, Ansgar, and Michael Basseler. "Literary Studies as a Form of Life-Science: The Knowledge of Literature." *New Theories, Models and Methods in Literary and Cultural Studies*. Eds. Greta Olson and Ansgar Nünning. Trier: Wissenschaftlicher Verlag Trier, 2013. 189–212.

Nünning, Ansgar, and Christine Schwanecke. "Crossing Generic Borders: Hybridisation as a Catalyst of Genre Development." *The Cultural Dynamics of Generic Change in Contemporary Fiction: Theoretical* Frameworks, *Genres and Model Interpretations*. Eds. Michael Basseler, Ansgar Nünning, and Christine Schwanecke. Trier: Wissenschaftlicher Verlag Trier, 2013. 115–146.

Nünning, Vera, and Ansgar Nünning. "On the Narrativity of Rituals: Interfaces between Narratives and Rituals and Their Potential for Ritual Studies." *Ritual and Narrative. Theoretical Explorations and Historical Case Studies*. Eds. Vera Nünning, Jan Rupp, and Gregor Ahn. Bielefeld: transcript, 2013. 51–75.

Nünning, Ansgar. "Towards Transnational Approaches to the Study of Culture: From Cultural Studies and Kulturwissenschaften to a Transnational Study of Culture." *The Trans/National Study of Culture: A Translational Perspective*. Ed. Doris Bachmann-Medick. Berlin: de Gruyter, 2014. 23–49.

Berning, Nora, Ansgar Nünning, and Christine Schwanecke (eds.). *Reframing Concepts in Literary and Cultural Studies: Theorizing and Analyzing Conceptual Transfers*. Trier: Wissenschaftlicher Verlag Trier, 2014.

Nünning, Ansgar. "Metaphors We Pay For, or: Metaphors of the 'Financial Crisis' Shaping the Cultural Life of Money." *Cognition and The Cultural Life of Money*. Eds. Helena Goncalvez da Silva and Isabel Gil. Berlin: de Gruyter, 2015a. 47–67.

Nünning, Ansgar. "My Narratology: An Interview with Ansgar Nünning." *DIEGESIS. Interdisciplinary E-Journal for Narrative Research / Interdisziplinäres E-Journal für Erzählforschung* 4.1 (2015b): 104–109. http://nbn-resolving.de/urn:nbn:de:hbz:468-20150520-121640-7 (12 January 2019).

Nünning, Ansgar. "'Experiments in Life': Literary and Cultural Studies as a Form of Life-Science." *Emergent Forms of Life in Anglophone Literature: Conceptual Frameworks and Critical Analyses*. Eds. Michael Basseler, Daniel Hartley, and Ansgar Nünning. Trier: Wissenschaftlicher Verlag Trier, 2015c. 53–73.

Nünning, Ansgar, and Christine Schwanecke. "The Performative Power of Unreliable Narration and Focalisation in Drama and Theatre: Conceptualising the Specificity of Dramatic Unreliability." *Unreliable Narration and Trustworthiness: Intermedial and Interdisciplinary Perspectives*. Ed. Vera Nünning. Berlin: de Gruyter, 2015. 189–219.

Nünning, Ansgar, Renate Stauf, and Peter Strohschneider. "Kriterien und Standards der Literaturwissenschaft: Debatten, Denkanstöße, Desiderate." *Kriterien und Standards der Literaturwissenschaft*. Eds. Ansgar Nünning, Renate Stauf, and Peter Strohschneider. *Germanisch-Romanische Monatsschrift* 65.1 (2015): 1–12.

Nünning, Ansgar. "(Nicht-)Beobachtbares, epistemologische Krisen und emergente Forschungsfelder: Methodologische Probleme und Perspektiven kulturwissenschaftlicher Erforschung von Gegenwartskultur(en." *Gegenwartskultur als methodologische*

Herausforderung der Kulturwissenschaft(en). Eds. Jürgen Joachimsthaler and Verena Thinnes. Frankfurt a. M.: Peter Lang, 2016. 27–61.
Nünning, Ansgar, and Vera Nünning. "Stories as 'Weapons of Mass Destruction,' or: George W. Bush's Narratives of Crisis as Paradigm Examples of Ways of World- and Conflict-Making (and Conflict-Solving?)." *Narrative in Conflict(s)*. Eds. Wolfgang Müller-Funk and Clemens Ruthner. Berlin: de Gruyter, 2017a. 189–232.
Nünning, Vera, and Ansgar Nünning. "How to Stay Healthy and Foster Well-Being with Narratives, or: Where Narratology and Salutogenesis Could Meet." *How to Do Things with Narrative: Political and Narratological Perspectives on Anglophone Texts*. Eds. Jan Alber and Greta Olson. Berlin: de Gruyter, 2017b. 157–186.
Nünning, Ansgar. "Bildung durch Wissenschaft als die Idee der Universität: Kohärenz und Korrespondenz durch forschendes Lehren und Lernen." *Universitäre Englischlehrerausbildung. Wege zu mehr Kohärenz und Korrespondenz*. Ed. Bärbel Diehr. Bern: Peter Lang, 2018.

Michael Basseler
Stories of Dangerous Life in the Post-Trauma Age: Toward a Cultural Narratology of Resilience

Abstract: This chapter argues that we are currently witnessing a shift away from the trauma paradigm toward a new, post-trauma paradigm that manifests itself most strongly in the concept of resilience. Among the potential meanings and possibilities of trauma, resilience is being hailed as the quality that individuals, communities, and whole societies must possess in order to survive and thrive in a world of ubiquitous risk and crisis. While it draws on recent research from psychology and the social sciences, the chapter primarily aims to contribute to an understanding of the ways in which resilience – both in the individual psychological and in the social-ecological sense – is significantly constructed through narratives. Discussing various literary (e.g., Chris Cleave's *The Other Hand*) and non-literary examples of resilience narratives, the chapter sketches out a cultural narratology of resilience that would enable us to come to terms with the narrative strategies and techniques as well as the cultural values, patterns, assumptions, ideologies, political agendas, and societal norms implicated in those stories.

1 Introduction: Are we entering a post-trauma age?

In *The Juridical Unconscious*, Shoshana Felman famously claimed that the twentieth century "was in effect a century of traumas and (concurrently) a century of theories of trauma" (2002, 1). In light of the various atrocities of two world wars, the Holocaust, Vietnam, totalitarian rule, but also feminist and other political movements that brought to the fore domestic violence and the "private horror" of "new forms of political, racial, and sexual persecution" (Felman 2002, 2), trauma has emerged as a "conceptual center" and an "essential dimension of human and historical experience" (Felman 2002, 2). Within literary and cultural studies, too, trauma theory has become one of the most widely cultivated and productive fields of recent decades, as scholars have turned to literature, film, and other media to gain insights into the paradoxical mechanisms of traumatic representation (see, e.g., Caruth 1995; Vickroy 2002; Whitehead 2004).

Now that we are already well into the twenty-first century, humankind has arguably neither become less prone to violence nor immune to trauma. In fact, the major conflicts and catastrophes of our own day – 9/11 and the ensuing 'war on terror', civil wars in Syria and Libya, the expulsion of the Rohingya from Myanmar, to name but a few – have produced their very own, distinct traumas, haunting individuals and societies alike. Moreover, as environmental concerns become more and more visible, new forms of "climate trauma" (Richardson 2018) are emerging, complementing the trauma canon of the twentieth century and requiring further theoretical work.

These developments notwithstanding, this chapter argues that we are currently witnessing a shift away from the trauma paradigm to a new, post-trauma paradigm that manifests itself most strongly in the (by now quite diverse and fuzzy) concept of resilience. Broadly, resilience can be understood as "the process of harnessing biological, psychosocial, structural and cultural resources to sustain wellbeing" (Panter-Brick and Leckman 2013, 335). One of the lessons learned from traumatology, one might claim, is that trauma needs to be handled proactively, or even prevented altogether. Political theorist David Chandler has recently pointed out with reference to the UK civil contingencies and trauma resilience training that "the resilience discourse encourages a shift from post-hoc programmes of trauma counseling to the inculcation of mental or subjective capacities to respond to crises without becoming traumatised" (Chandler and Reid 2016, 30). Another case in point is the "road to resilience" campaign of the American Psychological Association that was launched after the events of 9/11. The APA defines resilience as the "process of adapting well in the face of adversity, trauma, tragedy, threats or significant sources of stress [...]. It means 'bouncing back' from difficult situations" (American Psychological Association). While their "10 ways to build resilience" promote effective coping strategies for survival, as well as preventive measures in a time of perceived terrorist and other major threats, the campaign and its advice mainly served, as Insa Fooken (2016, 33) has pointed out, to influence the mental representation of 9/11 in its aftermath, creating an attitude that oscillated between acceptance of the unchangeable on the one hand, and activity orientation and certain types of action on the other.

Rather than constituting an opposite to trauma, however, resilience is in many ways tied to experiences of trauma as well as to trauma theory. Speaking about resilience in a '*post*-trauma age', therefore, does not imply the end of trauma, but may be more fruitfully understood in analogy to other 'post-'constructions in the history of critical theory, e.g. 'post-structural' or 'post-colonial'. A productive approach might be to conceptualize resilience in the context of more recent, "after trauma studies" (Kurtz 2018, 334) or "revisionist trauma theory" (Balaev 2014, 3), developments that move away from the traditional psychoanalytical, "universal pathological concept" (Balaev 2014, 3) which views trauma as essentially dissociative and thus ultimately unrepresentable.[1] Instead, a revisionist approach to trauma will employ a pluralistic theoretical and methodological framework to suggest that "extreme experience cultivates multiple responses and values" (Balaev 2014, 4). Against this backdrop, focusing on resilience as a new approach to traumatic experience means to foreground the values that are attached to trauma, as well as the meanings that can be (and frequently are) made of traumatic experience, which in turn are always "influenced by a variety of individual and cultural factors" (Balaev 2014, 4). Resilience might, then, be understood in this sense as a new form of traumatic representation that does not, as in the classical model, posit the unrepresentability of its source, but instead highlights the "narrative *possibility*, the potential for the configuration and refiguration of trauma in narrative" (Luckhurst 2008, 89). In short, resilience might be understood as one among the "multiple meanings" (Balaev 2014, 5) of trauma.

While life in the twenty-first century has probably not become less dangerous than in previous centuries – though the opposite might also be true – what seems to be changing is the way in which societies, governments, and organizations attempt to prepare themselves for the unpredictable yet inevitable catastrophes of the future. Rather than simply responding to trauma, the aim is to prevent it and to make people less vulnerable to it. This is what the concept of resilience is all about: "Resilience is currently propounded by liberal agencies and institutions as the fundamental property which peoples and individuals worldwide must possess in order to demonstrate their capacities to live with danger" (Evans and Reid 2014, 2). Hence the concept of resilience, though closely entwined with experiences and discourses of trauma, signals a shift toward what might be called a 'post-trauma age'.

Despite the rapid proliferation of resilience-thinking in various academic and societal fields, literary and cultural studies have so far not made any significant contribution to the fast-growing research in this area.[2] In light of this

---

[1] For further examples of these new approaches to literary and cultural trauma studies, see Luckhurst (2008) and Craps (2013) as well as the articles in Buelens et al. (2014). For a concise overview, see chapter 2.4 in Erll (2017).

[2] This lacuna becomes very obvious if one compares the total number of publications on 'resilience' in various disciplines. As the survey provided by Weiss et al. (2018, 23) shows, the humanities have produced by far the smallest number of publications, with less than 50 entries in 2015 as compared to about 1100 in medicine, 300 in ecology and 500 in the social sciences.

lacuna, the aim of this chapter is to contribute to an understanding of the ways in which resilience, as a central emerging concept and concern of the twenty-first century, is significantly constructed through narratives. Therefore, I will focus on two distinct if related notions of resilience, or strands of resilience theory, which have been formulated in their respective disciplines: individual (psychological) resilience and social-ecological resilience. The next section I will introduce the psychological concept of resilience and its narrative underpinnings, followed by some brief examples of literary and non-literary narratives that serve to demonstrate how psychological resilience is constructed in autobiographical and fictional life stories. These examples will illustrate how – explicitly or implicitly – notions of resilience shape narratives of loss and traumatic events, and how *vice versa* the very notion of resilience rests upon acts, processes, and structures of storytelling. Then I will turn to another research field in which the concept of resilience has featured prominently in recent years, namely the interface between political, social, and environmental sciences. While psychological resilience essentially refers to the capacity of an individual to overcome extreme stress and trauma, as a social-ecological concept resilience has been propounded as a "subjective and systematic state to enable each and all to live freely and with confidence in a world of potential risks" (Lentzos and Rose 2009, 243). Finally, I will sketch out some preliminary ideas and suggestions toward a "cultural narratology" (see Nünning 2000; 2009a) of resilience that might fruitfully complement and revise existing research in the literary and cultural study of trauma, risk and catastrophe, as well as in the interdisciplinary study of resilience.

2 Psychological resilience: Narrative as 'fog-lamp'

Among the earliest work on resilience, research from the field of psychology has been crucial in conceptualizing and popularizing resilience as a concept to describe how humans deal with severe disturbances. In particular, Emmy Werner's empirical work on the long-term effects of psychosocial risk factors on the development of Hawaiian children born in 1955 has been central in this respect (Werner and Smith 1982). However, while these early studies understood resilience primarily as an inner capacity of individuals, research since the 1980s has considered the dynamic interrelation of diverse biopsychosocial factors on various systemic levels. Today, resilience serves as a heuristic category to describe long-term processes of resistance, stabilization and transformation, as well as coping strategies in the wake of trauma (Fooken 2016, 30).

Within psychological research, resilience has in recent years importantly complemented and recalibrated the study of trauma (cf. Kent et al. 2014). As a resource-oriented concept with a decidedly positive conception of mankind (*Menschenbild*), it has already led to a significant change of perspective (Fooken 2016, 30). While traditional trauma studies tended to put a rather reductionist focus on the "exclusively pathogenic consequences of adverse life conditions, trauma and risk," research on resilience has broadened this perspective by accentuating "individual and social resources and hence the possibility of successfully dealing with aversive life events and of achieving a sufficient restoration of psychic stability" (Fooken 2016, 14, my transl.). From the perspective of traumatology, therefore, resilience means "efficacious adaptation regardless of significant traumatic threats to personal and physical integrity" (Agaibi and Wilson 2005, 199).

A central question concerns the 'normality' or frequency of resilience as an adaptive process to trauma. Arguing that "the majority of the U.S. population has been exposed to at least one traumatic event" without showing symptoms of PTSD, George Bonanno (2004, 106) claims that resilience and not trauma is the most common response to violent or even life-threatening events. Along the same lines, the French psychologist Boris Cyrulnik has described resilience as "anti-destiny" (2009, 19), arguing that "resilience is so common that it proves that we can survive" (2009, 14). As Fooken (2016, 40) reminds us, however, it is important to note that any development toward resilience does not happen because of, but despite adverse life circumstances, since these are not part of life's 'normal' challenges.

Researchers in the field of psychological resilience studies have only begun to shed light on the important role of narration as the central coping strategy or healing mechanism. Again, Cyrulnik provides some helpful first insights in this regard. As he explains in his book *Resilience*, "what we are at any given moment obliges us to use our ecological, emotional, and verbal environments to 'knit' ourselves. We might feel that, if a single stitch is dropped, everything will unravel, but in fact, if just one stitch holds, we can start all over again." (2011, 13) While his notion of "verbal environments" and the process of "knitting ourselves" already point toward the identity-making power of narrative, in *Talking of Love* he uses the example of the traumatic experiences of child-soldiers to note that "the way families and the cultural environment talk about wounds can either attenuate or exacerbate that suffering, depending on what stories they tell" (Cyrulnik 2009, 15). Stressing the function of storytelling, Cyrulnik employs the powerful metaphor of "narrative as fog-lamp" (2009, 37) to understand resilience as the process of narrative meaning-making and psychological healing in the aftermath of extreme suffering (2009, 116).

The significance of storytelling in the process of building psychological resilience has also been acknowledged by researchers in the field of narrative psychology. In one of the most systematic and illuminating contributions to date, Neimeyer and Levitt (2001) examine how, in a psychotherapeutic context, self-narratives enable people to overcome psychological crises and stress. They explore how people's life stories or "macronarratives" (Neimeyer and Levitt 2001, 49) are challenged by certain aversive life events, how stories of the self can even collapse in such situations, and how narrative repair can work effectively. Drawing on the work of Jerome Bruner, Donald Polkinghorne and others, they endorse a constructivist epistemology in which narration constitutes a fundamental anthropological need, and in which people regularly project and construct meaning and make their lives intelligible by telling personal stories.

Neimeyer and Levitt analyze a number of exemplary stories as to how they impose narrative structure in terms of setting, characterization, plot, theme, and "fictional goal" (2001, 59). All of these elements contribute, in one way or another, to the effectiveness of personal stories with regard to coping mechanisms and strategies, moving from the 'where and when', 'who' and 'what' of the narrative to its deeper meaning, the 'why' and 'wherefore'. The term 'fictional goal' refers to the "overarching teleology" (2001, 59) of the story, that is, the ways in which it is embedded in the macro-story of our lives. It is fictional "not because it is 'untrue' in some objective sense, but because it is fashioned or invented by the narrator" (Neimeyer and Levitt 2001, 59). In a series of case studies Neimeyer and Levitt demonstrate how "narrative ultimately serves a healing as well as heuristic function" as people "explore and rewrite life stories that have been shattered, undermined, or determined by difficult life experiences" (2001, 64).

Thus conceptualized, resilience is inextricably intertwined with narrative construction. Although they do not systematically define the term 'resilience', Neimeyer and Levitt (2001, 64) reason that

> resilience arises [...] from the double effort first to *describe* our coping responses in the micronarratives of our life story, and then to *inscribe* these as personal resources in the more or less coherent macronarratives that consolidate our sense of identity over time. 'Coping' then becomes a storied construction, created and sustained within a distinctively human meaning-making process.

As the result of successful coping processes through storytelling, resilience not only corroborates notions about "how our lives become stories" (Eakin 1999). In the context of autobiographical research – whether in literary studies or psychology – the concept also has the potential to provide new perspectives to the study of narrative identity (see Holler and Klepper 2013), and to challenge and refine existing notions of the 'storied self.'

While existing research on resilience narratives focuses on storytelling in a psychotherapeutic context, resilience also promises to be an important conceptual and heuristic category for analyzing literary narratives. Chris Cleave's *The Other Hand* (2009), for example, though mostly discussed with regard to its staging of ethical choices in a globalized world, lends itself particularly to a reading within a 'post-trauma' context. Presenting psychological coping essentially as a *storied* construction, *The Other Hand* emphasizes the role of narrative in individual and collective healing – or resilience – processes in the wake of traumatic experience. The novel takes as its political-historical context the conflict in the Niger Delta which, ever since the 1990s, has led to extreme violence and ethnic conflict as a result of the exploitative practices of international oil companies. It is told alternately from the perspectives of fourteen-year old Nigerian refugee, Little Bee, and Sarah O'Rourke, a journalist who lives with her husband, Andrew, and their only son in the leafy London suburb of Kingston upon Thames. The plot revolves around a traumatic incident on a Nigerian beach a couple of years before the narration sets in: The O'Rourkes had come to Nigeria for a holiday that was meant to salvage their marriage. On the beach, however, things went awry, as the couple suddenly found themselves surrounded by a band of soldiers who had kidnapped Little Bee and her sister. Confronted by the men, the situation quickly went out of control after Sarah tried to release the girls from the soldiers' power. While the O'Rourkes withdrew from the scene with deep shock and a severed finger (Sarah), Little Bee managed to escape with hardly more than her bare life after her sister had been raped, tortured, and then killed by the men. When the narration sets in, Little Bee has come to England as a refugee trying to find relief from her traumatic past. As she enters the O'Rourkes' life for the second time, however, Little Bee causes the guilt-ridden, clinically depressed Andrew to commit suicide.

Although a trauma constitutes the kernel of the plot, the perspective of the novel's main character suggests that *The Other Hand* is better understood as a fiction of resilience. A girl deeply unsettled by what she experienced in her home country, Little Bee is what Cyrulnik would call a resilient, "oxymoronic personality" who manages not only to survive, but even to develop hope for herself, as well as for others: "The oxymoron becomes characteristic of a personality that has been wounded but which still resists, that suffers but is happy enough to go on hoping despite everything" (Cyrulnik 2009, 22). In this instance, despite the "heavy cargo" (Cleave 2009, 67) of her traumatic memories, Little Bee finds a strategy to survive the two years of her incarceration in an English detention center. What enables her to do so, the novel suggests, is her imagination and her readiness to embrace language and narration as a means to overcome her trauma.

Through its use of bi-perspectival homodiegetic narration (see Ansgar and Vera Nünning 2000, 43–44) the novel aesthetically foregrounds storytelling as the key to both Sarah's and Little Bee's mourning and coping processes. Little Bee in particular uses narrative as her "fog lamp," as a means to ascribe meaning to her experience and overcome her trauma. As she announces in the first chapter: "I am here to tell you a real story. I did not come to talk to you about the bright African colours" (Cleave 2009, 12). Narration, as process and product of the storytelling act, is crucial for Little Bee's resilience; it signals her survival: "In a few breaths' time I will speak some sad words to you. But you must hear them the same way we have agreed to see scars now. [...] A sad story means, this storyteller is alive" (Cleave 2009, 14). However, in the course of the novel her story gradually intertwines with that of Sarah, and it becomes apparent that, as a single story, it is not enough to heal her trauma. Toward the end of the novel, therefore, Sarah and Little Bee travel through Nigeria to collect similar stories, for as Sarah explains to Little Bee: "'Our problem is that you only have your own story. One story makes you weak. But as soon as we have one hundred stories, you will be strong'" (Cleave 2009, 355). Narrative resilience, one might conclude, is conceived here as a collaborative (and arguably gendered) *narrative* project. Presenting the deeply entangled stories of two women who have been differently affected by the trauma of the 'Niger Delta Oil Wars', Cleave's novel does not privilege rupture and unspeakability as the aesthetic hallmarks of trauma narratives, but instead focuses on "narrative *possibility*" (Luckhurst 2008, 89) and the meaning of trauma, especially for Little Bee, its 'oxymoronic' protagonist.[3]

3 Social-ecological resilience: Naturalizing trauma in the risk society

As I have suggested elsewhere (Basseler forthcoming), resilience might be fruitfully conceptualized within social and ecological discourses as a response to what Ulrich Beck has dubbed the "risk society" (see Beck 2005, 2016).

---

3 One might object, though, that by letting the white, Western journalist Sarah take over the process of fostering resilience through storytelling, the novel risks complicity with what critics of resilience refer to as the pathologization of resilience, i.e. the notion that resilience builds upon "knowing what is better for lives whose lack of protection fully validates an interventionist response" (Evans and Reid 2014, 90).

Resulting from industrial (over-)production and technological innovation in a global capitalist framework, a plethora of unprecedented and incalculable ecological hazards is endangering "*all* forms of life on this planet" (Beck 2005, 22). Looking back at the defining events of our contemporary moment, these are to an increasing degree constituted by risks and crises: climate change, Chernobyl and Fukushima, the global financial crisis, 9/11, and ongoing terrorism around the world, military conflicts and wars, the loss of biodiversity, and so forth. In light of these global risks, Beck (2016, 15) diagnoses a "comprehensive meta-change of 'society'" as well as a "general cultural transformation." With the "self-endangerment of modernity" (Beck 2013, xvi), risk is no longer an abstraction or a state of exception, "but is instead the normal situation, and hence the motor driving a major transformation of society and politics" (Beck 2013, xix).

The rapid rise of the concept of resilience in social-ecological contexts (cf. Weiss et al. 2018) can be understood as a concerted response to the realities of the global risk society and its actual and potential traumas. It has been described as a new "ethics of responsibility" (Evans and Reid 2014, 6) which asks groups and individuals to come to terms – and ultimately feel at home – with the many risks of our age. The growing popularity of resilience-thinking in the past few decades points, therefore, to an increasing awareness and conceptualization of life on planet Earth as dangerous, contingent, complex, vulnerable and fraught with risk. Resilience, in its social-ecological variant, has been propagated in various contexts and research fields, from climate change (Gall 2013; Wapner 2016) and environmental crises (Goldstein et al. 2012), through terrorism and 'homeland security' (Flynn 2007), to economic and financial crises (Jansen 2013) and urban planning (Vale and Campanella 2005), and it has been discussed from multidisciplinary (Baggio et al. 2015; Weiss et al. 2018), postcolonial (O'Brien 2012; Murphy 2013; Habib 2016), and indigenous perspectives (Strand and Peacock 2003; Kirmeyer et al. 2011). It has been generally affirmed as a desirable societal goal, a guiding principle (Blum et al. 2016, 152), and a "cultural task" (Ostheimer 2018), as well as a new perspective on processes of societal transformation in the wake of natural catastrophes, terror attacks, epidemics, and other disasters, especially with regard to the analysis of processes and phenomena of preservation and regeneration (Endress and Rampp 2015).

Part of this transdisciplinary discussion, however, also entails a decidedly critical perspective on the notion of resilience. The most sustained critique so far has focused on the interrelation between resilience and neoliberalism. Vardy and Smith (2017, 175), for instance, summarize resilience as a "code word for 'business as usual' as industrial, military, and political elites rearrange their operations to acknowledge the reality of climate change while maintaining relations of power".

Oscillating between responsibilization pressures and political empowerment, resilience discourse tends to be complicit with neoliberal regimes (cf. Evans and Reid 2014; Chandler and Reid 2016). Resilient subjects, Evans and Reid argue, "have accepted the imperative not to resist or secure themselves from the dangers they face," and instead "adapt to their enabling conditions via the embrace of a neoliberal rationality that fosters a belief in the necessity of risk as a private good" (2014, 41–42). In their view, resilience constitutes a form of "neoliberal *interventionism*" (Evans and Reid 2014, 47) which "displaces any sense of social responsibility and pastoral care with a care for the self that naturalizes the conditions of vulnerability" (Evans and Reid 2014, 65).

It is in this context, also, that social-ecological notions of resilience are marked by a somewhat conflicted, ethically difficult, and perhaps even paradoxical relation to notions of collective trauma. While past traumas and the vulnerabilities exposed by them are an integral part of the resilience perspective, such a perspective risks reaffirming vulnerability and precariousness as a necessary step toward social transformation and progress (Evans and Reid 2014, 24; Blum et al. 2016, 162). Moreover, traumatic events of a collective dimension always render some groups more vulnerable and others more resilient. Hurricane Katrina has shown, for instance, that the traumatic effects of the disaster were unevenly distributed among various race, class, gender, and age groups.

Perhaps even more than in the realm of individual, psychological resilience, the meanings of traumatic events thus inevitably depend on the forms of representation they take. Who is represented as resilient (or vulnerable), and what are the underlying narrative patterns of such representations? From an urban studies perspective, Laurence Vale and Thomas Campanella have described these narrative mechanisms, pointing out that "[t]here is never a single, monolithic *vox populi* that uniformly affirms the adopted resilience narrative in the wake of disaster" (2005, 341). While resilience narratives in the wake of societal trauma are usually constructed by those in power, "marginalized groups or peoples are generally ignored in the narrative construction process" (Vale and Campanella 2005, 341). As a consequence, "[t]he power politics of any resilience narrative makes it inherently controversial, and changing power dynamics within each affected community will determine just how contested the construction of resilience becomes" (Vale and Campanella 2005, 341). Above all else, social-ecological resilience must therefore be conceptualized as a function of narrative. Narratives offer the interpretive framework in which the meanings of disasters and traumatic events are produced. As such they are always indicative of dominant power structures.

If we turn to literary fictions, we find a considerable body of work that presents social-ecological resilience narratives in connection with either actual historical events or entirely fictional scenarios. For instance, a number of novels dealing with Hurricane Katrina relate stories of resilience that complicate and critique the official narratives constructed by the government and mainstream media. Among those novels are Jesmyn Ward's myth-infused *Salvage the Bones* (2011) about the perseverance – or "dirty resilience" – of an impoverished African American girl whose home and community have been drastically affected by the storm (see Basseler forthcoming), Tom Piazza's *City of Refuge* (2008), which presents the stories of two fictional families – one black, one white – to highlight the ways in which socio-economic as well as racial categories affect resilience, and Dave Eggers's non-fiction novel *Zeitoun* (2009) about the Syrian-American Abdulrahman Zeitoun, whose decision to stay in New Orleans during the storm proved fatal. Showing how his personal resilience was thwarted by the failed disaster management of the authorities and by a general societal climate in which many immigrants from the Middle East and South Asia were discriminated against in the aftermath of the 9/11 attacks, the novel raises important questions about the 'unintended consequences' and efficiency of US national resilience programs. Other examples of contemporary "fictions of resilience" (see Basseler forthcoming) include Indra Sinha's *Animal's People* (2007), which takes as its historical reference one of the worst-ever industrial disasters, the Bhopal Gas Tragedy (see O'Brien 2012, Murphy 2013), Amitav Ghosh's *The Hungry Tide* (2005), which addresses the relationship between local knowledge and cosmopolitan intervention in environmental challenges (see Murphy 2013), and even post-apocalyptic novels such as Cormac McCarthy's *The Road* (2006), which stages a kind of minimal resilience in the wake of an imaginary environmental collapse.

Approaching social-ecological resilience from a cultural-narratological perspective will, then, allow us to analyze 'real-life' as well as fictional resilience narratives in order to gain a deeper understanding of how trauma and catastrophe are naturalized within a global risk society through the use of storytelling. In the final section of this chapter, I will, therefore, propose some steps towards a cultural narratology of resilience and provide some further examples to demonstrate how narrative is perhaps the major cultural and cognitive scheme through which notions of resilience are currently generated.

4 Towards a cultural narratology of resilience

At the beginning of the twenty-first century, our culture and society are pervaded with stories of psychological and social-environmental resilience, both real-life (*Wirklichkeitserzählungen*, see Klein and Martínez 2009) and fictional, from all walks of life and throughout all media. Resilience is being promoted by the UN in short narrative videos that tell how, for instance, Ethiopian farmers became more resilient by planting new crops in response to changing environmental conditions (see O'Brien 2017, 47); in blogs in which parents relate how they managed to cope with severe injuries and illnesses of their children (Assad 2017); in "success stories" by the Community and Regional Resilience Institute (www.resilientus.org); or by political advisors who use narrative scenarios to convince the public of the necessity to become 'more resilient' to terrorist threats (Flynn 2007). Moreover, resilient characters and communities increasingly populate fictional narratives in literature and other media, including those mentioned above, as well as Hollywood films and TV shows such as Benh Zeitlin's *Beasts of the Southern Wild* (2012) and David Simon and Eric Overmyer's *Treme* (2010–13).

While some scholars from the social sciences have already begun to point toward the role of storytelling in popularizing or even construing resilience in social-ecological contexts, virtually no efforts have been made so far to conceptualize resilience from a narratological perspective. More often than not, existing research on the narrative construction of resilience (e.g. in the context of urban design, see Goldstein et al. 2012) proceeds from a rather vague notion of 'narrative' as a wide umbrella term for any form of symbolic representation. I would argue, however, that a cultural-narratological perspective is crucial for a deeper understanding of the narrative forms, genres, strategies, and techniques underlying those narratives, as well as of their cultural functions. In light of the widely acknowledged yet undertheorized relationship between narrative and resilience, a cultural narratological framework would be highly conducive to an understanding of how narratives shape resilience and how resilience is essentially a narrative concept. After all, the very notion of resilience, as the capacity to 'bounce back' from stress and pain, rests intrinsically upon the narrative sequencing of events, responses, and adaptive processes.

At the same time, resilience offers an opportunity to test and refine the categories, concepts, and analytical tools of what Ansgar Nünning has dubbed 'cultural narratology.' As the present volume impressively documents, it is no doubt one of Nünning's most important contributions to literary and cultural studies to have outlined cultural narratology as an interdisciplinary approach that focuses on the "performative, reality-constituting, or worldmaking function of narration" (2012, 146), highlighting the connection between narratology and the study of culture (Nünning 2012, 160). As Nünning suggests, such an approach "shift[s] the emphasis from formal and structural aspects to those concerning content, context and functions of narratives, thus pushing the semantic dimension of narrative texts into the foreground" (2012, 158). As material expressions of culture, narratives become the locus for interdisciplinary cultural research: "In narrative texts and everyday stories mental dispositions are manifested, i.e. collectively prevailing ways of feeling and thinking, convictions, norms and values, and other mental dispositions that inform our narrative ways of worldmaking" (Nünning 2012, 162). In this sense, a cultural narratological approach conceives of narratives as "cognitive cultural forces" and explores "the ways in which the formal properties of narratives reflect, and influence, the unspoken mental assumptions and cultural issues of a given period" (Nünning 2012, 165). To approach resilience and its narratives – both individual-psychological and social-ecological – from the perspective of cultural narratology means, then, to look for the cultural values, patterns, assumptions, ideologies, political agendas, and societal norms etc. which are implicated in, or conjured up by, those narratives, be they affirmative or critical.

Although a short book chapter is certainly not the place to develop a substantial, systematic cultural narratology of resilience, I would like at least to sketch out some trajectories and make some tentative proposals here as to the contours of such an approach. While the primary interest of cultural narratological research, as Nünning has rightly emphasized, is in the content, context, and functions of narratives, structural and formal aspects nevertheless play an important role, as they also serve to shape cultural notions of resilience, e.g. by drawing on certain conventional generic patterns of narrative. A cultural narratology of resilience may benefit from the findings of literary trauma theory, and especially from research that analyzes the literary and narrative devices through which trauma is frequently staged (see Vickroy 2002; Whitehead 2004). Moreover, as resilience narratives – at least in some of their current forms – share a certain proximity to other prevalent kinds of narrative in which pathological notions of trauma are expanded and contested, they may be tentatively defined in a loose structural analogy to Ansgar and Vera Nünning's narratological definition of "broken narratives" (2016, 52–71).

The notion of resilience narratives as broken narratives, or "compromised-resilience narratives", has also been put forward by Susie O'Brien (2017, 59), who demonstrates, in what is one of the few serious interventions in the resilience discourse from the perspective of literary studies, how such narratives can become "effective tools for self-organization and self-repair" (2017, 58). Like broken narratives, resilience narratives are often characterized by certain structures revolving around a disruptive or even traumatic event and/or situation of perceived risk (individual or collective, often in combination) and resulting in a temporary (or even ongoing) "disruption of normal trajectories" (Nünning and Nünning 2016, 56). The "biopsychosocial spectrum" (Fooken 2017, 36) of such risks, negative life circumstances and particular events ranges from, e.g., death of a close relative, addiction, chronic illness, exposure to extreme violence (e.g. child-abuse, rape), poverty etc. to war and military or paramilitary conflicts, natural and 'man-made' disasters, political suppression and systematic (or even systemic) violence, forced migration, captivity/confinement, and extreme socioeconomic need.

Resilience narratives, in another analogy to 'broken narratives', often feature narrators who make a "sustained effort at reconstructing some kind of coherence and continuity" (Nünning and Nünning 2016, 56) and seek to return to a state of meaning and normalcy. *The Other Hand* is a case in point, as is Indra Sinha's *Animal's People*, in which the autodiegetic narrator remarks: "You have turned us Khaufpuris into storytellers, but always of the same story. [...] No way was I going to tell those stories. I've repeated them so often my teeth are ground smooth by the endless passage of words" (Sinha 2007, 5). Animal's metanarrative comment signals a shift from repetitive trauma narrative to a narrative of resilience and empowerment. The narrative act, therefore, appears as an effective tool in the adaptation process of 'bouncing back' from disaster and trauma, but at the same time as a way of worldmaking. Like broken narratives – or perhaps as a specific kind of broken, compromised narrative – resilience narratives "serve to reintegrate disruptive experiences and re-establish a sense of coherence" (Nünning and Nünning 2017, 167), thus allowing for the cultivation of the various responses, values, and multiple meanings of trauma.

In contrast to broken narratives – or to the many trauma narratives described by literary scholars as disruptive, fragmented, incoherent and so on – resilience narratives, however, typically present fairly coherent stories in which not the traumatic event or its dissociative cognitive repercussions, but the overcoming of trauma and a positive outlook take center stage. In this regard, the notion of salutogenesis as formulated in psychology and medicine (Wink 2016, 3) is closely connected not only with the concept of resilience but also expressly with that of narrative, inasmuch as the "salutogenetic power of narratives" (Nünning and Nünning 2017, 169) contributes indispensably to the well-being of both individuals and societies.

At the same time, however, and for allied reasons, (narratives of) vulnerability and trauma should not be seen as opposites, but as integral and complementary aspects of resilience narratives. Whether they affirm or critique such thinking, resilience narratives implicitly proceed from the notion that healing and even progress can be a possible, meaningful outcome of trauma and disaster. On the other hand, in the complex non-linearity of our age of unintended consequences, literary resilience narratives in particular not only tell stories of overcoming trauma and vulnerability, they also reveal ways in which certain measures toward adaptation can in fact produce new vulnerabilities.

Many resilience narratives, in 'real life' as well as in literature, stage various social and cultural resources, or "key cultural elements" (Murphy 2013, 166), which serve to increase the resilience of individuals, groups, communities, and even societies. Storytelling, as we have seen, can be one such resource of resilience. Other such elements include music (e.g. in *Treme*), myth (*Beasts of the Southern Wild, Salvage the Bones*), cultural traditions such as Maori woodcarving (e.g. in Patricia Grace's *Potiki* (1995), see Murphy 2013), or 'Mardi Gras Indian' ceremonies (*Treme*). Foregrounding such cultural techniques and traditions, these narratives highlight the degree to which resilience is ingrained in culture. Exploring such notions of "cultural resilience" (see Strand and Peacock 2003) is arguably still one of the most pressing tasks of contemporary resilience research, and one in which a cultural narratological approach might make an important contribution.

While these brief preliminary thoughts may suffice to demonstrate how a transdisciplinary narrative approach to resilience could draw on the conceptual and methodological frameworks established by research in literary trauma theory, as well as on recent interventions in cultural and historical narratology, I will conclude this chapter by sketching some trajectories and questions for further research.

Although resilience discourse is a global phenomenon promoted by international organizations such as the UN, a cultural narratological approach should be sensitive to the cultural specificity of resilience narratives and their embedment in larger cultural and national narratives. As, for instance, Kevin Rozario (2005) has persuasively argued, the narratives fabricated in the aftermath of such catastrophic events as the Chicago Fire of 1871 or the San Francisco Earthquake of 1906 were entrenched in modern American notions of progress and social transformation, serving as "self-fulfilling prophecies [...] that made material reconstruction viable" (2005, 40). The cultural specificity of resilience narratives also becomes visible in Stephen Flynn's essay *America the Resilient* (2008), in which he draws upon US American national myths (e.g. the Frontier myth) and other culturally available plots to remind his readers that the country has lost, and needs to regain, resilience as one of its key national strengths and cultural values. Analyzing those culturally specific patterns is thus crucial for a cultural narratology of resilience.

Drawing on Fredric Jameson's notion of the "ideology of form" (2002 [1981], 62), a cultural narratology of resilience should investigate how narrative forms coincide or collide with social forms, and particularly how aesthetic forms afford (and constrain) certain political notions of resilience. In this regard, recent 'neo-formalist' approaches (e.g. Levine 2015) provide helpful and stimulating methodological suggestions. While various scholars have pointed to the normativity of the concept of resilience, a formally sensitive approach to resilience narratives might well sharpen our understanding of how this normativity is produced or underpinned by specific aesthetic and narrative forms. How, for example, are narrative forms and configurations used in service of ideological and political notions of resilience, e.g. in a neoliberal or postcolonial context? Or how can turning points in resilience narratives be understood as key formal elements through which trauma and disaster are imbued with meaning (see Nünning and Sicks 2012) – especially if we acknowledge with Kevin Rozario (2005, 33) that the "configuration of narrative tends to pull disaster toward the middle of a story, encoding it as a principle of transformation"?

Along similar lines, a cultural narratology of resilience would have to pay close attention to the role of narrative genres in the construction of resilience. In keeping with recent work in genre theory that conceives genres not as neutral containers but as devices that "create effects of reality and truth, authority and plausibility" (Frow 2015, 2), it is arguable that genres play a much more central role in modeling our notions of resilience than is usually believed. Whether in autobiographical sub-genres, in historical progress narratives or in a post-apocalyptic novel like *The Road*, different kinds of resilience narratives are shaped, or prefigured, by certain culturally available genre conventions, while at the same time they refigure our understanding and cultural-cognitive models of resilience.

Also addressing the formal aspects of resilience-thinking, a cultural narratological and literary-theoretical approach could serve to better understand the metaphors that shape our notions of resilience. As Fooken (2017, 27–28) observes, psychological resilience discourse is characterized by the use of a variety of metaphors, from organic metaphors through metaphors of weight, of fighting and combat, and of space (especially road metaphors), to metaphors of containment, networking, and construction. In fact, the very concept of resilience, at least in the psychological and social-ecological domains, is radically metaphorical ('bouncing back'), not only in the sense of Lakoff and Johnson's "conceptual metaphors" (1980), but also in the sense of a "mini-narration" (Nünning 2009b). A literary and cultural approach to resilience should therefore explore the "metaphorical implications" (Nünning and Nünning 2016, 48) of notions of resilience in both literary and non-literary storytelling.

Apart from focusing on the forms and cultural specificity of resilience narratives, a cultural narratological approach should also contribute to historicizing resilience narratives. Susie O'Brien (2017) has recently alerted us to the similarities that some contemporary resilience stories (and, paradoxically, their critiques) still share with nineteenth-century novels by Dickens, Hugo and others, inasmuch as they present familiar stories in which characters (quite often children) through sheer moral integrity overcome the hardships, uncertainties and negative social effects of a rapidly changing society. As O'Brien points out: "It is worth recalling this history, not in order to sanctify our more sophisticated contemporary understanding of resilience [...] but to understand it as a compelling narrative to think through in relation to our own, even more precarious, future" (2017, 59). A cultural and historical narratology of resilience might, then, be conducive to fathoming the relation of both past and present narrative responses to trauma, risk, and catastrophe, along with respective cultural-historical notions of, for example, providence, exceptionalism, and individualism (e.g. the resilient 'self-made man').

In addition to the forms and historical dimensions of resilience narratives, a cultural narratological approach also needs to address the cultural work that these narratives perform in our societies. In this regard, especially literary texts serve to fulfill important functions as an "ecological force within culture" (Zapf 2016, 27). While Hubert Zapf's important work on 'literature as cultural ecology' provides more than a mere starting point and methodological framework for such a perspective, even his most recent monograph (2016) does not delve into resilience as an important new discursive field within ecocriticism and environmental humanities. Approaching resilience from such an angle could, however, yield crucial insights into how literary – as well as other – cultural narratives might serve as a "cultural-critical metadiscourse", "imaginative counter-discourse" and/or "reintegrative interdiscourse" (Zapf 2016, 103–114). Read alongside 'official' resilience narratives such as those propagated by the U.N., literary works such as Ishmael Beah's 2014 novel *The Radiance of Tomorrow* can serve to critique adaptationist and reductionist stories, as well as to reveal the neoliberal framework in which they are often embedded (see O'Brien 2017). Coming to terms with the cultural-cognitive functions of these narratives within both contemporary and historical resilience-discourse is one of the lacunae that a cultural narratological approach would help to address.

To conclude, a cultural narratological perspective promises important findings that are still markedly absent from multidisciplinary resilience research. Proceeding from the assumption that storytelling is one of the most powerful tools of social and cultural transformation available to us – indeed, as Ansgar Nünning's oeuvre so impressively demonstrates, that it represents an irreducibly cultural way of making meaning, making the self, and making the world – such a perspective could arguably make an important contribution to our understanding of resilience as an emerging ethical, political, and cultural concern of the twenty-first century – whether or not this might be referred to one day by historians as the post-trauma age.

References

Agaibi, Christine, and John Wilson. "Trauma, PTSD, and Resilience A Review of the Literature." *Trauma, Violence & Abuse* 6.3 (2005): 195–216.
American Psychological Association. *The Road to Resilience.* http://www.apa.org/helpcenter/road-resilience.aspx. Washington (29 August 2018).
Assad, Alicia. *The Stories We Tell: Resilience Gained Through Positive Narrative.* https://www.huffpost.com/entry/the-stories-we-tell-resilience-gained-through-positive_b_587510bbe4b0eb9e49bfbfa5. Huffington Post, 1 October 2017 (29 August 2018).
Baggio, Jacopo, Katrina Brown, and Denis Hellebrandt. "Boundary Object or Bridging Concept? A Citation Network of Resilience." *Ecology and Society* 20.2 (2015): 2.
Balaev, Michelle. "Literary Trauma Theory Reconsidered." *Contemporary Approaches in Literary Trauma Theory.* London: Palgrave Macmillan, 2014. 1–14.
Basseler, Michael. "Fictions of Resilience: Narrating (Environmental) Crisis and Catastrophe in Cormac McCarthy's *The Road* and Jesmyn Ward's *Salvage the Bones.*" *The American Novel in the 21st Century: Cultural Contexts – Literary Developments – Critical Analysis.* Eds. M. Basseler & A. Nünning. Trier: WVT, 2019 (forthcoming).
Beah, Ishmael. *Radiance of Tomorrow.* New York: Farrar, Strauss and Giroux, 2014.
Beasts of the Southern Wild. Dir. Benh Zeitlin. Fox Searchlight Pictures, 2012.
Beck, Ulrich. *Risk Society. Towards a New Modernity.* Los Angeles: Sage 2005 [1992].
Beck, Ulrich. "Foreword: Risk Society as Political Category." *The Risk Society Revisited.* Ed. Eugene Rosa, Aaron McCright, and Ortwin Renn. Philadelphia: Temple University Press, 2013. xii–xxiii.
Beck, Ulrich. *World at Risk.* Trans. Ciaran Cronin. Cambridge, MA: Polity, 2016 [2007].
Blum, Sabine, Martin Endreß, Stefan Kaufmann, and Benjamin Rampp. "Soziologische Perspektiven." *Multidisziplinäre Perspektiven der Resilienzforschung.* Ed. Rüdiger Wink. Wiesbaden: Springer, 2016. 151–77.
Bonanno, George. "Loss, Trauma, and Human Resilience: Have We Underestimated the Human Capacity to Thrive After Extremely Aversive Events?" *American Psychologist* 59.1 (2004): 20–28.
Buelens, Gert, Sam Durrant, and Robert Eaglestone (eds.). *The Future of Trauma Theory: Contemporary Literary and Cultural Criticism.* London: Routledge, 2014.
Caruth, Cathy (ed.). *Trauma: Explorations in Memory.* Baltimore: Johns Hopkins University Press, 1995.
Chandler, David, and Julian Reid. 2016. *The Neoliberal Subject.* Resilience, Adaptation and Vulnerability. London: Rowman & Littlefield.
Cleave, Chris. *The Other Hand.* London: Hodder and Stoughton, 2009.
Community and Regional Resilience Institute. Webpage. www.resilientus.org. Washington (6 November 2018).
Craps, Stef. *Postcolonial Witnessing: Trauma Out of Bounds.* New York: Palgrave Macmillan, 2013.
Cyrulnik, Boris. *Talking of Love. How to Overcome Trauma and Remake Your Life Story.* London: Penguin, 2009.
Cyrulnik, Boris. *Resilience: How Your Inner Strength Can Set You Free From the Past.* London: Tarcher/Penguin, 2011.
Eakin, Paul John. *How Our Lives Become Stories.* Ithaca: Cornell University Press, 1999.
Eggers, Dave. *Zeitoun.* San Francisco: McSweeney's Books, 2009.

Endreß, Martin, and Benjamin Rampp. "Resilienz als Perspektive auf gesellschaftliche Prozesse." *Resilienz im Sozialen*. Ed. Martin Endreß and Andrea Maurer. Wiesbaden: Springer, 2015. 33–55.

Erll, Astrid. *Kollektives Gedächtnis und Erinnerungskulturen. Eine Einführung*. Third rev. ed. Stuttgart: Metzler, 2017.

Evans, Brad, and Julian Reid. *Resilient Life: The Art of Living Dangerously*. London: Polity, 2014.

Felman, Shoshana. *The Juridical Unconscious: Trials and Traumas in the Twentieth Century*. Cambridge, MA: Harvard University Press, 2002.

Flynn, Stephen. *The Edge of Disaster. Rebuilding a Resilient Nation*. New York: Random House, 2007.

Flynn, Stephen. *America the Resilient: Defying Terrorism and Mitigating Natural Disasters*. https://www.foreignaffairs.com/articles/2008-03-02/america-resilient. Foreign Affairs March/April 2008 (28 August 2018).

Fooken, Insa. "Psychologische Perspektiven der Resilienzforschung." *Multidisziplinäre Perspektiven der Resilienzforschung*. Ed. Rüdiger Wink. Wiesbaden: Springer, 2016. 13–45.

Frow, John. *Genre*. New York: Routledge, 2015.

Gall, Melanie. *From Social Vulnerability to Resilience: Measuring Progress Toward Disaster Risk Reduction*. UN Institute for Environment and Human Security, 2013.

Ghosh, Amitav. *The Hungry Tide*. New York: HarperCollins, 2005.

Goldstein, Bruce Evan, Anne Taufen Wessells, Raul Lejano, and William Butler. "Narrating Resilience: Transforming Urban Systems Through Collaborative Storytelling." *Urban Studies* 52.7 (2012): 1285–1303.

Grace, Patricia. *Potiki*. Honolulu: University of Hawaii Press, 1995.

Habib, Maha. "Cultures of Trauma and Cultures of Resilience: Trauma and Survival in Jean Arasanayagam's *All Is Burning* and Shashi Deshpande's *The Binding Vine*." *South Asian Review* 37.2 (2016): 224–240.

Holler, Claudia, and Martin Klepper (eds.). *Re-Thinking Narrative Identity*. Amsterdam: John Benjamins, 2013.

Jameson, Fredric. *The Political Unconscious. Narrative as a Socially Symbolic Act*. New York: Routledge, 2002 [1981].

Jansen, Stephan A. "Resistenz durch Resilienz – Über die existenzielle Eleganz von Risiko-Organisationen." *Fragile Stabilität – stabile Fragilität*. Ed. Stephan A. Jansen, Eckhard Schröter, and Nico Stehr. Wiesbaden: Springer, 2013. 117–128.

Kent, Martha, Mary C. Davis, and John W. Reich (eds.). *The Resilience Handbook: Approaches to Stress and Trauma*. New York: Routledge, 2014.

Klein, Christian, and Matías Martínez. *Wirklichkeitserzählungen. Felder, Formen und Funktionen nicht-literarischen Erzählens*. Stuttgart: Metzler, 2009.

Kirmeyer, Laurence, Stéphane Dandeneau, Elizabeth Marshall, Morgan Kahentonni Phillips, and Karla Jessen Williamson. "Rethinking Resilience from Indigenous Perspecitves." *Canadian Journal of Psychiatry* 56.2 (2011): 84–91.

Kurtz, J. Roger (ed.). *Trauma and Literature*. Cambridge: Cambridge University Press, 2018.

Lakoff, George, and Mark Johnson. *Metaphors We Live By*. Chicago: Chicago University Press, 1980.

Lentzos, Filippa, and Nikolas Rose. "Governing Insecurity: Contingency Planning, Protection, Resilience." *Economy and Society* 38.2 (2009): 230–254.

Levine, Caroline. *Forms. Whole, Rhythm, Hierarchy, Network*. Princeton: Princeton University Press, 2015.

Luckhurst, Roger. *The Trauma Question*. London: Routledge, 2008.

McAdams, Dan P. *The Redemptive Self. Stories Americans Live By*. Oxford: Oxford University Press, 2006.

McCarthy, Cormac. *The Road*. New York: Vintage, 2006.

Murphy, Patrick D. "Community Resilience and the Cosmopolitan Role in the Environmental Challenge-Response Novels of Ghosh, Grace, and Sinha." *Comparative Literary Studies* 50.1 (2013): 148–168.

Neimeyer, Robert, and Heidi Levitt. "Coping and Coherence: A Narrative Perspective on Resilience." *Coping With Stress: Effective People and Processes*. Ed. C.R. Snyder. Oxford: Oxford University Press, 2001. 47–67.

Nünning, Ansgar. "Towards a Cultural and Historical Narratology: A Survey of Diachronic Approaches, Concepts, and Research Projects." *Anglistentag 1999 Mainz: Proceedings*. Eds. Bernhard Reitz and Sigrid Rieuwerts. Trier: WVT, 2000. 345–373.

Nünning, Ansgar. "Surveying Contextualist and Cultural Narratologies: Towards an Outline of Approaches, Concepts and Potentials." *Narratology in the Age of Cross-Disciplinary Research*. Eds. Sandra Heinen and Roy Sommer. Berlin: de Gruyter, 2009a. 48–70.

Nünning, Ansgar. "Steps Toward a Metaphorology (and Narratology) of Crises: On The Functions of Metaphors as Figurative Knowledge and Mininarrations." *Metaphors Shaping Culture and Theory*. Eds. Herbert Grabes, Ansgar Nünning, and Sibylle Baumbach. Tübingen: Narr, 2009b. 229–262.

Nünning, Ansgar. "Narrativist Approaches and Narratological Concepts for the Study of Culture." *Travelling Concepts for the Study of Culture*. Eds. Birgit Neumann and Ansgar Nünning. Berlin: de Gruyter, 2012. 145–183.

Nünning, Ansgar, and Kai Sicks (eds.). *Turning Points. Concepts and Narratives of Change in Literature and Other Media*. Berlin: de Gruyter, 2012.

Nünning, Ansgar, and Vera Nünning. "Multiperspektivität aus narratologischer Sicht: Erzähltheoretische Grundlagen und Kategorien zur Analyse der Perspektivenstruktur narrativer Texte." *Multiperspektivisches Erzählen: Zur Theorie und Geschichte der Perspektivenstruktur im englischen Roman des 18. bis 20. Jahrhunderts*. Eds. Vera Nünning and Ansgar Nünning. Trier: WVT, 2000. 39–77.

Nünning, Ansgar, and Vera Nünning. "Conceptualizing 'Broken Narratives' from a Narratological Perspective: Domains, Concepts, Features, Functions and Suggestions for Research." *Narrative im Bruch. Theoretische Positionen und Anwendungen*. Eds. Anna Babka, Marlen Bidwell-Steiner, and Wolfgang Müller-Funk. Göttingen: Vienna University Press, 2016. 37–86.

Nünning, Ansgar, and Vera Nünning. "How to Stay Healthy and Foster Well-Being with Narratives, or: Where Narratology and Salutogenesis Could Meet." *How to Do Things with Narrative: Political and Narratological Perspectives on Anglophone Texts*. Eds. Jan Alber and Greta Olson. Berlin: de Gruyter 2017. 157–186.

O'Brien, Susie. "Resilient Virtue and the Virtues of Resilience: Post-Bhopal Ecology in Animal's People." *Kunapipi* 34.2 (2012): 23–31.

O'Brien, Susie. "Resilience Stories: Narratives of Adaptation, Refusal, and Compromise." *Resilience* 4.2 (2017): 43–65.

Ostheimer, Jochen. "Die resiliente Gesellschaft. Überlegungen zu einer Kulturaufgabe im Zeitalter des Menschen." *Resilienz. Interdisziplinäre Perspektiven zu Wandel und*

Transformation. Eds. Maria Karidi, Martin Schneider, and Rebecca Gutwald. Wiesbaden: Springer, 2018. 327–346.

Panter-Brick, Catherine, and James F. Leckman. "Editorial Commentary: Resilience in Child Development – Interconnected Pathways to Wellbeing." *Journal of Child Psychology and Psychiatry* 54.4 (2013): 333–336.

Piazza, Tom. *City of Refuge*. New York: HarperCollins, 2008.

Richardson, Michael. "Climate Trauma, or the Affects of the Catastrophe to Come." *Environmental Humanities* 10.1 (2018): 1–19.

Rozario, Kevin. "Making Progress: Disaster Narratives and the Art of Optimism in Modern America." *The Resilient City*. Eds. Lawrence J. Vale and Thomas J. Campanella. Oxford: Oxford University Press, 2005. 27–54.

Sinha, Indra. *Animal's People*. London: Simon & Schuster, 2008 [2007].

Strand, Joyce, and Robert Peacock. "Resource Guide: Cultural Resilience." *Tribal College Journal* 14.4 (2003): 28–31.

Treme. Dir. David Simon and Eric Overmyer. 4 seasons. HBO, 2010–2013.

Vale, Laurence, and Thomas Campanella. "Conclusion: Axioms of Resilience." *The Resilient City: How Modern Cities Recover From Disaster*. Eds. Laurence J. Vale and Thomas Campanella. Oxford: Oxford University Press, 2005. 335–355.

Vardy, Mark, and Mick Smith. "Resilience." *Environmental Humanities* 9.1 (2017): 175–179.

Vickroy, Laurie. *Trauma and Survival in Contemporary Fiction*. Charlottesville: University of Virginia Press, 2002.

Wapner, Paul. "Climate of the Poor: Suffering and the Moral Imperative to Reimagine Resilience." *Reimagining Climate Change*. Eds. Paul Wapner and Hilal Elver. New York: Routledge, 2016. 131–149.

Ward, Jesmyn. *Salvage the Bones*. New York: Bloomsbury, 2011.

Weiss, Matthias, Silja Hartmann, and Martin Högl. "Resilienz als Trendkonzept. Über die Diffusion von Resilienz in Gesellschaft und Wissenschaft." *Resilienz. Interdisziplinäre Perspektiven zu Wandel und Transformation*. Eds. Maria Karidi, Martin Schneider, and Rebecca Gutwald. Wiesbaden: Springer, 2018. 13–32.

Werner, Emmy, and Ruth S. Smith. *Vulnerable But Invincible. A Longitudinal Study of Resilient Children and Youth*. New York: McGraw-Hill, 1982.

Whitehead, Anne. *Trauma Fiction*. Edinburgh: Edinburgh University Press, 2004.

Wink, Rüdiger. "Resilienzperspektive als wissenschaftliche Chance. Eine Einstimmung zu diesem Sammelband." *Multidisziplinäre Perspektiven der Resilienzforschung*. Ed. Rüdiger Wink. Wiesbaden: Springer, 2016. 1–11.

Zapf, Hubert. *Literature as Cultural Ecology. Sustainable Texts*. London: Bloomsbury, 2016.

Sibylle Baumbach
Mind the Narratives: Towards a Cultural Narratology of Attention

Abstract: Taking its cue from current discourses on anxieties of (in)attention, and from the connections between attention, culture, and narrative, this essay introduces the conceptual and methodological framework for a cultural narratology of attention. As I argue, selective attention is not only a biological necessity: it also guides the production and reception of literary texts, influences the cultural narratives we live by, drives the development of (new) genres, and gives rise to what I call 'attention narratives'. Focusing on Arthur Conan Doyle's *Sherlock Holmes* stories, this essay shows how these 'attention narratives' connect with cultural anxieties of attention and distraction, driven mainly by technological advancements, while challenging readers' attentional capacities. They do so by creating moments of 'inattentional blindness', which help increase readers' awareness of the mechanisms of attention, while exposing cultural attention narratives that have shaped and continue to shape our perception. Given the central role of attention in cultures and narratives, there is a strong need for a cultural narratology of attention that bridges cognitive psychology, cultural studies, and literary studies. This essay offers the foundation for such an approach.

1 Attention, please! Narratives in the attention economy

We live in a culture of distraction. Whether tending to our multiple selves in social media or reacting to relentless push-notifications on our smartphones, the lure of 24/7 connectivity has a firm hold on most of us. The effortless access to multiple different worlds and communication channels, coupled with the desire to stay connected and receive instant gratification for our actions, makes us as 'social animals' easy prey for what Jonathan Crary has referred to as "24/7 capitalism [...] in which multiple operations or attractions can be attended to in near-simultaneity, regardless of where one is or whatever else one might be doing" (2013, 84). While we are faced with a surplus of information propelled by digital communication techniques, our time and cognitive capacities are limited. Within the free market of "cognitive capitalism" (Moulier-Boutang 2011), attention has become both a key currency and scarce resource. The growing awareness of its limits has given rise to what has come to be known as the 'attention economy' (Davenport and Beck 2001), where the value of an object is defined by "the amount of (unpaid-for) [...] attention it has absorbed" (Beller 2006, 181).

These developments, coupled with novel opportunities afforded by digital technologies, have also affected practices of storytelling. Newly emerging genres, such as the 'internet novel', the 'email novel', or 'twitterature', tap the technological potential of digital communication. Furthermore, many of these narratives cater to what Katherine Hayles has defined as "hyper attention": a penchant for "switching focus rapidly among different tasks, preferring multiple information streams, seeking a high level of stimulation, and having a low tolerance for boredom" (2007, 187). According to Hayles, this lack of sustained attention is the antipode to "deep attention," "traditionally associated with the humanities [and] characterized by concentrating on a single object for long periods (say, a novel by Dickens), ignoring outside stimuli while so engaged, preferring a single information stream, and having a high tolerance for long focus" (2007, 187). As will be argued in this paper, however, anxieties of (in)attention as well as the strong link between attention and narratives are not a postmodern phenomenon. Instead, they are at the heart of both narratives and (information) cultures and can be traced across different eras.

In the following pages, I will briefly outline the concept of 'attention' and the connections between attention, culture, and narrative, before suggesting a framework for a (cultural) narratology of attention. In the latter part of the essay, I will turn to Arthur Conan Doyle's *Sherlock Holmes* stories as a prominent example of what I refer to as attention narratives. These narratives, in their time deeply embedded in the economy of attention, address and also counter anxieties of attention by disclosing the mechanisms of attention, conveying strategies of attentional focus, and involving readers in attentional challenges prompted by specific narrative devices. In responding to discourses on attention toward the end of the nineteenth century, Conan Doyle's stories revolve around key aspects of human (in)attention that remain relevant and, indeed, contribute to the stories' ongoing appeal.

While attention research is a growing area in psychology (see Nobre and Kastner 2014), philosophy (see Nanay 2016), and art history (see Crary 1999), literary and cultural studies have not yet deeply engaged with this field. Although some studies that explore what can be termed 'literary attention' exist, a (cultural) narratology of attention still needs to be established. For this approach, cultural studies and narratology must join forces. The objective of a cultural narratology of attention will be twofold: first, it will offer the tools for the systematic analysis of the narrative forms and structures that elicit (or inhibit) attention and their connection to the cultures of attention in which these narratives were created and communicated; secondly, it will assess the function of narratives in different attention economies, both within and across various eras, by examining the ways in which narratives have been shaped by, and have contributed to shaping, attention cultures.

The lack of such an approach is all the more surprising, given that principles of attention guide "social practices of real-world storytelling in different discourses and institutions" (Nünning 2012, 164). If, as claimed by Kenneth Rogers, attention can be conceptualized as "a *transactional reality*, which [...] shapes a transferential site where external technologies of power encounter the self" (2014, 20–21), narratives serve as an important means for reflecting upon technologies of attention, anxieties of (in)attention, and "the notion of an attention economy as a new human capital strategy" (2014, 194), while at the same time "negotiating a crisis of the self that is increasingly managed, mediated and controlled by technologies" (2014, 2).

In this context, the attention to attention and 'attention narratives' in particular, i.e. narratives that revolve around key aspects of attention and that challenge readers' attentional capacities, might be regarded as part of a counter-movement to the "internal (mental) and external (ecological) exhaustion" (Doran 2017, 52) effected by neoliberal capitalism, insofar as these narratives advocate the re-establishing of a "relation to the self" (Doran 2017, 56) by scrutinizing cultural anxieties of (in)attention and unveiling key strategies of attention and attention management. In fact, narratives of attention have often emerged from crises of attention. Their notable increase in recent decades can be explained on the one hand by the growing public awareness of cognitive impairments, partly driven by the "ADHD industry" (Rogers 2014, 166), and on the other by the increased attention being paid "to a contemporary form of governmentality conditioned by the resurgence of political and economic liberalism, the rise of biocapitalism, and the rapid mutations of media technology in the digital information economy" (Rogers 2014, 2). A cultural narratology of attention based on approaches from literary and cultural studies, therefore, is a profoundly cross-disciplinary endeavor drawing on existing research on attention in the disciplines of cognitive and cultural psychology, philosophy, art history, and media studies.

2 Attention, culture, and narrative

Although not a unitary phenomenon, and therefore hard to define, attention is generally conceived as referring to the selection of a subset of the multiple impressions perceived by the human senses. Bombarded with numerous and diverse stimuli that we cannot process in their entirety, our brain has to filter the sensory input to allow us to successfully navigate our environment. Attention has been conceived as "bottlenecks in perception" (Nobre and Kastner 2014, 1201), which regulate the information entering our working memory and prevent us from cognitive overload. It can, therefore, be regarded as a biological necessity.

To conceptualize the complex processes involved in attention, scholars distinguish between stimulus-driven or bottom-up, and goal-driven or top-down attention (see Pinto et al. 2013). Whereas the first type of attention is exogenous and involuntary, the latter is endogenous and more sustainable, as it is directed by voluntary control (see Carrasco 2011). While some – especially exogenous – processes in attention are considered universal (Pinto et al. 2013), patterns in endogenous attention are guided by "knowledge, expectation, motivation, feelings, values and goals" (Masuda 2017, 2) and are thus shaped by our cultural environments. This is confirmed by studies comparing attention patterns in participants from America and Japan. Involving various tasks that require the description of visual scenes, these studies suggest that American participants pay greater attention to focal objects and foregrounded information, while Japanese participants tend to integrate focal and contextual information. These findings connect with earlier studies that distinguish between two different thinking styles, the analytic and the holistic (see Nisbett 2003, also Masuda 2017) associated with Western and Asian cultures respectively (Nisbett 2003, 82).

What is particularly interesting is that these studies take "people's narrative styles as an indicator of their attention" (Masuda 2017, 2), claiming that "constructing narratives tends to activate culturally dominant modes of attention" (Masuda 2017, 3). There is, of course, a structural difference between spontaneously (re)produced narratives and carefully composed (literary) narratives that have gone through several editing processes. For the analysis of attention cultures, however, the latter might be even more revealing, as they constitute key "cultural products", which "reflect [a] culture's dominant meaning system" (Masuda 2017, 6) and "can also shape psyches, as they reinforce or prime particular ways of thinking, valuing, or feeling" (Morling and Lamoureaux 2008, 213).

In addition to providing insight into dominant notions of attention within a particular culture at a specific time, narratives may help shape readers' attentional capacities by promoting mindfulness. The latter has been described as "intentionally knowing and choosing what the attention is directed to" or "attention regulation" (Hassed 2014, 631). It is important to note that mindfulness and attention require both the ability to focus and the ability to let the mind wander. After all, tension cannot exist without its counterpart of (temporary) release: distraction "is not the opposite of attention [but] simply marks a disruption [...] in its rhythms" (Phillips 2016, 128).

A cultural narratology of attention must, therefore, not only take into account the different ways in which narratives respond to and negotiate cultural, political, psychological, and philosophical discourses on attention: it must also consider the interplay of attention and distraction created in these narratives in the interests of cognitive release, and even of mind-wandering – moments which are themselves, in addition to fostering creativity and problem-solving skills, a prerequisite for attention (see Baird et al. 2012).

3 Developing a cultural narratology of attention

Some initial starting points for developing a cultural narratology of attention are provided by recent approaches to 'literary attention' in contexts ranging from distraction in eighteenth-century literature (Phillips 2016) and the poetics of attention in eighteenth-century (Koehler 2012) and Romantic poetry (Gurton-Wachter 2016), through the desire for attention to the everyday in post-1945 American poetry (Epstein 2016), to attentive reading and the mega-novel (Letzler 2017). To establish a narratology of attention that contributes to the field of critical attention studies as represented by Crary (1999), Hayles (2007), Beller (2006), and Rogers (2014), the works by Phillips and Letzler – together with initial linguistic studies on devices used to control readers' attention (Emmott et al. 2013) – are particularly relevant.

Concerned with both literary attention and distraction, these studies confirm the close bond between narrative and attention. After all, ancient rhetoric revolved around strategies to draw in and bind listeners (see Möller 2013): all texts are essentially composed to attract attention. What characterizes narratives of attention, however, is their rooting in discourses of attention at a specific time. The poetics of attention in Romantic poetry, for instance, is closely linked with the late eighteenth-century political discourse of watchfulness and "the militarization of attention" (Gurton-Wachter 2016, 5) that was driven by fear of a possible French invasion – an anxiety countered at the time by literary attention, which "allow[ed] readers to notice the neutral, overlooked, or untouched" (Gurton-Wachter 2016, 193). In a similar vein, "the obsessive attention to concrete, daily experience" (Epstein 2016, 219) in post-WW2 American poetry expressed a "political critique of capitalist, consumerist American culture" (Epstein 2016, 220), insofar as it aimed "to puncture the aura of triviality that masks the political realities and profound truths of everyday life" (Epstein 2016, 274).

Considering the interconnection between aesthetic and political modes of attention and drawing on Frederic Jameson's notion of the "ideology of form" (1981, 90; see Nünning 2012, 167), I would argue that the development of literary genres is also fundamentally guided by changing discourses of attention. Although more research has to be conducted to substantiate the link between attention and genre development, the connection is confirmed, for instance, by Gothic fiction, which both prompts and exhibits forms of attentional excess, as well as the dangers of intense fixation (see Phillips 2016, 137–139) and fascination (see Baumbach 2015, Ch. 4). The focus on attention and its strategies in these narratives counters anxieties about the absorbing effects of reading, the monstrosity of modern technologies, and the crisis of perception, all of which revealed a growing awareness of the "constitutive role played by various forms of technical and cognitive mediation in the mind's perception of the external world" (Drury 2017, 145).

The rise of the short story is also closely connected with a crisis of perception and a concomitant anxiety of attention to which they responded not by encouraging attentional excess but by channeling and refining readers' attentional capacities. The proliferation of this genre in the late nineteenth century[1] coincided with the emergence of a modern "capitalist consumer economy" (Crary 1999, 33) and was accompanied by "an ongoing crisis of attentiveness" (Crary 1999, 13):

> [T]he changing configurations of capitalism continually push attention and distraction to new limits and thresholds, with an endless sequence of new products, sources of stimulation, and streams of information, and then respond with new methods of managing and regulating perfection. (Crary 1999, 13–14)

In our contemporary attention economy we can witness similar effects. Indeed, the crisis of attention in the nineteenth century went hand-in-hand with new theories of attention, most notably William James' *The Principles of Psychology* (1950 [1890]). The short story, which found the perfect home in periodicals, catered to shorter attention spans. This quality made it preferable to the novel which, as Edgar Allan Poe remarked, "cannot be read at one sitting", thus "depriv[ing] itself [...] of the immense force derivable from *totality*" (1863, 197). I will return to the connection between the short story and attention in the final part of this essay.

The analysis of attention narratives starts with the identification of "attractors". As defined by Peter Stockwell, "an attractor is a figural, trajector element

---

1 As H.G. Wells remarked in relation to the 1890s, "[s]hort stories broke out everywhere" (1914, v).

that claims most readerly attention on the basis of, among other factors, agency, topicality, human-scale, brightness, size, noisiness, danger, and so on" (2014, 24). Stylistic features that have been identified as capturing attention include foregrounding devices such as italics, alliteration, unusual metaphors, repetition, or fragmentation (see Emmott et al. 2013). For digital fiction, media-specific features such as sound, images, the level of reader participation, and interface design have to be taken into account (see Bell et al. 2013), as well as distractors, including hyperlinks, which interrupt the linear flow of reading and add to readers' cognitive load (see Hayles 2010, 68).

Further "attention-controlling" (Emmott et al. 2003, 21) mechanisms range from generic expectations to scripts and schemata that relate to readers' pre-knowledge and culturally-determined processes of understanding. Insofar as characters describe moments of deep attention or distraction, reveal some kind of attention deficit, comment on their own or other characters' proneness to distraction or their talent for (or lack of) concentration, and create moments of joint attention (see Tobin 2008) by directing the gaze to specific objects or other characters, they can also be regarded as attention-drawing and -controlling devices within a narrative.

Characters can further serve as attractors if they point to the narrative's attentional (or distractive) qualities in metafictional twists, as Laurence Sterne's Madam Reader does in *The Life and Opinions of Tristram Shandy, Gentleman* (1759) or Ian McEwan's Briony in *Atonement* (2001). Further attractors include images of attention, both literal and metaphorical, such as the microscope (Phillips 2016, 136) or the magnifying glass, which announce or prepare a scene of intense focus.

Attention is also the guiding principle in character construction and constellation, inasmuch as it regulates what Alex Woloch (2003) calls 'character-space', i.e. the space a character occupies at the expense of other characters. Characterization, therefore, should involve the analysis of the disjunctions between "a distributed pattern of attention" in the story and "the formed pattern of attention in the discourse" (Woloch 2003, 41), i.e. between the implied potential of a character and the space that character inhabits in a narrative compared to other characters. The results will yield important insights into the dynamics of character arrangement within narrative texts, in addition to the "social rhythms" (Levine 2015, 53) that regulate the tempi of social experience.

One of the hallmarks of attention narratives, as defined here, is their ability to draw attention to attention and its limitations – the latter property by violating strategies for keeping readers' attention. Paraphrasing Viktor Shklovsky's remark on *Tristram Shandy* (1759) – "it is the consciousness of form through its violation that constitutes the content of the novel" (Shklovsky 1991, 149) – one could argue that it is the consciousness of attention through its violation that constitutes attention narratives.

Violations of form include "layered syntax, plotlines, and cognitive breaks" (Phillips 2016, 99) of the sort that characterize non-linear or disrupted narratives. Cognitive breaks can be instigated by shifts in perspective, time, or space. They predominantly occur in first-person narratives and are often triggered by narrators' digressions. As in *Tristram Shandy*, these detours, which Sterne refers to as "the life, the soul of reading" (1832 [1759], 64), may be marked by dashes in the text which indicate "junctions between overlaid narrative threads and thoughts, building a sense of synchronous cognition" and suggest "the interruptions, or focal rests, produced as the mind becomes overloaded" (Phillips 2016, 104). What Phillips calls "[f]ragmented rhythms of scattered attention" (2016, 98) can also be traced in many modern and postmodern narratives from Virginia Woolf's *Mrs Dalloway* (1925) to David Llewellyn's *Eleven* (2006), where the aesthetics of fragmentation points to an attempt to refocus attention after the traumatic experience of war and terror.

In principle, such "multifocal narrative[s]" (Phillips 2016, 105) illustrate the possibility of "parallel processing" (Phillips 2016, 110) of information, demanding (and confirming readers' capacity for) divided attention, i.e. the ability "to perform two or more tasks or process two or more sources of information concurrently" (Zanto and Gazzaley 2014, 939). As scholars have argued, reading is essentially an act of "double" (Gurton-Wachter 2016, Ch. 1) or "divided" (Phillips 2016, 206) attention, for it includes several parallel processes from "letter [and] morpheme recognition, […] all the way up to conflict resolution within the lexicon" (Dehaene 2009, 51), as well as activities such as gap-filling (Iser 1978) and mental simulation (Green and Donahue 2012). Unless the narrative draws attention to these processes, they do not interfere with, but rather support immersion in a story.

Multifocal narratives, however, increase the cognitive load needed for processing and organizing the multiple pieces of information. The disruption of narrative flow with digressions may on the one hand point to the non-chronological nature of memory, but pushed to extremes it indicates an overload of (the narrator's) working memory and unduly stretches readers' cognitive capacities. Long, complex sentences, including "(1) multiple, incomplete syntactic units; (2) disorganized or poorly subordinated clauses; and (3) irregular rhythmic variations" (Phillips 2016, 114) which are impossible to parse at first reading can have a similar effect.

Though often less complex on the syntactic level, mega-novels, such as Eleanor Catton's *The Luminaries* (2013) or Karl Ove Knausgaard's six-part autobiography *The Struggle* (2009–2011), whose "ceaselessly compelling" narrative leaves you "interested [...] even when [...] bored" (Wood 2012), draw much of their success from their excessive demands on readers' attention. Connecting to Roland Barthes' remark that "it is the very rhythm of what is read and what is not read that creates the pleasure of the great narratives" (1975, 11), David Letzler has argued that mega-novels, characterized by a "distinctive combination of expansiveness and emptiness" (2017, 89), are training grounds for our attentional capacities because they strategically overstrain readers' working memory, forcing them to select: "Some passages should be processed closely and slowly, while others should be read more quickly; some are best read distantly, and others are best passed over entirely" (2017, 233). These shifts in attention, prompted by redundancies and repetitions, limited semantic complexity, an overload of long lists or references – e.g. encyclopedic fiction, such as Mark Z. Danielewski's *House of Leaves* (2000) – or narrative excess in representations of the quotidian (as so often in life-writing), are "cognitively beneficial" to the extent that they help readers "modulate attention in the mega-novel's controlled environment" (Letzler 2017, 233). According to Letzler, this ability is central for navigating "the more unrestrained cascades of information we regularly encounter in our everyday lives" (2017, 233). Stimulating both deep and skim reading, "the cruft of fiction" (Letzler 2017) might help nurture what Maryanne Wolf has recently described as a "'bi-literate' reading brain capable of the deepest forms of thought in either digital or traditional mediums" (2018, n. p.).

Free of any 'cruft', the short story represents the opposite trend in literary attention: it seems to have done the filtering for us, offering only the most relevant information and, "read at one sitting" (Poe 1863, 197), however intense, refrains from overstraining our working memory. Nevertheless, although short stories have become increasingly popular again, propelled by the award of the Nobel Prize in Literature to Alice Munro in 2013, the most read fiction in the UK in 2018 was crime fiction (Hannah 2018, n. p.), a genre whose success is grounded not so much in a yearning for justice as in the attention games it initiates.

As Catherine Emmott, Anthony J. Sanford, and Marc Alexander have argued, "[m]ystery and detective writing relies on the manipulation of readers' attention" (2013, 47). To this end it has four main strategies: "(1) burying information"; "(2) the use of distractors [...] to direct readers' attention towards a false trail"; "(3) the use of foregrounding devices"; and "(4) the use of false reconstructions at the denouement" (Emmott et al. 2013, 47). Its great success during the crisis of perception in the late nineteenth century suggests that crime fiction is both the product of, and an antidote to cultural anxieties of (in)attention.

To further explore its potential in terms of cultural attention narratives, I will briefly turn to what is arguably the most successful example of crime fiction: Arthur Conan Doyle's *Sherlock Holmes* stories. Sparked by their adaptation by the

BBC in England and CBS in America, these have lately experienced a revival. In addition to indicating "an ongoing crisis of attentiveness" (Crary 1999, 13), this revival, as Kyoko Takanashi has observed, "draws attention to Conan Doyle's texts as a rich site for exploring the politics of information culture" (2017, 250). It also draws attention to attention itself, as well as to the connection between attention, culture, and narrative, and in doing so confirms the current need for a cultural narratology of attention.

4 Defective attention and the detective turn

Targeted especially in *The Strand Magazine* to a mass readership, the *Sherlock Holmes* stories (1887–1927) were deeply embedded in a modern economy of attention. In fact, the very invention of the character of Sherlock Holmes was attention-driven. As Doyle recalled, "it had struck me that a single character running through a series, if it only engaged the attention of the reader, would bind that reader to that particular magazine" (Doyle 2012, 95). To keep readers interested in the narratives, even if they missed one installment, Doyle designed them as a series, as deeply interconnected, yet essentially independent. In addition to operating within the machinery of nineteenth-century seriality (see Wiltse 1998, 116), the *Sherlock Holmes* stories foreground the art of attention through their protagonist, who introduces himself at the outset of the series as "consulting detective" (Doyle 2006, 41), directs attention to what is frequently overlooked, and shows a precision in reasoning that verges on the superhuman.

As Dr. Watson, the scientific, yet crucially inattentive observer through whom the narratives are focalized, suggests, Holmes' "cold, precise but admirably balanced mind" makes him "the most perfect reasoning and observing machine that the world has seen" (Doyle, 2005, 5). Blending man, mind, and machine, the image underlines the attention mechanisms at work in these narratives and at the same time reflects late nineteenth-century anxieties which, as Crary suggests, went hand-in-hand with "the emergence of a social, urban, psychic, and industrial field increasingly saturated with sensory input" (Crary 1999, 13):

> Inattention, especially within the context of new forms of large-scale industrialized production, began to be treated as a danger and a serious problem, even though it was often the very modernized arrangements of labor that produced inattention. (Crary 1999, 13)

In addition to being a prime product of attention – a fact confirmed by the public outcry following Holmes' suggested death at the Reichenbach Falls in "The Adventure of the Final Problem" (1893) and the ensuing pressure exerted on

Doyle by readers and magazine alike to revive the popular character (which he did eight years later in *The Hound of the Baskervilles*) – Sherlock Holmes served (and serves) not only as a generator of attention but also as a source of insight into its mechanisms. Responding to late nineteenth-century anxieties, the attention machinery that drives Doyle's narratives can further be read as a literary training ground for challenging and refining readers' attentional capacities. The close link between these narratives and cognitive psychology is confirmed by recent studies on memory, deduction, and attention, which refer to Doyle's stories to illustrate information processing mechanisms (see Didierjean and Gobet 2008, and especially Konnikova 2013).

Although the word 'attention' hardly occurs in the stories, Holmes' image of the 'brain attic', proposed in *A Study in Scarlet* (1887), points to a strong focus on techniques of attention management. In this novel, which is the first story of the series and introduces Holmes' principles of 'the art of deduction',[2] Holmes compares the human brain to "a little empty attic, [which] you have to stock [...] with such furniture as you choose" (Doyle 2006, 32). The aim behind this mnemotechnic strategy is to avoid cluttering one's cognitive system, more precisely, one's long-term memory, with superfluous input:

> A fool takes in all the lumber of every sort that he comes across, so that the knowledge which might be useful to him gets crowded out, or at best is jumbled up with a lot of other things, so that he has a difficulty in laying his hands upon it. (Doyle 2006, 32)

This statement connects to a claim that William James would make three years later in *The Principles of Psychology* when he stated, "*My experience is what I agree to attend to.* Only those items which I *notice* shape my mind – without selective interest, experience is an utter chaos" (James 1950 [1890], 402).

Countering John Locke's conceptualization of the human mind as a blank slate upon which all sensual impressions are inscribed, both James and Doyle's Holmes advocate the necessity of filtering sensual input through controlled, voluntary attention; it is the latter that distinguishes 'observing' from 'seeing' (see Holmes' rebuke of Watson: "You see, but you do not observe", Doyle 2005, 10). Holmes' selection criteria do not follow any 'standards': The Copernican principle,

---

[2] The reference to 'the art of deduction' could also be read as a first test in readerly attention, for it turns out that Holmes' mode of reasoning is not based on deduction, but rather on abduction (see Rapezzi et al. 2005).

for instance, has no place in his 'brain attic', as it does not aid him in solving his cases.³ Instead, he follows the principle of choice, which resonates with James' statement that "[e]ach of us literally *chooses*, by way of attending to things, what sort of a universe he shall appear to himself to inhabit" (1950 [1890], 424).

The rejection of 'common knowledge' enables him to pay attention to what is overlooked, most notably by Dr. Watson or Scotland Yard, who rely on narratives that provide "reassurance and familiarity rather than discomfort and strangeness" (Takanashi 2017, 258). By pointing to information that might be strange yet deeply relevant, Holmes takes on the role of an indexer,⁴ representing a kind of "liberal professionalism [which] depends on striving for a 'cultivated detachment' in information management – one that [...] navigates the push-pull relation between data and narrative" (Takanashi 2017, 262). In this respect, the character of Sherlock Holmes might be read as introducing a new form of critical, individualized attention economy, where the ability to control and maintain one's attention, unaffected by the foci already set within "[t]he society of spectacle" (Debord 1967), reinforces the autonomous subject. The desire for autonomy in attention and attention management embodied by Holmes might well contribute to the enduring popularity of this figure.

In recent revivals of Doyle's stories, Holmes' capacities for "professional information management" (Takanashi 2017, 263) are accentuated insofar as his thought processes and cognitive databases are visualized as digital interfaces which he navigates through swiping movements that suggest controlled access to digital media. In the BBC series, produced by Steven Moffat and Mark Gatiss, Holmes' 'brain attic' becomes a 'mind palace', a metaphor which also draws on the mind-machine image inasmuch as it conceives the brain as a computer, a "hard drive" (BBC *Sherlock*, S1, E3: "The Great Game" (2010), 4:44–4:46) on which memories and knowledge can be stored, structured, and retrieved. Part of Holmes' 'mind palace' has been outsourced to his smartphone, which serves as an extended mind through which he can tap the full potential of the internet. Unlike the world wide web, but quite like the attic, the 'mind palace' has only limited storage space ("I have to delete something", BBC *Sherlock*, S3, E2: "The

---

3 Holmes' disregard of the Copernican system could also be read as a depreciation of a treatise by his adversary James Moriarty, who may have been modeled on the Canadian-American astronomer Simon Newcomb, who had published on *The Motion of the Moon* (1878) and *Popular Astronomy* (1878) (see Shreffler 1989).
4 Indices became increasingly popular towards the end of the nineteenth century, following the foundation of the Index Society which aimed "[t]o direct public attention to a neglected subject" (Wheatley 1878, 38; see Takanashi 2017).

Sign of Three" (2014], 01:13:06–01:13:10). The key difference between the 'brain attic' and the 'mind palace', however, is that the latter is made accessible to viewers, whereas the former is a closed mental space, albeit one whose design is suggested through descriptions (by both Watson and Holmes) and to some extent replicated in Doyle's narratives through an acute attention to detail.

What further complicates access to Holmes' brain attic is the fact that Doyle's stories are told from the viewpoint of Dr. Watson. Though the narratives include long sequences of direct speech by Holmes, which provide an impression of immediacy, these are recalled by the doctor. Watson, however, is a reliable narrator and attends closely to Holmes, which underscores the strong attraction exerted by the detective: "His very person and appearance were such as to strike the attention of the most casual observer. [...] His eyes were sharp and piercing [...] and his thin, hawk-like nose gave his whole expression an air of alertness and decision" (Doyle 2006, 29). While Watson presents Holmes as the embodiment of attention, he fears that he himself, however, might be regarded "as a hopeless busybody" (Doyle 2006, 30). As if to excuse himself for his infatuation with this figure, Watson urges us, his readers, to consider the attentional void that had dominated his life prior to the encounter with the detective: "how objectless was my life, and how little there was to engage my attention" (Doyle 2006, 30). Where Holmes serves as attractor, Watson adopts a dual position as both distractor and attractor. As narrator, he channels the reader's attention by zooming in and out of the center of attention and commenting on the detective's art of deduction; but he also creates instances of joint attention by recalling moments in which both Holmes and he attended closely to specific aspects of a scene.

The BBC series counters this mode of 'deep', singular and, to some extent, filtered attention by diminishing Watson's role as attention-controlling narrator of a blog he writes, thus providing viewers direct access to all the characters that appear and allowing them access to Holmes' 'mind palace'. Numerous cross-cut shots, overlaying graphics, floating texts, and slow-motion effects are used to visualize Holmes' thought processes and to blend searches in various mental databases and maps as a means to creating what appears to be an ideal human-technology interface. The image of the digitalized brain, tailored to an audience used to switching its attention between multiple media, further blurs the line between man and machine and presents instances of controlled attention. Coupled with stage shifts in (camera) perspective, reverse shots, and quick scene transitions, these techniques demand viewers' divided attention. As a result, they stimulate parallel processing to a greater extent (due to their more rapid succession) than multifocal narratives, and engage viewers in an 'attention machine' that caters to what Katherine Hayles (quoted above) has identified as a dominating trend toward "hyper attention" (2007, 187).

The hyper-attention scenes included in the BBC adaptation emphasize that the *Sherlock Holmes* stories continue to respond to a desire for attentional control – belying the fact, of course, that the BBC series (not unlike Doyle's stories) is part of a greater media machinery governed by the attention economy. That this point could be missed might be regarded as a form of 'inattentional blindness', which the *Sherlock Holmes* stories ironically try to expose and work against. The term, coined by Arien Mack and Irvin Rock (2000) in connection with experiments in visual perception, refers to the (natural) tendency to miss important information while focusing intensely on one specific task or aspect; after all, it is impossible to attend to all stimuli present. Christopher Chabris and Daniel Simons have illustrated this psychological phenomenon with the by now well-known 'gorilla experiment' (2010, 5–6) in which a video is played showing six people, three dressed in white, three in black. The two groups pass a basketball between them and viewers are asked to count the number of times the players in white pass the ball. While focusing on this task, half of the viewers fail to notice a person dressed in a full-body black gorilla costume who slowly walks across the scene and even stops in the middle of the action to thump its chest.

As argued by Chabris and Simons, 'inattentional blindness' is "not just limited to visual attention" (2010, 39), but exposes a widespread "illusion of attention" (2010, 41), which consists in the belief that we see everything, even though our attention is selective and highly restricted. This illusion of attention – which Chabris and Simons describe as "a necessary, if unfortunate, by-product of the normal operation of attention and perception" (2010, 38) – is exploited in detective and crime fiction. In fact, quite a few of Doyle's narratives include information that, if attended to, might have revealed the solution to a case quite early on in the story.

A prime example is "The Adventures of Silver Blaze", a short story published in *The Strand Magazine* in 1893, where Holmes investigates the case of a missing racehorse, Silver Blaze, and the murder of its trainer, John Straker. The short story includes multiple red herrings that might point to the murderer, including a group of Gypsies who disappeared after the events. As it turns out, however, the key to solving the case was obvious but overlooked. This is pointed out by Holmes in what is presented as an attentional challenge to the police officer, Inspector Gregory, who earlier in the story had already missed some evidence at the crime scene (see Doyle 2005, 404). The challenge begins with a clue provided by Holmes, consisting of the information that three sheep in the neighborhood of the crime scene had recently gone lame. It is followed by a hint concerning the non-reaction of the watchdog at the stables:

> "Gregory, let me recommend to your attention this singular epidemic among the sheep." [...] I saw by the Inspector's face that his attention had been keenly aroused. [...]
> "Is there any other point to which you would wish to draw my attention?"
> "To the curious incident of the dog in the night-time."
> "The dog did nothing in the night-time."
> "That was the curious incident", remarked Sherlock Holmes. (Doyle 2005, 411)

This short dialogue leaves the inspector, Watson, and also the reader baffled. Instead of offering an explanation, the next paragraph introduces a shift in time and place: "Four days later Holmes and I were again in the train" (Doyle 2005, 412). By zooming out of what is (almost) offered as the solution to the case, Watson leaves the reader time and space to solve the riddle before presenting its resolution toward the end of the story, when Holmes points out that the dog did not bark because it must have known the person who abducted the horse. This leads him to conclude that it must have been the trainer himself who kidnapped Silver Blaze. He adds that Straker must have turned against his employer and tried to prevent the horse from winning. Sensing the danger of being hurt, Silver Blaze lashed out, killing Straker, when he tried to nick its tendon – a method that he had previously tested on sheep, hence the lame sheep in the stable's vicinity (see Doyle 2005, 416–417).

The dialogue between Holmes and the Inspector centers on 'attention'. The repeated use of the noun emphasizes the need to focus (without overstretching the tension due to the playful tone of this exchange), while creating an instance of joint attention to three lame sheep and a dog's non-reaction – seemingly trivial aspects considering the kidnapping and murder that need to be solved. The foregrounding of 'attention' in this dialogue highlights its previous lack. At the same time, it reveals an instance of inattentional blindness on the part of the characters, but also of the reader, who could potentially have deciphered the "curious incident of the dog in the night-time" even before it was revealed by Holmes.

The planting of hidden clues that make the solution plausible is a common feature in well-crafted crime fiction. To a greater extent than readers of individual detective narratives, however, readers of a series such as the *Sherlock Holmes* stories, which are deeply infused with mechanisms of attention and attention management, become gradually attuned to attention-controlling mechanisms. Attention narratives such as "Silver Blaze", therefore, help increase readers' awareness of the clues dispersed across the narrative, refining their attentional capabilities, and also alerting them to the human proneness to inattention.

5 Conclusion and outlook

The potential of detective fiction to foreground issues of attention is further confirmed by twenty-first-century novels that draw on the success of the genre in this respect. Two popular examples are Mark Haddon's *The Curious Incident of the Dog in the Night-Time* (2003) and Emma Healey's *Elizabeth Is Missing* (2014). Both first-person narratives are written in the tradition of detective fiction and foreground minds that are commonly regarded as defective. Healey's narrator, Maud, suffers from dementia and is confined to her increasingly flawed perception of the world, which ironically belies her detective qualities, for it is these that lead to the solving of a long-forgotten murder. While *Elizabeth Is Missing* can be read as a plea for a change of perspective in our perception of attentional 'deficits', Haddon's narrative goes a step further. Although showing symptoms that might be associated with Asperger's syndrome, Christopher, the 15-year-old narrator in *The Curious Incident*, is acutely attentive to details which commonly go unnoticed. This also enables him to eventually solve the mystery surrounding the death of his neighbor's dog. Ironically, what aids him in his endeavor is narrative, more precisely "a murder mystery novel" (Haddon 2003, 5), which he composes following all the tricks of the trade, including a beginning "with something to grab people's attention" (Haddon 2003, 5). The multimodal narrative is suffused with numerous distractions provided by the narrator, which are, however, identified as such, as Christopher comments on his proneness to mind-wandering throughout the story.

As I have argued elsewhere (Baumbach 2019, forthcoming), Haddon's novel emphasizes the crucial role of storytelling in creating instances of attention and mind-wandering which expose mechanisms of attention, prompt shifts in perspective, and help readers reconsider and refine their attentional habits. Furthermore, the novel draws attention to our own attentional illusion. This is already indicated by the title, which is a direct reference to the attention scene in Doyle's "Silver Blaze" story described above, and as such announces an incident of inattention even before the narrative sets in. However, not only readers unfamiliar with that story tend to overlook the hint. Focusing on the 'mystery' and on signs of Christopher's cognitive 'impairment' to which the novel seems to draw attention, we may miss more than just the clue that the dog was killed by a person familiar to it: conditioned by the grand narratives of attention disorder from the "ADHD industry" (Rogers 2014, 166), we also tend not to notice that the narrative confronts us with our own misconception of attention 'deficits', exposing a perhaps more significant inattentiveness. This, Chabris and Simons argue, is also a product of our digital environment, prompted by "devices that require greater amounts of attention, more and more often, with shorter and shorter lead times" (2010, 37). They conclude that, although it is impossible to eliminate "the illusion of attention", it is crucial to become aware of it and "to take steps to avoid missing what we need to see" (Chabris and Simons 2010, 41).

By drawing attention to attention, narratives both record and create such an awareness. Deeply embedded in (changing) attention economies, they help unveil mechanisms of attention and attention management, while prompting but also countering tendencies to inattentional blindness. A cultural narratology of attention will provide the tools for examining the multiple levels upon which narratives have been deeply engaged in negotiating dominant discourses of attention and challenging readers' attentional capacities and illusions. It will enable us to scrutinize the attention narratives we live by, addressing, dissecting, and eventually overcoming our inattentional (but also attentional) blindness to the cultural, social, political, and individual attention deficits those narratives both conceal and expose. Ultimately, a cultural narratology of attention will confront us with our own attention complexes and makes us attend to them by urging us to "look for the invisible gorillas in the world around [us]" (Chabris and Simons 2010, 241).

References

Baird, Benjamin, Jonathan Smallwood, Michael D. Mrazek, Julia W.Y. Kam, Michael S. Franklin, and Jonathan W. Schooler. "Inspired by Distraction: Mind Wandering Facilitates Creative Incubation." *Psychological Science* 23.10 (2012): 1117–1122.
Barthes, Roland. *The Pleasure of the Text*. Transl. Richard Miller. New York: Farrar, Strauss and Giroux, 1975.
Baumbach, Sibylle. "The Attention Economy and the Novel." *New Approaches to the Twenty-First-Century Anglophone Novel*. Eds. Sibylle Baumbach and Birgit Neumann. Basingstoke: Palgrave Macmillan, 2019 (forthcoming).
Baumbach, Sibylle. *Literature and Fascination*. Basingstoke: Palgrave Macmillan, 2015.
Bell, Alice, Astrid Ensslin, and Hans Rustad. *Analyzing Digital Fiction*. New York: Routledge, 2013.
Beller, Jonathan. *The Cinematic Mode of Production: Attention Economy and the Society of the Spectacle*. Lebanon: University Press of New England, 2006.
Catton, Eleanor. *The Luminaries*. London: Granta Publications, 2013.
Carrasco, Marisa. "Visual Attention: The Past 25 Years." *Vision Research* 51.13 (2011): 1484–1525.
Chabris, Christopher and Daniel Simons. *The Invisible Gorilla. How Our Intuitions Deceive Us*. New York: Crown Publishers, 2010.
Crary, Jonathan. *Suspensions of Perception: Attention, Spectacle and Modern Culture*. Cambridge, Mass.: MIT Press, 1999.
Crary, Jonathan. *24/7. Late Capitalism and the Ends of Sleep*. London: Verso Books, 2013.
Danielewski, Mark Z. *House of Leaves*. New York: Pantheon, 2000.

Davenport, Thomas, and John Beck. *The Attention Economy. Understanding the New Currency of Business*. Brighton, Mass.: Harvard Business School Press, 2001.

Debord, Guy. *The Society of Spectacle*. Trans. Donald Nicholson-Smith. New York: Zone Books, 1967.

Dehaene, Stanislas. *Reading in the Brain: The Science and Evolution of a Human Invention*. New York: Viking, 2009.

Didierjean, André, and Fernand Gobet. "Can Sherlock Holmes Help Cognitive Psychology?" *The Psychologist* 21.10 (2008): 858–859.

Doran, Peter. *A Political Economy of Attention*. London: Routledge, 2017.

Doyle, Arthur Conan. *The New Annotated Sherlock Holmes. Vol. 1*. Ed. Leslie S. Klinger. New York: Norton, 2005.

Doyle, Arthur Conan. *The New Annotated Sherlock Holmes. Vol. 3*. Ed. Leslie S. Klinger. New York: Norton, 2006.

Doyle, Arthur Conan. *Memories and Adventures*. Cambridge: Cambridge University Press. 2012.

Drury, Joseph. *Novel Machines: Technology and Narrative Form in Enlightenment Britain*. Oxford: Oxford University Press, 2017.

Emmott, Catherine, Anthony J. Sanford, and L.I. Morrow. "Towards a Theory of Reading in the Age of Cognitive Science: Cross-Disciplinary Perspectives on Narrative from Stylistics and Psychology." *Belgian Journal of English Language and Literatures*, New Series 1 (2003): 17–30.

Emmott, Catherine, Anthony J. Sanford, and Marc Alexander. "Rhetorical Control of Readers' Attention: Psychological and Stylistic Perspectives on Foreground and Background in Narrative." *Stories and Minds. Cognitive Approaches to Literary Narratives*. Eds. Lars Bernaerts, Dirk de Geest, Luc Herman, and Bart Vervaeck. Lincoln: University of Nebraska Press, 2013. 39–58.

Epstein, Andrew. *Attention Equals Life: The Pursuit of the Everyday in Contemporary Poetry and Culture*. Oxford: Oxford University Press, 2016.

Green, Melanie C., and John K. Donahue. "Simulated Worlds: Transportation into Narratives." *Handbook of Imagination and Mental Simulation*. Eds. Keith D. Markman, William M.P. Klein, and Julie A. Suhr. New York: Psychology Press, 2012. 241–254.

Gurton-Wachter, Lily. *Watchwords: Romanticism and the Poetics of Attention*. Stanford: Stanford University Press, 2016.

Haddon, Mark. *The Curious Incident of the Dog in the Night-Time*. London: Vintage, 2003.

Hannah, Sophie. "It's No Mystery that Crime is the Biggest-Selling Genre in Books." *The Guardian*, 12 April 2018.

Hassed, Craig. "Training the Mindful Health Practitioner: Why Attention Matters." *The Wiley Blackwell Handbook of Mindfulness*. Eds. Amanda Ie, Christelle T. Ngnoumen, and Ellen J. Langer. Malden: Wiley and Sons, 2014. 630–648.

Hayles, N. Katherine "Hyper and Deep Attention: The Generational Divide in Cognitive Modes". *Profession* 1 (2007): 187–199.

Hayles, N. Katherine "How We Read: Close, Hyper, Machine." *ADE Bulletin* 150 (2010): 62–79.

Healey, Emma. *Elizabeth Is Missing*. New York: HarperCollins, 2014.

Iser, Wolfgang. *The Act of Reading: A Theory of Aesthetic Response*. London: Routledge and Kegan Paul, 1978.

James, William. *Principles of Psychology*. New York: Dover, 1950 [1890].

Jameson, Frederic. *The Political Unconscious: Narrative as Socially Symbolic Act*. Ithaca: Cornell University Press, 1981.

Koehler, Margaret. *Poetry of Attention in the Eighteenth Century*. Basingstoke: Palgrave Macmillan, 2012.
Konnikova, Maria. *Mastermind: How to Think Like Sherlock Holmes*. Edinburgh: Canongate, 2013.
Letzler, David. *The Cruft of Fiction: Mega-Novels and the Science of Paying Attention*. Lincoln: University of Nebraska Press, 2017.
Levine, Caroline. *Forms: Whole, Rhythm, Hierarchy, Network*. Princeton: Princeton University Press, 2015.
Llewellyn, David. *Eleven*. Bridgend: Seren, 2006.
Mack, Arien, and Irvin Rock. *Inattentional Blindness*. Cambridge, Mass.: MIT Press, 2000.
Masuda, Takahiko. "Culture and Attention: Recent Empirical Findings and New Directions in Cultural Psychology." *Social and Personality Psychology Compass* 11.12 (2017): e12363.
McEwan, Ian. *Atonement*. London: Vintage, 2001.
Möller, Melanie. *Ciceros Rhetorik als Theorie der Aufmerksamkeit*. Heidelberg: Winter, 2013.
Morling, Beth, and Lamoureaux, Marika. "Measuring Culture Outside the Head: A Meta-Analysis of Individualism-Collectivism in Cultural Products." *Personality and Social Psychology Review* 12 (2008): 199–221.
Moulier-Boutang, Yann. *Cognitive Capitalism*. Transl. Ed Emery. Cambridge: Polity Press, 2011.
Nanay, Bence. *Aesthetics as Philosophy of Perception*. Oxford: Oxford University Press, 2016.
Nisbett, Richard E. *The Geography of Thought*. New York: Free Press, 2003.
Nobre, Anna C., and Sabine Kastner. "Attention: Time Capsule 2013." *The Oxford Handbook of Attention*. Eds. Anna C. Nobre and Sabine Kastner. Oxford: Oxford University Press, 2014. 1201–1222.
Nünning, Ansgar. "Narrativist Approaches and Narratological Concepts." *Travelling Concepts for the Study of Culture*. Eds. Birgit Neumann and Ansgar Nünning. Berlin: de Gruyter, 2012. 145–183.
Phillips, Natalie M. *Distraction: Problems of Attention in Eighteenth-Century Literature*. Baltimore: Johns Hopkins University Press, 2016.
Pinto, Yair, Andries R. van der Leij, Ilja G. Sligte, Victor A.F. Lamme, H. Steven Scholte. "Bottom-up and Top-Down Attention Are Independent." *Journal of Vision* 13.16 (2013): 1–14.
Poe, Edgar Allan. *The Works*. 4 Vols., Vol. 3. New York: W. J. Widdleton, 1863.
Rapezzi, Claudio, Roberto Ferrari, and Angelo Branzi. "White Coats and Fingerprints: Reasoning in Medicine and Investigative Methods of Fictional Detectives." *British Medical Journal* 331.7531 (2005): 1491–1494.
Rogers, Kenneth. *The Attention Complex. Media, Archaeology, Method*. Basingstoke: Palgrave Macmillan, 2014.
Sherlock. "The Great Game" (S1, E3). Produced by Steven Mofatt and Mark Gatiss. BBC, 2010.
Sherlock. "The Sign of Three" (S3, E2). Produced by Steven Mofatt and Mark Gatiss. BBC, 2014.
Shklovsky, Viktor. *Theory of Prose*. Champaign: Dalkey Archive Press, 1991.
Shreffler, Philip A. "Moriarty: A Life Study." *Sherlock Holmes by the Gas-Lamp: Highlights from the First Four Decades of The Baker Street*. Ed. Philip A. Shreffler. New York: Fordham University Press, 1989. 263–270.
Sterne, Laurence. *The Life and Opinions of Tristram Shandy, Gentleman*. 2 Vols., Vol. 1. London: James Cochrane and Co., 1832 [1759].
Stockwell, Peter. "War, Worlds and Cognitive Grammar." *Cognitive Grammar in Literature*. Eds. Chloe Harrison, Louise Nuttall, Peter Stockwell, and Wenjuan Yuan. Amsterdam: John Benjamins Publishing, 2014. 19–34.

Takanashi, Kyoko. "Sherlock's 'Brain-Attic': Information Culture and the Liberal Professional Dilemma." *PMLA* 132.2 (2017): 250–265.

Tobin, Vera. *Literary Joint Attention: Social Cognition and the Puzzles of Modernism*. Univ. Diss.: University of Maryland, 2008.

Wells, H.G. *The Country of the Blind and Other Stories*. London: Thomas, 1914.

Wheatley, Henry B. *What Is an Index? A Few Notes on Indexes and Indexers*. London: Longmans, Green & co., 1878.

Wiltse, Ed. "'So Constant an Expectation: Holmes and Seriality." *Narrative* 6.2 (1998): 105–122.

Wolf, Maryanne. "Skim Reading is the New Normal." *The Guardian*, 25 August 2018.

Woloch, Alex. *The One vs. the Many: Minor Characters and the Space of the Protagonist in the Novel*. Princeton: Princeton University Press, 2003.

Wood, James. "Total Recall: Karl Ove Knausgaards's *My Struggle*." *The New Yorker*, 13 August 2012.

Woolf, Virginia. *Mrs Dalloway*. Oxford: Oxford University Press, 2008 [1925].

Zanto, Theodore P., and Adam Gazzaley. "Attention and Ageing." *The Oxford Handbook of Attention*. Eds. Anna C. Nobre and Sabine Kastner. Oxford: Oxford University Press, 2014. 927–971.

Marion Gymnich
The End of the World (as We Know It)? – Cultural Ways of Worldmaking in Contemporary Post-Apocalyptic Narratives

Abstract: The article explores the functions of selected post-apocalyptic narratives, i.e., of stories that can be categorized as a specific subset of 'narratives of catastrophe' on the basis of the criteria defined by Ansgar Nünning. Novels, films, TV series, and videogames about the end of the world as we know it have become increasingly popular across different media. The functions of this type of narrative arguably go a long way towards accounting for its striking popularity, and a comparison with older post-apocalyptic narratives in fact suggests a shift in terms of the functions of the genre in recent years. In contrast to 'last man' stories of the nineteenth century, the 1950s, and the 1960s, many contemporary post-apocalyptic narratives can be read as stories of survival. The notion of 'narratives as cultural ways of worldmaking' as described by Ansgar Nünning is an ideal framework for exploring the meaning-making processes that are at work in the different types of post-apocalyptic story with a view to their cultural relevance. In addition, drawing upon the concept of 'obligation-worlds' developed by Marie-Laure Ryan in the framework of narrative semantics allows a scrutiny of the moral implications of post-apocalyptic stories and provides a link to narrative ethics.

1 Introduction

Recent years have seen an increased interest in post-apocalyptic fiction across different media. Starting from the observation that "[a]pocalypse is by definition exceptional and fearful, yet imagining apocalypse is a pervasive cultural habit", as Christopher Palmer (2014, 158) has put it, a closer scrutiny of recurring narrative patterns and possible functions of post-apocalyptic fiction seems to be called for. The term 'post-apocalypse' has multiple meanings, as James Berger (1999, 5) pointed out, and has been used in theological as well as secular contexts.[1]

---

[1] Cf. Berger (1999, 5): "First, it is the *eschaton*, the actual imagined end of the world, as presented in the New Testament Apocalypse of John and other Jewish and early Christian apocalypses, or as imagined by medieval millenarian movements, or today in visions of nuclear Armageddon or ecological suicide. Second, apocalypse refers to catastrophes that resemble the imagined final ending, that can be interpreted as eschaton, as an end of something, a way

Post-apocalyptic fiction involves references to an event that meets the three criteria identified by Ansgar Nünning in his definition of narratives of catastrophe: (1) the event that is presented in post-apocalyptic fiction as a significant turning point[2] in the history of humankind is associated with a "moment of surprise or the extraordinary"; (2) the extraordinary experiences are of a collective nature; and (3) the event, "in contrast to mere occurrences [...] need[s] to have far-reaching and large-scale structural consequences which are perceived by protagonists and/or the observers as disastrous" (Nünning 2012b, 68). In other words, post-apocalyptic narratives may be categorized as a subset of narratives of catastrophe that depict or refer to particularly devastating events, typically involving the extinction of a substantial part of humankind.

Among the post-apocalyptic novels published since 2000 there have been critically acclaimed works and bestsellers such as Margaret Atwood's *MaddAddam* trilogy (2003–2013), David Mitchell's *Cloud Atlas* (2004), Cormac McCarthy's *The Road* (2006), and Max Brooks's *World War Z* (2006). Further examples of post-apocalyptic narratives include the comic series *The Walking Dead* by Robert Kirkman, Tony Moore, and Charlie Adlard (2003–), the eponymous AMC television series (2010–) – as well as the latter's spin-off *Fear the Walking Dead* (2015–) –, movies like *I Am Legend* (2007), *World War Z* (2013),[3] and the Australian film *Cargo* (2017). Moreover, there are video games with a post-apocalyptic premise, like the role-playing games *Fallout 1–4* (1997, 1998, 2008, 2015), which establish an alternative timeline and allow the player to explore a world that has largely remained a wasteland after a nuclear war and is now populated by ghouls and mutants as well as by the remnants of humankind.

---

of life or thinking. The destruction of the temple in 70 C.E. and the expulsion from Spain in 1492 worked in that way for Jews. And in our age the Holocaust and the use of atomic weapons against Japan have assumed apocalyptic significance. They function as definitive historical divides, as ruptures, pivots, fulcrums separating what came before from what came after. All preceding history seems to lead up to and set the stage for such events, and all that follows emerges out of that central cataclysm. Previous historical narratives are shattered; new understandings of the world are generated."

2 Post-apocalyptic narratives are, in fact, based on the assumption that the cataclysmic event they refer to constitutes the *ultimate* turning point in the history of humankind, while "the concepts of emergence and evolution" (Nünning and Sicks 2012, 16) often play an important role in dystopian fiction. For a more extensive discussion of the implications of turning points in literature, cf. Nünning and Sicks (2012) and Nünning (2012c).

3 Both *World War Z* and *I Am Legend* are based on novels, but the audio-visual adaptations differ considerably from the literary texts.

In the last few years, an increasing number of post-apocalyptic narratives have specifically addressed a very young readership. Evidence of this phenomenon is provided by numerous young adult novels in the vein of James Dashner's *Maze Runner* series (2009–2016), as well as by Piers Torday's *The Last Wild* trilogy (2013–2015), written for children and featuring a future in which the ocean "covers most of the planet" (Torday 2013, 53) – which leads to the conclusion that global warming must have changed the face of the Earth completely. Nothing is left of human civilization in *The Last Wild* (2013) except for "[f]our great cities, built to contain the world's refugees" (Torday 2013, 51). The countryside has been turned into a "Quarantine Zone" (Torday 2013, 53) due to a virus that has infected virtually all animals and has made most humans excessively afraid of wildlife and domestic animals alike; these are ruthlessly hunted down as carriers of the disease.

The success of post-apocalyptic fiction addressing particularly young adults and children, as well as the ubiquity of post-apocalyptic stories across different media, might raise the question whether post-apocalyptic stories have turned into a cultural 'master narrative' of the new millennium. As I hope to show in the following, many contemporary post-apocalyptic narratives can be read as stories of survival. This sets them apart from the majority of their predecessors in the nineteenth century, the 1950s, and the 1960s, which are on the whole more likely to imagine the total extinction of humankind. The emphasis on the survival of a few, which by and large seems characteristic of recent post-apocalyptic fiction, implies that these narratives constitute a somewhat ambivalent response to the fears generated by the "crises and catastrophes with which we are almost daily confronted in the media in what seems to be the age of crises and catastrophes" (Nünning 2012b, 60). Post-apocalyptic stories seem increasingly to mingle a belief in the resilience of humankind with predictions about large-scale disasters that feed upon widespread anxieties concerning war, terrorism, pandemics, global warming, and ecological collapse.

Even if the primary goal of this article is an analysis of recent post-apocalyptic fiction and its relation to contemporary culture, it seems appropriate first to take a closer look at some older works in this genre. A comparative approach will make it possible to delineate the features of post-apocalyptic narratives, as historically variable 'ways of worldmaking', a good deal more precisely. Thus, in Section 2, I will examine patterns that emerge in some prominent examples of earlier post-apocalyptic fiction. These can be subsumed under the label of 'last man' stories, because they conjure up visions of the end of all life on the planet or, at least, of the end of human life on Earth. In Section 3, I will argue that recent post-apocalyptic stories, by contrast, tend to project a future that makes survival of the human species seem possible after all, despite large-scale destruction and high fatalities. The struggle to survive in an extremely hostile environment may also bring about moral issues, encouraging individuals to renegotiate or even forego their values in order to ensure their survival. In the following, I will primarily make use of two narratological concepts that have proven highly productive for an analysis of post-apocalyptic narratives: first, the notion of 'narratives as cultural ways of worldmaking' described by Ansgar Nünning, and second the concept of 'obligation-worlds' developed by Marie-Laure Ryan in the framework of narrative semantics.

Drawing upon Nelson Goodman's study *Ways of Worldmaking* (1978), in which the American philosopher explores the implications of the notion of a "multiplicity of worlds" (Goodman 1978, 2), Ansgar Nünning has shown that "narration or storytelling itself is one of the most important cultural ways of worldmaking" (2012a, 154). The insight that narratives constitute "cognitive and cultural phenomena and [represent] an active force in their own right which is involved in the actual generation of ways of thinking, feeling and of attitudes and thus of something that stands behind historical developments" (Nünning 2012b, 84–85) has proven indispensable for cultural narratology, as it has for a profounder understanding of cultural processes of meaning-making in general. If narratives are "involved in the actual generation of ways of thinking, feeling and of attitudes", then both the omnipresence of post-apocalyptic fiction in recent (popular) culture and the shift from 'last man' stories to narratives of survival may shed light on reactions to what Nünning has called the current "crisis inflation" of "a media society of crises and catastrophes" (2012b, 64). This type of story is, after all, particularly likely to resonate with people already primed for crises and catastrophes by prevailing media discourses.

This also implies that post-apocalyptic stories of survival, like other "narratives of crises and catastrophes", are not "merely a passive vehicle that reproduces the ideology of the respective period" (Nünning 2012b, 84); in fact, they

> should be conceptualised as playing a creative role in shaping our cultural awareness and in constructing the ideological fictions that provide the mental framework of the cultural imagination or collective consciousness, or rather of what Fredric Jameson called 'the political unconscious'. (Nünning 2012b, 84)

Specifically, while reiterating widespread fears and anxieties, post-apocalyptic narratives of survival may also provide a way of coping with such fears by nurturing a belief in the resilience of humankind. In this context, it is worth mentioning that 'resilience' has recently become a buzz-word of popular discourse.

Marie-Laure Ryan's concept of 'obligation-worlds' complements the conceptualization of post-apocalyptic narratives as cultural ways of worldmaking by highlighting the moral implications of this type of story and thus providing a link to narrative ethics (cf. Phelan 2013). Ryan's approach is a possible-worlds theory that "describes narrative universes – whether fictional or not – as modal systems in which the external (i.e., physical) facts asserted by the narrator play the role of 'textual actual world.' Surrounding this ontological center are the little solar systems formed by the private universes of the characters" (Ryan 2014, 733). I will focus on one of the components of these 'private universes', the characters' obligation-worlds, since these prove particularly interesting for hypotheses concerning potential functions of post-apocalyptic narratives. Obligation-worlds encompass the "social rules and moral principles" (Ryan 1991, 116) of characters' private universes. In a post-apocalyptic scenario, this component of the characters' private universes is bound to be fraught with problems, since life in the aftermath of an apocalypse, in a world of extreme scarcity that has become the site of a desperate struggle for survival, can be expected to bring forth egoism rather than altruism and, in more general terms, a renegotiation of values and personal priorities. A scrutiny of what happens to the characters' obligation-worlds under these extreme circumstances will prove interesting from the point of view of narrative ethics.

2 The literary and cultural tradition of 'last man' stories

When examining the structures and functions of contemporary post-apocalyptic stories such as those mentioned above, one has to keep in mind that these are by no means the first narratives to speculate on the end of the world. There was, for instance, a veritable vogue of post-apocalyptic narratives in the 1950s, many of which reflect the fear of another nuclear war in the wake of Hiroshima and Nagasaki, including Richard Matheson's *I Am Legend* (1954), as well as Nevil Shute's *On the Beach* (1957) and its eponymous 1959 movie. Further examples of post-apocalyptic narratives can be found from the 1960s to the 1990s in the movies *Planet of the Apes* (1968), *Mad Max* (1979), *The Day After* (1983), *Waterworld* (1995), and *Postman* (1997), to name just a few. In the nineteenth century, literary works such as Lord Byron's poem "Darkness" (1816), Mary Shelley's novel *The Last Man* (1826), and H.G. Wells's *The Time Machine* (1895) imagined what the extinction of human life on the planet might look (and feel) like. Indeed, tales that address the annihilation of a large part of humanity and its aftermath appear among the world's oldest narratives, although the references to cataclysmic events – wars, pandemics, ecological collapse, etc. – of their nature reflect more recent cultural fears and anxieties.

The biblical story in the *Book of Genesis* of the survival of a select few – both humans and animals – in a flood that otherwise destroys all life on Earth is probably the most famous post-apocalyptic tale of Western culture,[4] though many ancient civilizations knew similar narratives.[5] The story of Noah's Ark has traditionally been among the first biblical (or at least Old Testament) stories taught to children of kindergarten age in the context of early religious education. Thus, generation upon generation of preschool and school children have been introduced to what is after all a post-apocalyptic narrative, albeit one whose outlook is at least partially optimistic, given its message that human (as well as animal) life on the planet *will* continue, even after a cataclysmic event.

However, many older post-apocalyptic stories do not focus on survival, detailing instead the end of humankind or even of all life on the planet. In Lord Byron's poem "Darkness" (1816), for instance, the death of the sun and the ensuing darkness on Earth cause universal despair, war, famine, and cannibalism and leave no survivors. The scenario evoked in Byron's poem can be seen as a response to the experience of the 'Year without Summer' of 1816, when the eruption of a volcano in Indonesia had a global impact on weather conditions, causing food shortages and giving rise to widespread fears.[6] Beyond responding to a concrete historical experience, however, the poem is also arguably informed by an interest in the (destructive) force of melancholy, deemed a key characteristic of Romanticism.

Responding to the fear of a nuclear war, Nevil Shute's *On the Beach* (1957) conjures a world in which all human and animal life on the planet comes to an end due to radiation spreading further and further south in the wake of a large-scale nuclear conflict in the northern hemisphere. The novel focuses on several characters waiting for death in Southern Australia. Unlike humankind in Byron's poem – and many characters in contemporary post-apocalyptic fiction – they stay remarkably calm and, by and large, seem to accept their fate. What Byron's poem and Shute's novel have in common, however, is their insistence on the horror caused by the thought of entire cities and regions where nobody survives. This is stressed in *On the Beach* in the description of a reconnaissance mission undertaken by an American submarine. The ship approaches Australian cities like Cairns in Northern Queensland, as well as the American west coast, only to

---

4 Over the centuries, the biblical story of the Flood has also inspired countless (re-)writings and works of art (by Jan Brueghel the Elder and Michelangelo among others), which supports the assumption that this particular narrative is firmly embedded in Western cultural memory.
5 For an overview of Flood myths in different cultures, cf. the essays in Dundes (1988).
6 For a discussion of the 'Year without Summer' and its impact on culture and literature, see Klingaman/Klingaman (2013).

discover that nobody is alive there anymore.[7] The novel is told by a heterodiegetic narrator using various (male and female) characters as focalizers, and the story ends when the last of these focalizers, who already suffers from radiation sickness, commits suicide. Although she is not the last human still alive at this point, there can be no doubt that all the others will die within a few days. *On the Beach* is thus a variation of the 'last man' narrative, which features a solitary survivor serving as witness to the final days of the human race.

Mary Shelley's *The Last Man* (1826) is a prime example of the 'last man' narrative: a novel that imagines a future in which humankind is being wiped out by the plague over the course of a few years. In the end, there is just one survivor, Lionel Verney, who seems immune to the disease, and whose consequent loneliness is described in vivid terms in his autodiegetic narration. Shelley's novel shows that neither 'last man' stories nor pandemics are a recent invention. Charlotte Sussman argues, in fact, that Shelley's novel "was part of a vogue for last-man narratives in the first decades of the nineteenth century, which included a novel translated from French called *The Last Man; or, Omergarus and Syderia, a Romance in Futurity* (Grainville; 1806) and Byron's poem 'Darkness'" (Sussman 2003, 286).

Strictly speaking, narratives about the extinction of humankind should pose a (logical and narratological) conundrum resulting from the fact that "there cannot be any narratives without a human (anthropomorphic) experiencer of some sort at some narrative level" (Fludernik 1996, 9). *On the Beach* (1957), as was mentioned above, leaves the reader to imagine the death of the last human and the ensuing empty space, once densely populated. Byron's "Darkness" (1816) categorizes the vision of the end of humankind as a dream (albeit perhaps a prophetic one). In a somewhat similar vein, a fictive introduction in Shelley's novel claims that Verney's written account of the end of humankind was found on leaves in the Sibyl's cave. In other words, this post-apocalyptic story was from the start classified as a prophecy.

In the case of Wells's *The Time Machine* (1895), the conundrum mentioned above is skirted by the ruse of sending a visitor from the past into a future where no other human witness remains. At first sight, then, *The Time Machine* might not seem a typical example of post-apocalyptic fiction, since there is no catastrophe in the sense described here in the introduction.[8] Still, Chapter 11 of Wells's

---

[7] Cf. Petter Skult (2015, 112), who argues that "the relative permanence of man-made yet inanimate things only serves to emphasize the vulnerability of life."
[8] The two audio-visual adaptations of the novel, made in 1960 and 2002, reinterpret the story along more obviously post-apocalyptic lines by referring to disasters of apocalyptic dimensions: a nuclear Third World War in the 1960 version and part of the moon crashing onto the Earth in the more recent one.

classic takes the time traveler "thirty million years" (Wells 2002 [1895], 97) into the future and describes a world in which humankind has become extinct. The only life form the traveler can spot is "a round thing, the size of a football perhaps, or, it may be, bigger, and tentacles trailed down from it; it seemed black against the weltering blood-red water, and it was hopping fitfully about" (Wells 2002 [1895], 99). In other words, the time traveler as a *de facto* 'last man' on Earth is confronted with a creature that defies categorization, indicating that this future is not 'his' world anymore. During earlier stops, he could still see "a thing like a huge white butterfly" (Wells 2002 [1895], 96) and gigantic crab-like creatures (cf. Wells 2002 [1895], 96), i.e., life forms that at least resembled what he was familiar with, even though their size made them appear grotesque. Chapter 11 in Wells's novel creates a haunting image of the otherness of a dying world, of complete silence and an "abominable desolation that hung over the world" (Wells 2002 [1895], 97), witnessed by that solitary human.

Loneliness is a major theme of post-apocalyptic fiction and links this type of narrative to the genre of the Robinsonade. More often than not, survivors in a post-apocalyptic scenario try to combat this feeling by revisiting old stories and/or by writing down their own account of their experience. The protagonist of Matheson's *I Am Legend* (1954), as well as his modern successor in the eponymous movie from 2007, regularly consume old stories representing a pre-apocalyptic world entirely different from the one they now inhabit; while Matheson's protagonist reads novels (for instance Bram Stoker's *Dracula*, 1897), his contemporary counterpart watches television programs he must have recorded in the early days of the pandemic. The references to literary texts and TV programs point to a world that is no more, and to outdated ways of cultural worldmaking inherent in the (fictional and non-fictional) narratives of pre-apocalyptic days. In this way, the feeling of loss is made even more poignant.

The premise of 'last man' stories – i.e., the imminent end of human life on Earth – implies that those who double as autodiegetic narrators must assume that their stories will never be read. Imagining the narratee as a void and the narrative as remaining without even the possibility of response enhances the horror of its impact for human beings, who have often been described as instinctive storytellers (see, e.g., Gottschall 2013): the lack of any kind of conceivable narratee reinforces the impression of utter solitude. As mentioned above, the protagonist in Shelley's *The Last Man* (1826), the sole survivor of the plague, who has to carry on in "a future in which nature flourishes while humanity is destroyed" (Sussman 2003, 295), is one such narrator who seeks solace in recording the last days of humankind, although he too doubts that his story will ever be read. Nevertheless, as the following passage illustrates, he appeals to the prospective reader's empathy in his retrospective account of the ever dwindling number of humans: "[...] it was not till the first of August, that we, the emigrants, – reader, there were just eighty of us in number, – entered the gates of Dijon" (Shelley 2008 [1826], 411). In his despair, Verney seeks compensation for the lack of fellow humans in at least *imagining* a future reader. In Nevil Shute's *On the Beach* (1957), by contrast, efforts to preserve an account of the last days of humankind are mentioned in passing but not taken very seriously, at least not by the characters on whom the novel focuses: they realize that narrative worldmaking is bound to come to an end once the last human is dead.

In all of these 'last man' stories, with the possible exception of *On the Beach*, the activities of reading and/or telling stories figure as the characters' – at times desperate – attempts to make sense of their situation, to create at least the illusion of some kind of company, and in doing so to cling to their humanity. In other words, these 'last man' stories subscribe to the idea that "telling stories is really a basic anthropological need felt by human beings and a central medium of creating identity" (Nünning 2012a, 154). In this vein, post-apocalyptic tales of survival may also endow storytelling with a crucial role in the process of rebuilding society or establishing new communities. For if such stories provide a certain hope, this is often closely linked to the potential for creating a meaningful account of the past and/or the present. It is to this aspect of post-apocalyptic narrative that I shall now turn.

3 Post-apocalyptic stories of survival: Challenging pre-apocalyptic obligation-worlds

By contrast with those older post-apocalyptic narratives which envisage the end of human life on Earth, more recent post-apocalyptic fiction shows a striking tendency to tell stories of survivors. Given its overall subject matter, post-apocalyptic "survival fiction" (Conrad 2017, 63) still typically depicts immense loss and unspeakable horrors, but it often also expresses a certain element of hope. At the beginning of *On the Beach* (1957), Shute quotes from T.S. Eliot's poem "The Hollow Men" (1925), which ends in the well-known lines "This is the way the world ends / Not with a bang but a whimper" (Shute 2009 [1957], n.p.). A substantial portion of contemporary post-apocalyptic fiction, however, is based on the premise that 'the end of the world as we know it' is not really an end at all: it is a new beginning, even if the conditions for human survival and for building a new community could hardly be more adverse:

> [...] nearly every apocalyptic text presents the same paradox. The end is never the end. The apocalyptic text announces and describes the end of the world, but then the text does not end, nor does the world represented in the text, and neither does the world itself. In nearly every apocalyptic presentation, something remains *after the end*. (Berger 1999, 5–6)

Brooks's *World War Z* and the eponymous movie, the TV and comic series *The Walking Dead*, the *Fallout* video games, the movie *Cargo*, Dashner's *Maze Runner* series, and Torday's *The Last Wild* trilogy – all of these (and many other contemporary post-apocalyptic stories) focus on small groups who struggle to survive in an extremely hostile environment that has been brought about by some sort of apocalypse.

In the case of Cormac McCarthy's *The Road* (2006) and the eponymous film (2009), the readers and viewers might suspect for a long time that both protagonists – father and son – are doomed to die in a world where everything is "[b]arren, silent, godless" (McCarthy 2007 [2006], 4). Yet, eventually, in what amounts to a *deus ex machina* ending, a family turns up immediately after the father's death and gladly accepts the newly orphaned boy as a new member. This act reveals "an interest in the welfare of others beyond kinship" (Johns-Putra 2016, 533) that is highly unusual in the world depicted in *The Road*: "The woman when she saw him put her arms around him and held him. Oh, she said, I am so glad to see you." (McCarthy 2007 [2006], 286) In moments like this, *The Road* shows a tendency that also informs many other contemporary post-apocalyptic narratives, albeit in varying degrees, namely the belief that, beyond a mere 'survival of the fittest', moral values and in particular compassion may also survive.

Perhaps as no other character in recent fiction, the son in *The Road* embodies the survival of compassion in this post-apocalyptic world. In an environment that has been rendered virtually uninhabitable, where some humans have even turned into cannibals due to a lack of food, the boy does not partake in the widespread "devastation of what makes humans humane" (Johns-Putra 2016, 521). He feels genuine pity for people he and his father encounter on their way south, and is even willing to share what little they have. Similar expressions of compassion and altruism can from time to time be found in other post-apocalyptic narratives mentioned above as well, for instance, in *The Last Wild* (2013), where the young protagonist Kester Jaynes discovers that he can communicate telepathically with animals. In a world where animals are shunned by most human beings, Kester proves capable of empathy across the human-animal divide: he not only listens to the animals' stories, he feels pity for their plight. Foregrounding "the ability of animals to experience pain and suffering" – a true "animal consciousness" (Nayar 2014, 87) – the novel thus certainly invites an ecocritical reading and possibly even a posthumanist stance. An emphasis on "empathy as a human resource in a post-apocalyptic world" (White 2015, 532) provides a glimpse of hope that is arguably as important as mere physical survival.

The potential of post-apocalyptic stories to address moral issues is an aspect of this type of narrative that can be further explored by drawing on the notion of 'obligation-worlds', a concept developed by Ryan in her narrative semantics. She defines this concept as follows:

> The obligation-world, or O-world of characters, is a system of commitments and prohibitions defined by social rules and moral principles. While the social rules are issued by an external authority, the moral principles may be defined by the characters themselves. These regulations specify actions as allowed (i.e., possible), obligatory (necessary), and prohibited (impossible). (Ryan 1991, 116)

In a post-apocalyptic scenario, the external authorities that guaranteed social rules in the pre-apocalyptic world (i.e., legislative and religious institutions, schools, the police force, etc.) have in all likelihood disappeared. Instead, post-apocalyptic fiction frequently features individual leaders who appropriate (and more often than not abuse) the role of external authority, seeking to impose their own rules on followers, victims and enemies alike. Cases in point include characters like General Bethlehem in the film *Postman* (1997), or the Governor and Negan in *The Walking Dead*.

In a post-apocalyptic scenario, moral principles that were generally accepted – and more often than not simply taken for granted – in the pre-apocalyptic world are apt to be challenged. The constant need to cope with extreme scarcity and to fight for survival may cause characters to reconsider and renegotiate their obligation-worlds, i.e., their individual, as well as collective, definitions of what is allowed, obligatory, and prohibited. Probably the most blatant example of the shift from 'prohibited' to 'allowed' lies in the references to cannibalism that can be found in *The Road* and *The Walking Dead* (as well as in Byron's "Darkness"). *The Road* suggests, however, that moral principles may in fact be preserved by revisiting stories that represent the values of the vanished world. Here the father tells old stories to his son – "a post-apocalyptic child born after the death of nature, [...] who has never known anything else" (Søfting 2013, 712) – in order "to inspire him and help him sleep more peacefully" (White 2015, 539). In this way, he contributes to shaping the boy's obligation-world in accordance with principles that may appear outdated in the changed environment, and the boy himself adheres to a moral code that distinguishes strictly between 'the good guys' and 'the bad guys' and is eager to be always on the side of the former. The ending of *The Road* expresses a glimpse of hope by intimating that the boy's moral principles are rewarded when he is adopted by a family who shares his values. The depiction of the boy's stance, his repeated musings on moral vs. immoral behavior, as well as the hopeful ending, contribute to what Vera Nünning identifies as one of the key functions of literary texts, i.e., "provid[ing] stimuli for empathic responses and help[ing] readers to recognise and distinguish between nuances of emotions" (2014, 119).

The concept of 'obligation-worlds' promises to be particularly useful for an analysis of correspondences and contrasts between both individual characters and groups in post-apocalyptic fiction, where a substantial part of the plot tends to revolve around conflicts triggered by different characters' or groups' moral universes. Though the zombies appearing in post-apocalyptic narratives such as *The Walking Dead*, *Fear the Walking Dead* and *Cargo* can be seen as the ultimate expression of a complete lack of moral principles, a similar deficit in human characters, where it appears, is even more horrifying. And it does so in the later seasons of *The Walking Dead*, when some groups of human survivors turn out to be even more deadly than the zombies.

From the point of view of narrative ethics, the depiction of the characters' obligation-worlds – i.e., the "ethics of the told" (Phelan 2013, para. 3) – may invite readers/viewers to speculate on their own moral choices. If characters' obligation-worlds are shown to shift or to be under pressure, we may wonder how stable our own moral principles might become under similarly extreme circumstances. Indeed, the fact that this elementary moral question is addressed in many post-apocalyptic stories may go a long way toward explaining the widespread fascination with this type of narrative. Time and again, readers and viewers are invited to ponder how they would act in similar situations, i.e., when their survival or that of their family and friends is at stake. In video games with a post-apocalyptic setting, the players, due to the interactive nature of the medium, at times face scenarios that force them to make moral decisions, while trying to assess what is allowed, obligatory, and forbidden within the textual actual world of the game. They may even experiment with moral choices that do not conform to ethical behavior, for instance by joining groups whose obligation-worlds differ fundamentally from what would be deemed socially acceptable today.

4 Forging new narrative communities

Wherever, in post-apocalyptic tales of survival, storytelling plays a vital role in building a new narrative community and establishing a new culture, we see the function of narrative affirmed on the text-internal level as a way of worldmaking;

for, as Nünning observes, "collectively shared narratives serve to shape cultural identities" (2012a, 145). A case in point is the section "Sloosha's Crossin' an' Ev'rythin' After", which constitutes the temporal vanishing point and structural core of Mitchell's *Cloud Atlas* (2004), a hybrid novel linking stories set on different time levels and informed by different genre conventions (from the travel narrative to the thriller and epistolary novel) in an account of the development of humankind toward a post-apocalyptic future.[9] In the remote future of this section, "long after humanity has *almost* completely obliterated itself" (Dimovitz 2015, 88; emphasis mine), storytelling has survived as a cultural practice. Here Zachry's autodiegetic narrative addresses the question of the survivors' identity in a world changed utterly from the pre-apocalyptic, whose meager relics – a globe or book – have become uninterpretable.[10] Presented as an oral narrative, a "fireside story" (Mezey 2011, 14), Zachry's tale offers the prospect of a new collective identity, and the short postscript by his son at the end of this section (Mitchell 2004, 324–325), added after Zachry's death, suggests that those stories are indeed being passed on from one generation to the next. The fictive post-apocalyptic community, like a real one, is being "forged and held together by the stories the members tell about themselves and their culture" (Nünning 2012a, 163).

In Atwood's *Oryx and Crake* (2003), storytelling as a way of cultural worldmaking and community-building is particularly apparent in the impact the stories told by one of the few human survivors of the apocalypse – Jimmy (a.k.a. the Snowman) – have on a group of post-humans. The latter crave stories and begin to develop their own culture on the basis of what they are told, unwittingly flouting the intentions of their scientist creator, whose virus had exterminated humankind. The group of 'designated survivors' he created at the same time are genetically engineered beings supposedly exempt from the flaws of humanity that had brought about the previous dystopian situation. Their intended state of innocence implies that they are also ignorant of traditional narratives, which enables Jimmy to invent, for instance, a new creation story for his attentive

---

9 Jason Howard Mezey (2011, 10) describes the intricate structure of *Cloud Atlas* as that of "six interlocking stories with a different, fully realized narrator in each one, and featuring a time scheme that moves forward across millennia and then doubles back on itself."

10 The enormous distance between the post-apocalyptic world and ours is stressed by certain linguistic features of Zachry's tale. The combination of "neologisms with frequent linguistic contractions and suggestive, onomatopoetic phrases" (Breidenbach 2018, 316), already visible in the title of this section, renders the central section of the novel quite challenging as a reading experience. At times, the reader is forced to guess the meaning of words and sentences, which rather slows down the reading process.

listeners.[11] While these post-humans, the Crakers, appear alien to the reader as well as to Jimmy, they seem to embody a certain hope for a better, more peaceful future after the excesses of the dystopian society, which the text sketches in extensive flashbacks. For this "tribe of Edenic post-humans" (Palmer 2014, 166), the process of forging a collective identity, like their own culture and belief system, is very much based on stories. Moreover, the transformation of old narratives provides at least a tenuous link with the pre-apocalyptic world, despite the Crakers' radical otherness.

In other texts, too, post-apocalyptic fiction links the idea of the survival of humankind (in whatever form) with a process of storytelling that serves to create a new collective identity, and this may also involve renegotiating the values agreed upon within the community. In the film *Postman* (1997), for instance, a tale made up by a survivor is sufficient to bring about a new society whose obligation-worlds are informed by a reactivation of the traditional values of (nineteenth-century) America. In some cases, however, what survives of humankind may only be a vague memory preserved in stories told by post-humans. Robert Neville, the protagonist of Richard Matheson's *I Am Legend* (1954), even seems to feel a kind of triumph when, in the moments before his death, he imagines that "the new people of the earth" (Matheson 2001 [1954], 160), vampire-like mutants whom he has killed by the dozen, will remember him as a bogeyman: "A new terror born in death, a new superstition entering the unassailable fortress of forever. I am legend." (Matheson 2001 [1954], 160)

5 Criticism, warnings, and the dissemination of values: Potential functions of post-apocalyptic fiction

Starting from the assumption that narratives are "cognitive cultural forces" (Nünning 2012a, 165), the emphasis on "various forms of adaptive continuity and survival that link the pre- and post-disaster worlds" (Pitetti 2017, 447) raises questions regarding the potential cultural functions of post-apocalyptic fiction. One might expect this genre to be a near relative of the dystopia and to express a similar warning, and Katherine V. Snyder does in fact see a possible

---

[11] The creation story begins as follows: *"Crake made the bones of the Children of Crake out of the coral on the beach, and then he made their flesh out of a mango."* (Atwood 2013 [2003], 110)

reason for the widespread fascination of post-apocalyptic narratives in their similarity with the extrapolating force of dystopian fiction:

> Post-apocalyptic fiction serves as rehearsal or preview for its readers, an opportunity to witness in fantasy origins and endings that are fundamentally unwitnessable. We are horrified and yet thrilled to see ourselves and our world in the unthinkable plight portrayed here, and even more horrified and thrilled to *see the origins of this plight in ourselves.* (2011, 479; emphasis mine)

Cases in which a dystopian scenario relentlessly paves the way for an apocalypse and a subsequent survivor story include Atwood's *Oryx and Crake* (2003) and Mitchell's *Cloud Atlas* (2004). But even if there is no obvious dystopian background, post-apocalyptic fiction may function as a powerful warning – possibly intensified by the focus on a "single overwhelming disaster on which the concept and frisson of apocalypse usually depends" (Palmer 2014, 169), in contrast to the manifold concerns typical of dystopian fiction. In this way post-apocalyptic narratives may fulfill the function of a *"cultural-critical metadiscourse"* (Zapf 2001, 93) highlighting the "typical deficits, contradictions and deformations in prevailing political, economic, ideological and utilitarian systems of civilisatory power" (Zapf 2001, 93).

Some features of recent post-apocalyptic fiction, however, render its straightforward reading as cultural-critical metadiscourse somewhat doubtful. Narratives focusing on characters whose survival in the face of catastrophe must be extremely unlikely actually contribute to downplaying any potential warning by implying that human life will – against all odds – continue. Moreover, if the apocalyptic event remains unspecified (as, e.g., in *On the Road*) or is a pandemic that has *not* been caused by scientific experiments, humanity is ostensibly exonerated from tangible guilt, for what could anyone do to prevent this type of apocalypse? And according to Palmer, the sheer number of post-apocalyptic stories entails the danger of trivializing very real threats:

> Nuclear disaster and ecological collapse are too important to be ignored – in fact they cannot be ignored because they haunt us in their demand not merely for emotional and imaginative response, but for action. But nuclear disaster and ecological collapse (and their many siblings regarding possible catastrophe) are easily drawn upon through reliable images and appeals. [...] Apocalypse threatens to become cliché because we have lived with it too long; its imagery and its impressive effects are too readily available. [...] The catastrophe as an event so devastating that it ought to be unique in fact has dozens and dozens of precedents and variants. It is both anticipated and *déjà*. There is, then, some cultural need for skepticism, if not about the real threat of disaster then about our habit of imagining it. (2014, 159)

One might thus speculate that the more post-apocalyptic novels, movies, TV series, comics, and video games are produced and consumed (as entertainment), the easier it becomes for readers/viewers/players to remain in denial regarding actual dangers in the form of global warming, natural disasters, terrorism, and wars threatening the future of life on this planet. The value of the post-apocalyptic narrative as a warning would then be virtually eliminated.

Yet strategies such as the shift toward presenting humans as the main antagonists in the later seasons of *The Walking Dead*, or highlighting the conflicts between characters' obligation-worlds, also stress that the warning offered by post-apocalyptic fiction may not only concern larger sociopolitical, economic and ecological issues. Stories about the end of the world as we know it may also raise the troubling question what individuals are prepared to do or are capable of doing in order to survive. The "ethics of the told", i.e., "the ethical dimensions of characters' actions" (Phelan 2013, para. 3), in post-apocalyptic narratives may thus serve as a reminder that survival is perhaps only desirable in a world that is worth living in precisely because moral principles and values persist. This message is timeless and applicable to countless situations in the readers'/viewers'/players' reality; it shows that post-apocalyptic fiction may fulfill what is one of the basic functions of literary texts: the investigation and dissemination of values.[12]

---

[12] For an exploration of this function of fiction, cf. for instance the contributions in Erll, Grabes, and Nünning (2008), and in Baumbach, Grabes, and Nünning (2009).

References

Atwood, Margaret. *Oryx and Crake*. London: Virago, 2013 [2003].
Baumbach, Sibylle, Herbert Grabes, and Ansgar Nünning (eds.). *Literature and Values: Literature as a Medium for Representing, Disseminating and Constructing Norms and Values*. Trier: WVT, 2009.
Berger, James. *After the End: Representations of Post-Apocalypse*. Minneapolis/London: University of Minnesota Press, 1999.
Breidenbach, Birgit. "Hybridisation and Globalisation as Catalysts of Generic Change: David Mitchell's *Cloud Atlas* (2004) and *The Bone Clocks* (2014)." *The British Novel in the Twenty-First Century: Cultural Concerns – Literary Developments – Model Interpretations*. Eds. Vera Nünning and Ansgar Nünning. Trier: WVT, 2018. 311–326.
Brooks, Max. *World War Z: An Oral History of the Zombie War*. New York: Crown, 2006.
Byron, George Gordon. "Darkness." *The Complete Poetical Works*. Ed. Jerome J. McGann. Vol. 2. Oxford: Clarendon, 1980. 302.
Conrad, Maren. "Beginning at the End: Romantic Visions of the Last Man in Post-Apocalyptic Robinsonades." *Apocalyptic Chic: Visions of the Apocalypse and Post-Apocalypse in Literature and Visual Arts*. Eds. Barbara Brodman and James E. Doan. Madison/Teaneck: Fairleigh Dickinson University Press, 2017. 63–75.
Dimovitz, Scott. "The Sound of Silence: Eschatology and the Limits of the Word in David Mitchell's *Cloud Atlas*." *SubStance* 44.1 (2015): 71–91.
Dundes, Alan (ed.). *The Flood Myth*. Berkeley/Los Angeles: University of California Press, 1988.
Erll, Astrid, Herbert Grabes, and Ansgar Nünning (eds.). *Ethics in Culture: The Dissemination of Values through Literature and Other Media*. Berlin/Boston: De Gruyter, 2008.
Fludernik, Monika. *Towards a 'Natural' Narratology*. London: Routledge, 1996.
Goodman, Nelson. *Ways of Worldmaking*. New York: Hackett, 1978.
Gottschall, Jonathan. *The Storytelling Animal: How Stories Make Us Human*. New York: Mariner Books, 2013.
Grainville, Jean-Baptiste Cousin de. *The Last Man; or, Omergarus and Syderia, a Romance in Futurity*. 2 vols. London: R. Dutton, 1806.
Johns-Putra, Adeline. "'My Job is to Take Care of You': Climate Change, Humanity, and Cormac McCarthy's *The Road*." *Modern Fiction Studies* 62.3 (2016): 519–540.
Klingaman, William K., and Nicholas P. Klingaman. *The Year Without Summer: 1816 and the Volcano that Darkened the World and Changed History*. New York: St. Martin's Press, 2013.
Matheson, Richard. *I Am Legend*. London: Golláncz, 2001 [1954].
McCarthy, Cormac. *The Road*. New York: Vintage, 2007 [2006].
Mezey, Jason Howard. "'A Multitude of Drops': Recursion and Globalization in David Mitchell's *Cloud Atlas*." *Modern Language Studies* 40.2 (2011): 10–37.
Mitchell, David. *Cloud Atlas*. London: Hodder and Stoughton, 2004.
Nayar, Pramod K. *Posthumanism*. Cambridge/Malden,MA: Polity, 2014.
Nünning, Ansgar. "Narrativist Approaches and Narratological Concepts for the Study of Culture." *Travelling Concepts for the Study of Culture*. Eds. Birgit Neumann and Ansgar Nünning. Berlin/Boston: De Gruyter, 2012a. 145–183.
Nünning Ansgar. "Making Crises and Catastrophes – How Metaphors and Narratives Shape their Cultural Life." *The Cultural Life of Catastrophes and Crises*. Eds. Carsten Meiner and Kristin Veel. Berlin/Boston: De Gruyter, 2012b. 59–88.

Nünning, Ansgar. "'With the Benefit of Hindsight': Features and Functions of Turning Points as a Narratological Concept and as a Way of Self-Making." *Turning Points: Concepts and Narratives of Change in Literature and Other Media*. Eds. Ansgar Nünning and Kai Marcel Sicks. Berlin/Boston: De Gruyter, 2012c. 31–58.

Nünning, Ansgar, and Kai Marcel Sicks. "Turning Points as Metaphors and Mininarrations: Analysing Concepts of Change in Literature and Other Media." *Turning Points: Concepts and Narratives of Change in Literature and Other Media*. Eds. Ansgar Nünning and Kai Marcel Sicks. Berlin/Boston: De Gruyter, 2012. 1–28.

Nünning, Vera. *Reading Fictions, Changing Minds: The Cognitive Value of Fiction*. Heidelberg: Winter, 2014.

Palmer, Christopher. "Ordinary Catastrophes: Paradoxes and Problems in Some Recent Post-Apocalypse Fictions." *Green Planets: Ecology and Science Fiction*. Eds. Gerry Canavan and Kim Stanley Robinson. Middletown, CT: Wesleyan University Press, 2014. 158–175.

Phelan, James. "Narrative Ethics." *The Living Handbook of Narratology*. Eds. Peter Hühn, John Pier, Wolf Schmid, and Jörg Schönert. http://www.lhn.uni-hamburg.de/article/narrative-ethics. Hamburg: Hamburg University, 2013 (6 October 2018).

Pitetti, Connor. "Uses of the End of the World: Apocalypse and Postapocalypse as Narrative Modes." *Science Fiction Studies* 44.3 (2017): 437–454.

Ryan, Marie-Laure. *Possible Worlds, Artificial Intelligence, and Narrative Theory*. Bloomington/Indianapolis: Indiana University Press, 1991.

Ryan, Marie-Laure. "Possible Worlds." *Handbook of Narratology. Vol. 2*, Second ed. Eds. Peter Hühn, Jan Christoph Meister, John Pier, and Wolf Schmid. Berlin/Boston: De Gruyter, 2014. 726–742.

Shelley, Mary. *The Last Man*. Oxford: Oxford University Press, 2008 [1826].

Shute, Nevil. *On the Beach*. London: Vintage, 2009 [1957].

Skult, Petter. "The Role of Place in the Post-Apocalypse: Contrasting *The Road* and *World War Z*." *Studia Neophilologica* 87 (2015): 104–115.

Snyder, Katherine V. "'Time to Go': The Post-Apocalyptic and the Post-Traumatic in Margaret Atwood's *Oryx and Crake*." *Studies in the Novel* 43.4 (2011): 470–489.

Søfting, Inger-Anne. "Between Dystopia and Utopia: The Post-Apocalyptic Discourse of Cormac McCarthy's *The Road*." *English Studies* 94.6 (2013): 704–713.

Stoker, Bram. *Dracula*. Harmondsworth: Penguin, 2003 [1897].

Sussman, Charlotte. "'Islanded in the World': Cultural Memory and Human Mobility in *The Last Man*." *PMLA* 118.2 (2003): 286–301.

Torday, Piers. *The Last Wild*. London: Quercus, 2013.

Wells, H.G. *The Time Machine*. New York: Signet Classic, 2002 [1895].

White, Christopher T. "Embodied Reading and Narrative Empathy in Cormac McCarthy's *The Road*." *Studies in the Novel* 47.4 (2015): 532–549.

Zapf, Hubert. "Literature as Cultural Ecology: Notes towards a Functional Theory of Imaginative Texts with Examples from American Literature." *REAL* 17 (2001): 85–99.

Jan Rupp
Plumbing Distant Spatiotemporal Scales: Towards an Econarratology of Planetary Memory in Narratives of the Global South

Abstract: This essay explores figurations of environmental memory in narratives of the Global South for the particular insights they offer into today's global climate crisis. It is located at the intersection between cultural narratology and postcolonial ecocriticism, highlighted by recent work on ecological and ethical dimensions of storyworlds, as well as on their potential for cross-cultural understanding. Narratives from the Global South, the essay argues, frequently elaborate storyworlds on distant spatiotemporal scales, allowing readers to gauge central long-term as well as world-encompassing developments of anthropogenic change. Emerging from areas and climate zones in which the current environmental crisis is most keenly felt, these narratives retrieve fundamental ecological insights that may sensitize readers everywhere to the planet's precarious present, and thus help work towards ensuring a viable future. Their depiction of wide-ranging environmental memories can be seen to offer a blueprint against lingering amnesia, as issues of environmental justice loom large and the task of generating a shared commitment to the world is becoming increasingly urgent.

1 Introduction

Like few others, today's global ecological crisis is a case in point for the cultural power of narrative. Narrative serves to both fathom and respond to this crisis, to project and drive home a sense of catastrophe, of time running out.[1]

---

[1] These opening observations, and indeed the essay as a whole, are greatly indebted to Ansgar Nünning's seminal work in the area of cultural narratology (e.g. A. Nünning 2004), in particular to his writings on the role of narrative and metaphor in constructing and grappling with crises, catastrophes, and turning points (e.g. A. Nünning 2009, A. Nünning 2012a, A. Nünning and Sicks 2012). Serving as narrative kernels or "mininarrations" (A. Nünning 2012a, 62), condensed metaphors like 'crisis' or 'catastrophe' provide fundamental "categories in terms of which we conceptualise and structure culture, cultural change, disastrous events and even our theories thereof" (ibid.), thus resonating strongly with recent cultural responses to environmental change and natural disasters.

https://doi.org/10.1515/9783110654370-005

Scholars and activists alike have highlighted the need for committed and persuasive storytelling, rather than bare scientific fact, if people are to be mobilized to work collectively towards ensuring the planet's future. Symptomatically, Al Gore's highly publicized documentaries *An Inconvenient Truth: A Global Warning* (2006) and *An Inconvenient Sequel: Truth to Power* (2017) capitalize on the power of narrative to both shock and inspire his audience. They deftly juxtapose the dystopian narrative of climate change with a story of community, hope, and wonder. The earth's beauty might yet be preserved and is epitomized, in the first documentary especially, by a lingering cinematic gaze at majestic images from outer space, such as Blue Marble and Earthrise. Tapping into American cultural narratives at large, Gore teaches his audience a lesson and at the same time offers an opportunity for redemption. Even at the last minute, the world can be made a better place again.

Conspicuously, memory is being enlisted in a similar way for environmental concerns. Lawrence Buell has built on his rich body of ecocritical scholarship by proposing a concept of environmental memory. This "uncommon term with no set definition" (Buell 2017, 96) seeks to capture "the sense [...] of environments as lived experience in the fourth dimension – *i.e.* the intimation of human life and history as unfolding within the context of human embeddedness in webs of shifting environmental circumstance" (Buell 2017, 96) of varying duration. Buell differentiates various "spatiotemporal scales" (2017, 97), ranging from the *longue durée* of biological memory in both human and nonhuman life to the individual and collective uses of environmental memory in communities and nations. The interplay and extension of scales connects Buell's endeavour to recent inquiries into "planetary memory" (Bond et al. 2017) and "memory after humanism" (Knittel and Driscoll 2017). The latter have likewise pushed boundaries of memory to the planetary expanse of past human impact, as well as beyond the human to explore its relations with other species and biotic systems. As Buell argues, "for the sake of the planetary future of humans and nonhumans alike" it is vital "to develop robust, shared conceptions of environmental memory that extend much further back in time than the history of *homo sapiens* itself, let alone the lifetimes of particular individuals" (2017, 97). To confront "the inertial force of what the environmental psychologist Peter Kahn, Jr., has called 'environmental amnesia'" (2017, 96), Buell highlights the role of "expressive media" such as narrative and literature for the retrieval and transmission of "effective environmental memory" (2017, 97).

In this essay, I will take my cue from the emerging field of narratological ecocriticism to explore figurations of environmental memory in narratives of the Global South: these hold a special potential to prompt ecological awareness by plumbing distant spatiotemporal scales. Recent work at the intersection between narratology and ecocriticism is part of the broader development of postclassical, cultural, and contextualist narratologies, as well as, more specifically, of cognitive and postcolonial approaches to narrative.[2] Ecocritical studies have foregrounded the reading process as embodied practice and highlighted the potential of narrative to transport readers into storyworlds as alternative environments in which to simulate the experiences of human and nonhuman others. I will especially draw here on Erin James's work, which points up empathy and cross-cultural understanding as ethical dimensions of narrative comprehension, focusing on postcolonial and nonrealist narratives for the particular insights these bring to the increasingly global discussion of environmentalism and environmental justice (see James 2015).

Notions of postcoloniality and the Global South clearly intersect, with both addressing legacies of colonialism in today's world.[3] However, the concept of Global South is particularly conducive to scaling planetary memory inasmuch as it reaches beyond regional, national, or even hemispheric frames to include the flow of people, ideas, and goods to and from the Global North.[4] As I shall argue, figurations of planetary memory from the Global South offer especially pertinent and persuasive narratives to address world-encompassing developments. Global South narratives contribute to meeting a central challenge of "ecological storytelling" (Heise 2005, 129) in the twenty-first century: "namely, developing modes of narration that convey a sense of ecosystems not only in their local and regional manifestations, but also in their global reach" (Heise 20005, 130). Emerging from contexts and climate zones in which the global environmental crisis is most keenly felt, these narratives retrieve fundamental ecological insights that may sensitize readers everywhere to the planet's precarious present, and thus help work towards ensuring a viable future.

---

[2] On these overarching developments in narratology and the increasingly interdisciplinary study of narrative see *inter alia* Heinen and Sommer (2009), Alber and Fludernik (2010), A. Nünning (2012b), and V. Nünning (2013).
[3] In postcolonial studies and other areas, the concept of Global South serves to highlight transnational entanglements, as well as moving beyond discriminatory discourse such as 'developing countries' or the First World/Third World distinction.
[4] On the dynamic of hemispheric exchange see Levander and Mignolo (2011) and Müller et al. (2018, 3).

2 Ecological storytelling: Interdisciplinary perspectives on narrative form and environment-oriented contextualism

More needs to be said about the recent dialogue between narratology and ecocriticism, which has forged a number of crucial conceptual openings in existing interpretive frameworks. Central here are James's (2015) project of 'econarratology', as well as the wide-ranging study of environmental narrative, broadly defined as "any type of narrative in any media that foregrounds ecological issues [...], often but not always with the openly stated intention of bringing about social change" (Weik von Mossner 2017, 3). The potential for instigating change lies in the way in which environmental narratives do not simply foreground ecological aspects but closely engage the reader, listener, or viewer on an emotional level. Stories about environmental issues call for a highly interdisciplinary approach, combining an interest in narrative form and environment-oriented contextualism with insights from cognitive science, psychology, and affect theory. Drawing from the latter, the act of reading has been fleshed out as a not just imaginative but full-scale immersive experience, involving mind, body, and embodied cognition in an all-encompassing process of comprehension.[5] Rather than to be read at arm's length, environmental or "eco-narratives" (Heise 2005, 129) are understood as engaging the reader intimately, mobilizing empathy and affect, and potentially inducing change with respect to the environment and ecological concerns far beyond the page or reading experience.

Like the broad definition of environmental narrative, econarratology does not presuppose a specific type of story or genre, but can reveal environmental imaginaries even where these do not seem the dominant concerns of a text. In works that lack extensive depictions of nature, a selective and highly subjective channelling of related issues in terms of narration and focalization might still, as James points out, constitute a substantial perspective on the environment. Moreover, in the narratives she deals with, environmental issues frequently cut across categories of race, ethnicity and gender, an intersection highlighted by discussions of eco-feminism in postcolonial writing. In this and other bodies of work, the result may well be an intricate interplay of environmental and identity politics, which in theory may find expression in any aspect of narrative

---

[5] See V. Nünning (2014) on the state of the art of cognitive approaches in narratology and more broadly the study of fiction.

form (see Lehtimäki 2013, 137). In this context, both micro- and macro-structures of narrative, such as archetypal set patterns, writing styles, and genres, can carry meaning.

As a central element of econarratology, James draws on David Herman's concept of 'storyworld', a term that aims to capture more adequately the multidimensional process of narrative and narrative comprehension (see Herman 2002, 9–24). For, by extending the long dominant understanding of 'story' as defined primarily in terms of time and sequentiality into the compound 'storyworld', Herman emphasizes the spatial dimension of narrative and its world-creating power. To delineate the interplay of the story's existents as they unfold in time and space, he interestingly uses the term 'ecology' (Herman 2002, 13–14), though not in a strictly environmental sense, as James notes (2015, xi). However, Herman's association of ecology and the concept of storyworld provide a felicitous point of entry for ecocritical projects like James's econarratology. Highlighting aspects of narrative space and place, these borrowings recall and chime with foundational concerns of literary ecocriticism.

Theories of narrative cognition teach us that readers will always bring their real-life environmental experience to a text, implicitly or explicitly comparing their own mental models with the storyworld presented to them in order to make sense of it. In this light, James locates the potential of eco-narratives for cross-cultural dialogue in comprehending and squaring entire storyworlds with one another, a process in which a host of local and culture-specific approaches can come together in what she metaphorically envisions as a 'storyworld accord' – the title of her 2015 study. By bringing one understanding of 'world' into dialogue with another, both narrative comprehension in particular and cross-cultural understanding in general are made possible. Eventually, getting to know about and analysing narrative storyworlds from around the globe stands to serve an important environmental cause. Rather than prioritizing some imaginaries and policies over others, they are assembled in their plurality and variety on a level playing field, with the ultimate goal of arriving at just such an 'accord'. The reference to the difficult business of negotiating climate agreements in environmental world affairs throws into relief the essentially political dimension of a project like econarratology in the context of global debates on environmental justice and environmentalism.

The latent plurality of storyworlds, engendered between one reader's mental models and the text, and multiplied by other readers and other texts, is a timely reminder of the challenges involved. At the same time, the process of narrative comprehension can serve as an example in miniature for consensus politics on environmental matters. In fact, another advantage of the concept of storyworld is the way in which the referent 'world' may be understood, quite literally, as 'the planet', so that analysing and entering into dialogue about storyworlds may also open up a conversation about diverse environmental memories and a shared commitment to planetary futures. To bring about this dialogue on environmental matters between equal partners, James highlights the potential of postcolonial and non-realist narratives, in contradistinction to the privileging of realist styles of nature writing so long dominant in Western ecocritical perspectives. While not striving for authentic representations in a straightforward sense, non-realist styles may very well be true to life by capturing a particular subjective experience. After all, by empirical standards the current scale of climate change and extreme weather events may indeed, above all to those exposed to it, be overwhelming, out of the ordinary, or simply 'unreal'.

The potential of narrative – in particular non-realist narrative – for creating an ecological awareness of interlocking local and global spheres bears some emphasizing in the light of ongoing scepticism over the representation, or indeed representability of phenomena like global warming. When Ian McEwan received a prize at the Guardian Hay Festival for his novel *Solar* (2010), which features a physicist on a quest to save the world from environmental disaster, he was quoted as expressing surprise at the paucity of writers tackling the issue of climate change. The reason, he suggested, was one of temporality, scale and solidarity with distant others.[6] As recently as 2016, the Indian novelist Amitav Ghosh struck a similar chord in his book-length essay *The Great Derangement*. For Ghosh, the realist novel in particular fails to fathom, let alone give form to the abrupt, extreme and often cataclysmic nature of climate change.[7] Thus Ghosh sees writers and readers alike sleepwalking into ecological doom, 'deranged' by a literary imagination that conceals rather than confronts the world's environmental crisis.

If sudden, cataclysmic, high-impact disasters can challenge or even defy the literary imagination – like the first-ever tornado to hit New Delhi in 1978, which is a central motif for Ghosh – the same goes for the gradual effects of toxicity and pollution such as those that followed the explosion of the Union Carbide chemical plant in Bhopal in 1984. As Rob Nixon warns in his *Slow Violence and the Environmentalism of the Poor*: "The representational challenges

---

[6] "I think it is a unique challenge to human nature. We are programmed for the short term and have to think about the long term, do favours for people we've never met." (McEwan qtd. in Flood 2010, n. p.)

[7] Ghosh's account of the realist novel emphasizes its connection with the rise of bourgeois society and nineteenth-century ideas of probability and rationalism. This may be only one version (or literary history) of the realist novel, but it is symptomatic of larger anxieties currently emerging over the representation and representability of climate change.

are acute, requiring creative ways of drawing public attention to catastrophic acts that are low in instant spectacle but high in long-term effects." (2011, 10) Accordingly, he calls on writers to "intervene representationally" in order to alert readers to the slow, hidden violence of environmental degradation (Nixon 2011, 10). To be sure, neither the environmentalist writing Nixon deals with, nor the growing body of climate change fiction, should be overlooked.[8] Yet it is also true that many of the works concerned belong in the area of science (and other genre) fiction, a category distinct from the literary mainstream that writers like McEwan and Ghosh have in mind.

3 Sense of place and planet: Narrating planetary memory in the Global South

If the novel, at least in its classical European incarnation, lags behind in envisioning climate change, it becomes all the more urgent to look further afield for alternative archives and bodies of work – hence my focus on eco-narratives of the Global South. These are informed by a different experience of reality, one that ominously foreshadows planetary futures at large and markedly deviates from the standards of probability Ghosh detects in much realist fiction. Works from the Global South tend to elaborate environmental memories in storyworlds of disaster and degradation, while frequently presenting alternative ecologies that might be adduced to imagine and cope with the mounting challenge of climate change. Moreover, arising from a century-long history of colonialism, displacement, forced labour, and successive waves of global migration, environmental imaginaries in narratives of the Global South tend to be dual in nature, at once local and global.[9]

In this connection, what the concept of Global South captures is on the one hand patent historical links between bodies of writing, and on the other facets

---

8 See Trexler (2015) and Irr (2017) on the trajectory of climate change fiction, which has also been traced back as far as the 1960s.
9 As with any large and geographically sprawling category, like 'Global South', care must be taken to avoid over-generalization. Literary traditions between as well as within, say, India, Africa and the Caribbean differ widely and merit attention by themselves, rather than being subsumed into an overarching constellation. My purpose here is by no means to gloss over differences, but to highlight convergences in depictions of environmental memory that envision an extension of spatiotemporal scales. For these, the hemispheric framework of Global South is a fitting correlative.

of the literary imagination beyond the local and national. For instance, Anglophone Indian and Caribbean narratives look back to an intricate and shared history of migration, with large numbers of indentured Indian labourers emigrating to the Caribbean after the abolition of slavery in the nineteenth century. In postcolonial times, India as the ancestral homeland has remained an imaginary, while at the same time becoming a real destination for Caribbean-born writers, as in V. S. Naipaul's Indian travelogues, which James includes in her study of econarratology.[10] There might be less of a return movement from the Caribbean to India than to Africa, both in terms of migration and the artistic imagination – all the more reason, then, for critical inquiry. Anglophone Caribbean and Indian narratives emerge from close historical entanglements and make for a fruitful case study of commonalities and convergences in narrating environmental memories of the Global South.

For one thing, Indian-English literature is widely regarded as a pioneering tradition of 'green' postcolonial writing (see Mukherjee 2010). Novels like Indra Sinha's *Animal's People* (2007) and Arundhati Roy's *The God of Small Things* (1997) explore both environmental risks in more recent, postcolonial times and the chthonic ecologies of indigenous communities, with a keen interest in memories of human-nature as well human-animal relationality. Amitav Ghosh has also addressed environmental matters in many of his works, albeit different in nature than the dramatic climate events he fears resist the novelistic imagination. His novel *The Hungry Tide* (2004) is a frequent point of reference for questions of environmental justice and the difficulty of finding or acknowledging common ground between various environmentalisms in the globalized world (see James 2015, 2–3). The novel depicts the life of settlers in the Sundarbans, an archipelago of islands in the easternmost part of India on the border to Bangladesh, where the community has been based for hundreds of years. In that deep time space, they have evolved ways of eking out a living in tune with a nurturing but often precarious environment, a place of dangerous waters, crocodiles, and man-eating tigers. As this scene is visited by Piya, an Indian expat from the U.S. on the track of rare river dolphins, and Kanai, a Delhi businessman who becomes a translator for Piya's local guide, Fokir, conflicting environmental experiences and attitudes loom large. In particular, the Sundarban people's age-old rural ways of living with, but also protecting themselves against wild animals, is questioned by the two metropolitan characters when a tiger encroaches on village grounds and is hunted down. In a nuanced dialogue gesturing towards

---

10 In his novel *Half a Life* (2001), for example, Naipaul draws a fictional portrait of India that centres on a character whose life moves between India, Europe and Africa.

cross-cultural understanding, Ghosh juxtaposes the environmentalist prerogative of sparing the tiger no matter what with an alternative vista of inter-species ecological cohabitation. While not solving this conflict in any definitive way, the novel suspends the hegemonies of western environmentalism and makes room for the possibility that the Sundarban inhabitants' environmental practices are not easily dismissable. In fact, they might ultimately be less threatening to the survival of tigers as a species than the consumerist lifestyles of civilized humanity, whose animal activism can also be seen as a measure of overcompensation and alienation from their own, as well as other species' habitats.

A similar tension between longstanding indigenous ecologies and modern uses (as well as abuses) of the environment characterizes Arundhati Roy's *The God of Small Things*. In Roy's prize-winning novel, the character who most closely resembles life in the Sundarbans is Velutha, a carpenter and handyman at the Paradise Pickles & Preserves factory in Ayemenem, Kerala. As an untouchable, he is an outsider to the community, but still occupies a special place in the Ipe family, who own the factory. He is a friend and mentor of the novel's two young protagonists, taking the twins Rahel and Estha fishing, for instance, and he crosses social as well as moral boundaries as the illicit lover of Ammu, their mother. Most important of all, Velutha retains a pivotal environmental memory, an intuitive connection to the local landscape and biotic life, a "river-sense" (Roy 1997, 30) that is also ascribed to certain parts of the built environment like Ayemenem House, the family home. Velutha is the novel's central representative of a holistic ecology of animated life across human and nonhuman spheres, richly evoked by Roy in vivid passages of magical realism, such as when the two forbidden lovers meet by the river: "As he rose from the dark river and walked up the stone steps, she saw that the world they stood in was his. That it belonged to him. The water. The mud. The trees. The fish. The stars." (Roy 1997, 333) Velutha not only belongs in this storyworld that has evolved from what seem to be times immemorial and extends as far as the cosmos, he is also shaped by his environment in a very material, non-metaphorical, and non-realist way: "As she watched him she understood the quality of his beauty. How his labour had shaped him. How the wood he fashioned had fashioned him. Each plank, each nail he drove, each thing he made, had moulded him." (Roy 1997, 334)

Time and again, Roy depicts animated environments and shared ecological agency across human and nonhuman spheres.[11] The sense of mythic, planetary

---

11 Roy's novel, like the other examples discussed, thoroughly reconfigures human-nature relationality. The passages quoted are non-realist or suggestive of magical realism precisely in this way, and thus should not be limited to familiar tropes of nature writing and "narrative realism" (Heise 2005, 130).

memory that has formed Velutha seems to vanish when he is killed, though some of it is passed on to Rahel, who is closely associated with Roy's evocation of cyclical time and non-linear storytelling. On her return to Aymenem as an adult, Rahel remembers her childhood days as the novel's beginning meditates on the turn of the seasons. However, she also witnesses environmental decline as industrial agriculture and a luxury resort have radically altered the landscape and dried up the river: "[W]hen Rahel returned to the river, it greeted her with a ghastly skull's smile, with holes where teeth had been, and a limp hand raised from a hospital bed." (Roy 1997, 124) With the river's transition from animated life to zombie, Roy's novel segues to the intrusion of modern land-use and environmental pollution, which is staged in even more dramatic fashion in Indra Sinha's *Animal's People*.

In Sinha's novel, a fictionalized account of the Bhopal disaster, the eponymous hero Animal roams a wasteland which is gradually taken back by the community and the town's biota. A hybrid between human and animal, the novel's protagonist represents the extent of ecological life affected, as well as the emergence, or retrieval of shared solidarities in the face of environmental crime. Sinha's novel and its unnatural, as well as highly unreliable protagonist-narrator epitomize the community-building power of environmental memory, in this case Bhopal's resilience and renaissance under the disaster's formative impact. In responding to this environmental catastrophe, the narrator and his community – 'Animal's people' – seem to recall a longer-standing memory of ecological togetherness and inter-species relationality, in Bhopal as well as on a larger, planetary scale.

If eco-narratives in Anglophone Indian writing gauge boundaries of memory beyond the local and human, the same holds true for the broad spatiotemporal imaginaries articulated in Caribbean narratives. Because of its postcolonial and historical outlook, Anglophone Caribbean writing frequently deals with environmental change on a long-term, truly planetary basis from New World discovery to modern global migration.[12] Caribbean environments have seen the most radical transformation anywhere, while being constantly exposed to elemental geophysical forces. According to notions of world-ecology and world systems theory, the Caribbean occupies a pivotal location as a theatre of global capitalism and its ecological repercussions, which developed in sync with European imperial dominance of the globe from the sixteenth century onwards (see Moore 2003).

---

[12] This space of time squares with scientific narrative projections that postulate 1492 as an ecological watershed (see Lightfoot et al. 2013).

While not strictly speaking a narrative genre, a prominent instance of planetary memory can be found in poetry as a major strand of Caribbean writing.[13] In Derek Walcott's New World epics, such as *Omeros* (1990) and *Tiepolo's Hound* (2000), as well as in his other poetry, origin narratives and tropes of the New World Adam serve as recurrent macro-structures and motifs (see Handley 2007). For Walcott, the Caribbean is anything but the virginal landscape of the European imagination. Instead, it is a heavily scarred terrain, suffused with memories of slavery and plantation labour. However, his poetry repeatedly envisages the archipelago's biota as a recuperative ecology. In Walcott's ecopoetics and "language of plants" (Savory 2010), the island flora, as well as major settings like the sea and beach, provide crucial means for the New World Adam to recompose and constitute himself, often picturing the reciprocal inscription of human and nonhuman life in very literal, magical and more-than-metaphorical ways.

In his poem "Punctuation Marks", Philip Nanton gives a telling account of the intricate interplay between Caribbean identities, the formative impact of island ecologies, and the literary imagination. Originally published under the title "I" in 1992, the poem is reprinted in his more recent publication *Frontiers of the Caribbean* (2017), a blend between historical study, sociological analysis and postcolonial critique. The poem presents an origin story in more than one sense, recounting the speaker's (and arguably Nanton's own) personal formation by introducing the landscape in which he was born and grew up. Thus it traces the speaker's identity, but also chronicles the genesis and continuous transformation of the Caribbean through geological forces. Both variants of the origin story are supported by the poem's earlier title and its two possible meanings, with "I" as first-person pronoun referring to the speaker's persona and identity, or to the Roman number one ('I') as a signal of narrative beginnings. The new title "Punctuation Marks" suggests more clearly the story the poem tells of literary creation and inspiration. References to punctuation and writing continuously inflect the speaker's account of his identity and his island world as the poem opens: "Where sea and land meet, begin there. / The ampersand, the join, is a fault / that caused jagged peaks to rise / from the ocean's floor / spanning a vacant gulf." (Nanton 2017, n. p.) As can be seen, the poem's first few lines oscillate between different scales and perspectives, starting from ground level at the shoreline and then zooming out to the far larger, essentially

---

[13] Transgeneric perspectives have been a highly fruitful impulse of postclassical and cultural approaches to narrative. On forms of narration in poetry and drama see Hühn and Sommer (undated).

planetary scale of the world map, from which the islands' "jagged peaks" are viewed: "On any map of the world they are footnotes / reminders of nature's force" (Nanton 2017, n. p.). A central move and motif throughout Nanton's text, this symbolical merging of frontiers between the local and global is performed again as the poem's final section zooms in again to return to land and sea: "Come nearer, focus on one dot of an island. / I was born there, on the rim of a volcano." (Nanton 2017, n. p.) Tellingly, Nanton's visual allusions project a sense of place and planet at the same time (see Heise 2008). They are indicative of a holistic, indeed planetary vision, which characterizes his as well as many other Caribbean texts and builds on environmental memories transcending both the local and the human as frames of reference.

The impact of tropical topographies and the ambivalent legacy of radically transformed as well as renewable landscapes are a mainstay of Caribbean prose narratives, too. Many early novels of the decolonization era foreground the experience of extreme weather events, such as rain and flood in George Lamming's *In the Castle of My Skin* (1953), or scorching heat in Andrew Salkey's *A Quality of Violence* (1959) and Shiva Naipaul's *A Hot Country* (1983). While these texts negotiate, and are usually studied for, other topics away from environmental matters, such as (identity) politics at the dawn of independence, it is interesting to note just how consistently they reference the region's climate. As a ground tone, they resound with Caribbean weather and geophysical forces – in the words of Kamau Brathwaite its "environmental experience," which he famously associated with the roaring of hurricanes (1981, 20). In the Caribbean literary tradition, the hurricane serves as a symbol of both destruction and regeneration, an overarching rallying cry of self-assertion entering into an alliance with liberation movements to fend off colonial and neo-colonial interests (see Deckard 2016) and including the islands' population, as is suggested by the programmatic "We roar" in the foreword to Nanton's *Frontiers of the Caribbean* (2017, n. p.).

Time and again, Anglophone Caribbean narratives attribute life and agency to seemingly inanimate environmental elements, and in so doing critically suspend the division of nature and humans found in the realist traditions of western nature writing. Another location where resistant ecologies of human and nonhuman life are prominently explored in Caribbean writing is the hinterland. Historically a place of refuge for slaves that escaped the plantation regime, the hinterland continues to figure as an important environmental memory of revolt and revisionist history. In both Erna Brodber's *Myal* (1988) and Pauline Melville's *The Ventriloquist's Tale* (1997), it is a dark storyworld peopled by zombies who have been left crippled by colonialism but are now invigorated by the retrieval of lost environmental alliances. To stage this recovery both novels employ a range of non-realist techniques, such as Melville's playful trickster figure as narrator, which enable them to chart alternative ecologies of the sort that characterize Global South eco-narratives overall.

4 Conclusion

Interestingly, the power and promise of narrative has been challenged and cast into doubt at just the present moment of climate crisis. In view of the aggravating heat and drought of global summers, there is a growing sense of doom far beyond the realm of world politics, with agreements such as the Paris Climate accord hanging in the balance. The world's ecological crisis is increasingly being felt as a crisis of culture, a failure to anticipate, envision and drive home the consequences of man-made climate change. There is certainly no shortage of environmental narratives, and phenomena like global warming are subject to competing versions of epistemic storytelling.[14] Yet scientists warn of narrative scaremongering, and writers like Ian McEwan and Amitav Ghosh point to the novel's shortcomings as the *genre royal* of narrative, expressing scepticism about its capacity to imagine climate change. The question, then, is not *whether*, but *which* narratives can be drawn on to fathom and respond to ongoing developments of environmental decline.

In this situation, narratives of environmental memory from the Global South hold a particular potential. Acutely informed by human interdependence with the land and other species, the non-realist experiments of Global South narratives frequently foreground the materiality of lived environmental experience and at the same time project a sense of local and planetary space. They contribute important non-Western ecologies and alternative environmental memories in what remains a highly asymmetrical world with respect to industrial waste, consumption of resources and carbon footprints. Simultaneously, the symptoms of climate change have begun to show, and to be perceived most keenly, in settings of the Global South. Narratives which circumscribe this experiential reality will not only have to be accommodated in a storyworld accord, as the task of generating a shared environmental commitment to the world is becoming increasingly urgent. Global South narratives might also provide orientation and a lost connection to sustainable lifestyles where, often

---

14 See Richter (2016), who detects "a crisis of environmental narrative in the Anthropocene" and argues that "[n]ew environmental narratives" are needed in this epoch of man-made climate change "to counter and enrich that of environmental declension" (Richter 2016, 97).

enough, environmental degradation is a symptom of civilization, as well as of people's alienation from erstwhile ecological habitats. Although specific to the Indian subcontinent and the Caribbean archipelago, the long, wide-ranging environmental memories in the texts discussed here can be seen to offer a blueprint against environmental amnesia, speaking to past and present, as well to the future of the planet at large.

Narratives from the Global South are, as I hope to have demonstrated, an exemplary subject for an ecocritical narratology that highlights the plurality of their storyworlds, their materiality and affective power, and the possibility they offer for cross-cultural understanding. Intersecting with the lived experience and memory of material environments on a hemispheric scale and beyond, they constitute a timely and at the same time readily expandable area of narratological inquiry. While scholars argue for the cultural significance of narrative beyond the text, the climate crisis and its challenge of survival for humanity and the planet emphasize the role of storytelling in the most existential way imaginable.

References

Alber, Jan, and Monika Fludernik (eds.). *Postclassical Narratology: Approaches and Analyses.* Columbus: Ohio State University Press, 2010.

Bond, Lucy, Ben De Bruyn, and Jessica Rapson. "Planetary Memory in Contemporary American Fiction." *Textual Practice* 31.5 (2017): 853–866.

Buell, Lawrence. "Uses and Abuses of Environmental Memory." *Contesting Environmental Imaginaries: Nature and Counternature in a Time of Global Change.* Ed. Steven Hartman. Leiden: Brill, 2017. 95–116.

Brathwaite, Edward Kamau. "English in the Caribbean: Notes on Nation Language and Poetry." *English Literature: Opening up the Canon.* Eds. Leslie A. Fiedler and A. Houston Baker, Jr. Baltimore: Johns Hopkins University Press, 1981. 15–53.

Deckard, Sharae. "The Political Ecology of Storms in Caribbean Literature." *The Caribbean: Aesthetics, World-Ecology, Politics.* Eds. Chris Campbell and Michael Niblett. Liverpool: Liverpool University Press, 2016. 25–45.

Flood, Alison. *Ian McEwan Collects Award for Novel That Tackles Climate Change.* https://www.theguardian.com/books/2010/may/28/ian-mcewan-hay-prize-solar. The Guardian, 28 May 2010 (10 August 2018)

Ghosh, Amitav. *The Hungry Tide.* New York: HarperCollins, 2004.

Handley, George B. *New World Poetics: Nature and the Adamic Imagination of Whitman, Neruda, and Walcott.* Athens: University of Georgia Press, 2007.

Heinen, Sandra, and Roy Sommer. *Narratology in the Age of Cross-Disciplinary Research.* Berlin: de Gruyter, 2009.

Heise, Ursula K. "Eco-Narratives." *The Routledge Encyclopedia of Narrative Theory.* Eds. David Herman, Manfred Jahn, and Marie Laure Ryan. London: Routledge, 2005. 129–130.

Heise, Ursula K. *Sense of Place, Sense of Planet: The Environmental Imagination of the Global.* Oxford: Oxford University Press, 2008.

Herman, David. *Story Logic: Problems and Possibilities of Narrative.* Lincoln: University of Nebraska Press, 2002.

Hühn, Peter, and Roy Sommer. "Narration in Poetry and Drama." *The Living Handbook of Narratology.* Eds. Peter Hühn, John Pier, Wolf Schmid, and Jörg Schönert. http://www.lhn.uni-hamburg.de (10 November 2018).

Irr, Caren. "Climate Fiction in English." *Oxford Research Encyclopedia, Literature.* Oxford: Oxford University Press, 2017. DOI: 10.1093/acrefore/9780190201098.013.4

James, Erin. *The Storyworld Accord: Econarratology and Postcolonial Narrative.* Lincoln: Nebraska University Press, 2015.

Knittel, Susanne C., and Kári Driscoll. "Introduction: Memory after Humanism." *Parallax* 23.4 (2017): 379–383.

Lehtimäki, Markku. "Natural Environments in Narrative Contexts: Cross-Pollinating Ecocriticism and Narrative Theory." *Storyworlds: A Journal of Narrative Studies* 5 (2013): 119–141.

Levander, Caroline, and Walter Mignolo. "Introduction: The Global South and World Dis/Order." *The Global South* 5.1 (2011): 1–11.

Lightfoot, Kent G., Lee M. Panich, Tsim D. Schneider, and Sara L. Gonzalez. "European Colonialism and the Anthropocene: A View from the Pacific Coast of North America." *Anthropocene* 4 (2013): 101–115.

Moore, Jason. "Capitalism as World-Ecology: Braudel and Marx on Environmental History." *Organization and Environment* 16.4 (2003): 431–458.

Müller, Gesine, Jorge J. Locane, and Benjanim Loy. "Introduction." *Re-Mapping World Literature: Writing, Book Markets and Epistemologies between Latin America and the Global South.* Eds. Gesine Müller, Jorge J. Locane, and Benjamin Loy. Berlin: de Gruyter, 2018. 1–12.

Mukherjee, Upamanyu Pablo. "Arundhati Roy: Environment and Uneven Form." *Postcolonial Green: Environmental Politics and World Narratives.* Eds. Bonnie Roos and Axel Hunt. Charlottesville: University of Virginia Press, 2010. 17–31.

Nanton, Philip. *Frontiers of the Caribbean.* Manchester: Manchester University Press, 2017. DOI: 10.26530/OAPEN_622381.

Nixon, Rob. *Slow Violence and the Environmentalism of the Poor.* Cambridge: Harvard University Press, 2011.

Nünning, Ansgar. "Where Historiographic Metafiction and Narratology Meet: Towards an Applied Cultural Narratology." *Style* 38.3 (2004): 352–375.

Nünning, Ansgar. "Steps Towards a Metaphorology (and Narratology) of Crises: On the Functions of Metaphors as Figurative Knowledge and Mininarrations." *Metaphor: Shaping Culture and Theory. REAL – Yearbook of Research in English and American Literature* 25. Eds. Herbert Grabes, Ansgar Nünning, and Sibylle Baumbach. Tübingen: Narr, 2009. xi–xxviii.

Nünning, Ansgar. "Making Crises and Catastrophes – How Metaphors and Narratives Shape Their Cultural Life." *The Cultural Life of Catastrophes and Crises.* Eds. Carsten Meiner and Kristin Veel. Berlin: de Gruyter, 2012a. 59–88.

Nünning, Ansgar. "Narrativist Approaches and Narratological Concepts for the Study of Culture." *Travelling Concepts for the Study of Culture.* Eds. Birgit Neumann and Ansgar Nünning. Berlin: de Gruyter, 2012b. 145–184.

Nünning, Ansgar, and Kai Sicks. "Turning Points as Metaphors and Mininarrations: Analysing Concepts of Change in Literature and Other Media." *Turning Points: Concepts and Narratives of Change in Literature and Other Media*. Eds. Ansgar Nünning and Kai Sicks. Berlin: de Gruyter, 2012. 1–28.

Nünning, Vera. *Reading Fictions, Changing Minds: The Cognitive Value of Fiction*. Heidelberg: Winter, 2014.

Nünning, Vera (ed.). *New Approaches to Narrative: Cognition – Culture – History*. Trier: WVT, 2013.

Richter, Daniel deB. "The Crisis of Environmental Narrative in the Anthropocene." *RCC Perspectives: Transformations in Environment and Society* 2 (2016): 97–100.

Roy, Arundhati. *The God of Small Things*. London: Flamingo, 1997.

Savory, Elaine. "Toward a Caribbean Ecopoetics: Derek Walcott's Language of Plants." *Postcolonial Ecologies: Literatures of the Environment*. Eds. Elizabeth DeLoughrey and George B. Handley. Oxford: Oxford University Press, 2011. 80–96.

Sinha, Indra. *Animal's People*. London: Simon and Schuster, 2008.

Trexler, Adam. *Anthropocene Fictions*. Charlottesville: University of Virginia Press, 2015.

Weik von Mossner, Alexa. *Affective Ecologies: Empathy, Emotion, and Environmental Narrative*. Columbus: Ohio State University Press, 2017.

Birgit Neumann
Narrative Forms in the Age of the Anthropocene: Negotiating Human-Nonhuman Relations in Global South Novels

Abstract: The essay proceeds from the assumption that the changes ushered in by the age of the Anthropocene pose a representational challenge to literature and put pressure on narrative forms. It argues that narrative literature, especially texts from the so-called Global South, creatively respond to these changes by modelling narrative forms that afford new, sustainable ways of approaching our planet. These forms express the interdependences that govern relations between humans and nonhumans and widen the scope of human history toward multispecies ecologies. A close reading of the 2013 novel *Dust* by Kenyan author Yvonne Owuor analyses narrative forms that engage with the changed political, economic, and ecological demands of the Anthropocene. Lastly, the essay identifies challenges these narrative forms pose to classical narratology, focusing on representations of time, events, and space.

1 The age of the Anthropocene – an extended question mark

"The Anthropocene," writes Timothy Clark in *Ecocriticism on the Edge*, "blurs and even scrambles some crucial categories by which people have made sense of the world and their lives. It puts in crisis the lines between culture and nature, fact and value, and between the human and the geological or meteorological" (2015, 9). The Anthropocene, I would add, also scrambles a number of customary narrative forms deployed in fiction to depict the complex and multifaceted relation between human agents and their environments. The material and conceptual changes ushered in by the Anthropocene pose a representational challenge to literature and put pressure on narrative forms, most importantly on representations of time, space, and events. Rather than proceeding from the widespread assumption that "the temporal and material contractions of the Anthropocene" (Yusoff 2015, 383) materialize in narrative collapses, disruptions, and a general sense of capitulation in the face of something unrepresentable, the present essay sets out to show how literature creatively responds to these contractions. More specifically, it argues that a number of Global South novels model narrative forms that afford new, possibly more sustainable ways of approaching our planet.[1] They give expression to the interdependences – rather than hierarchies – that govern relations between humans and nonhumans and widen the scope of human history toward geological temporalities and multispecies ecologies.

In the following, I will present a brief overview of current discourses on the Anthropocene, before going on to explore how these discourses have been tied to the study of narrative fiction (Sections 2 and 3). Focusing on the 2013 novel *Dust* by Kenyan author Yvonne Owuor, I will then move on to analyze how postcolonial novels from the Global South respond to concerns related to the Anthropocene. The reason for this focus is twofold. First, the Global South, due to histories of modern colonialism and capitalist globalization, is "particularly vulnerable" (DeLoughrey and Handley 2011, 26) to the environmental changes marked by the Anthropocene: colonial resource exploitation, the plantation economy, petro-imperialism, the dumping of outsourced toxic waste, and neocolonial tourism "disproportionately jeopardize" (Nixon 2011, 5) both human and nonhuman life throughout that region. Second, postcolonial literature from the Global South has long been engaged in configuring forms that seem better suited to react to the changed political, economic, and ecological demands of the Anthropocene. In the final section of my essay, I will identify some of the challenges that these narrative forms pose for narratology.

2 The Anthropocene as a traveling concept

The term Anthropocene was proposed by chemist Paul Crutzen and biologist Eugene Stoermer in 2000 to designate a new geological age, which Planet Earth entered around 1800 with the Industrial Revolution and the birth of the steam engine. To a much greater degree than in the preceding epoch, the Holocene, humans in the Anthropocene have become central geological and climatological

---

[1] The concept of the planet is frequently used as an alternative to that of the globe, which is closely connected with the unifying and quantifiable thrust of global capitalism. The planet subverts "the hegemony of the global: refusing to cede to capitalism the impulse toward totality, but instead thinking totality otherwise" (Wenzel 2014, 21).

forces, profoundly making, shaping and transforming the planet. And since 1945, the beginning of the so-called phase of Great Acceleration, the "human terraforming of Earth" (Morton 2013, 4) has picked up pace and "dangerous intensity" (Clark 2015, 1). The accelerated mutation of ecosystems has unleashed a number of effects which, "dispersed across space and time" (Nixon 2011, 10), are both incalculable and irreversible: global warming, resource shortages, pollution, species extinction, and eroding soils amply evince the scope of humanity's geological agency and underline that the Anthropocene is indeed "a world-historical phenomenon that has arrived" (Trexler 2015, 4).

To be sure, the Anthropocene is not a clearly defined concept. It is an admittedly fuzzy, messy, and open term, a traveling concept *par excellence* (cf. Bal 2002; Neumann and Nünning 2012), which Clark fittingly describes as an "intellectual shortcut and expanded question mark to refer to the novel situation we are in" (2015, 3). Probably precisely due to – and not despite – its conceptual openness, the term has, in the last fifteen years or so, rapidly moved beyond the boundaries of its original context and entered into various disciplines in both the sciences and the humanities. The humanities have considerably expanded the term's geological focus to discuss the new political, cultural, ethical, and aesthetic exigencies of the age (cf. Clark 2015, 2). In one way or another, these studies proceed from the assumption that the looming catastrophes of the Anthropocene are also political in nature (cf. Purdy 2015). Climate catastrophes, species extinction, rising oceans, and deforestation emerge as the unwanted effects of epistemic orders, political practices, cultural discourses, and economic patterns. After all, these are central ways of worldmaking, whose "performative force" (Nünning 2010, 191) defines how we perceive and approach reality. From this vantage point, the term Anthropocene calls for a new kind of self-reflexivity about humanity's impact on the planet and more deeply planetary modes of thinking – exemplified in the new critical approaches, novel concepts, and alternative narratives about the planet current in the contemporary humanities: "As the notion of a world beyond us has become difficult to sustain," Robert Macfarlane has observed, "so a need has grown for fresh vocabularies and narratives that might account for the kinds of relation and responsibility in which we find ourselves entangled" (2016, n.p.).

The conceptual changes and paradigm shifts that the idea of the Anthropocene has instigated in the humanities are pervasive, ranging from the politicization of nature and the collapse of "the age-old humanist distinction between human history and natural history" (Chakrabarty 2009, 201) to the allocation of agency to nonhumans. Many of these conceptual innovations crystallize in so-called flat or horizontal ontologies and an attendant reconceptualization of human life. Under the rubrics of new materialism, object-oriented philosophy, speculative realism, and actor-network theory scholars like Jane Bennett, Karen

Barad, Donna Haraway, Timothy Morton, Quentin Meillassoux, and Bruno Latour have, in different though interrelated ways, articulated the conceptual premises of flat ontologies. Reworking "the 'Anthropos' in the Anthropocene" (Pálsoon et al. 2013, 8), they offer newly relational accounts of human life, stressing its entanglement with the nonhuman. These approaches take issue with binary oppositions – between humans and nonhumans, mind and body, culture and nature – that underlie many western epistemologies, and that had – and still have – devastating repercussions. Since the European Enlightenment, western epistemologies typically build on Cartesian mind-matter dualism to claim human exclusivity and to degrade the nonhuman – nature, animals, and things – to the rank of 'others' (cf. Latour 1993). In this way, they make these 'others' available for exploitation and consumption. Against the backdrop of such hierarchical dualism, new materialism and object-oriented philosophy foreground a vibrant and "coextensive materiality" (Iovino 2012, 46) connecting the human with the nonhuman. In so doing, they radically redistribute agency across a continuum of diverse agents and work toward what Karen Barad has called an "agential realism" that engages with the dynamism of matter (Barad 2007, 135; Bennett 2010) to question the ontological exceptionalism of humans. Being human, in this perspective, does not index the capacity to "act autonomously"; rather it means to share agency with other actors (Latour 2014, 5). Humans can no longer be exclusively understood in terms of their social, biological, psychological, and cultural make-ups. Rather, as Dipesh Chakrabarty in a seminal essay on "Postcolonial Studies and the Challenge of Climate Change" (2012) puts it, "humans are now part of the natural history of the planet" (10); they have forfeited their distinct status and have joined the ranks of nonhuman forces such as "heatwaves, cyclones, ocean deserts, Antarctic ice [and] activation thresholds" (Baucom 2014, 136). Along similar lines, nature and culture are no longer conceived as opposites but as intermingling forces; they converge in so-called 'nature-cultures' (Latour 1993; Haraway 2007; Descola 2013). As Jedediah Purdy in *After Nature: A Politics for the Anthropocene* (2015) succinctly notes, "there is no more nature that stands apart from human beings" (3); humans, politics, nature, and culture are inextricably entwined in complex networks.

As the above remarks suggest, the Anthropocene inevitably involves radically new temporal scales that afford ecological and biocentric – rather than merely social – modes of understanding the world. Acknowledging humans as a geological force, Chakrabarty argues, also means grasping human life as "belonging at once to differently-scaled histories of the planet, of life and species, and of human societies" (2012, 14), and he even suggests giving up the "distinction between natural history and human history" (2009, 201) altogether, to account for the fact that human and natural forces intermingle and human intervention has assumed the qualities of a "force of nature" in shaping the terrestrial environment. For Chakrabarty, western histories of capitalism, the Enlightenment, and modernity therefore need to be complemented by histories of climate change, fossil-fuel use, and geology: "The mansion of modern freedom," Chakrabarty concludes, "stands on an ever-expanding base of fossil-fuel use. Most of our freedoms so far have been energy intensive" (2009, 207–208). Chakrabarty therefore urges historians to reveal how human history and so-called natural history intermingle to produce tensions and incommensurabilities that destabilize conventional humanist and anthropocentric modes of thinking (Chakrabarty 2012, 2). Such a rethinking requires that we considerably complicate conventional, human-centered, and event-focused accounts of history. It might also require that historians – including historians of literature – come up with radically new historical periodizations that allow for "scale shifting moves" (Baucom 2013, 125). Ian Baucom might indeed have a point when he notes that in the anthropogenic age we need "to periodize in relation not only to capital but to carbon, not only in modernities and post-modernities but in parts-per-million, not only in dates but in degrees Celsius" (2013, 125).

3 Literature and literary studies in the Anthropocene

In the last ten years, the concept of the Anthropocene has also gained currency in literary studies. A whole range of studies, many of which fall under the rubric of ecocriticism (see Frenzel and Neumann 2017), aims at exploring the multifarious interrelations between literature and the new geological age. Originally closely tied to Green Studies and its activist thrust (see Coupe 2000), many of these approaches are content-oriented, which ultimately means that they pay little attention to the specificities of literary form. Accordingly, they focus on how literature portrays climate catastrophes, resource shortages, and species extinction, and how it allocates agency to the nonhuman to imagine ethically sounder ways of engaging with the environment. The more conceptually oriented of these studies are dedicated to examining how literary texts may either strengthen or undermine those Euro-American patterns of thinking and acting that legitimate the exploitation of nature in the contexts of colonialism, decolonization, and global capitalism. These studies typically make much of the alleged didactic potential of literature, illuminating how literary works may act as agents of change and "expose" and even "correct 'flawed' ways of being in the world" (Banerjee 2016, 195). From this perspective, the main achievement of literature lies in its power to raise a new ecological awareness, an awareness that might also entail a change in ecological behavior.

While thematic approaches are certainly valuable for showing how literature responds to urgent environmental issues, they are both limited and limiting: they reduce literature to a more or less mimetic representation of reality, and in so doing gloss over many of literature's defining characteristics, most importantly its form. Astrid Bracke's understanding of novels "as lenses and mirrors" (2018, 8) of climate crisis illustrates what is at stake here. Literary forms, however, far from being neutral devices, are, as Ansgar Nünning has noted (1989, 2010), implicated in specific socio-political orders and contribute to the meanings and effects of literary texts. Because forms are polyvalent, they fundamentally disrupt the supposed homology between reality and its literary depiction. In other words, while narrative fiction is permeated by the knowledge, discourses, and concerns of what lies outside it, it always potentially exceeds the referents it evokes.

To overcome the obvious limits of thematically oriented approaches, a number of scholars – amongst them Timothy Morton (2007), Ursula Heise (2008), Adam Trexler (2015), and Pieter Vermeulen (2017) – have advocated greater emphasis on the role of literary forms in engaging with the Anthropocene and related ecological concerns. Broadly speaking, these approaches proceed from the assumption that the Anthropocene poses not only scientific challenges, but also imaginative and representational ones, concerning in particular the massive stretching of temporal and geographical scales that it implies: "[H]umanity's geological agency and the nature and extent of the changes we have wrought on the Earth system," Stef Craps (2017, 2) writes, "raise problems of scale for the human imagination, necessitating new ways of thinking that are vastly more global and historical in scope than the narrow spatio-temporal confines of our ordinary daily lives tend to allow."

Against this conceptual backdrop, Ursula K. Heise's *Sense of Place and Sense of Planet – The Environmental Imagination of the Global* (2008) pioneers the study of how literature, through its specific forms, shapes a new sense of eco-cosmopolitanism, a term she defines as "an attempt to envision individuals and groups as part of planetary imagined communities of both human and nonhuman kinds" (2008, 6). "Through their formal strategies, as well as their substance," (Heise 2008, 11) literary texts such as John Brunner's *Stand on Zanzibar* (1968) or Karen Tei Yamashita's *Through the Arc of the Rainforest* (1990) model forms of connectedness that move beyond local ties to develop planetary visions of solidarity between humans and nonhumans. According to Heise (2008), allegory, collage, and montage are among the literary forms employed by novels to render frequently invisible forms of environmental change across the planet and to foster a sense of eco-cosmopolitanism that enmeshes local and global ecological systems.

In his pervasive overview of 150 novels, *Anthropocene Fictions – The Novel in a Time of Climate Change,* Adam Trexler explores how literature's engagement with climate change, ecological devastation, and greenhouse gas emissions engenders new literary forms. Climate fiction, he argues, "has increasingly allowed nonhuman things to shape narrative" (Trexler 2015, 26). But although he starts from the premise that "novels composed in the Anthropocene challenge received literary functions, such as character, setting, milieu, class, time and representation" (Trexler 2015, 16), his study pays surprisingly little attention to narrative forms. Rather, it is preoccupied with generic innovations, most of which, he argues, take place in the field of popular science fiction. Proceeding from the assumption that in its shaping of environmental issues the novel is "a privileged form" (Trexler 2015, 27), Trexler's study highlights the way in which contemporary Anthropocene novels imagine "concrete projects and [...] political affiliations" (2015, 168) that may initiate political action. Significantly, both Heise and Trexler make much of the political usefulness of literature and suggest that its forms and generic conventions can provide weighty answers to the demands of the Anthropocene.

The forms that novels deploy to respond to the changes of the Anthropocene are, however, more varied than these scholars envisage. Contemporary novels not only model narrative interconnections between the local and global and invent generic forms for imaginable post-apocalyptic scenarios; on a more fundamental level they create radically new narrative forms that point toward alternative flat ontologies, to a new sense of time and a redistribution of agency, and in doing so they challenge many conventional narratological categories. This neither implies a breakdown of narrative forms in the face of crisis, nor does it sustain Pieter Vermeulen's assumption that life in the Anthropocene "is precisely that which cannot simply be subsumed under formal patterns, orders, and rhythms, as a force that resists even as it encounters form" (2018, 11). The novels in question here offer something different: new forms that estrange established notions of narrative and narrativity, above all the exclusive focus on human agents and intentions (cf. Bruner 1986).

Moreover, Heise's and Trexler's emphasis on the political usefulness of literature in the age of the Anthropocene would seem equally questionable. Timothy Clark drives this point home with the pithy comment that "[t]o exaggerate the importance of the imaginary is, in itself, to run the risk of consolidating a kind of diversionary side-show, blind to its relative insignificance" (2015, 21). Clark's point is that, in the face of massive geological, meteorological and economic change, literature can no longer claim to be a significant cultural force. For

Clark, the Anthropocene establishes a new context for literature, namely a "context that entails a chastening recognition of the limits of cultural representation as a force of change in human affairs" (2015, 21). Indeed, many novels concerned with the exigencies of the Anthropocene work to dismantle strong forms of agency, and self-reflexively explore their own limits in driving change. In a fine article on "Future Readers – Narrating the Human in the Anthropocene," Pieter Vermeulen argues that literature's engagement with its limits might paradoxically become a strategy for coming to terms with the new role humans assume as co-actants of cyclones and insects, of nature big and small:

> Anthropocene narrative, on this account, has a particular purchase on the diminished planetary role of the human – of the role of the human, that is, in a world that can no longer be conceived as a globe but must be apprehended as a stubbornly nonhuman planet. (Vermeulen 2017, 871)

Rather than self-consciously claiming an aggrandized efficacy, many recent novels refuse to be associated with a politics of resistance and change. If they do socio-political work, it is certainly a 'minor' politics committed to imagining new modes of thinking and being in the world while gesturing toward the limited purchase of contemporary fiction. With these reflections in mind, I will turn to Owuor's *Dust* to illustrate how new narrative forms can be imagined with which to approach "the novel situation we find ourselves in" (Clark 2015, 3).

4 Yvonne Owuor's *Dust* – the dynamics of matter

Yvonne Adhiambo Owuor's debut novel *Dust* is not explicitly concerned with the pressing topics commonly associated with the Anthropocene – i.e. with climate change, pollution, and species extinction. Rather, it is a revisionary historical novel, a fiction of memory, of a kind that is currently burgeoning in Eastern Africa (cf. West-Pavlov 2019). Largely made up of the protagonists' memories, the novel traces the story of a Kenyan family, the Ogandas. It is a story of loss, suffering and grief closely entwined with Kenya's colonial and post-independence past. Narration emerges from the pressures of largely repressed memories and the painful struggle to move beyond past injuries. Crucially, memory-work, in *Dust*, is not only retrospective but also prospective, even future-oriented as a means of "nurturing what might still be" (Haraway 2016, 2) beyond the failures of the post-colonial nation. And these new temporalities are made possible by mnemonic practices that are not exclusively human. Rather – and herein lies a major contribution to the Anthropocene imagination – they emerge from an ecology of memory that brings the vitality of matter into interaction with human agency, "crack[ing] open the carapace of human self-concern" (McGurl 2011, 380) and in doing so generating sensitivity for the material preconditions that humans and nonhumans share.

The heterodiegetic narrative begins with a loss, yielding a constitutive absence that propels the plot forward. In a poetically dense scene we witness the death of Odidi, son of the Oganda family, who is killed by the police in the sectarian 'post-election violence' of 2007 on the streets of Nairobi.[2] The novel links the weeks of violence following the contested inauguration of Mwai Kibaki to earlier historical atrocities such as the anti-colonial Mau Mau uprising in the 1950s, in which Odidi's father, Aggrey Nyipir Oganda, served as a loyalist police aide. Learning about Odidi's death, his sister Ajany, a painter, returns from Brazil, where she had settled to escape the stifling atmosphere of Wuoth Ogik, the family home. As the family reunites in their unloved home, located in the northern drylands around Lake Turkana, they receive an unannounced British visitor, Isaiah Bolton. Isaiah seeks to reconstruct the circumstances that led to the mysterious death of Hugh Bolton, a colonial settler, whom he believes to be his father. In frequently painful memory-work, the narrative gradually reveals that it was Nyipir, then working as Bolton's assistant, who killed him in the attempt to defend his future wife, Akai Lokorijom. Deeply mired in histories of violence and burdened by a persistent sense of guilt, all of the characters in the novel are haunted by memories. These ghosts, as they are repeatedly called, conjure up the many unspeakable secrets, lies, and betrayals of the past which they are incapable of forgetting: "*Memories are ghosts* [...]. Places are ghosts, too" (Owuor 2013, 123).

In *Dust*, the rapid shifts between the characters' thoughts, memories, and impressions give rise to a polyphonic, non-linear narrative which consists of a multiplicity of small accounts, focalized by different characters and only loosely held together by a heterodiegetic narrator. At times it becomes impossible to distinguish clearly between the characters' and the narrator's perspectives, and the different voices recurrently fuse into one another to produce an open, disjunctive narrative. Continually oscillating between the Mau Mau uprisings of the early 1950s, the political assassination of Tom Mboya in 1969 and the postelection violence of 2007, the bits and pieces refuse to congeal into a coherent, progressive narrative. Instead, what emerges is a multilayered, multidirectional tale in which the past, present, and future of different characters are bound into

---

2 In this section I draw on ideas developed in Neumann (2019).

many loops of relation. Time, in *Dust*, does not only move forward: it is what West-Pavlov (2019) calls 'backward-turning' and 'sideways-sliding.' According to the narrator, "[t]ime shifts, a chain of moments leading [...] across thresholds" (Owuor 2013, 64) – an expression that poignantly indexes the intractable presence of the past as a "shadowed historical persistence" (Boxall 2013, 62) evoking alternative, largely forgotten histories and undoing the conventional assumption "that things just keep going on" (Wenzel 2017, 5).

Importantly, however, in *Dust* the fragmentary account of personal and collective history is interspersed with a different history, namely with natural history. It quickly becomes clear that the discontinuous narrative is grounded not only in personal trauma but also in the peculiar vitality of the Kenyan landscape. *Dust* configures time, temporality, and history not as the 'others' of a static spatial environment, but as categories wrested from an active and dynamic nature (cf. West-Pavlov 2019) which constantly changes shape and refuses to remain immobile. Space here is a fluid site of becoming that resists mastery, control, and possession: there is "[t]oo much life; everything breathes here, even the damn stones. Too much space [...]" (Owuor 2013, 78), Isaiah remarks of the arid landscape of Wuoth Ogik. It is within the novel's poetics of time and space that the titular dust acquires its significance: as the narrative adds ever new semantic layers of particulate material, so does the dust itself become animated and dynamic, incorporating human and nonhuman elements and cutting across the distinction between time and space. Constantly changing its form and make-up, it references unpredictable movement, transformation, and interrelation. Its very essence is change.

In Owuor's novel, the agency of space and nature is embedded in an animist cosmology that takes seriously the many human and nonhuman forces that make up the world. Broadly speaking, this cosmology is based on the belief that all material phenomena – humans, animals, plants, rocks, mountains, river, thunder, wind, and shadows – possess a distinct spiritual essence and a corresponding agency. Animist cosmology rejects the mind-body dualism characteristic of western (above all Cartesian) thought and foregrounds the complex interconnections between what we conventionally call 'subjects' and 'objects'. For the characters inhabiting *Dust*'s fictional universe, nature offers valuable interpretations of the world: "People," according to the narrator, "listen to four winds" (Owuor 2013, 41). Nature in all its different manifestations produces its own kind of language and knowledge – but it also registers forgotten histories that destabilize the humanist framework of knowledge and memory: "[W]inds carry songs," (Owuor 2013, 110) "every crevice contains a story" (Owuor 2013, 43); and "Mount Kulal," the narrator notes, is "the storykeeper of this land" (Owuor 2013, 117). It is important here to recognize that this understanding of nature goes well beyond premises of 'the nonhuman turn' currently recalibrating memory studies (see, e.g., Bond et al. 2017). For, when scholars in the field of planetary memory state, for example, that geology functions as "an archive by which the past and future history of the Anthropocene might be remembered" (Crownshaw 2017, 3), what they suggest is that geology registers essentially human histories, or what Crownshaw calls "humanity's geophysical agency" (2017, 3). In this way, they confirm rather than subvert the dichotomy between human agency and natural passivity. *Dust*, by contrast, highlights geology's agency within a broader ecology of memory where its distinct, non-anthropocentric knowledge encourages humans to think beyond 'their' history to geological and planetary histories of which they form only "a contingent organic part" (Colebroke 2017, 10).

The novel's representation of the dynamics of space and nonorganic matter also has socio-political implications. First and foremost, it undoes the dualism of time and space which, broadly speaking, structures western epistemes. More specifically, *Dust* dispels the notion of the blank, passive, inert space that lent acceptance to colonialism and today appears to justify the ongoing exploitation of its environment. The decoupling of nature from history, as Mary Louise Pratt (1992, 15) has convincingly argued, helped obscure colonialism's histories of conquest, exploitation, and violence, and ultimately "naturalize[d]" the global European "presence" by construing space as an abstract, undifferentiated, and seemingly 'natural' entity – a space incorporating different places into the same universal order and hence paving the way for the transformation of local differences and non-synchronicity into the ideologically charged opposition of the modern with the premodern, the civilized with the uncivilized etc. (Chakrabarty 2009, 7). By highlighting the dynamics of space and matter, Owuor's novel, in contrast, resists the totalizing impetus of abstract space to render concrete the unassimilable force of local particularities and to acknowledge the localized, geologically grounded significance of experience, knowledge, and memory.

Moreover, the collapse of the conventional distinction between time and space, as well as between human and nonhuman agency, has ecological implications. *Dust* invites readers to consider human history from an ecological perspective – one that is enshrined in natural history and emphasizes the relations rather than hierarchies between different agents. Time is as much tied to human experience as it is to the generativity of the planetary and cosmic forces, and, conversely, human time is inscribed with the "mineralogical dimension of human composition" (Yusoff 2015, 789). Both relations encourage us to "to think [...] disjunctively about the human" (Chakrabarty 2012, 2), i.e., rethink the human from the perspective of planetary geology and terrestrial histories. In this sense, through its narrative depiction of time and space, *Dust* offers biocentric concepts of the planet and models new forms of solidarity across the human-nonhuman divide, which might be a serious alternative to the premises of modern science and economics.

The allocation of agency and temporality to matter become visible, too, in the novel's creative use of spatialization. The deliberately fractured make-up of the text, the many blanks, "staccato phrase[s]" (Owuor 2013, 117), and sentence fragments prompt readers to continuously move back and forth, bridging the emergent interstices between the paragraphs. The depiction of an actively mutable and transmuting planet calls for equally flexible, open reading practices: by setting its readers into a state of transition, the novel exposes the inherent creativity of spatial matter. These novelistic spaces open up various ways of interpretation, confronting readers with both a sense of openness and a constantly deferred finality and in their specificity performatively undoing the notion of a blank space – a notion that, after all, was central to imperial colonization. Showcasing the potentiality of matter, *Dust*, one can conclude, calls for a consideration of our own engagement with so-called blank spaces and their consumption as usable elements – be it for signification or other processes of creating (surplus) value.

5 A narratology for the Anthropocene?

A number of the formal strategies that Owuor's narrative thrives on can also be found in other postcolonial novels, such as Wilson Harris's *The Dark Jester* (2001), Indra Sinha's *Animal's People* (2007), Keri Hulme's collection *Stonefish* (2004), and Helon Habila's *Oil on Water* (2011). In one way or another, all these texts remodel the sequentiality of past-present-future relations to trace geological shifts across different scales of time and space, create new connections between the human and the nonhuman, between "then and there," and "here and now" (Bond et al. 2017, 862). Jointly, their formal innovations and reconceptualizations of human life, space, and time confirm the intuition that much Anthropocene fiction not only demands new theoretical approaches but also new formal and possibly narratological models to capture them.[3] More

---

[3] Curiously, David Herman, in an essay with the promising title "Narratology beyond the Human" (2014), hardly considers the question of how the narrative exploration of human-animal relationships in the larger biosphere compels us to review the categories of narratology. The essay analyzes representations of human-animal relationships in Lauren Groff's short story "Above and Below" (2011), focusing on the bearing of these interactions on conventional concepts of self-narrative. Though Herman convincingly demonstrates that human relatedness to animals "entails a rethinking of self-other relationships" (2014, 137), he

specifically, Gerald Prince's (2004) call for a substantial revision of narratological concepts in the face of the changes introduced by postcolonial fiction also holds, I would argue, for many Anthropocene novels: "[E]very category at the narrating level," Prince claims, "should be reviewed in the light of postcolonial affinities and, if necessary, revised to accommodate narrative structures and configurations which these affinities might call for or suggest" (2004, 379). In this final section, I will pursue this contention by pinpointing some of the changes and challenges that Owuor's novel poses for narratology.

On the most fundamental level, *Dust* questions narratology's underlying concept of narrative. Marie-Laure Ryan succinctly summarizes this in the following terms:

> Narrative must be about a *world* populated by individuated existents. This world must be situated in time and space and undergo *significant transformations*. The transformations must be caused by nonhabitual physical events. Some of the participants in the events must be intelligent agents who have a *mental life* and *react emotionally* to the states of the world. Some of the events must be purposeful actions by these agents, motivated by identifiable goals and plans. The sequence of events must form a unified causal chain and lead to closure. The occurrence of at least some of the events must be asserted as fact for the story world. The story must *communicate something meaningful* to the recipient. (Ryan 2006, 8)

With an eye to *Dust*, this definition of narrative – which Monika Fludernik and Greta Olson consider "the most flexible and least prescriptive" (2011, 14) of such postulates – begs a number of questions: What exactly are the individuated existents that inhabit the fictional world of *Dust*? Do space, dust and wind qualify as individuated existents, and can human characters that are so closely entwined with natural matter be considered as individuated? In other words, can the very concept of 'individuality' and 'individuation' claim validity in a fictional world that thrives on entanglements, relations, and connectivity? What socio-political implications does Ryan's privileging of intelligence, mental life, emotionality, and intentionality possess, and why should we exclude nonhuman (and non-mental) life if this exclusion is clearly contested in the novel, even shown to be destructive? Moreover, what do we do with Ryan's emphasis on sequentiality, causality, and closure in connection with a narrative that highlights the slow, emergent, and non-causal eventfulness of natural

---

suggests that nonhuman actors can be understood in essentially human terms, namely as "beings who share the capacity to experience the world from a particular perspective" (2014, 137) – an anthropomorphization that defines Herman's 'narratology beyond the human' as all too human-centered.

history and that undoes narrative sequentiality to reveal "the past's unrealized visions of a liberated future" (Wenzel 2017, 6)? For it is precisely such unrealized visions of memories yet to come, and the multidirectional terrestrialized temporality they entail, that in *Dust*'s imaginative universe offer sustainable and ethically sound conceptions of the planet. Finally, Ryan's claim that stories must communicate something meaningful begs many questions about the signifying potential of matter. As argued above, *Dust* uses the materiality of the page to "horizontalize" (Bennett 2010, 112) conventional hierarchies between matter and meaning and to restore significance to concrete material space. The signifying potential of matter typically resists translation into language and discursive meaning. Clearly, it does not "communicate something meaningful to the recipient" (Ryan 2006, 8). And yet, it would be reductive in the case of *Dust* to ignore the novel's strategies of spatialization, since they bear essentially on reading processes and acutely affect readers. The questions that Ryan's definition raises – and more could be added – emphasize that existing concepts of narrative are certainly inept for at least some Anthropocene novels – novels whose specificities make it necessary to move beyond concepts of narrative that privilege human agents over the nonhuman and to replace notions of sequentiality, causality, and closure with those of temporal multi-directionality, discontinuity and emergence.

A closer look at some standard narratological categories such as space, time, and event is apt to tangle the relation between *Dust*'s narrative forms and narratology still further. To illustrate what is at stake I will briefly zoom in on space. Broadly speaking, narratology defines space in narrative texts as the fictional environment in which characters move, act, and dwell (cf. Neumann and Nünning 2008). Manfred Jahn and Sabine Buchholz (2005, 552) understand narrative space in terms of the following parameters:
1. the living conditions it offers;
2. the objects it comprises;
3. the boundaries that separate it from other coordinate places;
4. the temporal dimension or historical context to which it is bound.

From this perspective, representations of space designate specific locations, typically locations at a specific moment in time, which are key elements of the 'setting' of a scene. The setting provides topological determination to events, characters, and states represented in the storyworld: "A setting," according to Ronen, "is the zero point where the actual story-events and story-states are localized" (1986, 423). Following this definition, space offers a more or less stable background against which the dynamics of time can unfold and characters can act. Time can move forward because space remains immobile. Along the same lines, characters can act because space is inert, passive, and predictable.

Dust, by contrast, shows that space is not a stable background but that, interlocked with time, it continually spins and evolves. Such a conception of space tallies with Karen Barad's understanding of spatiality as a process and illustrates her claim that "the iterative enfolding of phenomena and the shifting of boundaries entail an iterative reworking of the domains of interiority and exteriority, thereby reconfiguring space itself, changing its topology" (2001, 92). Space, on this account, assumes a sense of obdurate agency. In narratological terms, such a sense of agency might best be captured by the category of eventfulness. Eventfulness, as elaborated by Wolf Schmid (2007), is, among other things, defined by the criteria of factivity and resultativity. While factivity, within the framework of the fictional world, distinguishes events from those changes of state "that are only wished for, imagined, or dreamed of" (Schmid 2007, 2), resultativity means that an event "reaches completion in the narrative world of the text" (Schmid 2007, 2). In other words, events materialize in that world in concrete, measurable results.

But how can the resultativity of emergent space in its ever-changing geology and vibrant materiality be depicted and analyzed? Being closely entwined with time, space, in *Dust*, unfolds unevenly, cumulatively and unpredictably; it points toward radically expanded pasts and futures which compel us to consider both anxious anticipations and latent memories. While it clearly has a number of effects and repercussions, these are not yet fully realized and do not, therefore, materialize as fixed results. The agency of space produces temporal gaps – possibly of decades, centuries, or even millennia – that gesture toward the "messy intersection" (Wenzel 2017, 6) of "human terraforming" (Morton 2013, 4) in its belated geological manifestations and an equally belated human awareness of that conjunction (see Wenzel 2017, 6). To examine the agency of space in this context entails devising more complex and dynamic narratological categories that tie space to eventfulness, while decoupling the event both from its original cause and from its direct results by the discontinuous workings of time.

Along similar lines, the novel's configuration of time, its allocation of agency to matter, and its modeling of multispecies communities necessitate a thorough revision of established narratological categories, more specifically those of time and character. Broadly speaking, the emphasis of such a revision should be on processes rather than structures, on entanglements rather than individual existents, on horizontal rather than hierarchical relations, and on multidirectional temporality rather than sequential progression. Whether or not a narratology specifically for the Anthropocene is possible – and whether or not it would be useful – remains to be seen. What is clear, however, is that the formal innovations introduced by recent Anthropocene novels demand radically new categories, scales, and axes of analysis to match their ongoing imaginative developments. All of this is to say that there is still much work to be done!

References

Bal, Mieke. *Travelling Concepts in the Humanities: A Rough Guide.* Toronto: University of Toronto Press, 2002.
Banerjee, Mita. "Ecocriticism and Postcolonial Studies." *Handbook of Ecocriticism and Cultural Ecology.* Ed. Hubert Zapf. Berlin/Boston: de Gruyter, 2016. 194–207.
Barad, Karen. "Re(con)figuring Space, Time and Matter." *Feminist Locations: Global and Local, Theory and Practice.* Ed. Marianne DeKoven. New Brunswick: Rutgers University Press, 2001. 75–109.
Barad, Karen. *Meeting the Universe Halfway: Quantum Physics and the Entanglement of Matter and Meaning.* Durham: Duke University Press, 2007.
Baucom, Ian. "History 4°: Postcolonial Method and Anthropocene Time." *Cambridge Journal of Postcolonial Literary Inquiry* 1.1 (2013): 123–142.
Bennett, Jane. *Vibrant Matter. A Political Ecology of Things.* Durham: Duke University Press, 2010.
Bond, Lucy, Ben De Bruyn, and Jessica Rapson (eds.). "Planetary Memory in Contemporary American Fiction." *Textual Practice* 31.4 (2017): 853–866.
Boxall, Peter. *Twenty-First-Century Fiction: A Critical Introduction.* Cambridge: Cambridge University Press, 2013.
Bracke, Astrid. *Climate Crisis and the Twenty-First-Century British Novel.* London: Bloomsbury, 2018.
Bruner, Jerome. *Actual Minds, Possible Worlds.* Cambridge: Cambridge University Press, 1986.
Brunner, John. *Stand on Zanzibar.* New York: Doubleday, 1968.
Buchholz, Sabine, and Manfred Jahn. "Space in Narrative." *Routledge Encyclopedia of Narrative Theory.* Eds. David Herman, Manfred Jahn, and Marie-Laure Ryan. London: Routledge, 2005. 551–555.
Chakrabarty, Dipesh. "The Climate of History: Four Theses." *Critical Inquiry* 35.2 (2009): 197–222.
Chakrabarty, Dipesh. "Postcolonial Studies and the Challenge of Climate Change." *New Literary History: A Journal of Theory and Interpretation* 43.1 (2012): 1–18.
Clark, Timothy. *Ecocriticism on the Edge: The Anthropocene as a Threshold Concept.* London: Bloomsbury, 2015.
Colebroke, Claire. 2017. "The Intensity of the Archive. Memory Studies and the Anthropocene: A Roundtable." *Memory Studies* 11.4 (2018): 9–12.
Coupe, Laurence (ed.). *The Green Studies Reader: From Romanticism to Ecocriticism.* London: Routledge, 2000.
Craps, Stef. "Introduction. Memory Studies and the Anthropocene: A Roundtable." *Memory Studies* 11.4 (2018): 1–3.
Crownshaw, Rick. "Speculative Remembrance in the Anthropocene: Memory Studies and the Anthropocene: A Roundtable." *Memory Studies* 00.0 (2017): 3–5.
DeLoughrey, Elizabeth M., and George Handley. "Introduction: Toward an Aesthetics of the Earth." *Postcolonial Ecologies. Literatures of the Environment.* Eds. Elizabeth M. DeLoughrey and George Handley. Oxford: Oxford University Press, 2011. 3–39.
Descola, Philippe. *Beyond Nature and Culture.* Chicago: The University of Chicago Press, 2013.
Frenzel, Sonja, and Birgit Neumann (eds). *Environments, Ecocriticism and Ethics in Anglophone Literatures.* Heidelberg: Winter, 2017.
Fludernik, Monika, and Greta Olson. "Introduction." *Current Trends in Narratology.* Ed. Greta Olson. Berlin: de Gruyter, 2011. 1–33.

Groff, Lauren. "Above and Below." *The New Yorker*. 13 June 2011. https://www.newyorker.com/magazine/2011/06/13/above-and-below (14 March 2019).

Habila, Helon. *Oil on Water*. London: Penguin Books, 2011.

Haraway, Donna. *Staying with the Trouble. Making Kin in the Chthulucene*. Durham: Duke University Press, 2016.

Harris, Wilson. *The Dark Jester*. London: Faber, 2001.

Heise, Ursula K. *Sense of Place and Sense of Planet: The Environmental Imagination of the Global*. Oxford: Oxford University Press, 2008.

Herman, David. "Narratology Beyond the Human." *DIEGESIS* 3.2 (2014): 131–143.

Hulme, Keri. *Stonefish*. Auckland: Huia, 2004.

Iovino, Serenella. "Material Ecocriticism. Matter, Text, and Posthuman Ethics." *Literature, Ecology, Ethics. Recent Trends in Ecocriticism*. Eds. Timo Müller and Michael Sauter. Heidelberg: Winter, 2012. 51–68.

Latour, Bruno. *We Have Never Been Modern*. Cambridge, MA: Harvard University Press, 1993.

Latour, Bruno. "Agency at the Time of the Anthropocene." *New Literary History* 45.1 (2014): 1–18.

Macfarlane, Robert. *Generation Anthropocene: How Humans Have Altered the Planet for ever*. https://www.theguardian.com/books/2016/apr/01/generation-anthropocene-altered-planet-for-ever. The Guardian, 14 April 2016 (17 September 2018).

McGurl, Mark. "The New Cultural Geology." *Twentieth Century Literature* 57.3–4 (2011): 380–390.

Morton, Timothy. *Ecology without Nature: Rethinking Environmental Aesthetics*. Cambridge, MA: Harvard University Press, 2007.

Morton, Timothy. *Hyperobjects: Philosophy and Ecology after the End of the World*. Minneapolis: University of Minnesota Press, 2013.

Neumann, Birgit, and Ansgar Nünning. *Travelling Concepts for the Study of Culture*. Berlin: de Gruyter, 2012.

Neumann, Birgit, and Ansgar Nünning. *An Introduction to the Study of Narrative Fiction*. Stuttgart: Klett, 2008.

Neumann, Birgit. "The Worlds of Afropolitan World Literature – Modeling Intra-African Afropolitanism in Yvonne Adhiambo Owuour's Dust." *Afropolitan Literature as World Literature*. Ed. James Hodapp. London: Bloomsbury, 2019 (in print).

Nünning, Ansgar. *Grundzüge eines kommunikationstheoretischen Modells der erzählerischen Vermittlung. Die Funktionen der Erzählinstanz in den Romanen George Eliots*. Trier: WVT, 1989.

Nünning, Ansgar. "Making Events – Making Stories – Making Worlds: Ways of Worldmaking from a Narratological Point of View." *Cultural Ways of Worldmaking: Media and Narratives*. Eds. Vera Nünning, Ansgar Nünning, and Birgit Neumann. New York: de Gruyter 2010. 191–214.

Nixon, Rob. *Slow Violence and the Environmentalism of the Poor*. Cambridge, MA: Harvard University Press, 2011.

Owuor, Yvonne. *Dust*. New York: Random House, 2013.

Pálsoon, Gísli et al. "Reconceptualizing the 'Anthropos' in the Anthropocene: Integrating the Social Sciences and Humanities in Global Environments Change Research." *Environmental Science & Policy* 28 (2013): 3–13.

Pratt, Mary Louise. *Imperial Eyes: Travel Writing and Transculturation*. London: Routledge, 1992.

Prince, Gerald. "On a Postcolonial Narratology." *A Companion to Narrative Theory*. Eds. James Phelan and Peter J. Rabinowitz. Malden: Blackwell, 2004. 372–381.

Purdy, Jedediah. *After Nature: A Politics for the Anthropocene*. Cambridge, MA: Harvard University Press, 2015.
Ronen, Ruth: "Space in Fiction." *Poetics Today* 7.3 (1986): 421–483.
Ryan, Marie-Laure. *Avatars of Story*. Minneapolis: University of Minnesota Press, 2006.
Schmid, Wolf. "Event and Eventfulness; Papers of the conference 'Event, Eventfulness, Tellability'; Ghent 2007." *Amsterdam International Electronic Journal for Cultural Narratology* 4 (2007).
Sinha, Indra. *Animal's People*. New York: Simon & Schuster, 2007.
Trexler, Adam. *Anthropocene Fictions: The Novel in a Time of Climate Change*. Charlottesville, VA: University of Virginia Press, 2015.
Vermeulen, Pieter. "Future Readers – Narrating the Human in the Anthropocene." *Textual Practice* 31.5 (2017): 867–885.
Vermeulen, Pieter. "Beauty That Must Die: Station Eleven, Climate Change Fiction, and the Life of Form." *Studies in the Novel* 50.1 (2018): 9–25.
Wenzel, Jennifer. "Planet vs. Globe." *English Language Notes* 52.1 (2014): 19–30.
Wenzel, Jennifer. "Past's Futures, Future's Past. Memory Studies and the Anthropocene: A Roundtable." *Memory Studies* 00 (2017): 5–7.
West-Pavlov, Russell. "Temporality and Quantum Theory in the Contemporary Global South Novel." *New Approaches to the Twenty-First-Century Anglophone Novel*. Eds. Sibylle Baumbach and Birgit Neumann. Basingstoke: Palgrave Macmillan, 2019 (in print).
Yusoff, Kathryn. "Geological Subjects: Nonhuman Origins, Geomorphic Aesthetics, and the Art of Becoming Inhuman." *Cultural Geographies* 22.3 (2015): 383–407.

Sandra Heinen
Fact, Fiction, and Everything in-between: Strategies of Reader Activation in Postcolonial Graphic Narratives

Abstract: This essay deals with recent postcolonial graphic narratives which address social ills, such as discrimination and violence based on gender, ethnicity or caste, or the horrors of genocide and war. To achieve their unambiguous communicative goals, the most urgent of which are to convey a political stance, to stimulate readers to take sides, and to encourage active engagement in the cause they represent, these graphic narratives blur, undermine or transgress in different ways the border between factual and fictional storytelling. The strategic – and media-specific – combination of factual and fictional modes investigated here thus plays a pivotal role in the endeavor to influence readers' attitudes and consequent behavior.

1 Introduction

"To tell new stories one needs new languages" – this is the unanimous opinion of a group of experts commissioned, in Sarnath Banerjee's *The Harappa Files* (2011, 12), to identify the best way to communicate the findings of a government survey on contemporary India. Since *The Harappa Files* is a comic book, it comes as no surprise that the communication experts come to the conclusion that "the use of image and text" is "the most appropriate way to bring out [the survey's] complicated observations" (Banerjee 2011, 13) and that, more generally, "contemporary societal concerns could be best addressed by using the medium of comics" (Banerjee 2011, 14). One reason cited for this is the medium's position "between art and the everyday" (Banerjee 2011, 15), which encourages wide distribution. The main argument in favor of comics, however, seems to be their 'new language', the medium-specific forms of articulation, which reduce complexity and provide pointed visualizations of both concrete and abstract phenomena, making the genre "the sharpest butcher's knife," honed to cut reality into "thin chewable fillets" (Banerjee 2011, 15).

In dealing with serious real-world topics and calling attention to pressing social and political concerns, Banerjee's *The Harappa Files* is

https://doi.org/10.1515/9783110654370-007

representative of a growing number of graphic narratives from around the world.[1] These narratives stand in the tradition of Art Spiegelman's *Maus* (1980–1991), Joe Sacco's *Palestine* (1993–1995), or Marjane Satrapi's *Persepolis* (2000–2003) – all of them critically acclaimed graphic novels, prominent in the West, which have paved the way for the emergence of politically engaged graphic narratives in diverse geographical and cultural contexts. The present article will discuss some anglophone examples from India, where a particularly lively comics scene has developed since the turn of the millennium (see Nayar 2016, Dawson Varughese 2017), as well as from Canada and Australia. Because of their countries of origin and the issues they negotiate, these and similar publications have been subsumed by a number of scholars under the umbrella term 'postcolonial graphic narratives', a classification which sets them apart from the dominant comics production of the U.S., Europe, and Japan (see Dony 2014; Mehta and Mukherji 2015; Knowles et al. 2016). Despite the pitfalls of grouping a range of heterogeneous texts under a single heading – and one as contested as 'postcolonial' – I will follow this usage, mainly in order to foreground what I perceive to be the narratives' main commonality: their decidedly postcolonial politics.[2]

The fact that they are designed as platforms for specific causes, however, does not mean these publications lack in artistry, or indeed artfulness. On the contrary, postcolonial graphic narratives use the flexible potential of comics to serve their communicative purpose in very creative ways.[3] One facet of this, which can be observed in a variety of otherwise quite varied products, is the resourceful combination of fictional and non-fictional elements – *The Harappa Files*, where a fictitious survey serves to expose social inequality in contemporary, post-liberalized India, being a case in point. The comics discussed below all blur, undermine or transgress at some point, and in different ways, the border between factual and fictional storytelling. I will argue that this is not done for the sake of aesthetic innovation or postmodern playfulness, but to achieve specific communicative goals, the most urgent of which are to convey a

---

[1] Following the publication industry's common genre ascription, the term 'graphic novel' is used here of both fictional and non-fictional book-length graphic narratives. Graphic novels are, then, understood as a subgenre of graphic narratives (which can also be shorter) and 'graphic narratives' as narratives in the comic strip medium.

[2] For a more detailed discussion of the advantages and drawbacks of the classification see Heinen (forthcoming).

[3] See Heinen (2013) for a discussion of some aesthetically innovative Indian graphic narratives.

political stance, to stimulate the readers to take sides, and to encourage active engagement in the cause they represent. Thus, these graphic narratives present themselves not as autonomous works of art but as engaged, politicized interventions. When Ansgar Nünning (2012, 165) proposes to "conceptualise narrative as an active force in its own right which is involved in the actual generation of ways of thinking and of attitudes and, thus, of something that stands behind historical developments", he is referring broadly to the world-making potential of narrative fiction. With respect to political narratives like the postcolonial graphic narratives discussed below, this can be taken quite literally: as I hope to show, the combination of factual and fictional storytelling plays a pivotal role in the endeavor to influence readers' attitudes and consequent behavior.

In this sense, postcolonial graphic narratives lend themselves to investigations of the role of 'narrative in culture'. According to Ansgar Nünning such investigations should, in order to explore "the functional links between narratives and cultures" (2012, 169), "take into account both thematic and formal features of texts and the ways in which epistemological, ethical and social problems are articulated" (2012, 167). Since my analysis of narrative forms will be limited to those that bear on the distinction between factual and fictional narrative, I will in Section 2 briefly discuss the different potential of the two modes to engage and activate the reader, before turning in Section 3 to comics as a medium of factual narration. Section 4 will then focus on exemplary postcolonial graphic narratives combining both factual and fictional elements, and discuss their impact-related functions.

2 Fictional vs. non-fictional narratives

The nature of fiction, and the distinction between fictional and non-fictional narratives, are subjects that have been widely discussed by theorists from various academic fields, including narrative theory (Cohn 1990; Fludernik 2001; Martínez and Scheffel 2003; Ryan 2010; V. Nünning 2014). Although the border between the two modes is porous and frequently crossed – at least temporarily – from both sides in the practice of storytelling, I agree with Martínez and Scheffel's contention that it is "not only legitimate but necessary to draw an unambiguous *theoretical* distinction between fictional and non-fictional narratives" (2003, 228; emphasis added). This distinction is purely conceptual and stands in contrast to storytelling practices, since narratives can undeniably combine fictional and factual elements, or remain ambivalent with regard to their fictionality/factuality. This, however, does not render the differentiation irrelevant, because such practices are only describable in relation to the fundamental distinction.

The defining difference between non-fictional and fictional narratives lies in their relationship to reality. While non-fictional narratives are referential in the sense that they claim to make statements about the extra-textual world (statements which may be true or false), fictional narratives make no such claim. Irrelevant here are criteria such as constructedness or literariness, since both fictional and non-fictional narratives are constructed artifacts that make liberal use of literary, poetic or aesthetic devices (White 1980; Cohn 1990).

The classification of a text as fiction or non-fiction is usually indicated both contextually and paratextually (genre ascription, preface, cover). In addition, a number of narrative features – a narrator who is identifiably not the author, the representation of the consciousness of a character other than the narrator, counterfactual narration etc. – can on the textual level function as 'signposts of fictionality' (Cohn 1990). However, as has been repeatedly pointed out, none of these signals is absolutely reliable, since authors can employ techniques of fictional writing in non-fictional texts, or even aim to mislead the audience altogether – as in the well-publicized forgeries of *Bruchstücke*, Binjamin Wilkomirski's 'Holocaust memoirs', published in 1995 and revealed three years later not to be based on first-hand experience (see Martínez and Scheffel 2003, 228–229), or the 1999 film *Blair Witch Project*, which is constructed (and made its debut) as an authentic video document of a group of young people who supposedly died while investigating rumors of witchcraft in a Maryland forest (see Ryan 2010, 9). Fictionality and factuality are neither semantic nor stylistic properties of texts, but are discursively constructed and ascribed by readers or viewers in their interaction with individual texts.

However, the classification of a text as fictional or non-fictional influences the reading process, it "tells us what to do with text" (Ryan 10). Vera Nünning (2014, 67–84) provides a systematic survey of studies on how the reading of fiction differs from that of non-fictional stories. The differences, due in part to the characteristic textual features of the two modes and in part to the aesthetic convention according to which "readers do not expect the content of the work [of fiction] to correspond to their knowledge of the real world" (V. Nünning 2014, 73), include differences in reading speed (fiction is read more slowly) and focus (stylistic features receive more attention if they occur in fictional texts). Moreover, texts regarded as fictional are more likely to take the reader out of their immediate surroundings into a state of 'transportation' or 'immersion' (V. Nünning 2014, 83, 86),[4] while non-fictional narratives trigger a referential mode of reading, encouraging the reader to draw connections between the textual and actual worlds. Finally, and of particular relevance in the context of political narratives, fictional stories are exceptionally apt to elicit emotional responses such as empathy, while factual narratives are more likely to prompt action (V. Nünning 2014, 82). The awareness of a narrative's fictionality functions as a protective bulwark separating the narrative from reality, making unpleasant or dangerous occurrences, because they are only hypothetical, less threatening than their representation in a factual text – possibly even enjoyable. The following section will show how, in their combination of factual and fictional elements, the graphic narratives discussed there use the different strengths of the two modes of composition to affect their readership.

3 Non-fictional narration in comics

According to Hillary Chute, non-fiction comics was reinvented in the early 1970s as "a serious documentary mode" (2016, 153) with the early publications of Art Spiegelman in the U.S. and Keiji Nakazawa in Japan (2016, 151). These paved the way for non-fiction to become "the strongest genre of comics" (Chute 2016, 6), and for comics to take "center stage among a range of documentary forms [...] that innovate the parameters of documentary" (Chute 2016, 6–7).

The popularity of comics as a means to tell non-fictional stories is counterintuitive inasmuch as the medium's features – its visual representations – suggest a distance from the real world. To underline the selective, distorted nature of its drawings, comics images have frequently been compared with photographs. Orijit Sen, the author of the first Indian graphic novel, outlines the

---

4 Ryan (2010, 14) distinguishes 'immersion' from mere 'fictional recentering'. While all fictional texts require a fictional recentering, which is defined as a deliberately performed "logical operation" by which readers "transport themselves in imagination" into the foreign world represented in a piece of fiction, immersion is an experience which does not necessarily occur when reading fiction, nor is it limited to fiction. Ryan's concept of 'immersion' seems to be roughly identical with V. Nünning's concept of 'transportation', describing the state of "'feeling cognitively, emotionally and imaginally immersed in a narrative world' while bodily awareness and a sense of the surrounding gets lost" (2014, 44) – Nünning adopts the concept from cognitive psychology and in her definition quotes a study by Marc A. Sestir. Although reading fiction need not lead to immersion, V. Nünning (2014, 83) suggests that "fiction is more conducive to fostering transportation than factual stories."

difference between photographs and drawings in his preface to a recently published anthology of graphic non-fiction from India in the following terms:

> The photographic document captured through a mechanical device records everything, every little detail that falls within the photographer's frame, in an instant. But when the comic artist draws her frame, she includes only a very deliberate and subjective set of observations and ideas. (Sen 2016, 8)

The degree of abstraction varies between drawing styles and, as Martin Schüwer (2008, 355) points out with reference to Scott McCloud, comics images can move away from realistic representations in two directions. On the one hand, there is iconic abstraction, through which a drawing no longer primarily references an object in the real world, but is rather turned into a sign with meaning, very much like iconic signs in Peirce's sense. Non-iconic abstraction on the other hand undermines referentiality altogether and foregrounds images as images ('the picture plane'). Both forms of abstraction deviate from realist representations, which strive for objectivity, making comics "an inherently subjective medium" (Sacco 2012, X).

Their subjectivity contributes, as Sen (2016, 8) has argued, not only to the aesthetic appeal of comics but also to its suitability as a medium of political criticism:

> This is, perhaps, where the real appeal of non-fiction comics lies: the opportunity to enter another person's real world, but as they see it. In this way, comics gives its creators tremendous political agency to counter an established view. It allows readers and writers to re-enter their world through the rupture of a new visual lens, giving both an opportunity to break from the dominant narratives of the time.

That comics presents a "subjective truth" (Sen 2016, 8) rather than an objective one is no drawback; on the contrary, it marks its narratives as counter-narratives and contributes to a particularly forceful mediation of the message.[5]

Two specific visual forms frequently found in comics are crystallizations of the medium's particular relationship to reality: the exaggerated representation in caricature and the use of visual metaphors. Because of their political thrust, both devices occur frequently in postcolonial comics. While caricature is most effectively used in short graphic narratives or pointed

---

[5] That subjectivity is not to be confused with fictionality or untruth is also underlined by the well-known comics journalist Joe Sacco (2012, XI), for whom "facts [...] and subjectivity [...] are not mutually exclusive", so that he can strive "for accuracy within a drawn work's subjective framework". In a more general sense, the medium's reliance on drawings gives visibility to the subjectivity that is characteristic of all narration.

non-narrative cartoons,[6] visual metaphors can be extended to support a whole graphic novel. Arguably the most famous example of such a strategy is Spiegelman's representation of Nazis and Jews with the heads of cats and mice – a metaphor that immediately stirred discussion of the work's legitimacy, because of its adoption of Nazi racist imagery in presenting Jews as vermin (mice). Moreover, the work's title, *Maus*, places the Holocaust memoir jarringly within the pop cultural tradition of animal comics like *Mickey Mouse* or *Donald Duck*. Somewhat surprisingly, however, the animal shape of Nazis and Jews never interferes with the narrative's claim to authenticity. One reason for this might be that, through its form, *Maus* "acknowledges the inescapable inauthenticity of Holocaust representations in the 'realist' mode" (Huyssen 2000, 76).

A postcolonial graphic narrative whose representational strategies are directly influenced by Spiegelman is Malik Sajad's *Munnu: A Boy From Kashmir* (2015), a coming-of-age story set amid the violence of the Kashmir conflict. As in *Maus*, an animal metaphor is used throughout the narrative to represent a persecuted people, in this case the Kashmiris, who are drawn as *hanguls*, a Kashmiri subspecies of elks (see Fig. 1). As is made clear toward the end of the story, the *hangul* was chosen by Sajad not only because it is native to the region and the "national animal of Kashmir", but also as a species that is "endangered because its habitat's been wrecked by the army and deforestation" (Sajad 2015, 333). There are, however, marked differences between the metaphors of *hangul* and mouse: While Spiegelman appropriates the dehumanizing denigration of Nazi ideology through what Huyssen (2000, 75) calls a "mimetic approximation", Sajad opts for an animal linked to the Kashmiri self-image, with unequivocally positive connotations of innocence and victimhood.

In either case the visual metaphor functions as an estranging device and distances the narratives from the realist mode. Although any continuously employed drawing style will become unobtrusive after a while and cease to disrupt the reading process (Schüwer 2008, 374), the use of visual metaphors such as animal heads defines the level of mediation here as, in Chute's (2016, 17) words, "conspicuously artificial." In fact Chute's statement that comics "openly eschew any aesthetics of transparency" (2016, 17) is especially apparent in graphic narratives such as Spiegelman's *Maus*

---

[6] Graphic caricature is a central device in the work of the South African comics artist Anton Kannemeyer. Outstanding Indian examples are Sarnath Banerjee's *The Harappa Files* and Gautam Bhatia's *Lie. A Traditional Tale of Modern India* (2010). On the significance of caricature and satire in Indian comics see Nayar 2016, 155–189.

Fig. 1: Selective animal symbolism in *Munnu*: Kashmiris represented as deer, non-Kashmiris (here: members of the Indian army) human-shaped (Sajad 2015, 15).

or Sajad's *Munnu*.[7] Nevertheless, this does not undermine their authenticity. Given the fact that both narratives are autobiographical – although the Holocaust experiences are not the author's, but his parents', prompting Marianne Hirsch (1993) to speak here of 'postmemory' – the non-realist drawings can be easily naturalized, even without knowing their personal context, as a valid expression of subjective experience and interpretation of the past.

4 Functions of fact/fiction boundary transgressions

A number of recent postcolonial graphic narratives explore the potential of both modes of storytelling, transgressing the boundary between fictional and non-fictional narration in either direction. *Munnu* is a case in point. Initially,

---

[7] The smiling masks in Ghosh's graphic novel *Delhi Calm*, which are worn by all politicians and Emergency supporters, have a similar estranging effect and lend the images an "unreal air", while conveying an interpretation of Emergency politics as playing a role, keeping up appearances and staging normalcy (Nayar 2016, 32).

the story appears fictional, as the focalizing character is referred to in the third person. The fact that the protagonist is referred to as 'Munnu', while the author's name is Malik Sajad, increases the likelihood that readers will regard Munnu as a fictional character, although at the very beginning of the narrative 'Munnu' (which simply means 'the youngest') is already revealed to be the protagonist's nickname; his real name is Sajad (Sajad 2015, 2). As the story progresses, a number of elements, such as the protagonist's early interest in drawing, which gradually develops into a professional career, increasingly encourage an autobiographical reading despite the third-person narration. When, halfway into the graphic novel, Munnu's first cartoon is published, the author's name is given as "M. Sajad" (Sajad 2015, 166), and toward the end of the narrative the character Munnu is seen working on the graphic novel *Munnu* (Sajad 2015, 332–333), underlining its non-fictionality. This oscillation between fact and fiction enhances the text's political impetus: Telling the story from a third- rather than a first-person perspective, the visual representation of the Kashmiris as scarcely individualized deer, and the use of the generic nickname Munnu, which "extends the narrative to many other Munnus in the Valley" (Singh 2017, n.p.), make the story more representative of the general situation in Kashmir. At the same time, its autobiographical dimension vouches for the narrative's authenticity.

While *Munnu* can be said to strategically oscillate between fictional and non-fictional narration, other graphic narratives are more easily assigned to one or other of the two modes, although they may include elements of both.[8] All of the texts discussed below were commissioned by non-profit organizations dedicated to issues such as multiculturality, aftermaths of colonization, or discrimination based on gender, ethnicity, or caste with the intention of influencing readers' attitude toward these issues. Factual and fictional elements are strategically combined to serve this goal.

---

[8] Another graphic novel oscillating between fact and fiction is *Secret Path* (2016) by Gord Downie and Jeff Lemire, which – like *The Outside Circle*, which is discussed below – deals with the experience of First Nations in Canada. It professes to tell the story of Chanie Wenjack, a 12-year old First Nations boy who died in 1966 during his attempt to run away from a Canadian Residential School to be with his family. Downie wrote ten songs about the boy's imputed thoughts, feelings and memories. The lyrics, constituting the textual part of the novel, are complemented by Lemire's images, which foreground the boy's inner life during his flight. While the recreation of the boy's experience is necessarily fictional, the graphic narrative's back cover emphasizes that Chanie Wenjack's is a true story, and the outer events of the narrative correspond with the known facts. The fictionalizing form of the storytelling here clearly functions to increase the narrative's emotional impact. An animated version of the graphic narrative can be watched at https://secretpath.ca/.

One example of such a strategic combination of fictional and factual elements is *Bhimayana. Experiences of Untouchability* (2011), a graphic biography of Bhimrao Ramji Ambedkar (1891–1956), a lawyer and social reformer who campaigned against the discrimination of Dalits and is today remembered as the principal architect of the Indian Constitution. In contrast to his more famous contemporary Mahatma Gandhi, Ambedkar came from a Dalit background and experienced at first hand various forms of caste-related discrimination. *Bhimayana*, which literally means 'the path of Bhim', recounts selected episodes of Ambedkar's life, from early incidents of discrimination to his later work as a political activist. Largely based on his autobiographical writings,[9] the story is embedded in a fictional frame which takes the form of a conversation between two women friends who have contrary opinions about the situation of Dalits in contemporary India. One of them believes that caste discrimination is a thing of the past, while the other tries to convince her that it remains strongly in force. The dispute provides not only the context for relating Ambedkar's story, but also for creating awareness of numerous recent instances of caste discrimination referred to by the characters; information about these is provided via press statements inserted in the graphic narrative. The main function of the fictional frame is clearly to draw a connection between the historical narrative and present-day violence. At the same time, it stages a conversation in the course of which one of the characters develops respect for Ambedkar. Although even at the end of their conversation she still falls short of fully agreeing with her friend, her change of opinion suggests she might take that final step later – as might others who learn more about the sway of caste oppression through *Bhimayana*.

Another, media-specific form of transgression of the fiction/non-fiction divide occurs when photographs are reproduced in fictional drawn comics. Schüwer (2008, 374) argues that comics drawing style can be compared to a pair of glasses through which readers see the storyworld: it colors how we perceive the story, yet in itself becomes unobtrusive after a short while. Because abrupt changes of style tend to foreground the medium and disrupt the illusion, they are usually avoided in mainstream comics.[10] Aesthetically, the comic book

---

9 Although S. Anand (2011, 103) admits that "some liberties have been taken" in the telling of Ambedkar's life in the main part of this graphic novel, I still consider it to be essentially a non-fictional narrative.

10 This is not necessarily the case in other works. Sarnath Banerjee's first graphic novel *Corridor* (2004), for example, uses the juxtaposition of images from various visual cultures as a stylistic principle (see Heinen 2013). That the combination of drawings and photographs does not necessarily disrupt illusion also becomes apparent in the aesthetically more conservative

The Outside Circle (2015) is a fairly mainstream graphic novel with fully colored, mostly realistic drawings. Yet at one point in the narrative, two black-and-white photographs are inserted to illustrate a particular aspect of the story (see Fig. 2). This tells of a young Aboriginal Canadian involved in gang-related crime who lands in jail after murdering his drug-addicted mother's boyfriend, but finds a way out of the cycle of poverty, violence and crime by participating in an Aboriginal rehabilitation program, whose promotion is arguably one of the main aims of the graphic novel. Participants in this program not only face their personal past but also the traumatic history of their tribes from the arrival of the first Europeans to the present day. In this context the two photographs illustrate the supervisor's remarks on residential schools, in which, during the nineteenth and twentieth centuries, indigenous children who had been taken from their families by Canadian authorities were raised with the set purpose of disconnecting them from their own cultural heritage and assimilating them to the dominant White culture.

It is significant that the images of the residential school are reproduced to look like actual photographs rather than drawn images. Although photographs have in the digital age lost much of their "evidential force" (Barthes 1981, 89) and their uses in comics today are many and various (Pedri 2015), in political graphic narratives they still often fulfill a classic documentary function, bearing irrefragable witness to the existence of what they represent: "Thanks to their technological objectivity, photos [...] offer a much more convincing testimony of the objects or events they represent than images created by the human hand, or verbal descriptions" (Ryan 2010, 16). As Roland Barthes (1981, 76) famously stated in *Camera Lucida*, the photograph's testimonial function is based on its indexical relationship to its referent:

> Photography's referent is not the same as the referent of other systems of representation. I call 'photographic referent' not the *optionally* real thing to which an image or a sign refers but the *necessarily* real thing which has been placed before the lens, without which there would be no photograph. Painting can feign reality without having seen it. Discourse combines signs which have referents, of course, but these referents can be and are most often 'chimeras.' Contrary to these imitations, in Photography I can never deny that *the thing has been there*. There is a superimposition here: of reality and of the past.

In order for comics photographs to generate such a superimposition, they must retain their original form rather than be converted into drawings, as they are, for example, in Karlien de Villiers's *Meine Mutter war eine schöne Frau* ('My

---

graphic narratives *Priya's Shakti* (2014) and *Priya's Mirror* (2014), in which all the images are composed of drawn characters in front of a photographic background.

Fig. 2: Insertion of historical black-and-white photographs into the drawn comic narrative in *The Outside Circle* (LaBoucane-Benson and Mellings 2015, n.p.).

Mother was a Beautiful Woman', 2006), a memoir of the author's childhood in apartheid South Africa. While the drawn photographs function there as signals of the graphic narrative's non-fictionality, they cannot provide 'evidence' of the reality of past events (see Fig. 3). In contrast, the photographs inserted in *The Outside Circle* remind the reader that, although the somewhat formulaic story of a hero rising from ruins is clearly fictional, the information it contains about the past and present situation of First Nations in Canada is not, and that reconciliation and healing are ongoing projects. The stylistic rift the photographs impose on the narrative flow might disrupt the illusion, but this is no drawback, as such disruption can only strengthen the comics' impact.

Fig. 3: Drawn photograph from *Meine Mutter war eine schöne Frau* (de Villiers 2006, 83).

A similar use of photographs can be observed in the Australian interactive graphic novel *The Boat* (2015), which is based on a work of fiction, Nam Le's short story of the same name. Here fictionality is predetermined by the source text, although the narrative unquestionably relates to the real world, as it tells the experiences of the so-called 'boat people' who fled from Vietnam in the 1970s. In 2015, the year of its publication, *The Boat* also functioned as a timely commentary on current migration movements. Published on the Internet, the work is aesthetically remarkable for a number of reasons, prominent among which are its use of image movement and sound to match the unfolding plot. The main feature that justifies the label '*interactive* graphic novel' is that readers steer their own way through the text, with regard not only to reading/viewing speed, but also to the path taken. They follow the main plot line by scrolling down, but can at four points in the story leave the main path to explore a side story (see Fig. 4). While the main plot line is consistently presented in drawn images, the side stories are told against the background of historical photographs of Vietnamese refugees (see Fig. 5). Here, history is quite literally the backdrop of the fictional narration: the photos, many of which show masses of people, with only a few focusing on individuals, not only authenticate the historical information provided in the text but also create an awareness of the numerical dimensions of loss and uprooting sustained in the war.

Fig. 4: Thought bubble containing a photograph, from which readers can access a side story in the interactive graphic novel *The Boat* (Le and Huynh 2015, n.p.).

While the interactive element in *The Boat* (2015) is designed in such a way that the narrative flow is never interrupted (the side stories provide additional information rather than alternative routes), in *Priya's Shakti* (2014) and *Priya's Mirror* (2014) interactivity takes a different form. These two fictional graphic narratives focus on victims of gender-based violence – rape in the case of *Priya's Shakti* and acid attacks in that of *Priya's Mirror* – who overcome shame and fear and discover their innate courage and strength. Spicing the formulaic plot, the appearance of deities and demons lends the stories an air of the unreal and fantastic. However, their clearly fictional conception is disrupted by additional material accessible through an augmented-reality app installed on a smartphone: when the reader looks at the comics visuals through the app, texts,

Fact, Fiction, and Everything in-between — 123

Fig. 5: Side stories in *The Boat* are told against the background of historical photographs of Vietnamese refugees (Le and Huynh 2015, n.p.).

images and links to videos are superimposed on them, providing information about real-world gender-based violence. Figure 6 shows, for example, on the left a page from the actual comic narrative *Priya's Mirror* with its fictional characters, and on the right the same page as seen through the augmented-reality app. This adds photographs of Monica Singh, a social activist fighting violence against women who became the victim of an acid attack after rejecting a marriage proposal when she was nineteen. Readers are also directed through the app to other real-life sources: a video of Monica Singh, an interview with other acid attack survivors, or a clip in which Bollywood director Farhan Akhtar speaks up against gender-based violence.[11] Thus the app – along with various community-centered events hosted in connection with the comics – functions to undercut the detachment of fiction from reality.

Fig. 6: Page 27 of *Priya's Mirror* on the left; on the right the same page as seen through an augmented-reality app.

---

11 Although the videos can be accessed through a direct link from the augmented-reality app as described, they are not part of the graphic narrative but of the reader's real-world media environment: they are hosted on external websites such as YouTube, have various producers, and can also be accessed in other ways.

5 Conclusion

In telling their story, all the graphic narratives discussed here seek to create an awareness of specific social ills, from discrimination and violence based on gender, ethnicity or caste to the horrors of genocide and war. To achieve this end they mix factual and fictional modes in various ways, strategically employing the different potentials of the two modes to strengthen their impact.

Priya's Shakti, *Priya's Mirror*, *The Boat* and *The Outside Circle* tell their stories of violence, social exclusion, displacement and oppression in the fictional mode. We can assume that this has to do with the particular features of fiction, not least with the creators' freedom to arrange and structure the narrative: whatever aspect seems relevant can find a place in the story, and a fictional narrative can be plotted and dramatized to maximize the intended effect. An example for this would be the plot development in *Priya's Shakti*, *Priya's Mirror* and *The Outside Circle*, which all tell a tale of characters overcoming adverse circumstances. An optimistic ending is chosen so that the stories can offer hope and point out escape routes for readers in similar circumstances. Relevant for the choice of fiction might also be that fictional characters can function more easily than real people as representatives: their experience can be easily thought of as shared by many. Fictionality thus facilitates identification. Moreover, in the case of *The Outside Circle* and the *Priya*-narratives, fictionality allows the narrative to be fashioned in line with existing comics genres, which is likely to increase the work's appeal. Thus *The Outside Circle* (at least initially) resembles crime comics, a global mainstay of the medium, while *Priya's Shakti* and *Priya's Mirror* are reminiscent of *Amar Chitra Katha* (*ACK*), arguably the most influential comic book series in India, consisting of over 440 titles on Indian history and mythology.[12]

Despite these advantages, fictionality carries the danger of removing a story from reality into the realm of the 'merely' invented. To underline the fact that, although the stories they tell may be fictional, the social ills they represent are not, *The Boat* and *The Outside Circle* include recognizably non-fictional elements, and the *Priya* comics add the non-fictional dimension via the augmented-reality app. In all these cases the momentary shift from fiction to fact is brought about – and signaled – by a change of medium, a turn from drawn images to photographs, or in the case of the *Priya* narratives also to film. Inverting

---

[12] While the *ACK* series is notorious for its conservative representation of gender roles, promoting female devotion and self-sacrifice, it also includes a number of issues dedicated to strong, combative heroines like *Chand Bibi* or *Rani Durgavati* (see Sreenivas 2010) who provide a mold for the *Priya* narratives.

Cohn's phrase, one might, therefore, say that the medium changes function here as signposts of an underlying non-fictionality – i.e. one that is not actualized in the narratives themselves. Anchoring the narratives in the cultural context from which they have emerged, the photographic insertions create an awareness of their non-fictional background and stimulate readers to adjust their real-world behavior.

A different route is taken by the creators of *Bhimayana*, who opted to tell a non-fictional story. The main reason for this choice is perhaps the general intention to inform readers about the historical Ambedkar, to whose writing and ideas the publishing house Navayana is dedicated.[13] Adapting Ambedkar's autobiography to the popular comics medium is ostensibly an attempt to keep the fading memory of the influential politician alive. The addition of a fictional frame narrative to the autobiographical core ultimately serves the same purpose, since the frame narrative's main voice argues that the historical account is of great relevance for Indian society today. In contrast to the other graphic narratives I have discussed, which use fiction to increase immersion, identification or emotional appeal, fiction in *Bhimayana* builds a bridge to the readers' world. The contrast in the way fictional and non-fictional elements are used in these texts underlines the impossibility of determining the narrative function of the two modes at a general level. Especially in a medium as open to experimentation as comics, that function is case- and context-specific.

---

[13] See Navayana's self-description on the company's website: "Deriving its name from B.R. Ambedkar's anti-metaphysical interpretation of Buddhism, Navayana is a publishing house that focuses on the issue of caste from an anticaste perspective. Founded in 2003, Navayana publishes general and academic nonfiction, graphic books, poetry and literary translations. It is best known for its finely curated list of books by and on Ambedkar" (Navayana Publishing, n. p.).

References

Anand, S. "A Digna for Bhim." *Bhimayana: Experiences of Untouchability*. Durgabai Vyam, Subhash Vyam, Srividya Natarajan, and S. Anand. New Delhi: Navayana, 2011. 100–104.
Banerjee, Sarnath. *The Harappa Files*. New Delhi: HarperCollins India, 2011.
Barthes, Roland. *Camera Lucida. Reflections on Photography*. Transl. Richard Howard. New York: Hill and Wang, 1981.
Bhatia, Gautham. *Lie. A Traditional Tale of Modern India*. New Delhi: Westland Books, 2010.
Chute, Hillary. *Disaster Drawn: Visual Witness, Comics, and Documentary Form*. Harvard: Harvard University Press, 2016.
Cohn, Dorrit. "Signposts of Fictionality: A Narratological Perspective." *Poetics Today* 11.4 (1990): 775–804.
Dawson Varughese, Emma. *Visuality and Identity in Post-Millennial Indian Graphic Narratives*. London: Palgrave Macmillan, 2017.
de Villiers, Karlien. *Meine Mutter war eine schöne Frau*. Zürich: Arache Coeur, 2006.
Devineni, Ram, Vikas K. Menon, and Dan Goldman. *Priya's Shakti*. http://www.priyashakti.com. New York: Rattapallax, 2014 (18 July 2018).
Dony, Christophe. "What is a Postcolonial Comic?" *Chronique de Littérature Internationale*. 7 November 2014. 12–13.
Downie, Gord, and Jeff Lemire. *Secret Path*. Toronto: Simon and Schuster, 2016.
Fludernik, Monika. "Fiction vs Non-Fiction: Narratological Differentiations." *Erzählen und Erzähltheorie im 20. Jahrhundert. Festschrift für Wilhelm Füger*. Ed. Jörg Helbig. Heidelberg: Winter, 2001. 85–103.
Ghosh, Vishwajyoti. *Delhi Calm*. New Delhi: HarperCollins India, 2010.
Heinen, Sandra. "'Indigenizing the Comic Book Medium': Techniques of Storytelling in Indian Graphic Novels." *Anglistentag 2012 Potsdam: Proceedings*. Eds. Katrin Röder and Ilse Wischer. Trier: WVT, 2013. 269–283.
Heinen, Sandra. "Postcolonial Perspectives." *Handbook of Comics and Graphic Narratives*. Eds. Sebastian Domsch, Dan Hassler-Forest and Dirk Vanderbeke. Berlin: de Gruyter, forthcoming.
Hirsch, Marianne. "Family Pictures: *Maus*, Mourning, and Post-Memory." *Discourse: Journal for Theoretical Studies in Media and Culture* 15.2 (1993): 3–29.
Huyssen, Andreas. "Of Mice and Mimesis: Reading Spiegelman with Adorno." *New German Critique* 81 (2000): 65–82.
Knowles, Sam, James Peacock, and Harriet Earle. "Introduction. Trans/formation and the Graphic Novel." *Journal of Postcolonial Writing* 52.4 (2016): 378–384.
LaBoucane-Benson, Patti, and Kelly Mellings. *The Outside Circle*. Toronto: House of Anansi, 2015.
Le, Nam, and Matt Huynh. *The Boat*. http://www.sbs.com.au/theboat/. SBS, 2015. (18 July 2018).
Martínez, Matías, and Michael Scheffel. "Narratology and Theory of Fiction: Remarks on a Complex Relationship." *What Is Narratology: Questions and Answers Regarding the Status of a Theory*. Eds. Tom Kindt and Hans-Harald Müller. Berlin: De Gruyter, 2003. 221–238.
Mehta, Binita, and Pia Mukherji. *Postcolonial Comics: Texts, Events, Identities*. Abingdon: Routledge, 2015.
Navayana Publishing. *About*. https://navayana.org/about/. New Delhi, 2017 (18 July 2018).

Nayar, Pramod K. *The Indian Graphic Novel: Nation, History and Critique*. Abingdon: Routledge, 2016.

Nünning, Ansgar. "Narrativist Approaches and Narratological Concepts for the Study of Culture". *Travelling Concepts for the Study of Culture*. Eds. Birgit Neumann and Ansgar Nünning. Berlin: de Gruyter, 2012. 145–183.

Nünning, Vera. *Reading Fiction, Changing Minds*. Heidelberg: Winter, 2014.

Pedri, Nancy: "Thinking about Photography in Comics." *Image & Narrative* 16.2 (2015): 1–13. http://www.imageandnarrative.be/index.php/imagenarrative/article/view/802/607 (28 October 2018).

Ryan, Marie-Laure. "Fiction, Cognition, and Non-Verbal Media". *Intermediality and Storytelling*. Eds. Marina Grishakova and Marie-Laure Ryan. Berlin: de Gruyter, 2010. 8–26.

Sacco, Joe. "Preface: A Manifesto Anyone?" *Journalism*. London: Jonathan Cape, 2012. XI–XIV.

Sajad, Malik. *Munnu: A Boy from Kashmir*. London: Fourth Estate, 2015.

Schüwer, Martin. *Wie Comics erzählen. Grundriss einer intermedialen Erzähltheorie der grafischen Literatur*. Trier: WVT, 2008. 8–9.

Sen, Orijit. "Preface." *First Hand. Graphic Non-Fiction from India*. Eds. Orijit Sen and Vidyun Sabhaney. New Delhi: Yoda Press, 2016.

Singh, Amrita. *'Inside Out'. Autobiography, History, and the Comic Form in Malik Sajad's Munnu: A Boy from Kashmir*. https://cafedissensus.com/2017/02/20/inside-out-autobiography-history-and-the-comic-form-in-malik-sajads-munnu-a-boy-from-kashmir/. Café Dissensus, 20 February 2017 (28 October 2018).

Sreenivas, Deepa. *Sculpting a Middle Class. History, Masculinity and the Amar Chitra Katha in India*. New Delhi: Routledge, 2010.

Vohra, Paromita, Ram Devineni, and Dan Goldman. *Priya's Mirror*. https://www.priyashakti.com/priyas_mirror/. New York: Rattapallax, 2014 (18 July 2018).

Vyam, Durgabai, Subhash Vyam, Srividya Natarajan, and S. Anand. *Bhimayana: Experiences of Untouchability*. New Delhi: Navayana, 2011.

White, Hayden. "The Value of Narrative in the Representation of Reality." *Critical Inquiry* 7.1 (1980): 5–27.

Carola Surkamp
'It's Not Our Opinion, It's the Opinion of Our Roles' – *Fremdverstehen* Revisited or: Where Foreign Language Education and Narratology Can Meet

Abstract: Theories and concepts of intercultural learning and *Fremdverstehen* have been discussed for decades in foreign language education. However, we still know only little about their actual realisations in the classroom: What exactly happens, for example, when learners are asked to put themselves in the situation of another person and tell a story from that person's perspective? And how can narrative texts by learners be assessed, i.e. when can a change of perspective be considered 'successful'? This contribution aims at exploring these questions on the basis of empirical data and by drawing on insights from cultural narratology. It shows how the framework of cultural narratology can also be used beyond text analysis in order to explain learners' actions and evaluate their work in classes focusing on intercultural learning.

1 Introduction

Central to cultural narratology (see Nünning 2012), the analysis of different forms and cultural functions of storytelling is also an indispensable resource in foreign language, literature and culture education (see Sommer 2000). Concepts such as the semantization of literary forms and the perspective structure of narrative texts, like the semiotic turn in understanding culture at the end of the 1990s and in the early 2000s, have led to the development of new learning objectives, models and methods in this field. Ansgar Nünning's work has played a vital role in these developments. On the one hand, he has put the concept of *Fremdverstehen* (intercultural understanding) in concrete terms for working with narrative texts. On the other hand, he has shown how, by negotiating meaning and contextualizing literature, foreign language teaching can go beyond merely dealing with cultural facts to include the mental dimension of cultures.

However, many concrete questions remain. What exactly happens, for instance, when learners are asked to work with texts and with the knowledge they gain in that process to take on the role of another person, producing a new text from that person's perspective? In other words: how does the process of intercultural understanding take place in a classroom context in which encounters with 'the other' are often only possible through various media? And when can a learner's change of perspective be considered successful?

The present article will discuss these and related questions. First, an overview of the relevant concepts of intercultural learning with narrative texts will be given. In a second step, empirical data gathered in an English lesson of an eighth grade German high school will be presented and discussed. Finally, the question will be raised as to how the framework of cultural narratology can be used – beyond text interpretation – to evaluate learners' actions and the work they produce. I aim to show, therefore, how cultural narratology, in combination with empirical research, can contribute to developing the concepts, processes, and assessment of intercultural understanding.

2 Teaching culture with literature in the foreign language classroom

In the classroom, foreign language learners often experience the target culture through different types of texts and media, including literary texts, which can provide valuable insights into the realities of different cultures – not as exact representations of cultural reality but as versions of reality that enable us to distance ourselves from preconceived opinions and stereotypes. Cultural narratology is especially useful in clarifying the concept of culture, the relationship between a literary text and the reality outside the text, and the significance of modes of representation to the interpretative process (see Surkamp and Nünning 2016, 38–44).

Considered by Nünning (2012) to be the basis for the connection of storytelling and culture, a multidimensional definition of culture such as that proposed by Posner (1991, 64) can lead to the inclusion of mental aspects of a target culture – patterns of thinking and feeling, values and norms, collective experiences, states of knowledge etc. – in the foreign language classroom. Drawing on the semantization of literary forms (see Nünning 2012, Ch. 4), cultural narratology considers texts as transmitting information of cultural relevance not only on the level of content but also on that of representation. This broadens the focus from cultural questions explicitly articulated in dialogues between the characters in a text to the manner in which something is presented through formal means such as the narrative situation, perspective structure, or representations of place and time.

A dynamic interrelationship between the text and the reality outside the text is presupposed, and this reality can also be critically questioned or even reinterpreted depending on the topic that is selected and the stylistic devices of the text.

3 Intercultural learning with literary texts

Understanding a foreign culture also implies a willingness and ability to undergo a change of perspective, to put oneself in the position of someone else and understand their feelings and reasons for acting as they do. Intercultural understanding is in this sense a process of creative learning to open oneself to the new and foreign (see Bredella 1987, 247).

The concept of 'perspective' entails a model of individual values and norms, psychological disposition, biographical background, culturally influenced behavior, needs, knowledge, and skills that have to be reconstructed in the process of changing perspective (see Surkamp 2005). To reconstruct the perspective of another person will encourage learners to see the world differently; it will make them aware of the subjectivity and relativity of their own point of view and enable them to reflect critically on both their own and the 'other' perspective:

> On the one hand, it is necessary to recognize how the other person perceives the world and, on the other hand, to what extent this point of view appeals to me and challenges me. Both these instances are necessary and indicate that intercultural understanding is a process that also brings about change in the learner. (Bredella 1995, 20; my translation)

Foreign language education seeks to determine how students' willingness and ability to engage in such a change of perspective can be concretely encouraged and fostered. In order to answer this question, Ansgar Nünning (2000) differentiates between two levels of intercultural understanding proper to literary texts: that articulated by the characters and that which occurs in the reception process, when learners/readers interact with the text. Here the narrative perspective of the text plays an important role, for in order to judge the events of a storyworld, it is important to know from whose point of view they are related: from a male or female perspective, for example, or from that of an ethnic majority or minority. From whatever angle it comes, the point of view confronting a reader will always be biased.

Applying Jean Piaget's term 'decentration' to the context of intercultural understanding, Ansgar Nünning (2000, 110) also distinguishes between the ability to differentiate perspectives, the willingness to take over a perspective, and the coordination of perspectives – i.e. the ability to integrate different perspectives on a meta-level. An important factor here is historical understanding, that is, the ability to put oneself in the place of historical characters, in their situations and living conditions (see Hartmann et al. 2009, 324), and a further aspect of this is critical reflection on comparable aspects of one's own culture and time.

From a didactic point of view, new developments in narratology exploring the potential of insights from psychology and the neurosciences can also contribute to refining the concept of changing perspective. Thus Vera Nünning (2014, 21, 25–26) differentiates between two types of change: understanding others by attributing thoughts and emotions to them, and understanding others by sharing their feelings. While the first type refers to so-called 'theory-of-mind abilities', which implies being able "to relate different perspectives, to recognise similarities and contrasts between them, and to assess the ways in which such relations influence the feelings, beliefs and intentions of those taking part in an interaction" (Nünning 2014, 162), the second type is based on empathy, i.e. the ability to feel as another person feels. Intercultural understanding requires both types (Nünning 2014, 26).

4 Action-orientation as method

From a methodological viewpoint, action-oriented foreign language teaching is thought to have great potential for fostering changes of perspective (see Surkamp and Nünning 2016, 70–71). This notion is based on the general assumption that teachers who exclusively focus on the acquisition of knowledge or the practicing of linguistic forms do not sufficiently prepare learners for communicative situations with people from different cultures (see Bach and Timm 2013). In order to learn how to communicate in a way that is appropriate for the partner and situation, students should be trained with action-oriented methods like role plays, simulations, or debates that enable them to use the foreign language as an instrument (e.g. to deal with conflicts, to negotiate meanings, or to express feelings; see Bach and Timm 2013, 12–13). In this way, they can also include their own interests, thoughts and feelings. Thus, changes of perspective are not only the goal but also an essential part of the classroom method in creating communicative situations in which learners can discover, take over and reflect on different points of view (see Surkamp 2005).

However, there is little empirical evidence for the value of action-orientation in this context. Investigating whether and to what extent foreign language classes dealing with literature foster students' intercultural competencies,

Britta Freitag-Hild (2010) came to the conclusion that, despite great discrepancies, students' abilities to take on different perspectives can be influenced in this way. Action-oriented tasks prove beneficial when students are encouraged to reflect on differences between a foreign perspective and their own (see Freitag-Hild 2010, 353), but learners have less difficulty taking on the point of view of a character whose norms, values and ways of thinking resemble their own (see Freitag-Hild 2010, 336). With regard to the level of difficulty in taking over a particular perspective, the selection of texts for classroom activities also, therefore, plays an important role, the specific traits of fictional personae making them more or less approachable for the learner.

5 Intercultural understanding put to the test

In order to explore the function and value of action-oriented tasks for processes of text reception and changes of perspective in foreign language classes a team from Göttingen University's Department of Teaching English as a Foreign Language conducted a study at a high school in the city from 2012 to 2013. We observed a teaching unit in an eighth grade (thirteen to fourteen year-olds) bilingual English class in which students, on the occasion of the US-American Thanksgiving celebration, were tasked to write and present a speech either from a Native American perspective or from that of descendants of the first white settlers. On the basis of texts written by the students in partner work, their discussions, and the actual speeches they held – all of which were videotaped – we analyzed to what extent action-oriented teaching encourages changes of perspective. The research question was how exactly these changes occur, what challenges students face in the process, and according to what parameters a change of perspective could be deemed successful in terms of intercultural learning. For this purpose, passages from the students' work and interactions were selected, transcribed, and interpreted.[1]

---

[1] The transcription follows the content-focused rules proposed by Kuckartz et al. (2008, 27). Movements in the classroom and other non- or paraverbal elements were recorded when they appeared relevant to the analysis. I would like to thank Katharina Delius, Ann-Kristin Eckhart, Ann-Christin Rudolf, and Svenja Straus for their invaluable assistance with the recording and preparation of the video material, Sonja Lewin for her help in interpreting and discussing the material, and Natalie Erkel for finalizing the manuscript. The six-month project was financed by the State of Lower-Saxony's Ministry of Science and Culture.

The assignment and its two perspectives were briefly outlined on a worksheet by the teacher. Students who chose to present the perspective of a Native American should mention in their speech what their ancestors had done for the white settlers and how they had been treated by them. Students who chose the white settlers' perspective should praise the accomplishments and courage of their ancestors. The tasks thus clearly assigned not only roles but values with regard to Thanksgiving and US-American colonial history: critical and disapproving (Native Americans), or supportive and praising (descendants of settlers).

In order to write their speeches, students could draw on information from texts on which they had worked in small groups in history and English classes. These looked more closely at the historical beginnings of the Thanksgiving celebration, focusing on different thematic areas chosen by the teacher, all of which – e.g. through historical eyewitness accounts – gave greater prominence to the Native American perspective than to that of the white settlers. Much emphasis was put, for example, on atrocities committed against Native Americans, such as their forced removal to reservations in what would be known as the Trail of Tears. As will be shown later in more detail, the selection of texts proved crucial for the process of adopting another perspective.

Action-oriented learning of this kind provides students with an opportunity to transform newly acquired knowledge into actual speech acts. A quasi-authentic situation is simulated in which the foreign language is used to express an opinion and convince an audience. This fosters not only speaking skills and personal identification with a topic, but also the concentration required to assimilate background information and familiarize oneself with the historical role context.

In the following pages, I will examine to what extent these factors were taken into account in the teaching unit and what processes of learning were triggered. The analysis follows the course of the class in a predominantly chronological way: First, I will focus on the negotiation of meaning among the students in their (sometimes struggling) attempt to take on a certain perspective. In a second step, I will analyze how they wrote, structured, and presented their speeches rhetorically and what this reveals about the degree to which they really changed their perspective. Finally, the findings of both processes will be scrutinized in combination with the feedback students received from their peers and the English teacher.

5.1 Partner work I: "We are Indians"

Students Sw3 and Sw4 received the task to write a speech from the Native American perspective. This required, first of all, the willingness to take on a foreign perspective. From the start, Sw4 had no difficulty in identifying with her role. This first became evident when her partner did not correctly remember the texts they had previously read, and wrongly assumed that the settlers had taught the Native Americans how to plant corn, not vice versa:

Sw4: (*louder, with emphasis*) We are Indians!

Sw3: Yes.

Sw4: We live there (*very loud, emotional facial expression*). And the others came and didn't know anything.

Sw3: (*laughs*)

Sw4: We helped them. (2) They (.) we – we lived there for hundreds of years. We knew everything how to grow corn.

Sw3: (*shakes her head*) Then I understood something wrong. OK.

This interaction shows that Sw4 strongly identified with the perspective of the Native Americans (or rather with the image of Native Americans created in the previous English and history lessons) and that this perspective was the key to writing her speech. Instead of giving student Sw3 an answer to her question concerning the cultivation of corn, her first reaction was an emotionally charged comment indicating her newly assumed role. The assertion "We are Indians" seems to imply that the role already contains all the information one needs. Only when her partner still does not grasp what she is trying to say does Sw4 explain the differences between the Native Americans, who had inhabited the continent for centuries and were well versed in the cultivation of corn, and the helpless foreign settlers. The fact that she uses the term "Indians", however, can also be viewed critically. Rather than sounding authentically Native American, her statement reveals, from a linguistic point of view, the reproduction of, and identification with a stereotype.

Nonetheless, Sw4 does undertake a change of perspective, as is illustrated in her use of personal pronouns. Initially she uses "We" to refer to herself and her partner, as well as to their fictitious roles as Native Americans. Her first exclamation "We are Indians" refers to their joint role in the English assignment; her following statement "We live there" already refers to the Native Americans as 'we'; and when she says "we – we lived there for hundreds of years", the personal pronoun refers to the Native Americans in their historical tradition, as a people. The adoption of the new perspective is so strong that it blends together her identity as a student and her fictitious role.

For Sw3 and Sw4, the process of identifying with their role is closely linked to a process of dissociation from the role of their opponents: the white settlers.

The connotations used to describe the white settlers are exclusively negative and by constructing them as a group that they refer to as "the others" they set them apart linguistically from their own roles. In the course of the partner work, this polarization has an impact on their rhetoric: they begin to construct the audience as the enemy:

> Sw3: OK. // You started pushing us around like crap. (*makes a gesture with her hand*) Like we're not people like you.
>
> Sw4: Um (2) about two centuries later (.) we (.) we were put in reservations
>
> Sw3: //
>
> Sw4: No. we were put into the bad, into the worst piece of // of America. And we had to sit there. [...]
>
> Sw3: Wait-wait-wait! We cannot understand how you could put us in the reservations like animals, like we were not (2) (*sticks out her tongue*) like we were not people like you. Is that right?
>
> Sw4: Yeah.

The fact that the assignment offers no details about the specific communicative situation enables the students to imagine a situation where they as victims can vehemently argue against their enemies. This clearly motivates their rhetoric, which includes a noticeable level of rephrasing. Thus, while Sw4 first states in an objective, factual way that the Native Americans were relocated in reservations, she soon corrects herself and chooses structures of comparison to dramatize her statements: the treatment of Native Americans is finally so inhumane that they are compared to animals. These stylistic devices show that Sw3 and Sw4 have inwardly adopted their new perspective, and this also becomes evident in other emotional traits, not only of the text of the speech but also of its manner of presentation, in which nonverbal communicative signs play an important role.

> Sw3: (*points at herself with both her hands*) "I (*emphasized*) am a Native American, and I want to tell you something (.) (*points at class*) so listen! (*laughter in class*) (2) 391 years ago (.) (*begins to walk through the classroom, points at herself*) our ancestors helped your ancestors (*points away from herself*) to survive. (.) We showed you (*points at class*) how to grow corn and because of that you had a great harvest and survived the winter. (.) So (.) and (*begins to walk a couple of steps*) the next year we celebrated Thanksgiving together the first time (*stands still*) (.) but from then on things changed. Our life got worse and worse (.) you put us (*voice goes up, higher pitch*) in reservations (*emphasized, almost shrill, spreads out her hands*) like we were animals (*stretches out arm to the side*) like we (*joins her hands in front of her chest*) were not people like you

(*points at class with her hand*) (2) If you ask me that is really unfair. (2) But aren't (*emphasized*) all men created equal? Today (.) it's still like it was some centuries ago. It's like (.) you would hunt a pig an – in the forest (*starts to walk*) and you will kill it and thank for it that you can eat it and survive but the pig (*right hand to her side*) is dead anyway. (*claps hands together*) Is that fair?" (2) That's it.

Content-wise, the student speaking first of all verbalizes her own role, establishes the 'white settlers', who are represented by the class, as the enemy, and gives an overview of the historical background, namely the helpfulness and co-operativeness of the Native Americans, the first Thanksgiving feast and the ensuing conflicts. Finally, Sw3 points out the continuing inequality between the descendants of the two segments of the population. The speech is a strong plea against the unjust treatment of the Native Americans and it can be seen as an attempt of the victims to find their own voice against the perpetrators – possibly even to implore them to change their conduct.

The fact that the students identify strongly with the perspective they are supposed to assume also becomes evident in the manner in which the speech is rendered. Through her gestures, Sw3 constructs her identity as a Native American by establishing a clear line between her own role and that of the white settlers. Her pitch also changes in the course of the speech: the more emotional the speech and the stronger her accusations, the shriller her voice becomes. Her gestures and intonation underline her strong identification with her role and have their due effect on the audience. The class and teacher emphasize the successful change in perspective and the authenticity and passion with which the speech was presented:

> Teacher: Yeah (.) I'd very much like to agree (.) very authentic (2) for-for // by far the biggest part of your speech we had the feeling you knew (*emphasized*) ye-you-you were giving it be-because there was something you want (*emphasized*) to tell us you would (.) again

It cannot, then, be denied that this sort of partner work vindicates action-oriented learning tasks. It can be questioned, however, if that is sufficient in the context of intercultural learning (see Ch. 5.3).

5.2 Partner work II: "It isn't our real opinion"

In contrast to Sw3 and Sw4, students assigned to the 'white settler' group had difficulty engaging in a change of perspective. From the start, Sw1 refused to take on an uncritical perspective toward the US-American past and there was a process of negotiation between the two of them concerning the 'right' perspective for writing the speech, the consequences of which can also be seen in the final product. Sw2 considered the fact that they were supposed to write a positive Thanksgiving speech from the perspective of the white settlers to be a distinct change of the previously learned 'facts' in class and viewed it as a form of denial of the atrocities committed against the Native Americans. She was, however, willing to accomplish the task:

> Sw2: We should, we should do it, um (.) about that point (*points at the worksheet*) [...] we should, we should do it like (*makes a gesture with her hand*): yeah, the Native Americans
>
> Sw1: //
>
> Sw2: They-they-they, they died because of something else, because we, we fought against them (.) so we should (*makes a gesture with her hand*) we should um
>
> Sw1: //
>
> Sw2: Well, we should change the truth.

Student Sw2 wants to express the perspective of the descendants of the white settlers by praising the actions of the white settlers – and this also corresponds with the explicit task ("you are very proud of your ancestors"). So she suggests explaining the deaths of the Native Americans, for which her ancestors are responsible, in a different way and summarizes her strategy at the beginning of the speech as 'changing the truth'. She is willing to take on a position that she considers to be dishonest in order to convincingly undergo a change of perspective; and she has already assumed this new perspective by using "we" to refer to her partner and herself as well as to their fictitious roles. Sw1, however, opposes the strategy of her partner and clearly displays more distance toward her assigned role:

> Sw1: (*waves her hands in a negating way*) It doesn't matter but I think she would really she would talk about the bad things, too, if she would be a descendant
>
> Sw2: Of course, but she will, she would
>
> Sw1: I would do it if I would be – be the people who – who had to do it I would // talk about that [...] because this I would think that I'm not happy about the things that um – um (.) I don't know (.) my – my grandmother, the grandmother of my grandmother
>
> Sw2: //
>
> Sw1: voted um voted Hitler. So I – I, so you know? So I would give, I wouldn't be happy about this so that's the same. And I don't think that they are happy about it now there are reservates and so

Student Sw1 refuses to take on the perspective of the settlers: she does not believe that a descendant of the white settlers would be so uncritical of the past. To illustrate her point, she compares the crimes committed by the settlers with the crimes committed by the Nazis and equates her own condemnation of the actions of her ancestors in Nazi Germany with the point of view of the speaker. Simply taking on the perspective of the perpetrators is out of the question for her.

In history education, such a way of thinking is called the "illusion of superiority" (von Borries, qtd. in Hartmann et al. 2009, 324; my translation): the idea that the present is necessarily superior to the past. This presupposed superiority becomes obvious in student Sw1's general assumption that people learn from their mistakes and that the crimes of the past would not be committed today. She fails to realize that there are alternative ways of viewing historical conflicts. To this day, there are people in the U.S. who consider it patriotic to be proud of their colonial history. Likewise, there are Germans who have right-wing political views despite the atrocities committed by the Nazis. Sw1's illusion of superiority denies the viability of such a perspective, which entails the risk of forming an uncritical attitude toward the interface of present and past in one's own culture.

Sw1 finally manages to assert herself and the two of them work on the speech from the perspective of a descendant of white settlers who is critical of her ancestors' actions. Thanks to the open nature of the assignment, the students can develop an ambivalent role construction, and they quickly adapt their situation to their own world and their alternative interpretation of critical settler descendants:

Sw1: Yeah, I said that because I thought that we are sisters who [...] and that father said um

Sw2: We could be twins (*laughs*)

Sw1: Yeah OK (*laughs*) it doesn't matter (.) that we have to give a speech about that (.) and then we don't know what we had to do because – because we are (.) we don't actually, actually // know anything about that not – not much, not very much um and then we looked up on the internet and so // [...]

Sw2: How are we begin. You can't say: "Dear (.) they family", that sounds I don't know

Sw1: Maybe it's a good (.) if we say when our father told that we had to do a speech

Sw2: We could say: "Dear family now we want to tell you something about Thanksgiven – Thanksgiving and how it was in sixteen twenty-one because our father told us to

Sw1: give a speech

Sw2: to – to inform us about it a bit more because in school we don't – we don't learn the right things" (.) or the whole thing

Sw1 makes the perspective they are to assume more concrete by imagining her and her partner to be sisters whose father has told them to give a speech. The students thus blend their own and the fictitious situation by having recourse to relationship constellations they already know from their own lives. This brings their assigned role a good deal closer to their own perspective and in that sense runs counter to achieving any real change of perspective. In what follows Sw1 contextualizes the historical background by giving an overview of the initial conditions of the settlement. Strictly speaking, a change of perspective does not occur. Instead of speaking of her ancestors, Sw1 refers to them as "settlers" or, more generally, as "they". She goes on to recount their bloody conflict with the Native Americans, and the ensuing Trail of Tears, again without mentioning them as people with whom she is related. In fact she portrays them in a distanced way as faceless institutions.

> Sw1: "And um so in 1830 the USA the US government passed a law that says um every Indian tribe is forced to leave their land and go to a reservation in west America (2) in the desert (*spreads out left hand*). I don't want to go the desert when I living in the um (3) I forgot the word (*laughs*) in the place and (3) ja. So the Indians don't want to do it, too. They don't want to leave their spiritual and physical home but the army forced them and (2) so the long, long way began. In (*sighs*) um the last the people arrived in 1838 and many of them died many of the Indians died. It's called the Trail of Tears. // [...]"

Here she uses the personal pronoun "I" in her speech, clearly assuming a Native American perspective and expressing solidarity with them in the context of the atrocities committed against them. She shows understanding toward their resistance against being forcibly relocated, implying that she would have acted in a similar way. On the one hand, this display of empathy can be considered a positive factor in intercultural learning; on the other hand, however, it can be viewed critically, since Sw1 takes her own point of view as the norm and evidently considers it powerful enough to effectively defend the Native Americans. Instead of engaging in an actual change of perspective, she actually displays a form of paternalism directly contrary to the goal of intercultural competence, using her own perspective as a default mode, i.e. assuming that the other feels as she would in a similar situation (see Nünning 2014, 180).

Toward the end of her speech, Sw1 refers to the present and the current Thanksgiving dinner. Here she finally finds her role as a descendant of the white settlers.

> Sw1: "And now they're still living there. Not every Indian but many of them (*moves hand to stress every single word*). Do you think this is good? (*louder*) Do you think it is good that we (*emphasized*) forced the Indians to do that? Is it good to kill so many Indians and years before we were happy sitting together? I think

that's not good. So raise your glasses (*raises left hand*) and thank God and don't forget the Indians and think about the false and good things of our settlers." (*Pretends to hold up a glass*)

Here Sw1 finally manages to talk about the conflict between the two groups from the white-American perspective, but instead of assuming the assigned role of a proud patriot, she maintains her negative view of her ancestors' actions; she does, however, now include herself in this collectively guilty group. She uses rhetorical questions to make the audience aware of their historical complicity, briefly switching to a moralizing 'I' that reflects her self-declared role as a critical young descendant and re-establishes her as a moral instance distinct from her peer group.

In contrast to the rest of the speech, this passage is presented in an increasingly emotional way and shows a change of perspective which is underlined by the fact that Sw1 now speaks more loudly and that her emphasis is more nuanced. The audience is included in rhetorical questions that demand a moral judgment. At the same time, these questions may be a way for Sw1 to reflect on her own culture and country of origin. The ambivalence between belonging to and setting oneself apart from a group is illustrated by the switch between the personal pronouns "we" and "I". Moreover, toward the end of the speech an entirely new perspective appears: Sw1 extends the personal pronoun "we" to include all who were part of the first Thanksgiving celebration, both Native Americans and settlers. Unlike Sw3 and Sw4, who retain a consistently clear distinction between the Native Americans and the white settlers, Sw1 rejects such dichotomous thinking, reminding her audience of peaceful times before the fighting, and her concluding plea for understanding between different cultures is phrased as an appeal to her relatives.

While Sw3 and Sw4 were praised by both their peers and the teacher for their successful change of perspective, the class is critical of the performance of Sw1 and Sw2 and their interpretation of the role of descendants of the white settlers:

> Sm: I liked your speech in the way you present it um but I think you character wasn't well a white settler but sometimes it looks like you were an Indian because you you (1) said so many good things about the Indians.

This feedback shows a certain ambivalence toward their classmates' attempt to change perspective, which they see as deviating materially from the assignment. A comparison of the two partner performances will show, however, that it would be overly simplistic to conclude that intercultural competence was not fostered by their presentation.

5.3 Discussion of the two partner performances

Although action-oriented tasks like the one described above clearly encourage changes of perspective, engaging students on an emotional level, and creating situations in which they use the target language for communication, the evidence from the Göttingen school class shows that they do not automatically guarantee success. It is not enough to focus on the students' final products: we need more complex interpretations of the processes entailed in their genesis. How, for instance, did students use their historical and cultural knowledge of Thanksgiving? More specifically: What challenges did they meet, what solutions did they find, and what role did their own backgrounds, thoughts, and feelings play in all this?

First of all, it appears particularly difficult for school students to assume a different perspective if this stands in stark contrast to their own system of norms and values. But that is a vital aspect of intercultural learning. It is to some extent a simple question of knowledge: as Nünning (2014, 182) points out, successful perspective taking "presupposes that a person knows enough about the traits, attitudes, feelings and beliefs of the other." From this point of view, the selection of texts used to prepare the Göttingen students for the unit was not ideal, as the texts all focused one-sidedly on the Native Americans, which made it easier to relate to their perspective: the settlers were almost exclusively presented there as ruthless perpetrators. Moreover, while the texts offered commentaries and included eye-witness accounts as examples for the role of the Native Americans, the perspective of the white settlers was ignored, thus preventing the students from receiving any real insight into their array of emotions and reasons for acting as they did. Analyzing the texts for their content and perspective, as cultural narratology demands, and discussing this with the class, would from the start have led to a different selection, and may well also have led to the realization that modes of representation have a guiding function and can prove culturally and historically one-sided.

Interpreting all this against the background of cultural narratology indicates that the students could hardly help identifying with the Native American perspective, an effect that is reminiscent of Alison Landsberg's concept of 'prosthetic memory', a phenomenon that "emerges at the interface of a person and a historical narrative of the past" (qtd. in Erll 2011, 158). According to Landsberg, "the person does not simply apprehend a historical narrative but takes on a more personal, deeply felt memory of a past event through which he or she did not live" (qtd. in Erll 2011, 158). Adopting a narrative – here that of the Native Americans – with which one is presented is just such an act of transcultural memorizing, and it would then seem extremely difficult to imaginatively switch to the opposite perspective, let alone to present it – here the story of the white settlers – in a quasi-authentic speech.

Secondly, the analyses raise the question of the criteria for considering a change of perspective successful in terms of intercultural learning. A closer look at the results shows that a simple division of the students' work into successful and unsuccessful is problematic. From an intercultural point of view, the speech from the perspective of the Native Americans that received high praise from both students and teacher is not entirely faultless. Conversely, the second group work, which did not run so smoothly, and where the students even partly refused to change their perspective, can in some ways be considered to have successfully fostered intercultural competence. It is, for example, striking that the first group primarily identified with the Native Americans by distancing themselves from a negatively presented enemy group whom they simply saw as violent perpetrators. While this was understandable in light of the texts read for the assignment, it remains highly problematic from an intercultural standpoint to define oneself exclusively by distancing oneself from others. The dichotomy between Native Americans and white settlers leads to a stereotypical presentation of 'good' victims against 'bad' perpetrators which makes it difficult to develop a differentiated point of view or a complex notion of a person's identity.

Moreover, unlike Sw3 and Sw4, Sw1 and Sw2 reflect critically on the perspective they were tasked to assume. In this case, their working process is more important than their finished product: the negotiations between the two students allowed them to autonomously discuss the historical period and the moral issues that arose from it. Furthermore, that Sw1 also subjects her own cultural history to critical analysis accords with accepted principles of intercultural competence. Finally, by uniting the Native Americans and white settlers as a joint collective at the end of her speech, Sw1 pleads for peace and mutual respect and goes beyond the binary idea of settlers vs. Native Americans presented by Sw3 and Sw4.

All in all, the examples from the Göttingen classroom show that intercultural understanding consists of different sub-competencies which may stand in tension or even contradiction toward each other. Ability and willingness to undergo a change of perspective are crucially important, yet intercultural understanding also requires the ability to differentiate between perspectives, to reflect on them from a distance, compare them, and negotiate between them. In this sense, Lothar Bredella's differentiation between inner and outer perspectives adds an important note to the discussion:

> The inner perspective is necessary to overcome ethnocentrism, and the outer perspective is necessary to prevent oneself from simply being exposed to the 'other' inner perspective without engaging with it in a critical way. A well-reflected, nuanced intercultural understanding is guaranteed when the tension between inner and outer perspective is properly developed. (Bredella 2001, 12; my translation)

In these terms, while Sw3 and Sw4 portray an emotional (if somewhat one-sided) 'inner' Native American perspective, Sw1 and Sw2 stand out by taking a critical 'outer' perspective – the problematic aspect is that they also do so in a phase when they are meant to assume an inner perspective. This may well be due to their fundamental disagreement with this perspective. Sw1 cannot cope with the tension arising from this situation – unlike Sw2, who continuously emphasizes the difference between their own opinion and that of the characters they are portraying: "It's not our opinion, it's the opinion of our roles".

But then again, the mixing of inner and outer perspectives may also be due to the classroom setting and overall lesson design. The Göttingen students were not given the opportunity to distance themselves from their roles and critically comment on their speeches – taking on this type of outer role after their speech might have made them more willing to fully assume the inner perspective in the speech itself. The second group tries to mix outer and inner perspectives, whereas Sw3 and Sw4 do not assume an outer perspective at any point during their task – in the concrete context they are under no pressure to do so. It could also be argued that the genre of the speech as such invites totalizing messages with a strong emotional appeal. A different genre for the assignment might have led to a more differentiated version from the Native American perspective, too.

One could go even further and question (in the given example) the very task of taking on the perspective of white settlers. The analysis of the results suggests that intercultural learning classes should not aim at a change of perspective per se. The question is rather what changes in perspective are meaningful to the particular class and make sense from an educational point of view. As König (2018, 67–68) points out, intercultural learning in the classroom should always give thought to different levels of power when choosing an assignment: the adoption of historically or culturally hegemonic perspectives can lead to confirming already privileged voices and suppressing less dominant ones. Not that intercultural learning classes should avoid dealing with hegemonic points of view, but tasks should focus on the differentiation and coordination of perspectives rather than on change of perspective as such. Only then will different positions and the relations between them become visible and discussable.

Moreover, in choosing the perspective from which students should tell a story, intercultural learning classes should also take into consideration what in narratology is called 'tellability' (see Baroni). Thus, in the example above, the question arises if the story of the white settlers is worth reporting in the first place. Should a Thanksgiving speech in class really praise the accomplishments of white settlers? If only "tellable materials can stimulate interest culturally, socially, personally, or with some combination thereof" (Baroni, paragraph 7), tasks like this run the risk of counteracting the very goals they were intended to serve. Perspective taking in class is not primarily an intellectual game but closely linked to the students' own identities, values, and feelings. For these students, Native American history – far more than that of the white settlers – generates emotions and empathy, and for that very reason becomes tellable.

6 Conclusion

Analysis of the empirical data collected during the project shows, on the one hand, that action-oriented processes need to be well prepared in order to guarantee that important steps reflecting the different types of decentration outlined in Section 3 can successfully take place. On the other hand, Nünning's model of different levels of intercultural understanding – together with other insights from cultural narratology – underlines the need for a second step of reflection in which students can coordinate different perspectives. Only then will they be able to differentiate between the cultural dimensions and perspectives presented in the texts they read, whether in history or English classes. Such coordination, however, also requires the ability to analyze one's own perceptions when reading and discussing a text, and this in turn means encouraging affective as well as analytical modes of understanding, fostering empathy as well as intellectual ability. Only if there is a reflection phase after an action-oriented phase will students have the opportunity to process and verbally communicate what their experience with a change of perspective was like.

Especially after a potentially difficult and challenging change of perspective, this exchange in class will allow students to assume an outer perspective from which they can assess their role perspective alongside their own point of view. In the example unit on Thanksgiving, for instance, Sw1's moral condemnation of the white settlers, her critical assessment of the historical incidents, and the parallel she draws between Nazi Germany and the atrocities committed by the white settlers could have been interesting topics for the whole class to discuss. Had the learners been encouraged to perform perspective changes in both an 'engaged' and a 'detached' mode (see Nünning 2014, 27), as well as to question their own culture and become aware of the historical limitations of their own perspective, they might have benefited even more from the action-oriented assignment. In other words, applying insights from narrative theory to the foreign language class can promote a better understanding of intercultural learning processes and open up new ways to improve established concepts and methodological approaches.

References

Bach, Gerhard, and Johannes-Peter Timm. "Handlungsorientierung als Ziel und als Methode." *Englischunterricht: Grundlagen und Methoden einer handlungsorientierten Unterrichtspraxis*. Eds. Gerhard Bach and Johannes-Peter Timm. Fifth ed. Tübingen: Francke, 2013. 1–22.

Baroni, Raphaël. "Tellability." *The Living Handbook of Narratology*. Eds. Peter Hühn et al. Hamburg: Hamburg University. http://www.lhn.uni-hamburg.de/article/tellability (15 November 2018).

Bredella, Lothar. "Die Struktur schüleraktivierender Methoden: Überlegungen zum Entwurf einer prozeßorientierten Literaturdidaktik." *PRAXIS des neusprachlichen Unterrichts* 34.3 (1987): 233–248.

Bredella, Lothar. "Verstehen und Verständigung als Grundbegriffe und Zielvorstellungen des Fremdsprachenlehrens und -lernens." *Verstehen und Verständigung durch Sprachenlernen?* Ed. Lothar Bredella. Bochum: Brockmeyer, 1995. 1–34.

Bredella, Lothar. "Zur Dialektik von Eigenem und Fremdem beim interkulturellen Verstehen." *Der Fremdsprachliche Unterricht Englisch* 35.53 (2001): 10–14.

Erll, Astrid. *Kollektives Gedächtnis und Erinnerungskulturen: Eine Einführung*. Second ed. Stuttgart: Metzler, 2011.

Freitag-Hild, Britta. *Theorie, Aufgabentypologie und Unterrichtspraxis inter- und transkultureller Literaturdidaktik*: British Fictions of Migration *im Fremdsprachenunterricht*. Trier: WVT, 2010.

Hartmann, Ulrike, Michael Sauer, and Marcus Hasselhorn. "Perspektivenübernahme als Kompetenz für den Geschichtsunterricht: Theoretische und empirische Zusammenhänge zwischen fachspezifischen und sozial-kognitiven Schülermerkmalen." *Zeitschrift für Erziehungswissenschaft* 12 (2009): 321–342.

König, Lotta. *Gender-Reflexion mit Literatur im Englischunterricht: Fremdsprachendidaktische Theorie und Unterrichtsbeispiele*. Stuttgart: Metzler, 2018.

Kuckartz, Udo, Thorsen Dresing, Stefan Rädiker, and Claus Stefer. *Qualitative Evaluation: Der Einstieg in die Praxis*. Second ed. Wiesbaden: VS, 2008.

Nünning, Ansgar. "'Intermisunderstanding' – Prolegomena zu einer literaturdidaktischen Theorie des Fremdverstehens: Erzählerische Vermittlung, Perspektivenwechsel und Perspektivenübernahme." *Wie ist Fremdverstehen lehr- und lernbar? Vorträge aus dem*

Graduiertenkolleg *"Didaktik des Fremdverstehens"*. Eds. Lothar Bredella, Franz-Joseph Meißner, Ansgar Nünning, and Dietmar Rösler. Tübingen: Narr, 2000. 84–132.

Nünning, Ansgar. "Narrativist Approaches and Narratological Concepts for the Study of Culture." *Travelling Concepts for the Study of Culture*. Eds. Birgit Neumann and Ansgar Nünning. Berlin: de Gruyter, 2012. 145–183.

Nünning, Vera. *Reading Fictions, Changing Minds: The Cognitive Value of Fiction*. Heidelberg: Winter, 2014.

Posner, Roland. "Kultur als Zeichensystem: Zur semiotischen Explikation kulturwissenschaftlicher Grundbegriffe." *Kultur als Lebenswelt und Monument*. Eds. Aleida Assmann, and Dietrich Harth. Frankfurt/M.: Fischer, 1991. 37–74.

Sommer, Roy. "Fremdverstehen durch Literaturunterricht: Prämissen und Perspektiven einer narratologisch orientierten interkulturellen Literaturdidaktik." *Fremdverstehen zwischen Theorie und Praxis*. Eds. Lothar Bredella, Herbert Christ, and Michael K. Legutke. Tübingen: Narr, 2000. 18–42.

Surkamp, Carola. "'The Essence of the New Way of Looking is Multiplicity – Multiplicity of Eyes and Multiplicity of Aspects Seen': Perspektivenwechsel als Lernziel und als Methode im fremdsprachlichen Literaturunterricht." *Perspektivenvielfalt im Unterricht*. Eds. Ludwig Duncker, Wolfgang Sander, and Carola Surkamp. Stuttgart: Kohlhammer, 2005. 33–48.

Surkamp, Carola, and Ansgar Nünning. *Englische Literatur unterrichten 1: Grundlagen und Methoden*. Fourth ed. Seelze-Velber: Klett-Kallmeyer, 2016.

Hanne Birk
Narrative and Visual Resources of Culture in Contemporary Indigenous Children's Books from Australia

> A *narrative* [...] is a representation of a process that produces change, whether in a fictional world or our world. (Kafalenos 2016, 152)

Abstract: In response to Ansgar Nünning's (2012) explorations of possible interfaces between narratology and cultural studies, this contribution presents a conceptualization of an analytical approach to Indigenous picturebooks from Australia. Following Nünning's arguments, it asks how the media-specific narratological tools developed for illustrated texts could be extended by a concept that allows for more culturally sensitive interpretations. After a short sketch of pertinent narratological approaches the argument shifts to the question how picturebooks can be understood as 'semanticized' visualisations of (selected dimensions of) culture(s). In consequence, the concept of 'visual resources' is introduced and employed in an analysis of three Indigenous Australian picturebooks. The discussion highlights the poietic potentials of the texts as well as the cultural relativity and transculturality of semanticized narrative and visual forms and thus the heterogeneity and transculturality of 'narrative worldmaking'.

1 Introduction

Picturebooks seem to be complex time-traveling transcultural storytelling phenomena. We encounter them in various centuries and (almost) all over the globe, and some of them tend to accompany us all our lives; first encounters during childhood may result in later re-readings (with some of them even having transgenerational effects). Not surprisingly, narratological research has established precise and useful concepts for analyzing these "generic hybrid crossover[s] between text and image" (Beckett 2012, 309). But these concepts, whether developed for picturebooks as such – or all the more so in the case of illustrations and text-image relations – may at least partly constitute examples for a problem which Nünning (2012, 145) identifies as follows:

> Although there is widespread agreement among many scholars working in a wide range of disciplines in the humanities and social sciences that cultures and narratives are closely interlinked, the complex connections between the interdisciplinary fields known as narratology and the study of culture have not yet been gauged, let alone systematically explored.

In consequence Nünning (2012, 146) uses "the insight into the performative, reality-constituting, or worldmaking function of narration" as a starting point to conceptualize interfaces between narratology and cultural studies, elaborating "key concepts for a cultural narratology and a narrativist study of culture." These invoke on the one hand "the notion of a cultural semanticisation of narrative forms," and on the other "the functions that narrative can fulfil as a cultural way of self-, community and worldmaking" (Nünning 2012, 147).

Following this line of argument, it is only fair and timely to ask how the useful narratological tools that have been developed and that have already been specifically modified for the "supergenre" (Lewis 1990, 142) picturebook can be complemented by concepts which allow for more culturally sensitive interpretations, acknowledging, for example, the (trans-)cultural contexts of production and configuration of the texts and their (trans-)cultural potential effects. This will be the main focus of the present article, which will first provide an introduction to the phenomenon of the picturebook as well as a short sketch of some narratological approaches especially apt for interpretations of text-image relations. Secondly, using selected narratological research results as a starting point, the focus will then shift to the question how images in picturebooks can be read as 'semanticized' visualizations of (selected dimensions of) culture(s). As one possible response the concept of 'visual resources'[1] will be introduced and, in a third step, employed in the discussion of three Indigenous picturebooks from Australia, highlighting their poietic potentials.

---

[1] The term 'visual resources' (echoing the concept of 'textual resources', Wertsch 2002) was devised jointly by Marion Gymnich and the present author. Marion Gymnich applied the concept in her presentation on "(Trans)Cultural Negotiations of Indigenous Visual Resources in Māori and Inuit Children's Books" (Birk and Gymnich) at the 43rd Annual Children's Literature Association Conference in Columbus, Ohio in 2016, and we referred to it in our presentation at the GAPS conference in Augsburg (2016).

2 On narratological approaches to picturebooks

Since the 1990s transdisciplinary research on picturebooks has been a thriving and fast evolving field of studies at the crossroads of several approaches originating in e.g. media studies, literary studies, the cognitive sciences, and sociology (see e.g. Colomer et al. 2010; Doonan 1992; Hunt 1990, 2004; Lesnik-Oberstein 1998; Nikolajeva and Scott 2001; Nodelman 1988; Schwarcz and Schwarcz 1991; Sipe and Pantaleo 2008). A range of reasons for this trend can be identified: Firstly, Beckett (2012, 2) refers to the dual (visual-textual) code of picturebooks and states that "[t]his unique feature of picturebooks is what makes them one of the most exciting and innovative contemporary literary genres." But not only the narrative code of picturebooks is double, analyses tend to take the specific dual heterogeneity of the (default) readership into account: "[p]icturebooks offer a unique opportunity for a collaborative or shared reading experience between children and adults, since they empower the two audiences more equally than other narrative forms" (Beckett 2012, 2).

Secondly, precisely this strict division between the two potential audiences, and the implied assumption that picturebooks mainly appeal to children and that the adults involved merely function as 'reading assistants' have been criticized as arbitrary or imprecise: "The perception that picturebooks are essentially a genre for children is shifting" (Beckett 2012, 3) and they are increasingly recognized as all-ages literature. Thirdly, and in consequence, the number of innovative "crossover picturebooks" is rising, rendering the picturebook "an extraordinarily rich field of literary and artistic creation" and "an exceptionally vibrant and transformative genre" (Beckett 2012, 308). This rise relies at least partly on the fact that the picturebook may function as "a motley, a ragbag of different genres, types, manners and modes," which is able "to absorb and ingest other, more closed and 'finished' forms" (Lewis 1990, 142 qtd. in Beckett 2012, 309). Accordingly, Beckett (2012, 316) describes the future development of the genre as follows: "In a graphically-oriented society where culture in general is shifting away from age as a defining category, picturebooks are an increasingly important mode of communication." This development is in line with the hypothesis that in general "our narratives across all media are only going to be more visual." (Losowsky 2011, 7) In conclusion, it may be assumed that picturebooks will continue to represent focal points for narrative innovation.

As could be expected, narrative research has responded to these developments by "[e]xtending [the] concept of fiction to other media" (Ryan 2010, 15), and a range of 'postclassical' narrativist approaches (see Passalacqua and Pianzola 2016), especially within the frameworks of inter- or transmedial narratology (e.g., Herman 2004; Ryan 2004; Thon 2016; Wolf 2005a, 2005b), has provided highly useful concepts for analyses of the avant-garde genre of the picturebook (see Bateman 2014, 72–90). A necessary premise for such endeavors is the idea of an interaction between codes, as well as the claim that narrative theory can 'do the job', as McHale (2010, 27) puts it:

> Narrative theory tends to treat non-narrative organization in narrative texts as supplemental, a little 'something extra,' auxiliary to narrativity; and it does so even in cases of mixed or hybrid texts, such as narrative poems or graphic novels, in which narrativity competes with other forms of organization, or may even be subordinated to them. [...] [T]his sort of interaction should be regarded not as incidental to narrative theory, but rather as a dimension of narrative form that a sufficiently capacious theory should be able to accommodate.

That narrative theories have, in fact, been able to negotiate the "other forms of organization", some of which we encounter in picturebooks, will be illustrated by the following sketch of some of the main issues surfacing in the respective research discourse. First of all, the phenomenon of interaction addressed by McHale is a defining characteristic of the 'aesthetic whole' of picturebooks as formulated by Sipe (2012, 4): "Picturebooks are highly sophisticated aesthetic objects, worthy of study and research by readers and viewers of all ages. As aesthetic wholes, picturebooks combine words and visual images (and occasionally other modalities) in complicated ways to produce this unity." There is a range of various "typologies or taxonomies that describe the diverse ways in which words and pictures interrelate in picturebooks" (Sipe 2012, 5), but there is also a widespread consensus that the relation between text and image is highly dynamic – an assessment that Sipe (1998) refers to by the term 'synergy'. One of the most prominent models in this respect was proposed by Nikolajeva and Scott (2001, 12); the main body of whose typology includes (1) "symmetrical interaction," where the narratives are "mutually redundant"; (2) "complementary picturebook[s]", in which words and images "fill[...] each other's gaps"; (3) the "expanding" or "enhancing" mode, where "visual narrative supports verbal narrative" (which itself "depends on [the] visual narrative"); (4) 'counterpointing interaction', where both components are "mutually dependent"; and (5) the "sylleptic" mode, which is characterized by independent narratives.

In addition to the text/image relation, it is, secondly, also necessary to consider the sequentiality of the double-coded narrative. Although the following statement by Boillat and Revaz (2016, 128) originally refers to comic strips, it also applies to some extent to picturebooks:

> [W]e wish to insist upon the need for an approach to the narrative sequence that takes into account its dual nature: both structured, coherent, and organized into a whole and, at the same time, dynamic, emergent, and unpredictable. Indeed, each strip in the series offers a narrative sequence that can be considered, on the one hand, a finished product (the tabular dimension of the page) and, on the other, a succession of panels progressively apprehended by the reader-interpreter.

Although the arrangement of images in picturebooks may not be as obviously sequential as in the individual panels of a comic strip, analyses of images in picturebooks do need to take into account not only the actual page but also the dynamic flow of images throughout the reading process.

Thirdly, zooming in on the individual images, the question surfaces as to "what there is to consider" (Doonan 1997, 68) from a narratological perspective. According to Doonan (1997, 68–69), analyses discuss especially "graphic elements" such as "[s]tyle – medium – abstract elements (line, shape, colour, and their arrangement on the picture plane)", "[l]ayout," which refers to the "[a]rrangement of illustrations and text" and includes issues such as the "harmony of the page opening," the "use of grid," and the "page-turn placement of text and pictures in relation to each other"; other features referred to include "the page opening," the "spacing of words, length of line, scale of lettering," and "how the text is being presented – on labels, in balloons, separately?" Furthermore, Doonan (1997, 68–69) suggests that attention should also be paid to the mode of "integration as a visual-verbal entity" – i.e. the "range of relationships between images and text," "the arrangement of illustration and placement of text," and the "creation of mood"; the "physical format" of the picturebook, its "size and shape – portrait or landscape – jacket – cover – end papers – paper stock – typeface" can, Doonan continues, also be taken into account. Moreover, a closer look at the individual "picture plane" is required, "imagin[ing] a picture as being a view seen through a window or a representation of 'space' [...]"; the picture plane is then "the view you are given" Doonan (1997, 71). But as the picturebook images depict 'space', not only is depth perception simulated (allowing for the analysis of 'foreground', 'middle ground' and 'background'), but a range of narratological concepts specifically developed for the visual code in film narratology can be drawn upon.[2] Taking

---

2 In order to account for the fact that, like a film, a picturebook can also be understood as "a composition structuring a large amount of heterogeneous information flowing from different channels" (Jahn 2003, n. p.) it may be useful to modify Jahn's concept of the FCD (filmic composition device) accordingly. The picturebook composition device (PCD) could then be defined as "[t]he theoretical agency behind [a picturebook's, HB] organization and arrangement [...]. The [PCB, HB] selects what it needs from various sources of information and arranges, edits, and composes this information for telling a [...] narrative" (Jahn 2003, n. p.).

the text-image relation into account, these include not only the distinction between homodiegetic and heterodiegetic narration, and between perspective and focalization, but also between various 'shots' (such as 'close shots' or 'full shots', see Jahn 2003, n. p.; Doonan 1997, 71).[3]

It is obvious that so far the approaches addressed have focused on text-internal features. However, the production and reception of picturebooks are also naturally embedded in cultural contexts, and these can be subdivided into social, mental, and material dimensions (Posner 1991; 2003). In order to conceptualize the complex ways in which picturebooks respond to their cultural contexts of production and reception it seems useful to analyze their relations to both textual and visual cultural resources. The term 'textual resources' was coined by James Wertsch in his study *Voices of Collective Remembering* (2002) and adapted by Birk (2008) to refer to the products of culturally and historically variable narratives and narrative practices, as well as to narrative patterns circulating within heterogeneous/hybrid, plural, and dynamic culture(s). Indigenous children's books draw on the textual resources of their cultures, including oral and written narratives, but also (if they are published in English) words or sentences from Indigenous languages. The concept of 'visual resources' constitutes a complementary category encompassing the heterogeneous, plural, diachronically variable and hybrid visual heritage of a culture. But, like the text, the images may draw upon a cultural repertoire in many different ways; hence these visual resources include artistic styles and practices, as well as artifacts and non-linguistic semiotic systems.

3 Visualizing culture(s): An analysis of illustrations in First Australian children's books

The following discussions of selected illustrations of Indigenous picturebooks from Australia do not represent the attempt at providing an analysis of text-image relations that is as exhaustive as possible; instead, they will only focus on selected strategies of 'visualizing culture(s)'. The first attempt at employing the concept of 'visual resources' discusses the picturebook *The Quinkins* (1978),

---

[3] For more precise accounts of tools for image analysis (including temporal dimensions and motion), see Cadden 2010; Kress and van Leeuwen (2006 [1996]); Painter et al. (2013).

a picturebook by Dick Roughsey and Percy Trezise that won the 1979 Picture Book of the Year Award (see Foster et al. 1995, 48) and was turned into a film in 1982 (see Lees and MacIntyre 1993, 355).

Dick Roughsey, whose skin name[4] Goobalathaldin can be translated as 'rough sea', was born in 1924 near Mornington Island in the Gulf of Carpentaria (see Lees and MacIntyre 1993, 369). He was "[o]ne of the most important illustrators in Australia from the late 1970s into the 1980s" (Foster, Finnis and Nimon 1995, 204) and chairman of the Aboriginal Arts Board in 1976. His twenty-four-year long collaboration with the pilot Percy Trezise (see Lees and MacIntyre 1993, 369) was a very productive phase, also documented in the *Storymaker* series (see Lees and MacIntyre 1993, 370).[5] As Lees and MacIntyre (1993, 370) observe: "Roughsey and Trezise's retellings of traditional stories were among the first picture-books to present Aboriginal culture to children. The graphic storytelling and pictures, which depict a wide range of Australian landscapes, ensure an enduring appeal" (see Ross Johnston 2017, 169–170). Readers encounter Quinkins in two narratives which belong to the Yalanji people of Cape York, *The Quinkins* (1978) and *Turramulli the Giant Quinkin* (1982).

Quinkins are figural elements featured in the textual and visual resources of the Yalanji tribe, whose homeland is in the Cape York region of Queensland. As Trezise (1969, 85) points out: "Quinkans [sic] have many shapes and forms and as many names"; so it is not surprising that they are anything but easy to interpret.[6] Referring to his First Australian sources, Trezise sees Quinkins mainly as ancestral beings who played important roles in initiation and burial ceremonies (see Trezise 1969, 132). In his reference work *Aboriginal Mythology*, Mudrooroo (1994, 138–139) addresses the various spellings of their name and calls them "spiritual embodiments of lust"; he highlights their relevance in Indigenous Dreamtime stories and their close relation to the Mimi spirits of North Australia, and mentions that they can be found in the rock art galleries at Laura, Cape York (see Mudrooroo 1994, 106–107).

The relevance of these Quinkin caves can be grasped more clearly by drawing on the research of Percy Trezise. Trezise and Dick Roughsey/Goobalathaldin

---

[4] The term 'skin name' refers to certain subsections within the highly complex First Australian systems of clanship/kinship, see Morphy (2000).

[5] For an account of Roughsey/Goobalathaldin's life and publications, see Lees and MacIntyre (1993, 369–370); for biobibliographical information on Percy Trezise, see Lees and MacIntyre (1993, 419–420).

[6] Mainly due to the fact that pre-contact First Australian cultures were predominantly oral, various notations and names exist for the Quinkins. Even in Trezise's publications different spellings are used without marking any semantic differentiation.

played a key role in the re-discovery of the Quinkin rock art galleries in Cape York in the 1960s. Scholars assume that this kind of rock art in North Queensland flourished during the so-called 'Great White Phase', i.e. 5000–8000 years ago (see Trezise 1993, 119). But radiocarbon dating by Alan Watchman showed other drawings in the same area, for example the back wall of the Sandy Creek site, to be even older. Trezise (1993, 196) remarks: "Watchman obtained a series of radiocarbon dates which show that the wall was painted by Aboriginal artists on at least three occasions – 6500 years ago, 16,000 years ago and 24,600 years ago. This is the oldest dated evidence for rock painting in Australia." In other words, the images of the mythical Quinkins are tens of thousands of years old.

But these images did not remain inside the caves: what is relevant here is that they became visual resources for a children's book. Already the first sentence of *The Quinkins* reads "From the beginning the Yalanji tribe belonged to the beautiful country of Cape York" (Trezise and Roughsey/Goobalathaldin 1978, n. p.). This, in combination with the sunrise in the background, conveys the idea that the Yalanji and their homeland have been closely linked since the dawn of time, or better: since 'deep time',[7] and affirms that the people belong to the land – not the other way round. Readers can already spot the very first Quinkin of the book on the painting on the wall of the cave.

This is not only an impressive beginning for a story, it also makes a clear political statement. In order to put the argument more clearly, it is necessary to see the representation of Quinkins as elements of First Australian visual resources in light of the *terra nullius* doctrine as explained by Irene Watson (2007, 17):

> The belief in European supremacy legitimized the violent theft of all things Aboriginal – our lands, our lives, our laws and our culture. It was a way of knowing the world, a way which continues to underpin the continuing displacement of Aboriginal peoples. The legal foundation of the Australian state was based on the white supremacist doctrine of *terra nullius*, […] and the idea of backward black savages roaming over vast tracts of open wastelands. Until the High Court decision in *Mabo*, […] *terra nullius* applied in Australian law. The doctrine applied even though Aboriginal people had been here for many thousands of years; our histories were long. *Terra nullius* made black invisible; the question of 'Aborigines' being free to roam was irrelevant, for in law we were non-existent.

This means that in the context of Australian colonial history with its *terra nullius* doctrine as legitimizing fiction for the appropriation of an entire continent, for the establishment of European ownership of the land, any reference to the

---

[7] See Kennedy and Nugent (2016, 65): "The concept of deep time has particular purchase in the context of Indigenous scales of memory in Australia, which precede written history, and which through the notion of 'country' extend offshore to encompass the sea and its creatures."

fact that the country had been inhabited by people before the Europeans arrived, exemplified here by the use of the Quinkins as visual resources, must, then, be a subversive strategy challenging the colonial master narrative. Taking the fact into account that *The Quinkins* was published in 1978, it can be concluded that many years before the so-called 'Mabo decision' by the Australian High Court in 1992 overturned the *terra nullius* doctrine, this First Australian picturebook already took a stand.[8]

But this is not the only functional potential of text-image synergy in this picturebook. Readers are not only invited into a fictional construction of a First Australian world but are also provided with opportunities to learn about Indigenous cultures – about the Quinkins for example. This is partly due to the framing strategies in *The Quinkins*; William Moebius emphasizes the significance framing techniques may have on the reader's perception of a story. Moebius (1996, 150) argues: "The code of the frame enables the reader to identify with a world inside and outside the story. Framed, the illustration provides a limited glimpse 'into' a world. Unframed, the illustration constitutes a total experience, the view from 'within'." In terms of frames, *The Quinkins* seems to be somewhere between the two opposites identified by Moebius. The text is set off from the image on a white background. But due to the double-page layout the images are huge and impressive, and are thus in all likelihood what captures the reader's imagination first.

Consequently, the text can firstly provide both Indigenous and non-Indigenous readers with a "glimpse 'into' a world" (Moebius 196, 150) by explanations; as a matter of fact quite a lot of information is provided, for example, on the differences between the various kinds of Quinkins. Trezise differentiates between two main Quinkin shapes, both of which can be seen on the cave wall depicted in the picturebook: the thin, abstract line figures called Timara, and the smaller Imjim with claws and often enlarged (possibly genital) extremities. These two Quinkin manifestations are found, for example, in the Giant Horse Gallery, the Quinkin Mountain Gallery, and the Quinkin Cave (see Trezise 1993, 198). But not only the illustration presents both kinds of Quinkins, in the caption below they are also introduced and commented on:

> The Imjim were small, fat-bellied, bad fellows, with large ugly heads, long teeth and claws. They stole children and took them to their cave in the great red mountain called Boonbalbee. [...] Timara was the name of the other Quinkins. They were humorous, whimsical spirits who liked to play tricks on people, but they didn't like the Imjim

---

[8] On the relevance of narratives for appropriation processes of (home-)land, see Said (1993, xiii) and Ching and Pataray-Ching (2018, 290).

> stealing children and always tried to stop them. The Timara were very tall – almost as tall as the trees – and so skinny that they lived in the cracks of the rocks. (Trezise and Roughsey/Goobalathaldin 1978, n. p.)

This strategy of mediating cultural knowledge to the readers is complemented by the technique of 'inviting' the reader in, and here the text provides "a total experience, the view from 'within'" (Moebius 1996, 150). For the Quinkins do not remain on the cave walls: later in the story, the Timara come out of their cracks in the rocks and confront the Imjim in order to save the children. In these scenes, the Quinkins are situated on the same ontological level as the protagonists; they are as visible and 'alive' as the human characters. In turn, the readers are allowed to watch what is happening from 'within' as if they were positioned right behind a rock in the narrated world. Consequently, it can be stated that the synergy between text and image in *The Quinkins* may support processes of transgenerational cultural and intercultural learning by providing, for example, in-depth knowledge on Quinkins as well as by affirming the vitality of the Indigenous culture.

The second set of picturebook examples refers to text-image synergies drawing on First Australian visual resources that can be associated with the evolvement of Papunya Tula Art, which is related to so-called 'sand dot painting'. This episode is intimately connected with the issue of White influence on Australian Indigenous art. In Papunya, First Australians

> had been resettled from their ancestral lands and found in painting ways to preserve their Dreamings and pass them on to the next generation. [...] Geoffrey Bardon was the first one to make available to that end the wall of the school building and then materials such as paint and canvas, and this is considered one of the original sparks, even a *sine qua non*, for the development of contemporary Aboriginal art. (Wolf et al. 2010, 15)

But, in order to avoid the perpetuation of the master narrative (namely that White influence was required for Indigenous art to flourish) on the origins of contemporary First Australian art, these authors are careful to state that the beginnings of this art cannot be reduced to "Geoffrey Bardon's activity as a teacher in Papunya in 1971." For, "important as that event was, it is merely the beginning of one of many different traditions of contemporary art by Indigenous Australians" (Wolf et al. 2010, 14). A little later "the Indigenous-organized artists' cooperative Papunya Tula Artists was founded" (Wolf et al. 2010, 15), and this has been active up to the present day.

In the picturebook *Roughtail: The Dreaming of the Roughtail Lizard and Other Stories Told by the Kukatja* (Greene et al. 1992), Papunya Tula-style illustrations are only one of the many strategies employed to stimulate the awareness of the Indigenous cultural heritage and to advance transgenerational cultural and intercultural learning. The Dreamtime stories taken from the textual resources of the Kukatja of Malarn, Yaka Yaka and Wirrumanu communities are introduced by a map which ties the stories to the region of their origin – an impression which is further strengthened by the information the authors give about themselves in short first-person comments at the end of the book. All narratives are provided in Kukatja and English so that, together with a pronunciation guide and a word list, they can encourage language acquisition. Complementary chapters include 'stories and kinship', with comments on the relevance of storytelling in the communities and an elaborated explanation of Kukatja kinship systems, while 'notes on Kukatja' allows readers to gain insights into the sound system of Kukatja and offers a pronunciation guideline. But it is especially the use of recurring visual elements (representing, e.g., 'creek' or 'fire') and their explanation that contributes to the mediation of cultural knowledge. Readers can learn the meaning of certain sign complexes, which may even help them understand images by other artists. In other words, the illustrations support a specific visual literacy: the ability to 'read' the images, to unlock their 'visual code' – a powerful instance of text-image synergies.

My final example is taken from Danny Naiura's *Tales of My Grandmother's Dreamtime* (2002). This is again a text which works with First Australian oral traditions. The narratives, including First Australian linguistic items, are part of the textual resources of the Burramadagal Clan of the Dharrug (Parramatta River area, New South Wales). They often explain the shape and behavior of animals and are illustrated with images that are also reminiscent of the Papunya Tula style. Moreover, like *Roughtail*, the text offers an explanation of single image elements, a 'reader's guide', about which Naiura (2002, 7) comments: "[I]t should not be considered comprehensive nor absolute, because various tribal interpretations and individual expression is not [sic] rigidly bound." But this is not the only support the author offers for understanding the stories. On some pages the illustrations are far less abstract than those in the previous example; the dots do not correspond to signs, but are grouped together in a way which almost turns them into a mosaic. In this book the images seem to help – especially from the point of view of non-Indigenous readers – to gain an understanding of and access to First Australian art.

While these images may certainly appear attractive to younger children, they are by the same token vulnerable to appropriation by the tourism and advertising industries. With reference to Graham Huggan's (2001) concept of the 'postcolonial exotic' the question needs to be asked whether some First Australian children's books may constitute elements in "the worldwide trafficking of culturally 'othered' artifacts and goods" (Huggan 2001, 28). Alternatively, the use of Indigenous art forms in children's books by Indigenous writers and artists can be seen as an act of reappropriation of art that has been commodified. The characteristic synergy of picturebooks, with their complex and highly dynamic relationship between text and image, may, in fact, counteract any simple "commodification of cultural difference" (Huggan 2001, 33). Only a close scrutiny of the text-image synergy in the individual text can provide a valid basis for hypotheses regarding the functions the book might fulfill.

4 Conclusion

As the examples have shown, the synergy between text and image and the relation of these two components to the textual and visual resources of a given culture can perform considerable cultural work. Cultural or collective functional potentials of representations of visual resources in First Australian picturebooks include, e.g., the subversion of one of the prevalent master narratives of colonial Australia, the *terra nullius* doctrine, the affirmation of the vitality of First Australian cultures, and the support of intercultural learning processes. On an individual level, 'reading' the illustrations and text-image relations certainly reinforces, for example, the transgenerational transfer of cultural knowledge, as well as the development of a specific competence, 'visual literacy' (see Brill and Branch 2007; Saada-Robert 1997), which, in light of the reading material drawn upon, needs to be conceptualized not merely as an ability rooted in specific cultural contexts but also as a transcultural competence.

In a final step it remains to be asked how this is relevant to cultural narratology or to the research area of narrativist studies of culture. Instead of pretending to be able to answer this question, let me rather return to the discussion by expressing the hope that the concept of 'textual' and 'visual resources' may be useful, for example, for highlighting the complex cultural relativity and transculturality of semanticized narrative and visual forms as well as for drawing the readers' attention to the fact that 'narrative worldmaking' may be understood less as a single 'planetary' process but rather in an 'interstellar' sense, as a potential referring to many (transcultural) 'worlds'.

References

Bateman, John A. *Text and Image: A Critical Introduction to the Visual/Verbal Divide*. London: Routledge, 2014.
Beckett, Sandra L. *Crossover Picturebooks: A Genre for All Ages*. New York: Routledge, 2012.
Birk, Hanne. *AlterNative Memories: Kulturspezifische Inszenierungen von Erinnerung in zeitgenössischen Romanen indigener Autor/inn/en Australiens, Kanadas und Aotearoas/Neuseelands*. Trier: WVT, 2008.
Boillat, Alain, and Françoise Revaz. "Intrigue, Suspense, and Sequentiality in Comic Strips: Reading *Little Sammy Sneeze*." *Narrative Sequence in Contemporary Narratology*. Eds. Raphaël Baroni and Françoise Revaz. Columbus: The Ohio State University Press, 2016. 107–129.
Brill, Jennifer M., and Robert M. Branch. "Visual Literacy Defined – The Results of a Delphi Study: Can IVLA (Operationally) Define Visual Literacy?" *Journal of Visual Literacy* 27.1 (2007): 47–60.
Cadden, Mike (ed.). *Telling Children's Stories: Narrative Theory and Children's Literature*. Lincoln: University of Nebraska Press, 2010.
Ching, Stuart, and Jann Pataray-Ching. "The Centrality of Hawaiian Mythology in Three Genres of Hawai'i's Contemporary Folk Literature for Children." *The Routledge Companion to International Children's Literature*. Ed. John Stephens. New York: Routledge, 2018. 289–299.
Colomer, Teresa, Bettina Kümmerling-Meibauer, and Cecilia Silva-Díaz (eds.). *New Directions in Picturebook Research*. New York: Routledge, 2010.
Doonan, Jane. *Looking at Pictures in Picture Books*. South Woodchester: Thimble Press, 1992.
Doonan, Jane. "Sharing Picture Books with Adolescent Students: A Training in Visual Literacy." *Die Wahrnehmung von Bildern in Kinderbüchern – Visual Literacy*. Ed. Schweizerisches Jugendbuch-Institut. Zürich: Chronos, 1997. 53–72.
Foster, John E., Ern Finnis, and Maureen Nimon. *Australian Children's Literature: An Exploration of Genre and Theme*. Wagga Wagga: Centre for Information Studies, Charles Sturt University, 1995.
Greene, Gracie, Joe Tramacchi, and Lucille Gill. *Roughtail: The Dreaming of the Roughtail Lizard and Other Stories Told by the Kukatja/Tjarany: Tjaranykura Tjukurrpa ngaanpa kalkinpa wangka tjukurrtjanu*. Broome: Magabala Books, 1992.
Herman, David. "Toward a Transmedial Narratology." *Narrative Across Media: The Languages of Storytelling*. Ed. Marie-Laure Ryan. Lincoln: University of Nebraska Press, 2004. 47–75.
Huggan, Graham. *The Postcolonial Exotic: Marketing the Margins*. New York: Routledge, 2001.
Hunt, Peter (ed.). *Children's Literature: The Development of Criticism*. New York: Routledge, 1990.
Hunt, Peter (ed.). *International Companion Encyclopedia of Children's Literature*. New York: Routledge, 2004.
Jahn, Manfred. *A Guide to Narratological Film Analysis. Poems, Plays, and Prose: A Guide to the Theory of Literary Genres*. http://www.uni-koeln.de/~ame02/pppf.htm. Version: 1.7. English Department, University of Cologne, 2003 (8 August 2018).
Kafalenos, Emma. "Narrativizing the Matrix." *Narrative Sequence in Contemporary Narratology*. Eds. Raphaël Baroni and Françoise Revaz. Columbus: The Ohio State University Press, 2016. 151–160.

Kennedy, Rosanne, and Maria Nugent. "Scales of Memory: Reflections on an Emerging Concept." *Australian Humanities Review* 59 (2016): 61–77.
Kress, Gunther, and Theo van Leeuwen. *Reading Images: The Grammar of Visual Design*. London: Routledge, 2006 [1996].
Lees, Stella, and Pam MacIntyre. *The Oxford Companion to Australian Children's Literature*. Oxford: Oxford University Press, 1993.
Lesnik-Oberstein, Karin (ed.). *Children in Culture: Approaches to Childhood*. Basingstoke: Macmillan, 1998.
Lewis, David. "The Constructedness of Texts: Picture Books and the Metaficitive." *Signal* 62 (1990): 131–146.
Losowsky, Andrew. "Introduction." *Visual Storytelling: Inspiring a New Visual Language*. Eds. Robert Klanten, Sven Ehmann, and Floyd Schulze. Berlin: Gestalten, 2011. 4–7.
McHale, Brian. "Narrativity and Segmentivity, or, Poetry in the Gutter." *Intermediality and Storytelling*. Eds. Marina Grishakova and Marie-Laure Ryan. Berlin: de Gruyter, 2010. 27–48.
Moebius, William. "Introduction to Picturebook Codes." *Word & Image* 2.2 (1996): 141–158.
Morphy, Howard. "Kinship, Family, and Art." *The Oxford Companion to Aboriginal Art and Culture*. Eds. Sylvia Kleinert and Margo Neale. South Melbourne: Oxford University Press, 2000. 60–67.
Mudrooroo. *Aboriginal Mythology*. London: Thorsons and HarperCollins, 1994.
Naiura, Danny. *Tales of My Grandmother's Dreamtime*. Mascot: Bartel, 2002.
Nikolajeva, Maria, and Carole Scott. *How Picturebooks Work*. New York: Garland, 2001.
Nodelman, Perry. *Words about Pictures: The Narrative Art of Children's Picture Books*. Athens, GA: The University of Georgia Press, 1988.
Nünning, Ansgar. "Narrativist Approaches and Narratological Concepts for the Study of Culture." *Travelling Concepts for the Study of Culture*. Eds. Birgit Neumann and Ansgar Nünning. Berlin: de Gruyter, 2012. 145–183.
Painter, Clare, J.R. Martin, and Len Unsworth. *Reading Visual Narratives: Image Analysis of Children's Picture Books*. Sheffield: Equinox, 2013.
Passalacqua, Franco, and Federico Pianzola. "Conclusion: Epistemological Problems in Narrative Theory: Objectivist vs. Constructivist Paradigm." *Narrative Sequence in Contemporary Narratology*. Eds. Raphaël Baroni and Françoise Revaz. Columbus: The Ohio State University Press, 2016. 195–217.
Posner, Roland. "Kultur als Zeichensystem: Zur semiotischen Explikation kulturwissenschaftlicher Grundbegriffe." *Kultur als Lebenswelt und Monument*. Eds. Aleida Assmann and Dietrich Harth. Frankfurt a.M.: Fischer, 1991. 37–74.
Posner, Roland. "Kultursemiotik." *Konzepte der Kulturwissenschaften: Theoretische Grundlagen – Ansätze – Perspektiven*. Eds. Ansgar Nünning and Vera Nünning. Stuttgart: Metzler, 2003. 39–72.
Ross Johnston, Rosemary. *Australian Literature for Young People*. South Melbourne: Oxford University Press, 2017.
Ryan, Marie-Laure (ed.). *Narrative across Media: The Languages of Storytelling*. Lincoln: University of Nebraska Press, 2004.
Ryan, Marie-Laure. "Fiction, Cognition, and Non-Verbal Media." *Intermediality and Storytelling*. Eds. Marina Grishakova and Marie-Laure Ryan. Berlin: de Gruyter, 2010. 8–26.

Saada-Robert, Madelon. "The Child's Cognitive Representation of Picture-Text Literature: A Constructivist Approach." *Die Wahrnehmung von Bildern in Kinderbüchern – Visual Literacy*. Ed. Schweizerisches Jugendbuch-Institut. Zürich: Chronos, 1997. 107–123.

Said, Edward. *Culture and Imperialism*. New York: Vintage Books, 1993.

Schwarcz, Joseph H. and Chava Schwarcz. *The Picturebook Comes of Age: Looking at Childhood through the Art of Illustration*. Chicago: American Library Association, 1991.

Sipe, Lawrence R. "Revisiting the Relationships between Text and Pictures." *Children's Literature in Education* 43.1 (2012): 4–21.

Sipe, Lawrence R. "How Picture Books Work: A Semiotically Framed Theory of Text-Picture Relationships." *Children's Literature in Education* 29.2 (1998): 97–108.

Sipe, Lawrence R., and Sylvia Pantaleo (eds.). *Postmodern Picturebooks: Play, Parody, and Self-Referentiality*. New York: Routledge, 2008.

Thon, Jan-Noël. *Transmedial Narratology and Contemporary Media Culture*. Lincoln: University of Nebraska Press, 2016.

Trezise, Percy J. *Quinkan Country: Adventures in Search of Aboriginal Cave Paintings in Cape York*. Sydney: Reed, 1969.

Trezise, Percy J. *Dream Road: A Journey of Discovery*. St. Leonards: Allen and Unwin, 1993.

Trezise, Percy J. and Dick Roughsey/Goobalathaldin. *The Quinkins*. Sydney: Collins, 1978.

Trezise, Percy J. and Dick Roughsey/Goobalathaldin. *Turramulli the Giant Quinkin*. Milwaukee: Gareth Stevens, 1988 [1982].

Watson, Irene. "Settled and Unsettled Spaces: Are We Free to Roam?" *Sovereign Subjects: Indigenous Sovereignty Matters*. Ed. Aileen Moreton-Robinson. Crows Nest: Allen and Unwin, 2007. 15–32.

Wertsch, James V. *Voices of Collective Remembering*. Cambridge: Cambridge University Press, 2002.

Wolf, Falk, Emily Joyce Evans, and Kasper König. "Remembering Forward – Introduction." *Remembering Forward: Australian Aboriginal Painting Since 1960*. Eds. Kasper König, Emily Joyce Evans, and Falk Wolf. London: Museum Ludwig and Paul Holberton Publishing, 2010. 8–19.

Wolf, Werner. "Intermediality." *The Routledge Encyclopedia of Narrative Theory*. Eds. David Herman, Manfred Jahn, and Marie-Laure Ryan. New York: Routledge, 2005a. 252–256.

Wolf, Werner. "Pictorial Narrativity." *The Routledge Encyclopedia of Narrative Theory*. Eds. David Herman, Manfred Jahn, and Marie-Laure Ryan. New York: Routledge, 2005b. 431–435.

Stella Butter
Troubling Justice: Narratives of Revenge

Abstract: Taking its cue from the current popularity of the revenge tale, this article investigates the cultural functions that the revenge genre fulfils as a distinct way of worldmaking. Giorgos Lanthimos' film *The Killing of a Sacred Deer* (2017) serves as an exemplary case study for this purpose due to its complex engagement with revenge templates. A brief historical sketch of the revenge genre helps delineate how Lanthimos' film carefully up-dates generic conventions in its engagement with wounded masculinity, flawed bourgeois ideals of the good life, and the alienated world of modernity. *The Killing of a Sacred Deer* ultimately sets itself up as an operating theater dispassionately dissecting the anatomy of storied retributive violence through grotesque defamiliarization. Far from presenting violence as a cure for social or individual malaise, Lanthimos' references to mythic and religious templates suggest that the complexity of social life and violence resists neat translation into culturally available plots. Not only is the relationship between revenge and justice troubled in the film, but the narrative transformation of violence into vengeance and justice is also critically foregrounded. The discussion of the revenge genre in the article demonstrates how cultural narratology deepens our understanding of the cultural work performed by genres over time.

1 Setting the scene: The craze for revenge stories in past and present

Contemporary culture is marked by a craze for revenge stories. In politics, a spirit of revenge is fueled by populist movements across Europe and the United States, whose crude political message "avoids the inherent complexities of public policy-making and offers hope, or change, or simply revenge" (Gaston 2016), as it taps into people's anxieties and sense of disenfranchisement in an age of globalization. The populist leader typically adopts the role of "the defender and the avenger" (Anselmi 2018, 43) of the common people against 'the elites' – a fact that has not been lost on the press or political analysts, who characterize populist politicians as "the new

https://doi.org/10.1515/9783110654370-010

avengers"[1] and frequently explain the support for populist movements as an act of revenge against the establishment.[2] A case in point is the threat issued by the Hungarian Prime Minister Viktor Orban during an election rally on 15 March 2018. Orban presented himself as an avenger of the common people against the global elite and announced that after the elections "moral, legal and political revenge" would be taken on his opponents, who had been colluding with foreign powers to undermine his administration's efforts to prevent an influx of migrants (Deutsche Welle, n. p.). The craze for revenge stories and action further feeds on the strong presence of fundamentalist discourses and the reverberations of the rhetoric of counter-terrorism in the wake of 9/11, with its calls for blood revenge against evil-doers. How easily a retributive rhetoric is reactivated can be seen in Donald Trump's notorious statement in 2017 that Kim Jong-un's threats against the USA would be "met with fire and fury like the world has never seen" (Pramuk 2017, n. p.). Further examples of the topicality of revenge in contemporary culture can easily be found in many different areas, e.g. lively debates concentrating on the misuse of the internet for heinous acts such as revenge porn, which entails the uploading of sexually explicit or nude pictures or videos to exact revenge on a chosen victim.

Popular culture reflects and shapes this widespread obsession with revenge. One need only think of the high ratings of television series such as *24* (2001–2010; see season eight, episodes 17–20) and *Revenge* (2011–2015), blockbusters like *V for Vendetta* (2005) and *John Wick* (2017), or the continued popularity of rape-revenge movies, e.g. the remake of *I Spit on Your Grave* (2010) with its three further parts (2013; 2015; planned release of the third part in 2018). Prize-winning independent movies such as the horror-comedy *From Jennifer* (2017), which depicts the female protagonist on a vengeance mission after having become a victim of revenge porn, contribute to the varied mix of revenge stories in circulation. The pronounced obsession with revenge tales and

---

[1] Fieschi (2004) with reference to UKIP and the BNP. See also, for instance, the characterization of Marine le Pen as "the blonde angel of vengeance" in the German press (Veiel 2017, n. p.; my translation).
[2] Scholars have commented on the "three-part plot structure" of populist narratives, which speak "of 'a glorious past, a degraded present, and a utopian future'" (Levinger, 2013, p. 123). By articulating 'highly stylized and exaggerated visions of the nation's past, present, and future conditions,' such mythic histories create 'emotional tension that can be used to mobilize the participants in the movement to avenge the nation's suffering' (Ibid; see also Levinger & Lytle, 2001)" (Levinger 2017, 5). On the "strikingly coherent narrative based on blame, victimhood and revenge" (Gerodimos 2013, 614) propagated by far left populism in Greece, see Gerodimos (2013).

vengeful actions has even induced scholars such as Kyle Wiggins to describe our times as "a vengeful age" (2018a, 16).[3]

If we do indeed live in such an age, then the need to take a closer look at how revenge is imagined through storytelling in popular culture takes on added urgency, no matter how ostensibly unpolitical many of these stories may seem. It is through storytelling that violence is transformed into vengeance, and the narrative of revenge typically concentrates on a specific type of violence – one that is concerned with questions of justice, fairness and punishment. Narrative patterns embed violent acts into a chain of causality, endow them with a distinct meaning and emotional charge (e.g. experienced violence as tantamount to a painful loss of honor or as indicative of intolerable social injustice), distribute roles (the offender, the victim, the avenger) and in this way enable individuals and collective bodies to make sense of past violence in such a way that further violence may be incited or legitimized. Revenge stories provide orientation in times of crisis or conflict precisely because their configuration of "past, present and future in a comprehensible plot" (Nünning 2012b, 75) "sketch[es] out the future course of action" (Nünning 2012b, 74) in terms of exacting payback.[4] Hence analyzing current tales of revenge promises insight into how revenge functions as a cultural narrative.

Approaching the genre of the revenge story from the perspective of cultural narratology means identifying how this genre becomes contemporary at different times. In his conceptualization of cultural and historical narratology, Ansgar Nünning (2012a) persuasively argues that "[w]hat is needed for the development of a fully-fledged cultural narratology is both a narrative, or narrativist, theory of culture, [...] and a culture-oriented theory of narrative that considers the dimensions of cultural contexts" (161). Especially pertinent for such an agenda, Nünning goes on to explain, is the question how culturally generic repertoires and plots help "turn experiences into meaningful narratives" (2012a, 164). Taking its cue from Nünning's agenda as outlined in these passages, the present article reflects on how the time-honored genre of revenge narrative speaks to contemporary audiences through its "cultural way of worldmaking" (Nünning 2012a, 166).

Genres do not become contemporary simply by being recycled in the present: what we perceive and categorize as 'contemporary', Theodore Martin urges, is based on "a strategy of mediation" (2017, 5) between present and past. Genres

---

3 For an excellent overview of revenge as a prominent theme in contemporary American literature and film, see the contributions in Wiggins (2018c).

4 Ansgar Nünning (2012b) does not refer to revenge stories, but to how metaphors and narratives construct what we call 'crises' or 'catastrophes'. Nevertheless, many of his astute observations also have a bearing on the structure and functions of revenge as a cultural narrative.

unfold such a strategy inasmuch as they "contain the entire abridged history of an aesthetic form while also staking a claim to the form's contemporary relevance" (Martin 2017, 6).[5] The genre of the revenge story provides continuity on the one hand in the form of familiar explanatory blueprints for violence and on the other by adapting these blueprints to an array of present needs.

Ever since antiquity, critics of the revenge story have traced its mutating forms and functions – i.e. its 'contemporariness'; and it is a genre that tends to become especially popular in times of socio-political transformation and instability. This was the case, for example, with the crowd-pleasing Renaissance revenge tragedy. In Early Modern England, concerns were raised due to the "largely informal, unwritten and unsystematic body of law" (Pollard 2012, 60), the push of the Tudor state toward the establishment of a centralized system of power, which stripped aristocratic classes of specific prerogatives and rights (e.g. the right to exert legitimate violence), and the development of a market economy, to name just a few key factors (see Pollard 2012, 60; Steenbergh 2009, 169). The Early Modern revenge tragedy dealt with these worrisome upheavals by updating older generic traditions, especially the Senecan model of tragedy, which saw true revenge as not just balancing the account through symmetrical payback but required the avenger to surpass the original offense. This explains the high body-count in many revenge tragedies. The legacy of the revenge tragedy is noticeable in the history of film and television genres. Lesel Dawson draws attention to how 1960s gangster films hark back to Renaissance forms by featuring a male "socially isolated figure with whom the audience feels an uneasy sympathy" (2014, 121), the failure of social institutions, a focus on family reputation and codes of masculinity, and a "revel[ing] in 'male-dominated violence and excessive body counts' [Griggs 121]" (2014, 121). In this way, the gangster film both modernized and encapsulated an 'entire abridged history' of the revenge story.

As the example of the gangster movie shows, sexual politics loom large in revenge films. Given the traditional strong association between violence and masculinity and the feminization of the victim position, this is hardly surprising. Indeed, many revenge films transform revenge into a means for healing modern wounded and fragile masculinity. In contrast, the rape/revenge-movies from the 1970s onward granted the female avenger, the furious woman meting out retribution for her sexual violation, center stage. This emergent variant of the revenge story does not, as critics emphasize, simply coincide with the women's movement, but was enabled by it (see Clover 1993, 77). By presenting the

---

5 On the challenges of writing a history of genre(s), see Neumann and Nünning (2007). For a helpful discussion of criteria that may be used to define genres, see Nünning (2007).

victim's perspective on rape (see the extended depiction of rape scenes in, e.g., *I Spit on Your Grave* (1978)), these films unflinchingly foreground the horrifying female experience of living in a 'rape culture.'[6] While the extent of the feminist politics in many of these rape/revenge-movies remains debatable, their mutation of the revenge genre prompts audiences to reflect on the violence inherent in the unjust gender system and what it takes to make necessary changes there.

A more recent trend in the revenge genre on screen is the spate of US films that envision private revenge as a valuable service to the general public. Kyle Wiggins discusses how films such as *Batman Begins* (2005) set up villains as embodiments of failures in complex systems so that the execution of vengeful punishment appears as a cure for systemic dysfunctionality (2018a, 16). These films address modern anxieties over the perceived uncontrollable complexity of an age of networks whose sprawling socio-political structures and institutions seem impervious to individuals or groups seeking redress for their grievances. Here the "interpersonal (or clan-based) blood feuds of classical revenge tragedies [are replaced] with a trope of symbolic transfers" (Wiggins 2018b, 155) where the villains stand in for perplexing institutional and organizational structures. The vengeful urge is no longer sutured to defending one's self-worth or self-esteem, as in many other revenge stories, but instead transmutes into "a measure of structural injustice" (Wiggins 2018b, 155).

Wiggins uses these two variants of vengeful desire to distinguish between different traditions of revenge story, which he dubs talionic and ultionic. Talionic stories (from *lex talionis* – the 'eye-for-an-eye' principle) are primarily concerned with "sat[ing] the damaged self" (Wiggins 2018b, 159), whereas the ultionic tradition directs the focus onto "systemic retribution" (Wiggins 2018b, 155). Wiggins's choice of the term 'ultionic' (from the Latin *ultio* = 'revenge'), was inspired by a passage from George Bernard Shaw's play *The Admirable Bashville* (1901), in which a police officer seeks revenge "on behalf of a [disembodied] principle", namely "the broken law", thereby establishing revenge as a selfless "act undertaken for the citizenry" (Wiggins 2018b, 160). Unlike Shaw's play, American ultionic stories, Wiggins remarks, typically fuse a selfish interest in personal payback with the need to settle a collective injustice so that revenge appears as simultaneously "selfish and selfless" (2018b, 160).[7]

While the preceding historical sketch of the revenge genre is far from offering an overview of its manifold varieties and functions, these pointers will help situate

---

6 For an in-depth analysis of sexual politics in *I Spit on Your Grave* and on transformations of the low brow rape-revenge movie, see Clover (1993).
7 For an in-depth discussion of the *ultion* in modern American literature and film, see Wiggins (2018b).

individual revenge films within the broader field of generic continuity and change. In the remainder of this article, I will discuss Giorgos Lanthimos' *The Killing of a Sacred Deer* (2017), a UK-Irish co-production, as an especially intriguing example of how contemporary Western cinema critically engages with the genre of the talionic revenge story as "a way of worldmaking, i.e [an emotive and] cognitive force in its own right" (Nünning 2012a, 160). Lanthimos' film sets itself up as an operating theater where the anatomy of violence, revenge, and sacrifice is dissected, thereby troubling both popular notions of retributive justice and bourgeois ideals of the good life. My analysis of the film will first concentrate on how it embodies the "accretive history of [the revenge] genre" (Martin 2017, 6), before probing its specific reworking of revenge templates.

2 *The Killing of a Sacred Deer* as an unsettling tale of revenge

For those versed in Greek mythology, the title of Lanthimos' film already conjures up revenge as a central theme. It was Agamemnon who killed one of Artemis's sacred deer, which provoked the goddess to punish him by putting all the winds to rest so that he and his army could not sail to Troy. As only the sacrifice of his daughter Iphigenia would appease vengeful Artemis, Agamemnon, after some initial reluctance, has her killed. The underlying structure of this myth, namely transgressive killing by an offender and the retributive blackmailing of this offender into the sacrifice of an innocent family member, is replicated in *The Killing of a Sacred Deer*.

In Lanthimos' film the affluent cardiologist Steven Murphy, who lives and works in Cincinnati, befriends the teenager Martin to assuage the guilt he feels over his botched surgery of Martin's father three years ago, which left the father dead on the operating table. Although Steven never confesses his surgical error, the film provides clear indications of his guilt. The anesthetist who assisted at the operation, for example, insists that Steven operated under the excessive influence of alcohol. This backstory of malpractice is, however, only gradually revealed, so that a sense of mystery prevails: for a long time it remains unclear what connects the successful surgeon with the bland teenager. While Martin seems initially to nurse hopes of restoring his nuclear family by playing matchmaker between his mother and Steven, he morphs into Steven's nemesis when these hopes are thwarted, calmly informing Steven that if he does not kill a member of his own family – i.e. his wife Anna, his 14-year-old daughter Kim or his 12-year old son Bob – then all of Steven's family will fall sick and die within days. After finally acknowledging that the paralysis of his children and their bodily degeneration are indeed a manifestation of Martin's vengeance, Steven decides to meet Martin's condition. He leaves the choice of his victim up to chance by blindfolding himself before pointing his shotgun at the family members gathered around him. After Bob's death, the remaining child, Kim, is restored to health, just as Martin had determined.[8]

These bare bones of the story already offer evidence as to how *The Killing of a Sacred Deer* retains specific structural elements of the Greek intertext but also departs from it in important ways. While Lanthimos' film reproduces the vengeful demand for sacrificial payment, it eschews the spiral plot structure that marks subsequent events in the Greek intertext. In the ancient myth, Iphigenia's sacrifice sparks off a whole chain of vengeance: vengeance for her daughter's death is one of the motives that drives Clytemnestra to murder her husband; Agamemnon's death is then avenged by Orestes, who kills his mother. Such a spiral structure suggests that revenge begets revenge in a never-ending cycle. Precisely this vicious circularity is foregrounded, for instance, in Seneca's *Agamemnon*, which gloomily relinquishes all hopes of social renewal (see Schiesaro 2014). Although the plot structure of *The Killing of a Sacred Deer* avoids such a spiral of vengeance in favor of a single retributive act, its reference to the Greek myth points to the lurking danger of unbounded revenge that cannot easily be broken: vengeful killing *per se* does not stop. By invoking this alternative development as a haunting presence, Lanthimos' film questions the ideological premise of a specific strand of revenge narratives, namely that the act of retribution can offer closure and protection from further harm (see, for example, *The Virgin Spring* [Swedish: *Jungfrukällan*] (1960); *An Eye for An Eye* (1996)).

The Killing of a Sacred Deer is strongly indebted to the talionic revenge genre, whose many tropes it carefully rehearses.[9] On the level of plot, revenge typically entails the repetition of the original transgressive act. In authoring his revenge plot, the godlike Martin departs from the Senecan model of excessive revenge by emphasizing the perfect symmetry of his master-minded retribution. Having murdered a member of Martin's family, Steven must now "balance

---

[8] Despite its title, deer play absolutely no role in Lanthimos' film, but he does include images of them in his mise-en-scène. The wood paneling of the restaurant where the main characters meet at the beginning and end of the film displays elements of nature, among them deer. A further reference to the myth is Kim's school paper on Iphigenia.

[9] The following brief discussion of generic features is based on a large body of research on revenge tragedy and contemporary revenge films, in particular Kerrigan (2000), Greenblatt (1997), Dawson (2014), McHardy (2008), Pollard (2012), and Clover (1993).

things out" (Lanthimos 2017, 48:20) by losing kin himself. Vengeance takes on the guise of a "repeat with a difference" (Dawson 2014, 123). One aspect of this difference is that Martin's target must know exactly what is happening and why. He is told that he is undergoing a fitting punishment for a previously perpetrated crime. It is precisely this fittingness that differentiates the avenger's deed from vulgar crime: it is an act not simply of common murder but of customized punishment, and as such it must be placed in the open by commenting on it (see Kerrigan 2000, 16–17). The avenger, then, has the "impulse to display, where the murderer's urge is to conceal" (Kerrigan 2000, 17).

However, the driving force of the revenge plot is typically not only a "desire for essential equilibrium" (Kerrigan 2000, 10), but also a need for restoration. The aspiration to restore the past through revenge is foregrounded in Lanthimos' film when Martin abruptly replaces the romance mode, geared toward resurrecting his lost nuclear family through a union between his mother and Steven, with that of revenge. The effortlessness of this replacement points to how "[r]evenge tragedy [or stories] and romance both [...] engage with fantasies of restoring what has been lost" (Dawson 2014, 123),[10] the repetition of the past being guided by the impulse to change it and in doing so to rewrite the painful present. This point is driven home when we learn that *Groundhog Day* (1993), a movie that depicts the redemptive change of the present through altering the past, is not only Martin's favorite film, but also the movie he plays when arranging a film evening between Steven and his mother in pursuit of his attempted matchmaking.

The Killing of a Sacred Deer shares with many other contemporary revenge narratives the concern with a wounded masculinity that needs to be restored. Martin appears desperate for a father figure. The masculine self is shown to be based on emulation: all the male characters in the movie at one point compare themselves to their fathers or to a surrogate father figure. The strong identification with the father is highlighted when Martin explains his compulsion to take revenge by literalizing what he calls a metaphor. He first fiercely bites Steven in the arm and then bites a piece of flesh out of his own arm to demonstrate that the only way to feel better about a wrong one has suffered is by having the deed repaid in kind. His action also establishes a nexus between revenge and sacrifice: the debt can only be absolved through the 'sacrifice' of one's own flesh or kin, as in the Agamemnon story. And as Martin is at this point

---

10 For a fascinating analysis of how the interplay between the genres revenge tragedy and romance shapes conceptualizations of revenge, see Dawson (2014).

justifying his revenge, the act of biting flesh out of his own body visualizes his perception of his father as an extended self. Losing him meant losing part of himself, and he conceives his revenge as redressing this loss. Given the imbrication of his juvenile fantasy of restorative violence with emulative masculinity, it seems only logical that the sacrificial victim should be Steven's son Bob rather than his daughter Kim. It is worth noting, however, that emulative masculinity not only provides orientation in the film, but is also depicted as a source of anxiety, e.g. when Steven bizarrely shares with his son the secret that as an adolescent he was frightened at the amount of semen his father ejaculated.

Martin's approach to the *lex talionis* principle illustrates the logic of compensation that marks revenge tales: revenge is about payback. Despite the pronounced economic register in revenge discourse, this compensation must be paid in kind: it cannot simply be replaced with money. Thus while Martin accepts Steven's presents and money, this does not assuage his thirst for revenge. Such a *lex talionis* conceptualizes justice as solely retributive: the wrong has been righted if offenders are made to suffer in proportion to their crime. In contrast, notions of restorative justice do not concentrate on punishment or suffering, but on what the offender could do to make amends to the victim. It is entirely in keeping with the idea of retributive justice when Martin insists that murdering a family member will enable Steven to start with a "clean slate" (Lanthimos 2017, 1:25:28). Critics have been quick to point out that the typical structure of repetition in revenge tales, the re-enactment of the original crime, suffuses this kind of retributive justice with moral ambiguities. Martin acknowledges such an ambiguity by introducing a split between justice and fairness. When Anna complains that she does not understand why she and her children should have to pay the price for what her husband has done, he answers: "I don't know if what is happening is fair, [...] but it is the only thing I could think of as close to justice" (Lanthimos 2017, 1:14:16–1:14:25).

This dialogue not only complicates notions of 'justice', but also indicates how core values of individuals and society are shaped by the history of genres, in this case by the talionic revenge story. Given the long tradition and continued pervasiveness of this genre in Western societies, it is no coincidence that Martin could only think of ensuring something 'close to justice' in terms of classical retribution. Moreover, he perceives the retribution plot as the "only one way to make you [= Steven] and me both feel better" (Lanthimos 2017, 1:26:21). Exemplified in the Iphigenia myth, the genre of the talionic revenge story provides Martin with a template with which to transform the devastating loss he has suffered into a coherent narrative and, by doing so, to gain a script for what he considers curative action. This is not simply retributive violence, it is *storied* retributive violence.

If Martin acts from a generic script to make himself feel better, then this conjures up an admittedly warped version of what Ansgar and Vera Nünning have discussed as the "salutogenetic power or potential of narratives" (2017, 169). The term 'salutogenesis' was coined by the sociologist Aaron Antonovsky to theorize how health and wellbeing (salutogenesis) depend on one's ability to deal with stress, which in turn hinges on one's sense of coherence. The latter requires "narrative competence" (Nünning and Nünning 2017, 169):

> [N]arrative is among the crucial ways in which human beings comprehend what is happening in their lives [...] by creating mental models of the characters, contexts, events, and settings that constitute a story (see Emmott 1997). [...] [S]torytelling and the acquisition of narrative authority [...] is also a way of [...] enhancing one's sense of manageability. (Nünning and Nünning 2017, 167)

The scene in which Martin bites Steven and himself is not only a metaphor of the alleged healing power of action in fulfillment of the *lex talionis*, it also highlights his way of transforming literary templates such as metaphors, or the revenge story genre itself, into flesh and blood. Authoring a talionic revenge plot allows Martin to wield absolute control and to impose a clear generic order on his world. However, the film questions this chosen strategy of resilience by casting a dubious light on the ability of the revenge genre formula to ensure justice and a quick curative fix for the ruptured, disconnected (male) self.

In Lanthimos' film, the probing of the revenge genre as a curative-redemptive formula is closely tied to a diagnosis of modern alienation. One of the most striking features of the film is the stilted, banal and at times bizarre dialogue, rendered in monotonous voices, between the main characters. These mechanical dialogues bespeak an estranged world devoid of any lasting emotional or cognitive intimacy, an absence that becomes obvious in Steven's constant lying. Even sexual intimacy between the Murphy couple is only achieved when Anna mimics an anesthetized body, equating sexual intercourse with necrophilia. The impression of an alienated, isolating world is intensified by the visual leitmotif of glass, which suggests invisible walls between characters, or that they are dealing with reflections and shadows rather than with real persons (see Fig. 1). Moreover, characters are frequently portrayed as lost in the vast spaces of a built environment that seems inhospitable to human scale (see Fig. 2). At the same time, the sound design of the film introduces an ominous, foreboding quality that one reviewer has called "auditory migraine" (Scott 2017).

It is important to note that this alienated world is not devoid of violence. Significantly, most of the scenes take place in the hospital where Steven works as a cardiologist, and in the Murphy home. The sterile hospital takes on gothic qualities due to the eerie sound design in combination with the depiction of vast labyrinthine spaces; characters walk through empty corridors whose length is emphasized by the use of deep focus (see Fig. 3). The labyrinthine nature of this space is visualized by a picture of a maze hanging on the wall of a hospital corridor (see Fig. 3). The hospital, a synecdoche for the modern world of systemic, scientific rationality, is transformed into an impenetrable repetition of the ever same, and it is precisely in this inhospitable space that the transgression of bodily prohibitions becomes socially accepted: the integrity of the human body is routinely violated as bodies are cut open, organs taken out, etc. While the horror movie genre has long capitalized on the two-edged nature of hospitals as sites of healing and bodily 'violation' (e.g. *Hospital Massacre* (1982)), Lanthimos' film eschews gory excesses and replaces them with the beheading and gutting of a fish in preparation for a meal – a coded presentation of routine surgical procedures as acts of violence. The gutting of a fish is performed by Matthew Williams, the anesthetist who had assisted at the botched operation on Martin's father, under the watchful eye of Steven, whom he had invited over with Anna for a barbecue. As Matthew prepares the fish, his wife passes him a knife with the words "There you go, doctor" (Lanthimos 2017, 34:00) – a scene suggesting that Martin's father was gutted like a fish, with equally cold efficiency, on the operating table. The dismal imagery leaves no doubt that the godlike doctors (see the religious music in the film) are harbingers of death rather than salvation.

Ultimately, the brutalizing hospital environment can be seen to encapsulate the alienating quality of a modern life-world. It is telling that the distinction between hospital space and home space becomes increasingly blurred when the Murphy family home is transformed into a medical care-home for their paralyzed children. As both the hospital (site of malpractice) and family home (site of Bob's murder) ultimately emerge as crime scenes in Lanthimos' film, there is no haven or reprieve from the violence of modernity.

It is in keeping with the trope of modernity as a condition of alienation that the American Dream is presented as sugar-coating violence, class hierarchies, and zombification. The affluent Murphy family live the American Dream, complete with a luxurious suburban home in an upper-class white neighborhood, two well-achieving children, and successful careers as doctors. This bourgeois version of the 'perfect life' can only be maintained by living an insulated existence behind glass: living, so to speak, in a real-life metaphor, where – and perhaps where alone – the awareness of the corruption and emotional sterility of that world can be repressed. With his quest for vengeance, Martin disrupts these empty scripted routines and strategies of evading uncomfortable truth. Not only does he represent the aggressive attack of a lower social class, whose own home is located well away from the Murphy neighborhood, he also indexes the return of the repressed corrupt past in the form of Steven's lethal malpractice. All in all, the revenge theme is instrumental to the films social critique of zombified life in contemporary America, with its false promise of comfortable, protective insulation against the pressures and pitfalls of modernity.[11]

In contrast to political propaganda or many other revenge films, *The Killing of a Sacred Deer* does not offer revenge and sacrifice as a quick solution to individual and social malaise. Instead, it unfolds a troubling anatomy of the relentless logic that drives vengeance plots, thereby estranging narrative vengeance patterns themselves. Retributive violence is no longer ideologically naturalized or rendered just; instead, the film's strategies of defamiliarization, especially the distancing of the audience from the characters through the stilted dialogues and, for instance, god-shots (see Fig. 2), encourages viewers to adopt a reflective attitude to what they are witnessing. And what they see is that revenge is neither cathartic nor curative, but grotesquely, implacably continuous. A closer look at the plot and character development makes this clear. Thus when Steven finds it impossible to decide which family member to murder, he places all three in a half circle around him, blindfolds both them and himself, then spins quickly in a circle, so that the choice of his target is left to chance or fate. While the impossibility of choosing his victim is understandable, the fact remains that this set-up is geared toward relieving Steven from at least some responsibility for his action: the murder of his son is not *per se* deliberate – which simply perpetuates his pattern of not accepting full accountability for his actions.

Spinning in a circle implies that nothing has changed on a deep structural level, and this motif, too, runs through the whole film. The replaceability of family members is discussed by Anna when she tells Steven that it would be logical to kill one of their children because they could have another one. Indeed, the sacrifice Martin requires only brings the egoism of the family members to the fore, as each is set on surviving at the cost of the others. Kim's offer to sacrifice herself for her family rings hollow in this respect, because it sounds as if she is frantically rehearsing the obligatory script of a good daughter to win her father's favor, for fear of having angered him by her attempt to escape the cursed family home. The ending of the film also appears as oddly anti-climactic. After the murder of Bob, the family sits calmly in the diner where Steven used to meet Martin. The parents look haggard and drawn. Martin comes in, significant looks are exchanged, and the Murphys leave. The plates of fast food

---

[11] Many reviewers have picked up on the critical staging of a zombified or sterile modernity in *The Killing of a Secret Deer*, see e.g. Lane (2017).

in front of them, onto which Kim squirts copious amounts of blood-red ketchup, can be read as an indication that the endless cycle of violence, conformity and sameness will remain. Moreover, there are no clear signs that Martin feels better after having exacted his revenge. In this light, the auditive framing of the movie with music referencing Christ's redemptive crucifixion and resurrection is at first glance puzzling: the film begins with "Jesus Christus schwebt am Kreuzel" from Schubert's *Stabat Mater* and ends with "Herr, unser Herrscher" from Bach's *St. John Passion*.[12]

Reviews and online discussions of the film show many viewers grappling with this puzzling quality. Some reviewers, for instance, wonder whether Martin is supposed to represent Artemis and if it makes sense to see Bob as Jesus sacrificed by the loving Father. However, neither the storyline of Agamemnon's sacrifice of Iphigenia nor the references to Christ's crucifixion can be seamlessly applied to the film's constellation of characters and its unfolding plot. Instead of vainly trying to pigeonhole the characters into such preset roles, it is more helpful to think of the intertextual allusions as an implicit commentary on revenge narratives and the appropriate response to violence.

The Greek allusions firmly locate the replacement of the judicial system with a vengeful sacrificial system in a mythic world, and by the same token bring out the 'otherness' of blood revenge in the world of modern systems of power and knowledge. At the same time, however, the reference to antiquity in a modern tale of blood revenge suggests that the desire for revenge is a basic human trait – witness its preeminent place in the history of Western storytelling. Moreover, the intertextual allusion highlights the role of templates and models in legitimizing vengeful violence. The references to Christ's crucifixion in the film's musical score, for instance, establish a jarring contrast to the revenge myth. After all, the New Testament is all about teaching forgiveness instead of revenge – a clash of approaches that foregrounds the urgent need to reflect on the patterns and plots we use to respond to and make sense of violence. Finally, a corollary of the fact that neither the mythical plot nor the religious framework can be neatly applied to the character constellation of *The Killing of a Sacred Deer* raises our awareness that the complexity of social life evades neat translation into templates.

Ultimately, *The Killing of a Sacred Deer* sets itself up as an operating theater that dispassionately dissects the anatomy of storied retributive justice through grotesque defamiliarization. The opening scene of the film, an extreme close-up

---

[12] At first glance, the opening scenes of the film, in which the depiction of heart surgery is overlaid with sacral music, serve to establish medicine (or science) as the modern equivalent to religion, complete with its own gods (the doctors). As the analysis has shown, such a view is then, however, thoroughly undermined.

of a heart undergoing operation, highlights the color blue of the surrounding medical fabric (see Fig. 4). The dominance of blue throughout the movie, ranging from blue clothes and interior décor to details such as the name of the restaurant – the Blue Jay – where Steven (and later his family) meet Martin, may then be read as highlighting how the fabric of the film, its narrative universe, is equally engaged in a delicate operation that cuts to the heart of Western culture – an operation revealing the deep entrenchment there of narrative templates of revenge and sacrifice.

3 Conclusion: The filmic anatomy of revenge

The Killing of a Sacred Deer suggests that a curative dimension for the malaise of modernity and fragile (male) selves lies not in easily applicable revenge formulas or catharsis but rather in pushing audiences into asking critical questions about how narrative templates shape our understanding of, and response to, violent retribution and sacrifice. Given the simplistic formulas of revenge – as an act of justice, as redemptive catharsis, or as individual and/or social cure – touted in contemporary political rhetoric and flaunted in many mainstream revenge movies, Lanthimos' film serves as a valuable intervention in the troubling tales we tell ourselves about achieving justice and healing.

It is a sign of our turbulent times that the revenge narrative is wide-spread in contemporary literature and film. Fictions of payback are arguably well-suited both to gauging the socio-political and economic inequalities that bedevil societies in a globalized world and to projecting the wish-fulfillment that the suffering individual can actually achieve justice through violent means of his or her own (cf. Wiggins 2018a, 11). While my case study has concentrated on the popular talionic motif, it is worth noting a proliferation in our own century of ultionic storytelling, with its concern for a wider structural redress of violence and injustice. A film like *Law Abiding Citizen* (2009), for example, portrays the corrupt American legal system as a target for revenge. The upsurge of *ultio* in contemporary revenge tales has even prompted Kyle Wiggins to call this model "the new revenge story" (Wiggins 2018b, 155).

A distinction that cuts across talionic and ultionic storytelling concerns the question whether a revenge tale nods to the redemptive restoration of order – or even to a better order – after vengeance is satisfied. *The Killing of a Sacred Deer* is not the only text that departs from this hallmark of most traditional revenge stories; an ever-growing number of current revenge tales does so, too. "In the stories America tells", Kyle Wiggins notes, "revenge has evolved from violent satisfaction into inexhaustible desire" (2018a, 2), as avengers go on a murderous spree that makes their addiction to killing blatantly manifest (e.g. *John Wick: Chapter 2* (2017)). One might add that popular television series such as *Game of Thrones* (ongoing since 2011) suggest that the thirst for revenge is never sated, its infectious cycle demanding an ever-mounting death toll. Here too we see that the many variants within the vengeful storytelling genre assess the possibility of achieving closure or equilibrium through vengeance very differently.

All in all, the revenge genre, through its imaginative exploration and evaluation of the psychosocial dynamics of vengeance, performs important cultural work. From a cultural-narratological perspective it shapes "communities of values" (Nünning 2012a, 174) inasmuch as shared revenge narratives "not only serve social communication about values and norms" surrounding retributive violence "but also ensure that cultural [revenge] models are archived and remembered in cultural memory" (Nünning 2012a, 174). In an age obsessed with revenge narratives, both in the realm of fiction and beyond, the need to critically dissect the narrative patterns activated to legitimate retributive violence becomes all the more pressing. Far from being simple entertainment, many fictions of revenge provide valuable prompters for reflecting on the troubled relationship between revenge and justice.[13]

---

[13] My warm thanks in this respect go to Dorothee Birke, Marcus Menzel, and the editorial team for their helpful feedback on an earlier version of this article.

Appendix: Images from *The Killing of a Sacred Deer*

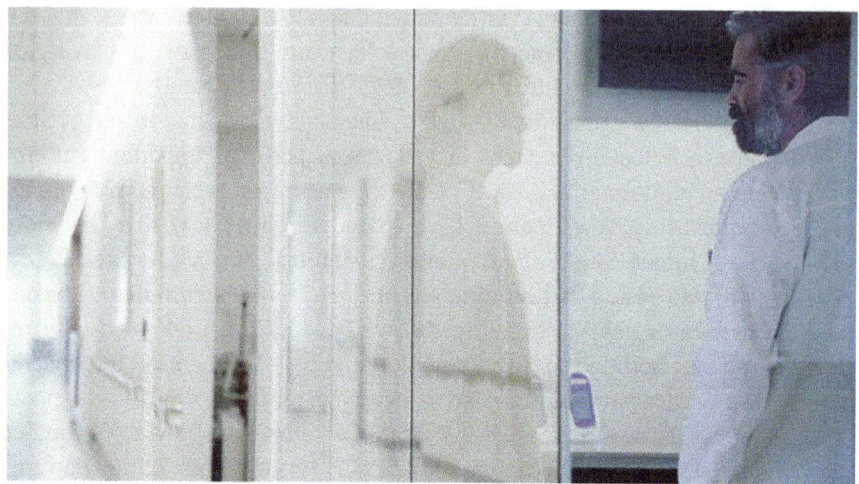

Fig. 1: Shadow Selves.

Fig. 2: Looking at Specimens.

Fig. 3: Gothic Labyrinth.

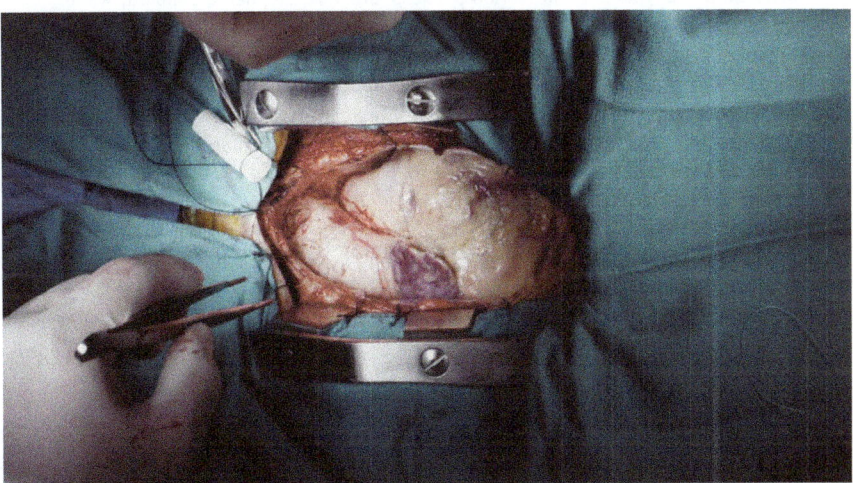

Fig. 4: Heart Operation.

References

Anselmi, Manuel. *Populism: An Introduction*. London: Routledge, 2018.
Clover, Carol J. "High and Low: The Transformation of the Rape-Revenge Movie." *Women and Film. A Sight and Sound Reader*. Eds. Pam Cook and Philip Dodd. London: BFI and Scarlet Press, 1993. 76–85.
Dawson, Lesel. "Revenge and the Family Romance in Tarantino's *Kill Bill*." *Mosaic* 47.2 (2014): 121–134.
Deutsche Welle. *Hungary's PM Viktor Orban Warns of Immigration Threat at National Day Rally*. https://p.dw.com/p/2uQA0. 15 March 2018 (6 October 2018).
Emmott, Catherine. *Narrative Comprehension: A Discourse Perspective*. Oxford: Clarendon Press, 1997.
Fieschi, Catherine. *The New Avengers*. https://www.theguardian.com/politics/2004/jun/15/thefarright.uk. The Guardian, 15 June 2004 (12 June 2018).
Gaston, Sophie. *Honest Speaking in the Post-Truth Politics Age*. https://www.demos.co.uk/blog/honest-speaking-in-the-post-truth-politics-age/. The Demos Blog, 9 August 2016 (14 September 2018).
Gerodimos, Roman. "The Ideology of Far Left Populism in Greece: Blame, Victimhood and Revenge in the Discourse of Greek Anarchists." *Political Studies* 63.3 (2013): 608–625.
Greenblatt, Stephen. "Hamlet." *The Norton Shakespeare*. Eds. Stephen Greenblatt, Walter Cohen, Jean E. Howard, and Katherine Eisaman Maus. New York: Norton, 1997. 1659–1667.
Kerrigan, John. *Revenge Tragedy: Aeschylus to Armageddon*. Oxford: Clarendon Press, 2000 [1996].
Lane, Anthony. *'The Killing of a Sacred Deer' and 'The Square'*. https://www.newyorker.com/magazine/2017/10/30/the-killing-of-a-sacred-deer-and-the-square. The New Yorker, 30 October 2017 (16 September 2018).
Levinger, Matthew, and Paula F. Lytle. "Myth and Mobilisation: The Triadic Structure of Nationalist Rhetoric." *Nations and Nationalism* 7.2 (2001): 175–194.
Levinger, Matthew. *Conflict Analysis: Understanding Causes, Unlocking Solutions*. Washington, DC: United States Institute of Peace, 2013.
Levinger, Matthew. "Love, Fear, Anger: The Emotional Arc of Populist Rhetoric." *Narrative and Conflict: Explorations of Theory and Practice* 6.1 (2017): 1–21. https://journals.gmu.edu/NandC (3 October 2018).
Martin, Theodore. *Contemporary Drift: Genre, Historicism, and the Problem of the Present*. New York: Columbia University Press, 2017.
McHardy, Fiona. *Revenge in Athenian Culture*. London: Duckworth, 2008.
Neumann, Birgit, and Ansgar Nünning. "Einleitung: Probleme, Aufgaben und Perspektiven der Gattungstheorie und Gattungsgeschichte." *Gattungstheorie und Gattungsgeschichte*. Eds. Marion Gymnich, Birgit Neumann, and Ansgar Nünning. Trier: WVT, 2007. 1–28.
Nünning, Ansgar. "Kriterien der Gattungsbestimmung: Kritik und Grundzüge von Typologien narrativ-fiktionaler Gattungen am Beispiel des historischen Romans." *Gattungstheorie und Gattungsgeschichte*. Eds. Marion Gymnich, Birgit Neumann, and Ansgar Nünning. Trier: WVT, 2007. 73–100.
Nünning, Ansgar. "Narrativist Approaches and Narratological Concepts for the Study of Culture." *Travelling Concepts for the Study of Culture*. Vol. 2. Eds. Birgit Neumann and Ansgar Nünning. Berlin: de Gruyter, 2012a. 145–183.

Nünning, Ansgar. "Making Crises and Catastrophes – How Metaphors and Narratives shape their Cultural Life." *The Cultural Life of Catastrophes and Crises*. Eds. Carsten Meiner and Kristin Veel. Berlin: de Gruyter, 2012b. 59–88.

Nünning, Ansgar, and Vera Nünning. "How to Stay Healthy and Foster Well-Being with Narratives, or: Where Narratology and Salutogenesis Could Meet." *How to Do Things with Narrative: Political and Narratological Perspectives on Anglophone Texts*. Eds. Jan Alber and Greta Olson. Berlin: de Gruyter, 2017. 157–186.

Pollard, Tanya. "Tragedy and Revenge." *The Cambridge Companion to English Renaissance Tragedy*. Eds. Emma Smith and Garrett A. Sullivan Jr. Cambridge: Cambridge University Press, 2012 [2010]. 58–72.

Pramuk, Jacob. *Trump Warns North Korea Threats 'Will Be Met with Fire and Fury'*. https://www.cnbc.com/2017/08/08/trump-warns-north-korea-threats-will-be-met-with-fire-and-fury.html. CNBC, 8 August 2017 (6 October 2018).

Scott, A.O. *Review: 'The Killing of a Sacred Deer' Depicts Familiar Torment*. https://www.nytimes.com/2017/10/19/movies/the-killing-of-a-sacred-deer-review-colin-farrell-nicole-kidman.html. New York Times, 19 October 2017 (14 September 2018).

Schiesaro, Alessandro. "Seneca's *Agamemnon*: The Entropy of Tragedy." *Pallas* 95 (2014): 179–191. http://journals.openedition.org/pallas/1726 (7 October 2018).

Steenbergh, Kristine. "Green Wounds. Pain, Anger and Revenge in Early Modern Culture." *The Sense of Suffering: Constructions of Physical Pain in Early Modern Culture*. Eds. Jan Frans van Dijkhuizen and Karl A. E. Enenkel. Leiden: Brill, 2009. 165–188.

The Killing of a Sacred Deer. Dir. Yorgos Lanthimos. Element Pictures, A24 and Film4, 2017.

Veiel, Axel. *Marine Le Pen: Der blonde Racheengel der Rechten*. http://www.fr.de/politik/marine-le-pen-der-blonde-racheengel-der-rechten-a-1247259. Frankfurter Rundschau, 27 March 2017 (6 October 2018).

Wiggins, Kyle. "Introduction." *American Revenge Narratives: A Collection of Critical Essays*. Ed. Kyle Wiggins. Cham: Palgrave Macmillan, 2018a. 1–19.

Wiggins, Kyle. "The Modern American Revenge Story." *American Revenge Narratives: A Collection of Critical Essays*. Ed. Kyle Wiggins. Cham: Palgrave Macmillan, 2018b. 153–173.

Wiggins, Kyle (ed.). *American Revenge Narratives: A Collection of Criticial Essays*. Cham: Palgrave Macmillan, 2018c.

Guido Isekenmeier
Erin Burnett in Mali: Bardic Television and the Genealogy of Cultural Narratology

Abstract: This article traces back some of the concerns of a cultural narratology (namely, its emphasis on the narrative construction of world models and cultural communities) to earlier engagements with the ideological dimensions of mass-mediated narratives in cultural studies. Drawing on Fiske and Hartley's theory of 'bardic television', it highlights the complexities of context for news narratives and the persistence of cultural configurations supporting them, in an attempt to come to terms with the transformation of news culture in the wake of new digital media formats framing current events. In an analysis of a 2013 CNN piece on the situation in Mali, it demonstrates the continued deployment of bardic television's strategies in recent television news reporting, which indicates an adherence to journalistic standards made obsolete by internet, media. This, in turn, seems to explain some of the problems of traditional news media in adapting to the changes in political discourse over the last decades (most pervasively in the Trump era).

1 Introduction

The "project of a cultural narratology" (Nünning 2009, 63) entails a double move away from purely formalist considerations of narrative technique and from codified bookish variants of narrative (as found in literature, historiography, etc.). Instead, the focus is on the ideological work performed by narratives and the perennial formats of "small stories" (Bamberg and Georgakopoulou 2008). Within this framework, it seems plausible to look back to (British) cultural studies approaches to the analysis of 'minor' narratives, which have always focused on ideological import. In a genealogy of cultural narratology of sorts, such a backward glance o'er travel'd roads (to borrow from Whitman) might serve as a reminder that some of the functional hypotheses formulated as a result of the "opening of narratology to cultural history" (Nünning 2009, 64) have at least partly been anticipated by earlier attempts to address the cultural workings of narrative.

https://doi.org/10.1515/9783110654370-011

As news media are among the most routine producers of culturally significant stories, I suggest to revisit Fiske and Hartley's (1989) analysis of news narratives, which takes the perceived similarities between contemporary television and the traditional bard as its starting point. Their model of 'bardic television' provides a useful account of the complexities of actual narrative situations involving not only typical formal features (narrative modalities), but also socio-institutional framings, discursive positionings, and mediatized formalities. Only by coming to terms with the way these variables sediment into conventional narrative forms can narratology lay claim to a delineation of the culturality of narrative.

Incidentally, the emergence of the idea of bardic television tells a story about the origins of cultural studies of narrative that differs from the 'polygenetic' origin story of cultural narratology. While the latter emphasizes that each of the "disciplinary traditions of narrative research" (Nünning 2012, 150), for instance in linguistics, literary studies, historiography, psychology, etc. has "developed its own narrativistic approach and established its own research fields and traditions" (Nünning 2012, 157), Fiske and Hartley's point of departure is a concept – bardic literature – already established in another disciplinary field – Celtic studies – where it has been used to shed light on the forms and functions of storytelling in the transition from oral to literary culture. Transferred to television news, the concept serves to elucidate aspects of the cultural function of news narratives – their socially centripetal orientation – currently at stake in the transition from a television-centered mediascape to one gravitating around internet media that are redefining the nature of mass communication.

The brief outline of the theory of bardic television provided in this article, and its application to a near-contemporary example (taken from CNN's *Erin Burnett OutFront*), constitute an attempt to delineate the contours of a media landscape radically changed by the advent of 'social' media, with the opportunities they afford for data mining and the manipulation of public opinion, from targeted advertising to election meddling. If ever there was a question as to whether they were going to change the parameters of public discourse, the 2016 US presidential election and the UK's Brexit referendum have demonstrated their revolutionary effects. Above all, they testify to the demise of television as the primary news medium. And yet, the following look at what *was* bardic television might contribute obliquely to a history of the present state of the news inasmuch as it tries to answer the question why the traditional news media are in crisis (conceptually rather than financially) and have yet to find a working model for the age we live in.

2 Bardic television

Fiske and Hartley's attempt to come to terms with the ideological work of television – and of television news in particular, from which their only extended example is drawn ("Here is the news", 1989, 91–100) – envisages television as "a social ritual [...], in which our culture engages in order to communicate with its collective self" (Fiske and Hartley 1989, 85). The general framework for their approach is thus anthropological: television performs the work of 'ritual condensation', "converting ideas, products of the mind (mentifacts) into material objects" (Leach 1976, 37; cit. Fiske and Hartley 1989, 90). And their overall emphasis is functional: they are concerned with the effects of ritual condensation on the television audience, and their concern culminates in ordered lists enumerating such effects, for example: "2. To *implicate* the individual members of the culture into its dominant value systems"; or "6. To *convince* the audience that their status and identity as individuals is guaranteed by the culture as a whole" (Fiske and Hartley 1989, 88).

When it comes to the structure of the communicative acts of television (news) and of the 'material objects' which make up the program, Fiske and Hartley have recourse to a model of literary, if not wholly literate, provenance: "the idea of television as our own culture's bard" (1989, 85). The stratagem is as simple as it sounds, drawing an extended parallel between contemporary television and the Anglo-Saxon *scop* (the Old English minstrel): "When we use the term *bard* it is to stress certain qualities common both to this multi-originated message and to more traditional bardic utterances" (Fiske and Hartley 1989, 85). In other words, 'bardic television' is a "comparative concept, proposing a similarity between the social role of television and that of the bardic order in traditional Celtic societies" (Hartley 2002, 16). In functional respects, television is the modern equivalent of the "maker and teller of tales in oral cultures" (Hartley 1988, 104).

As is typical for a conceptual transfer of this kind, some aspects of the model have to be modified, even when they are located in a dimension generally figured as analogical. Take, for instance, the double position of the (traditional) bard, whose task is to mediate on the one hand "between the rulers and patrons who license and pay them, and society at large" (Hartley 2002, 17), and on the other between "the audience with which it [the bardic role] communicates and the reality to which it refers" (Fiske and Hartley 1989, 86–87). That reality, however, in the case of the bardic epic, is a more or less distant, more or less mythologized past – think of *Beowulf*'s dealing with the heathen Danish ancestors of the Christian Anglo-Saxons to which it was addressed – while in the case of television news, it is the spatially distant, but temporally recent news-cycle of current events (for an application of Fiske and Hartley's concept to a 'historiographic' television genre see Stephenson 1983). At the same time, while the actors involved in the production and reception of the bardic message have changed – from rulers and patrons and a courtly audience to media institutions and broadcasting audiences – its function is still to mythologize (in Barthes' sense, 2009) culturally prevalent attitudes in a way that makes them appear natural. The bard's role is invariably to "guarantee that the meanings constructed [...] are not mere propaganda, either for the government, the 'establishment' or anyone else" (Hartley 1988, 106) by implicating the audience in that construction in such a way that the articulation of "(dominant) 'reality'" (Hartley 1988, 106) need not be "consciously apprehended by the viewer in order to have been successfully communicated" (Fiske and Hartley 1989, 87).

Although they occasionally refer to the various bards as "storytellers" (Hartley 1988, 103), Fiske and Hartley's use of terms commonly associated with communications studies ('message') or social anthropology ('ritual') might seem to question the view that the concept of bardic television encompasses narrative, or indeed any formal characteristics at all. The closest they get in their theoretical formulations to explicating such features is in their references to a "specialised rhetorical language" (Hartley 2002, 17) employed by television (news), which, however, has only a very rough correspondence with traditional bardic forms: "The traditional bard rendered the central concerns of his day into verse. We must remember that television renders our own everyday perceptions into an equally specialised, but less formal language system" (Fiske and Hartley 1989, 86).

In fact, Fiske and Hartley seem largely unfamiliar with the scholarship in 'oral-formulaic theory', which originated in Milman Parry's studies of Homer in the 1930s (Parry 1987), was carried over into an Old English context starting with Lord's 1949 dissertation (2000) and subsequently produced rich narratological material revolving particularly around the various points of view employed in *Beowulf* (from, say, Culbert 1963 to Richardson 1997 and beyond; see, for Homer, de Jong 2001, 2004). At best, they take note of this strain of criticism indirectly and belatedly, for instance via its appropriation in cultural studies by, for instance, Raymond Williams, whom Hartley (1988, 104) sees as having "put our notion of the bardic function back into the historical context of traditional Celtic societies". This may be taken to indicate that the concept was already 'on the move' before arriving in Fiske and Hartley's work, but it also makes one painfully aware of the shortcomings of their presentation of it.

One of the central features they ascribe to both bardic constellations, for example, is that "the bardic voice is oral" (Fiske and Hartley 1989, 86). But this was not even true of the original bardic utterance, which survives in a form that is the product of a literate culture, albeit one still closely modeled on oral patterns (just as early printed books followed the layout of manuscripts), and is thus at most 'oral-derived' (see Foley 1990). And it certainly is not true of television news, whose 'speakers' are essentially readers of precomposed written material. Paradoxically, however, the analogy does hold in the light of Ong's later argument about 'secondary orality' – "essentially a more deliberate and self-conscious orality, based permanently on the use of writing and print" (Ong 1982, 133), which makes both bardic voices readable as versions of simulated orality. That they are "oral, not literate" (Fiske and Hartley 1989, 86), though, is a patently misleading statement. As for the formulaic aspect of television news: I will return to that in my sample analysis.

Fiske and Hartley's theoretical argument bypasses more narrowly narrative matters, but these surface again in their analysis of two segments from ITN's *News at Ten* of January 7, 1976. One concerns an event involving a British and an Icelandic naval ship (the *Andromeda* and the *Thor* respectively) during the so-called 'Cod Wars'. ITN's Norman Rees gives a report of this incident in which "eyewitness language changes abruptly into reporter language" (Fiske and Hartley 1989, 98) in a way reminiscent of the flexible focalization found in *Beowulf*. Rees was aboard the Icelandic boat when the incident unfolded and gives a first-person account: "I *saw* the *Andromeda* approaching *us* at high speed from the stern of the gunboat. It overtook *us* with both vessels on a converging course" (Fiske and Hartley 1989, 97, italics in the original), only to switch to reported speech at the crucial moment: "*According to Thor's skipper* ... *he* dropped his engine speed and tried to turn away to avoid a collision. But *he claims* that the frigate herself turned at the last moment so that *Andromeda*'s stern *would* sideswipe the gunboat's bow" (Fiske and Hartley 1989, 98, italics in the original).

In Fiske and Hartley's perceptive interpretation, this apparently needless change of mode (because Rees "must have been able to observe the changes in direction of each ship just as well as the skipper", Fiske and Hartley 1989, 98) serves to "mask intentional aggression on the part of the British frigate" (Fiske and Hartley 1989, 98). It culminates in an indefinitely focalized account of the impact: "The *Thor*'s deck shook under the force of collision ..." (Fiske and Hartley 1989, 98). Even more fundamental than this orchestration of perspectives, though, seems to be the replacement of the Old English bard's 'I heard' formula, which is an appeal to the authority of oral transmission (see Rumble 1964), with the 'I saw' formula of television's bardic figure. Narrative authority in the reporting of current events is founded in vision, and any account of what is going on depends on either pictures or on-site reporting for its authentication. Hence, while evidently unwilling – given that he was catering for a British audience – to report, "even at the expense of his own observation" (Fiske and Hartley 1989, 98), that the *Andromeda* had rammed the *Thor*, Rees had to begin with a first-hand account simply to establish that something did indeed happen. Only then could he go on to obfuscate the events. I will return to a still more fallacious application of the 'I saw' formula below.

Another narrative peculiarity inherited from the bardic tradition – again, with a twist resulting from their orientation toward the immediate present – is that news narratives manipulate the proairetic code, that is, they tamper with the nature of narrative as an account of a series of decisions taken and actions performed which appears consequential when looked at from its end result. Where in the bardic epic, this takes the form of exploring alternative outcomes ("and now x would have happened, had not y intervened", Louden 1996, 346), the bardic drama of television news partly depends on narrative speculation about what *will* happen (next). Such musings on the future course of events ironically tend to the conclusion that in the end nothing of consequence will happen.

That is, at least, the inference that Fiske and Hartley draw from their analysis of the other segment of the ITN news bulletin, which has ITN defense correspondent Peter Snow projecting the course of action of the Special Air Service (SAS), which was being deployed to Northern Ireland at the time. They comment: "When Snow comes to describe what the SAS will do, we are, as it were, taken behind the scenes at Battalion HQ, and initiated into the logistical minutiae of detailed planning [...]. But at the same time, the object of all this activity is systematically avoided. In every case the action is aborted into formulaic and negating phrases" (Fiske and Hartley 1989, 93). They conclude that "[a]s Snow closes his piece with the words 'that's why they, the SAS, believe that if anyone can find the killers who strike by stealth, they can', we are driven by the way the message itself is constructed towards the response 'but they can't'" (Fiske and Hartley 1989, 93–94). Such narrative defeatism, I will argue below, can also be applied to the process of decision-making itself. In fact, if Snow's account had been given in response to the question whether the SAS should be deployed at all, the (implicit) answer would have had to be 'No'.

At any rate, as narratologists, we might deplore the lack of narratological concepts in the design of Fiske and Hartley's theory, even of the term 'narrative' itself. We might also criticize that while their analyses pay due attention to *narrative form*, they are devoid of the terminological precision aspired to by narratology, and somewhat disconnected from their theoretical groundwork in addressing features of narrativity and narrative mediation. It is well-nigh impossible to ignore, though, that we are confronted here with a cultural study of narrative whose considerations of the *functions of narrative* are on the one hand inspired, however remotely, by a literary (or at least proto-literary) model, and on the other produce formulations that anticipate the functional hypotheses of cultural narratology.

Cast in the bardic role of a storytelling medium, television "articulate[s] the main lines of the established cultural consensus about the nature of reality" and "transmit[s] by these means a sense of cultural membership" (Fiske and Hartley 1989, 88) – statements which mirror (albeit in more generalized terms) Nünning's twofold claim (2012, 172) that "cultures communicate their stories in order to reach a consensus about what can be considered as normal within a given cultural framework," and that the generative function of narratives with regard to "social and cultural coherence consists in giving the audience an opportunity [...] to join a social and ideological group through storytelling" (2012, 172).

On a related note, narratives "are never merely mimetic reflections of the real world, but rather actively create models of the world" (Nünning 2012, 169); they are "involved in the actual generation of attitudes, discourses, ideologies, hierarchies of norms and values, and structures of feeling and thinking" (Nünning 2012, 160). Similarly, bardic television was meant to "overcome previous conceptualizations of the media, which concentrated on the way they were/are meant to reflect society," by emphasizing "the way the media take their mediating role as an active one" (Hartley 1988, 17) – active in the sense that it "tends to articulate the negotiated central concerns of its culture, [...] ideologies, beliefs, habits of thought and definitions of the situation" (Fiske and Hartley 1989, 89).

Cultural narratology's emphasis on the "performative power of narration" (Nünning 2012, 154) ties in well, therefore, with older cultural studies approaches to narrative that frame, for instance, the "socio-centrality" (Fiske and Hartley 1989, 89) of bardic television. The following example will illustrate the narrative complexities illuminated by that concept, while preparing a consideration of its shortcomings in the current theoretical and cultural situation.

3 War in Mali: Erin Burnett out front

The lead story of CNN's news program *Erin Burnett OutFront* on 14 January 2013[1] reported on the situation in Mali, where the French military had just begun a military intervention codenamed 'Opération Serval' following the capture of the central Malian town of Konna by Islamist forces four days previously. The account begins with an introduction using the set-up typically

---

[1] The 2:20 segment analyzed here is available at https://edition.cnn.com/videos/bestoftv/2013/01/14/exp-erin-us-and-war-in-mali.cnn (29 November 2018).

Fig. 1: *Erin Burnett OutFront*, 14 January 2013, 0:04.

employed in television news to visually represent the position of the 'television bard' (Fig. 1).

The arrangement features the aptly named 'anchor' in the studio, surrounded by the paraphernalia of CNN's corporate identity (reminiscent of Erin Burnett's 'patrons', if you like) in the lower third of the frame, backed by a picture representing the event she is reporting (the 'reality' to be mediated). She addresses the audience in classical news style and gives a summary lead answering basic questions about the event: "Good evening everyone, I'm Erin Burnett. *OutFront* tonight: War in Mali. A deadly conflict between al Qaeda-linked militants and the Malian government is escalating. And the United States is getting involved."

While the picture changes to a rudimentary map of Western Africa, which geographically situates the event in a country divided into a north-eastern half shaded in red and labeled 'Islamic Radicals Territory' and a south-western half in green registering only the location and name of the capital city, she continues: "Islamic militants who have controlled Northern Mali for months, are now threatening to take control of the entire country." This threat is captured on the map by placing the country's name, Mali, on a red background across the frontier of the two areas, visualizing the outreach of the Islamists into government-controlled territory.

Cutting to Reuters footage of French soldiers being deployed in Bamako, Burnett switches to her signature informal register to declare: "The militants' move towards the capital, Bamako, prompted France to take action over the weekend. France put boots on the ground and went all-in, bombing rebel training camps and other targets. So what will the United States do?" The poker jargon of going all-in neatly fits the familiar cognitive metaphor of war as a game/sport, but also begs the question of what exactly is at stake in this conflict – for France obviously, but also for the US. Thus Burnett arrives at what, from the point of view of CNN's American audience, is the central concern of the report ("what will the United States do?").

As with ITN's report on the deployment of the SAS to Northern Ireland, Burnett's handling of the future course of events is only partly a matter of representing official policy decisions, mediating between the tentative stance of the Obama administration on Mali – and indeed on preventive military action in general (see Woocher 2017) – and the various attitudes that might prevail among her audience, favoring anything from hawkish intervention through humanitarian assistance to detached non-interference. Her task is to cast the current situation and, in particular, its prehistory, in such a way as to forge a consensus on the likely outcome of decisions when all things are considered. This is done by a careful orchestration of official statements, the voice of the other, and Burnett's own unique and authoritative perspective, which work together toward a tacit message on the advisable course of action.

The program's reflection on the question of what the US will do starts (and ends) with the administration's stance: "A Pentagon official told me this afternoon that the US 'will participate in Mali, but' – and I wanna make sure I put quotes around this – 'is still deciding what that looks like'". Note how, besides an implied exclusivity of access ("told *me*"), the communication is carefully relayed and the policy kept at a distance by multiple quotation marks – the statement is given on-screen in inverted commas, as well as being intonationally marked by Burnett and explicitly referred to as a quote in her commentary – indicating that this might not yet be the socio-central mindset toward which her account is working.

Next up is a reminder, already anticipated by the use of military slang ("put boots on the ground"), that the American news anchor is hardly content with the role of news*reader* to which German or British television audiences are accustomed. Abruptly changing from reporter to eyewitness language (in Fiske and Hartley's formulation), Burnett explains: "Now when we went to the Mali border last summer, I saw first-hand how dangerous the situation is." The seemingly contradictory use of past perception to validate a present state of affairs ("I *saw* first-hand how dangerous the situation *is*") is legitimized by the narrative of an event unfolding over an extended period of time (remember that the Islamists "have controlled Northern Mali for months"). Similarly, it does not matter that the pictures shown of Burnett at a refugee camp in Burkina Faso (dated July 24, 2012), in which she is seen serenely talking to a woman surrounded by children, seems disconnected from what she claims to have seen ("how dangerous the situation is"). All that matters is that they support her status as witness, as one who has been in the field, out front, to directly observe what is (or rather, was) going on.

Back to the immediate present and to the reporting mode, we are presented with an attempt to give the other side of the story, as required by the journalistic code of impartiality which also produced Rees's apparent blindness in ITN's Cod War story (see Fiske and Hartley 1989, 98): "Today, we spoke to some of our sources on the ground, including the military commander of the al Qaeda-linked Islamic group Ansar Dine. He told us that the militants are – his word – 'excited' and would – his word again – 'welcome U.S. troops on the ground'. He also said the French bombs have killed civilians and that France is 'signing a death warrant for French people around the world, opening the gates of hell'. Omar says the militants will fight to the end and that this will be 'long war' 'more dangerous than Afghanistan or Iraq'." The 'source' in this instance is Omar Ould Hamaha, who acted as spokesman for both Ansar Dine and the Movement for Oneness and Jihad in West Africa (MOJWA), militant groups linked to the Algeria-based Al-Qaeda in the Islamic Maghreb (AQIM). Needless to say, it is difficult to imagine how such a figure could be "clawed back into a socio-central position" (Fiske and Hartley 1989, 87) for an American audience. Yet his words are treated just like those of the unnamed Pentagon official earlier on, verbally ("his word", "his word again") as well as visually (Fig. 2).

While Hamaha's peripheral status or "subordinate identity" (Fiske and Hartley 1989, 89) is preserved in the portrait – with a Homeric epithet exploiting his henna-dyed goatee beard and his *nom de guerre*, which derives from the AK-47 rifle, lurking at the back: red-bearded Hakka – his statements, while grotesquely hyperbolic, are rendered as matter-of-factly as the cautious announcements of a government representative. In stark contrast to his earlier portrayal as an outlandish fanatic who refuses to speak to Burnett because she is a woman ("Why Mali Matters: Al Qaeda on the Rise", 24 July 2012[2]), she now seems willing to endorse his threats, as he supplies a crucial component of the anti-interventionist yarn she is spinning, namely the prospective association of a military engagement in Mali with the ineffective wars fought in both Afghanistan and Iraq.

---

[2] Online at https://www.youtube.com/watch?v=djhaem3kDIk [2018–11–29].

Fig. 2: *Erin Burnett OutFront*, 14 January 2013, 1:16.

This reading of the events as foreboding another precipitate US intervention is reinforced shortly after (I skip a sequence on Ishmael, the Tuareg fighter) by another reference – illustrated with undated and unlocated archival footage of Islamist fighters – to the prolonged and complicated prehistory of the current moment of crisis: "The United States has already tried to help Mali. The United States trained Malian army commanders, some of whom defected to fight with the Islamists." Thus, the United States has already interfered without success in Mali, it is (being) reminded of other unsuccessful operations in the so-called War on Terror and, finally, it is always in danger of bringing about another terrorist attack on American soil, as the concluding soundbite of a US official clarifies: "So, if the United States becomes more involved in the War, will Islamists threaten the US directly? Secretary of State spokeswoman Victoria Nuland was asked that very question today: 'I think we are all well aware of the requirement to be vigilant about our own security including in the homeland, but that's why it's so important to get this operation done and get it done right'."

Without ever saying so, the *OutFront* segment, while seemingly sticking to the predictive announcement of an imminent US mission in Mali ("the United States is getting involved", "the US 'will participate in Mali'"; "'it's important to get this operation done'"), manages to construct a narrative of the futility of such an undertaking by infusing it with the myth of ineffective intervention, whose "articulation does not have to be consciously apprehended by the viewer in order to have been successfully communicated" (Fiske and Hartley 1989, 87).

Apart from casting the current events as simply the escalation of a situation that has been around for some time ("Islamic militants [...] have controlled Northern Mali for months" and "The United States has already tried to help Mali"), another means used to communicate that myth is repetition and variation – characteristic features of oral-formulaic style (see Lord 1995, Ch. 5).

The quintessence of Burnett's report can thus be seen to reside in her gradual modification of the sentence addressing the prospective US activity in Mali in the form of an assertion ("the United States is getting involved"), first into a question ("what will the United States do?"), and finally into a conditional ("*if* the United States becomes more involved"), thereby aborting the action "into formulaic and negative phrases" (Fiske and Hartley 1989, 93). In line with this, the actual U.S. involvement in Mali turned out to be limited to supportive operations such as aerial refueling missions for French aircraft, as the administration decided to stick to the argument that "U.S. policy prohibits direct military aid to Mali because the fledgling government is the result of a coup" (Formanek and Ford 2013, n. p.). It seems indeed as if the bardic narrative of television news, intent on providing its audience with a sense of cultural membership, has relayed and qualified administrative positions which could then be fed back into official policy as representative of a cultural consensus on military intervention in Mali.

4 Conclusion

More than 25 years after the FCC (Federal Communications Commission) started to repeal the fairness doctrine (a process completed in 2011), which required broadcasters to present fair and balanced coverage of controversial issues, the CNN program was still trying to not only cover both sides of a conflict but also to enable all foreign-policy factions within the US (from hawkish war-on-terror advocates to pacifist non-interventionists) to relate in one way or another to its suggested 'solution' on the question of American involvement. As late as 2013 Burnett remains faithful to the idea of bardic television, which, as I have argued, encompasses a culturally sedimented constellation including (1) socio-institutional settings: the bardic order / the videosphere (see Debray 2003, 65); (2) discursive positionings: the epic bard / news anchor as mediator between audience, reality, and ruling class (see Hartley 1988, 105); (3) mediatized formalities: oral-formulaic variation / news-style and concomitant pictoriality; and (4) narrative situations and modalities: variable focalization and divine intervention / reporter-witness transitions, suspended proairesis.

While the enduring 'mainstream' model of bardic television news helps us realize, therefore, that in order to address "specifically cultural phenomena" (Erll 2005, 89), cultural narratology has to move beyond a binary association of narrative forms with cultural functions to explore the actual configurations of narrative acts in cultural contexts, it must be said that – at the present cultural moment – the particular constellation Fiske and Hartley envisaged is a thing of the past. Television is no longer the electronic hearth around which the audience (as national family) assembles – not only because it lost its status as leading news medium sometime after 9/11, but also because social and political divisions have made it inconceivable that people any longer huddle around a single campfire. When political parties and populations are increasingly adrift and there is no longer a position of socio-centrality, you can either cater to a particular audience – and replace the mediation of reality with filter bubbles and suspended proairesis with paranoid projection, as Fox News has done – or find yourself sitting on the fence, caught between a hostile administration and a reality increasingly in doubt (see Moore 2018).

References

Bamberg, Michael, and Alexandra Georgakopoulou. "Small Stories as a New Perspective in Narrative and Identity Analysis." *Text & Talk* 28.3, 2008: 377–396.

Barthes, Roland. *Mythologies*. London: Vintage, 2009 [Fr. 1957].

Culbert, Taylor. "Narrative Technique in Beowulf." *Neophilologus* 47.1 (1963): 50–61.

Debray, Régis. *Introduction à la Médiologie*. Paris: Presses Universitaires de France, 2000.

de Jong, Irene J.F. *A Narratological Commentary on the 'Odyssey'*. Cambridge: Cambridge University Press, 2001.

de Jong, Irene J.F. *Narrators and Focalizers: The Presentation of the Story in the 'Iliad'*. Second ed. London: Bristol Classical, 2004 [1987].

Erll, Astrid. "Cultural Studies Approaches to Narrative." *The Routledge Encyclopedia of Narrative Theory*. Eds. David Herman, Manfred Jahn and Marie-Laure Ryan. London: Routledge, 2005. 88–93.

Fiske, John, and John Hartley. "Bardic Television." *Reading Television*. London: Routledge, 1989 [1978]. 85–100.

Foley, John Miles. *Traditional Oral Epic: 'The Odyssey', 'Beowulf', and the Serbo-Croatian Return Song*. Berkeley: University of California Press, 1990.

Formanek, Ingrid, and Dana Ford. "U.S. steps up involvement in Mali." https://edition.cnn.com/2013/01/26/world/africa/mali-unrest/index.html. *CNN World*, 28 January 2013 (29 November 2018).

Hartley, John. *Understanding News*. London: Routledge, 1988 [1982].

Hartley, John. "Bardic Function." *Communication, Cultural and Media Studies: The Key Concepts*. Third ed. London: Routledge, 2002. 16–17.

Leach, Edmund. *Culture and Communication*. London: Cambridge University Press, 1976.

Lord, Albert B. *The Singer Resumes the Tale*. Ed. Mary Louise Lord. Harvard: Harvard University Press, 1995.
Lord, Albert B. *The Singer of Tales*. Eds. Stephen Mitchell and Gregory Nagy. Second ed. Harvard: Harvard University Press, 2000.
Louden, Bruce. "A Narrative Technique in *Beowulf* and Homeric Epic." *Oral Tradition* 11.2 (1996): 346–362.
Moore, Suzanne. "The US Press Corps has to Learn to Stand Up to Trump." https://www.theguardian.com/commentisfree/2018/nov/08/us-press-corps-trump-journalists-press-conferences. *The Guardian*, 8 November 2018 (29 November 2018).
Nünning, Ansgar. "Narrativist Approaches and Narratological Concepts for the Study of Culture." *Travelling Concepts for the Study of Culture*. Eds. Birgit Neumann and Ansgar Nünning. Berlin: de Gruyter, 2012. 145–183.
Nünning, Ansgar. "Surveying Contextualist and Cultural Narratologies: Towards an Outline of Approaches, Concepts and Potentials." *Narratology in the Age of Cross-Disciplinary Narrative Research*. Eds. Sandra Heinen and Roy Sommer. Berlin: de Gruyter, 2009. 48–70.
Ong, Walter J. *Orality and Literacy: The Technologizing of the Word*. New York: Methuen, 1982.
Parry, Milman. *The Making of Homeric Verse: The Collected Papers of Milman Parry*. Ed. Adam Parry. Oxford: Oxford University Press, 1987.
Richardson, Peter. "Point of View and Identification in *Beowulf*" *Neophilologus* 81.2 (1997): 289–298.
Rumble, T.C. "The *hyran-gefrignan* Formula in *Beowulf*." *Annuale Mediaevale* 5, 1964: 13–20.
Stephenson, William. "The Bardic Drama of Television's Narrative Histories." *Journal of Popular Film and Television* 11.3 (1983): 131–134.
Woocher, Lawrence. "Missed Opportunities for Prevention? A Study of U.S. Policy and Atrocities in Syria since 2011". https://de.scribd.com/document/358210798/SUMMARY-OF-FINDINGS-MISSED-OPPORTUNITIES-FOR-PREVENTION. *United States Holocaust Museum Syria Study*, 2017 (29 November 2018).

Dorothee Birke
New Media Narratives: Olivia Sudjic's *Sympathy* and Identity in the Digital Age

Abstract: This chapter reflects on the status of novels in the age of social media by examining Olivia Sudjic's *Sympathy* (2017) as a case study. Hailed as "the first great Instagram novel" by reviewers, *Sympathy* offers a meditation on the impact of social media on subjectivity and intimacy. The chapter examines how narrative techniques are employed to reflect on wide-spread hopes and fears concerning the digitalization of communication. It then complements this discussion with a historical perspective, arguing that by focusing on the interplay between media and identity, Sudjic's book updates a double claim which is as old as the genre of the novel: that the media we consume have a formative impact on who we are, and that narrative fiction deserves a prominent place in a hierarchy of different media formats because it offers privileged insights into the workings of the human mind. In interpreting *Sympathy* as one of the latest installments in an ongoing campaign asserting the special status of novels in a digitalized media environment, the chapter demonstrates how narratological analysis can be fused with media-ecological and media-archeological approaches.

1 Introduction

'On or about February 4, 2004, human character changed' – or so we might be led to believe by those commentators who see the rise of social media, exemplified in the date when Mark Zuckerberg launched Facebook, as fundamentally altering the way in which we relate both to others and to ourselves. Virginia Woolf's much quoted aphorism from "Mr Bennett and Mrs Brown" (here brought forward almost a century) reminds us that there is nothing very new about the idea that modernization has an impact on how we understand subjectivity. Woolf's main interest in her essay is in the artist's – more specifically, the novelist's – role in mediating such an understanding. Her belief in the ability of the novel to create truthful visions of human character stands as a challenge to her successors to keep rethinking the genre, a challenge that is arguably complicated by the perception that in the age of Facebook, Instagram and Twitter, novel writing and reading are rapidly disappearing cultural practices.

This chapter presents a case study of a work by a novelist who has taken up this challenge. Olivia Sudjic's *Sympathy* (2017) has been hailed as "the first great Instagram novel" (Livingstone 2017b) and "the best fictional account [...] of the way the internet has shaped our inner lives" (Preston 2017).[1] Sudjic's novel exemplifies the continuing claim of the genre to reflect on and contribute to an understanding of 'human character' at a particular moment in time, in this case the age of social media. This claim, premised on the idea that media play a central role in the formation of identity, can be seen as a fundamental credo of the novel since its establishment as a major narrative form in the eighteenth century.[2] The cultural work performed by a book like *Sympathy* can, in this light, best be understood by linking a broadly cultural narratological perspective with a media-historical approach. This means paying attention not just to the form and content of narratives, but also to the way in which they materialize as concrete media objects, made meaningful through media practices within a particular cultural context.

There are several ways in which this approach is indebted to what Ansgar Nünning has dubbed "cultural narratology" (2012). Firstly, Nünning's insistence on the "cultural semanticisation of form" (2012, 147) underlies a narratological analysis, in particular of temporal structure and narrative perspective, that will show how the form of storytelling reflects a particular take on contemporary identity. Secondly, I will examine how Sudjic's novel stages the "performative, reality-constituting [...] function of narration" (Nünning 2012, 146), in which the protagonist transforms experience into narration and the reader is invited to follow, participate in, but also to critically question this transformation. Thirdly, I would like to complement what Nünning and Jan Rupp (2011) have summed up

---

1 I would like to thank the participants of the master's seminar 'Reflections on Digital Culture in Literature and TV' at the University of Freiburg for the stimulating discussions that have shaped my thinking about this novel.

2 The Enlightenment idea that minds are formed through education, and that the choice of reading material is of the utmost importance, has been reflected throughout the history of the novel since the appearance of Cervantes' crazed reader, Don Quijote. As a popular medium, the novel was long suspected of exerting a negative influence on its readers: in *The Reading Lesson*, Patrick Brantlinger argues that as late as the nineteenth century, the genre labored under an "inferiority complex," featuring material that contributed to its own condemnation (1998, 2–3). However, the 'anti-novel' discourse in question (exemplified in the recurrence of Quixotic reader figures) can also be seen as asserting a belief in the superior (rather than inferior) potential of narrative fiction to shape its readers, if only they make the right choice of material (see Birke 2016). William Warner's *Licensing Entertainment* (1998) demonstrates that eighteenth-century novelists, most prominently Samuel Richardson and Henry Fielding, established the novel as a morally respectable genre, and since then the novel has been extraordinarily efficient in advertising its own merits (see Birke 2016).

as the "medialisation of narrative" in contemporary novels with an investigation into what might be called a 'narrativization of media'. That is, I see *Sympathy* as engaging with some particularly potent cultural narratives *about* media: namely the notion that media – determined by the affordances of the particular medium – play a central role in shaping identity, and, based on this premise, that they can be divided into those with predominantly positive and those with predominantly negative effects. Sudjic herself remarks on the historical and cultural dimension of such evaluations when she points to the moral panic surrounding novel reading in earlier centuries: "Now novels are good and it's Instagram that's bad. Every single time a new format comes up for identifying with other people, we all throw up our hands thinking it's a disaster" (O'Brien 2017). However, while some aspects of *Sympathy* reflect this analytical attitude toward media hierarchies, on other levels the novel is itself suffused with them.

2 Digital panic

Sudjic's book could be described as a Bildungsroman (or maybe anti-Bildungsroman) of the internet age. Set mainly in 2014, it tells, in retrospect, the formative misadventures of the narrator-protagonist, Alice Hare, a 23-year-old Londoner who comes to New York to visit her grandmother, seek out her origins and determine what she wants to do with her life. She then discovers the pleasures of social media and becomes fixated on Mizuko Himura, a Japanese writer nine years her senior. One of the things that make the novel remarkable is its invention of a lyrical vocabulary which makes palpable Alice's mounting obsession with her mobile phone. She is propelled into an online simulacrum of reality, just as her namesake, Lewis Carroll's Alice, falls down the rabbit hole. The novel's epigraph, a quote from *Through the Looking-Glass*, frames the protagonist's quest into the world of social media both as driven by a need for community and as perilous: "I wouldn't mind being a pawn, if only I might join."

Throughout, as I will show, *Sympathy* engages with the hopes and fears – predominantly fears – attending the rise of social media. Not all of these worries are new. A central one – catchily labeled 'digital dementia' by the German psychiatrist Manfred Spitzer (2012) – is that surfing the internet has a deteriorating effect on cognitive capacities. The idea that online media promote only superficial engagement with information and thus, over time, leach their users' ability to concentrate, is reminiscent of nineteenth-century discussions like the Victorian intellectual Samuel Smiles' critique of reading for amusement. Smiles is concerned about a tendency toward "multifarious reading" rather than single-minded study:

"The evil is a growing one, and it operates in various ways. Its least mischief is shallowness; its greatest, the aversion to steady labour which it induces, and the low and feeble tone of mind which it encourages" (1897, 320). Where, for Smiles, the problem was the rise of easy-to-read literature, not least novels, contemporary media pessimists like Spitzer and Sven Birkerts point to the proliferation of shallow and unreliable material on the internet, as well as the enticement to click from hyperlink to hyperlink rather than to engage in a linear, concentrated perusal.

What further unites past and present critiques is particularly a concern about the media practices of young people whose habits and abilities are still under formation. The idea that the rise of social media threatens the development and well-being of a whole generation is summed up in the American psychologist Jean M. Twenge's formula of 'iGen' – 'I' as in 'internet' and 'iPhone,' but also 'individualist,' 'insecure' and 'in person no more' (see Twenge 2017, 2–3). Subtitled *Why Today's Super-Connected Kids Are Growing Up Less Rebellious, More Tolerant, Less Happy – and Completely Unprepared for Adulthood*, Twenge's book proposes, among other things, that members of the iGen are marked by a "decline in inperson social interaction" that is likely to lead to "having inferior social skills" (2017, 90), and that their internet activities foster a navel-gazing individualism rather than community involvement (Twenge 2017, 176–177). Similar concerns had already been voiced by the social psychologist Sherry Turkle in her widely influential *Alone Together: Why We Expect More from Technology and Less from Each Other*, which cautions against the alienating effect of digitalization, as "our networked life allows us to hide from each other, even as we are tethered to each other" (2011, 1). The concern about growing social ineptitude is complemented by worries about online anonymity on the one hand and loss of privacy on the other. Online anonymity opens up a whole range of ways to invent yourself, but also to deceive others. At the same time, digitalization makes all of us transparent in unprecedented ways, making possible data collection and use of personal information of every kind. Significantly, the interplay of anonymity and visibility has been linked with a rise in threatening behavior – typically stalking and cyberbullying – an issue addressed by the journalist Jon Ronson in *So You've Been Publicly Shamed* (2015), which analyzes the internet as the new public pillory.

This is highly controversial territory, where alarmist statements about the detrimental effects of new media receive far more public attention than cautious and balanced analyses. The long-term individual and social effects of digitalization are certainly far from being comprehensively charted or understood. What literary and media history can teach us is that discussions about media effects tend to be emotionally charged, and that there is a constant bias toward seeing the newest formats and technologies in black and white terms, as either heralding progress or as a threat.

Fictional representations of media practices have long been part of the debate on media change, imaginatively exploring how we can be transformed by the cultural products we consume. Elsewhere, I have examined the role of such self-reflections in the history of the novel, which teems with characters like Cervantes' protagonist Don Quijote, whose character and life are fundamentally altered by his reading (Birke 2016). Today, some of the most widely received reflections on media use can be found outside the pages of books, prominently for example in the digital dystopias of the British TV series *Black Mirror*, launched on Channel 4 in 2011 and picked up by Netflix in 2016. A narratological approach helps to see how rhetorical and aesthetic choices – selection of material, temporal organization, point of view, characterization, representation of place etc. – shape the image of the media changes represented in such texts, and how they tap into larger cultural narratives about media. The greatest influence on these cultural narratives is exerted by popularized science in the vein of Spitzer and Turkle – which is why I focus on these rather than on more complex accounts such as José van Dijck's *The Culture of Connectivity* (2013).

What a media-conscious perspective adds to the narratological view is the awareness that the particular media context in which a story is represented in itself already adds a whole dimension to the narrative of media that is offered. I do not simply mean that different media afford different possibilities of representation – e.g. that film is audiovisual where the novel is not, although this is, of course, an important issue taken up by transmedial narratology (see e.g. Ryan and Thon 2014). Nor is my main interest in the fascinating topic of how the rise of new media has influenced the formal development of the novel (see e.g. Nünning and Rupp 2011). Rather, my point is that any novel, TV series, or drama is itself implicated in the media developments and hierarchies on which it reflects – there is no 'neutral' vantage point from which the relative merits of different media could be assessed. *Black Mirror*, for example, is representative of a wider tendency in TV to depict online culture as shallow, freaky or sinister (series like *The Good Wife* and *Sherlock* are cases in point), and could therefore be seen as cementing the ongoing cultural upgrading of TV as a new highbrow medium (see the notion of 'quality TV'). Narratives of media, then, need to be contextualized from the perspective of both media ecology and media archeology. For one thing, attention should be paid to the way in which specific forms participate in a negotiation of their own status in the ever evolving network of environments and relationships, that is, in their media ecology (see e.g. Hoskins 2014, 662–663). Secondly, a media-archeological perspective will focus on the historical dimension of these interconnections, facilitating "a way to investigate the new media cultures through insights from past new media" (Parikka 2012, 2).

Considering the novel from the vantage point of media ecology and archeology brings home one central point: that it is by no means merely a dinosaur, a remnant of an old media environment. While some media have no doubt become obsolete – we need only think of the VHS cassette and the DVD (see e.g. Benzon 2013) – the novel remains an integral part of the contemporary media landscape. One could argue that this is because novels are not media in the same sense as DVDs or video cassettes, and that it is their transferability to a new carrier, from book to e-reader or even smartphone, that secures them a place in a digitalized world. Yet this is only one aspect of the picture. In fact, the case can be made that the novel's special position in today's media ecology rests on its very association with the allegedly obsolete medium of the book. In his ground-breaking study *Bring on the Books for Everybody* (2010), Jim Collins shows how, rather than being pushed to the margins, novel reading has become the hub of new media constellations. While these involve digital media technologies and agents such as amazon.com, the Kindle e-reader, and internet book blogs, the printed book, with its intrinsic materiality, not only retains pertinence and significance, but even becomes a hallmark of refined media sensibility. "Popular Literary Culture", as Collins describes it, is on the one hand the result of a convergence of literary and digital cultures, but on the other hand revolves around "a celebration of [...] reading as a transformative cultural activity that occurs only in books and nowhere else in the hypermediated culture where that reading takes place" (2010, 82). The fetishization of the book within digital culture is closely tied to a fetishization of the novel as a genre, to the extent that 'book reading' and 'novel reading' have become synonymous (see Birke and Fehrle, 2018).

True to the self-reflexive stance of their eighteenth-century forebears, contemporary novels continue to participate in the larger conversation about media hierarchies. Digitalization has, it transpires, furnished the genre with yet another way of rethinking its own potential and asserting its status. Accordingly, I shall in what follows read *Sympathy* as a particularly innovative and complex exploration of what the latest turn in media development means for human identity and interaction – not forgetting that the novel itself is an interested party in this discussion.

3 *Sympathy* and the narrativization of digitalized subjectivity

At a time when internet use is often regarded as diametrically opposed to the literary book culture it threatens to supplant, the description of *Sympathy* as the "first great Instagram novel" may sound to some ears oxymoronic.³ After all, Instagram, with its focus on images rather than text, presented in a grid of 'tiles' that can be juxtaposed for aesthetic impact, has been seen as epitomizing what is wrong with the internet: offering snippets rather than a sustained story or argument; being shallow, obsessed with glossy surfaces rather than content; fostering a narcissistic selfie culture (see e.g. Livingstone 2017a) – everything, in fact, that literary culture is not supposed to be, as one of *Sympathy*'s first reviewers on the *Amazon* website opined: "This unfocused narrative ultimately breaks down due to the superficiality of internet culture. When the book is not directly referencing the internet it is replete with its own overlay of asinine internet culture effluvia. [...] Brace yourselves – I suspect this is the future of 'literature'" (Lloyd 2017).⁴

More approving reviewers find that evoking the experience of living your life online is one of the novel's strengths. What to Lloyd is "unfocused" is to others successfully semanticized form: "*Sympathy*", writes Marta Bausells (2018) in a review for the online site *Literary Hub*, "reads like a fever dream, blending consciousness and paranoia and dreams, and jumping back and forth through time – like you do on the gram."

The temporal structure of the novel is indeed a striking feature, making for a quite disorienting reading experience. While the overall framework follows a familiar blueprint for first-person fiction, with present-self Alice recollecting and commenting on her past-self experiences, this past is not told in a linear fashion, but in spurts and circles. One storyline, related in an overall chronological sequence, is concerned with Alice's arrival in her terminally ill grandmother Silvia's apartment in New York, moving in with Silvia's friends, the Rooiakker family, after Silvia is admitted to hospital, getting involved with the Rooiakker's acquaintance Dwight, and finally, after Silvia's death, going back to England. However, this account is overlaid and interspersed with the story of Alice's mounting obsession with Mizuko – an episode which, in the chronology of the plot, fits into a fairly small slot between her involvement with Dwight and her return to England, but which in terms of the novel's discourse spills out on all sides. Alice's narrative keeps circling around this relationship in a non-chronological way, weaving episodes into the strand about her earlier backstory and her time with Silvia and the Rooiakkers in passages that are so extensive that the narratological concept of 'prolepsis' (foreshadowing), with its suggestion of subordination to a main timeline, cannot do them justice. It is these events – Alice unfollowing Mizuko on

---

3 For a more sustained discussion of the prevalence and implications of a juxtaposition between book and internet culture, see Birke and Fehrle (2018).
4 Sudjic was so struck by this review that she commented on it in an interview: "Scott, many thanks, I hope to use your final line as a quote for the paperback" (Sudjic 2017b).

Instagram, their first meeting in a café, their first night together – that dominate the narrative, reflecting her obsession. It is a long time, however, before it is actually revealed how the two women came to meet. Nestled in the middle of the novel as in the eye of a hurricane (in Chapter 16 of 32), are the description of the moment "when the obsession began" (Sudjic 2017a, 225) and the explanation of how the Silvia/Rooiakker and Mizuko plot lines converge. Even though the media experiences of reading the novel and of scrolling through Instagram are hardly identical, the first half of *Sympathy*, with its use of what one could call 'hyper-prolepsis', could be said to mimic an internet user's serendipitous progress through the social media feed of a new acquaintance.[5]

The nonlinear rendering of the narrative strand concerned with Mizuko contributes moreover to the impression that Alice's narrative style reflects her own subjective moods and obsessions. While such an emphasis on subjectivity is hardly a new feature in the history of the novel (one need only think of Virginia Woolf's 'stream of consciousness' focus on reflector figures, or of Kazuo Ishiguro's anxiously self-seeking first-person narrators), *Sympathy* updates it by presenting it as an expression of the protagonist's preoccupation with social media. Alice's relationship to Mizuko is virtual to a degree that would make her a model subject for Twenge's iGen, with its eschewal of face-to-face interaction and poor social skills. What we find out in the middle of the novel is that Alice first encountered Mizuko's name through an online service offering genetic testing and matching (reminiscent of the real-life service of the biotech firm 23andMe). Alice is the only character who knows that this Japanese stranger is Robin Rooiakker's biological daughter. Monitoring Mizuko's Instagram account, she begins to see parallels to her own life – not least that they have both gravitated to New York – and after lurking around Mizuko in virtual space for a while she engineers a 'coincidental' meeting in a café. Subsequently, the internet becomes "a tool designed for the sole purpose of observing her [Mizuko]. It was the only way I could have been brave enough to approach her in real life, having dissected the pictorial equivalent of her DNA in advance" (Sudjic 2017a, 76). After surveillance on social media, the next step is to take control of Mizuko's mobile phone: Alice finds out the password, goes through all the private information saved on the device, and even tries to police Mizuko's contacts with other people, deleting messages from her estranged boyfriend in the hope of becoming the sole focus of her attention.

Alice appears as an unreliable narrator with questionable norms and values, not least because many of the sociopathic activities of her past self are related by

---

5 For the concept of hyper-prolepsis I am indebted to Carolin Gebauer, who has proposed that this type of achronic narration is typical of contemporary present-tense novels.

the present self in a matter-of-fact, unapologetic way: "If you are wondering whether I had looked at everything on her [Mizuko's] phone while I had it, then: of course. I thought that would be obvious, but maybe you're not like me" (Sudjic 2017a, 268). While it seems that the present self is more self-aware than the past self, it is questionable whether there has been a real advance in maturity and control over her life: present-self Alice, back in England, seems to spend most of her time sitting in front of the computer, trawling the internet for signs of Mizuko, even after their relationship has blown up. On the one hand the protagonist-narrator thus comes across as sinister and creepy, representing the exploitative aspects of social media, while on the other hand she is characterized as isolated and vulnerable. She arrives in New York friendless and clueless, and lets herself be mistreated both by her temporary boyfriend Dwight, who uses her for sex and as a captive audience for his vanities, and by Robin, who turns out to be a serial sexual harasser. But most of all, for much of the story she desperately tries to ignore the fact that her 'relationship' with Mizuko is completely one-sided, that she has fallen in love with a projection rather than a real person. Only at the end of the novel does she acknowledge the virtual character of her experience: "My reflections amount to a love story that is mostly made up, from memories that are mostly false, between people who were mainly not there" (Sudjic 2017a, 405). Alice turns to social media to forge the close connections she never experienced. However, the connectivity promised by social media, the novel suggests, can foster only an illusion of intimacy.

The phantasmagorical character of online relationships is also reflected in the narrator-protagonist's particular take on identity, in which the borders between body and technology become fluid. This theme is already introduced in the first sentences of the novel:

> I wasn't with her when the fever started. I didn't even know she was sick. I'd known nearly everything about her until then, and could have recalled the smallest detail of any given day, whether she'd spent it with me or not. For months her presence, and telepresence, had given shape to my new life in New York. Now, with the stroke of a finger, it had gone. (Sudjic 2017a, 1)

'Physical presence' and 'telepresence', for the narrator, seem to amount to the same thing. The absence referred to in the first sentence, as we realize by the end of the first paragraph, could thus refer to either. "Being with somebody", in Alice's world, does not necessarily mean being in the same room: Sudjic stages a mindset where the act of un-following a social media account is experienced as an incisive physical loss, and the writerly act of 'making strange' the vocabulary of physicality suggests that in a world governed by digital media, intimacy itself has been reconfigured. In the course of the novel, the motif comes up time and again: when Alice first encounters Mizuko in person, "[i]t felt strange that I couldn't stretch out my hand through her body, push it out the other side, or turn her over in my palm" (Sudjic 2017a, 8). Holding her friend's phone "felt kind of like holding her brain" (Sudjic 2017a, 268). However, Alice also comes to realize that "while I had direct access right now to Mizuko's mind through her device, only Rupert [her ex-boyfriend] had access to the rest, even though I was the one there, right next to her" (Sudjic 2017a, 303). Mizuko stays unavailable not just on an emotional level but also on a physical one: tellingly, the moment of the most intense bodily proximity between the two women, a kiss, becomes "hyperreal", a precious memory reproduced "so many times I no longer know that it *did* happen" (Sudjic 2017a, 270).

In fact, the last third of the novel features a turning point which revolves around a double failure on Alice's part to overcome the limitations both of physical reality and of social relations by means of digital self-invention. In a shocking sequence of events, she is abandoned by Mizuko at a party where she is drugged, drawn into a hazily rendered group sex cluster and (being too sluggish to run away like most of the other guests) arrested for drug possession and disorderly conduct. Back home, she is aghast when she sees the marks left on her body by the night's encounters: "I was covered in bruises: some small and distinct as grapes, some faint and stippled, others cloudy and creeping like rot – finger marks, bites, grazes" (Sudjic 2017a, 324). It is only then that the reader, together with Alice, realizes that what happened to her amounts to sexual assault. While this clearly illustrates the extent of the protagonist's inability to delineate physical boundaries and take care of herself, the second part of the scene goes even further in emphasizing the primacy of bodily experience. Alice suddenly discovers that she is bleeding violently in the termination of a pregnancy she has so far managed to ignore. She retrieves the fetus from the toilet, takes a picture and sends it to Mizuko, who never replies. The futility of this frantic attempt to salvage some meaning from the episode by means of social media starkly exposes the misguidedness of Alice's attempts to invent a new, virtual self.

4 *Sympathy* and the history of the Novel

By questioning the idea that media offer access to another human being and foster intimacy, *Sympathy* reverses a trope that in the eighteenth century was central to shaping the novel as a genre. Maybe the most prominent instance of such an understanding is Samuel Richardson's bestseller *Pamela* (1740), in which the eponymous servant girl records, in letters to her parents, the trials and tribulations she suffers from the advances of her employer, the rakish landowner Mr. B.

At the turning point of the novel, B. seizes the letters, and Pamela thinks she is undone: "[N]ow he will see all my private thoughts of him, and all the secrets of my heart. What a careless creature am I!" (Richardson 1980 [1740], 263) Instead, B. is so impressed by the virtuous emotion he encounters in the correspondence that he proposes marriage. *Pamela* reflects the specific historical and cultural significance of the letter – understood as an authentic expression of feeling and a means of fostering affection and friendship – in the 'cult of sensibility' that took off in the mid-eighteenth century.

Sympathy is equally interested in the relations between contemporary media practices and self. It updates the discussion by critically investigating the potential of social media to reflect an authentic self and to foster close connections with others. The time-transcending relevance of this topic is already signaled in the book's title, which, as Sudjic explains in an interview, was originally conceived as a historical reference to a seventeenth-century polymath with an obsession for 'Sympathy Powder', a medicine that "could link people and things across time and space" (Wright 2017). While the initial idea for the novel's setting was completely transformed, what remains is an interest in human connection as a driving force behind technological invention.

I have already addressed the way in which the novel casts doubt on the idea that digital media afford community or closeness. Their role in representing a true self is even more ambivalent. On the one hand, digital technology reveals a host of facts about an individual: Mizuko's preferences, the biographical details she has shared online, her movements through the city, which can be deduced from her postings on Instagram – all this and more is readily available. On the other hand, Alice realizes that for Mizuko, "the internet was primarily a tool of self-promotion and reinforcement for her multiple selves" (Sudjic 2017a, 76). That she herself can never hope to be more than an extra in this self-fashioning spree becomes clear in a scene when the two are on a road trip. Alice takes a picture of Mizuko, but is forbidden to upload it on her own Instagram account because Mizuko wants to post the photograph as "part of a carefully crafted post-breakup narrative" (Sudjic 2017a, 290), intended to make her ex-boyfriend Rupert believe that she is on the road with a new lover. Nor is the use of social media as a self-promotion tool confined to Mizuko. Alice herself, when she has just met Dwight and discovered Instagram, enjoys posting pictures that craft an image of herself as a hip socialite: "'Alice Hare,' I imagined people I no longer knew saying to each other, 'is living in New York, is definitely not a virgin, has a boyfriend in tech, and hangs out with tattooed young people who drink black drinks that have charcoal as an active ingredient'" (Sudjic 2017a, 130).

While this critical depiction of the characters' social media habits strongly resonates with the real-life criticism (especially of Instagram) mentioned above, it should not be forgotten that the problem of authenticity concerns any medium that can be used for self-presentation. *Pamela* can actually be regarded as a case in point: famously, Richardson's rival Henry Fielding read the novel against the grain and responded with the parodistic rewriting *An Apology for the Life of Mrs. Shamela Andrews* (1741), in which the protagonist exposes herself as a scheming fraud and the letters published in *Pamela* as an instrument of pure self-fashioning. Fielding's book not only questions the notion that ego-documents reflect an authentic version of the self, but also reframes the relationship between such media and the novel. While Richardson's *Pamela* suggests a congruence between the media of letter and novel, the epistolary format providing the reader with the same kind of intimate access to the workings of another mind that the letters give Mr B., *Shamela* posits an incongruent relationship between the two media. Here the self-image a character projects in fictional ego-documents is deconstructed by juxtaposing it with the image presented by the novel as a whole. Throughout the history of the novel, the interest in such multi-layered explorations into subjectivity has been a driving force for the modification and refinement of narrative technique. Two types that have been especially prominent are multiperspectivity (as in *Shamela*, which features letters from different writers) and unreliable narration (as in *Sympathy*, which casts doubt on the moral-ethical trustworthiness of its narrator-protagonist).[6]

Against the background of this tradition, Sudjic's book appears not so much as confronting a completely new media phenomenon, but rather as playing a variation on an old theme, namely the staging and critical exploration of the use of media to construct a narrative of self. *Sympathy* thus actualizes a central claim on the behalf of the novel as a genre: that by combining the impression of immediate access to the mind of another person, however fictional, with the superordinate presentation (explicit or implicit) of a value system for judging and making sense of that character, the novel becomes a key medium of insight into the workings of the human mind.

***

Sympathy is highly reflexive about its own interventions in the discussion of media development and hierarchies. While it takes seriously the question what a change in media habits might mean for individual and social development, it also parodies a simplistic juxtaposition of media-addicted youth with a well-adjusted older generation. Strikingly, it is the media junkie Mizuko who voices a theory about her superior media competence:

---

[6] Ansgar Nünning has done pioneering work in systematizing both concepts and in mapping their semanticizations. See Nünning (1998) and Nünning and (Nünning 2000).

> She had led a class about how my *generation* couldn't physically cope with books anymore; they had been rewired and could now learn only through "gamification". These little morons, she explained, had to be able to interact and adapt and insert themselves somehow into everything; otherwise it wasn't worth knowing. "I'm a Digital Immigrant," she said primly. "You're a Digital *Native*." (Sudjic 2017a, 77–78)

It is true that the most positive character in the whole book, the no-nonsense Silvia, who is the only person to show real kindness toward the protagonist, is characterized by her complete rejection of the digital. She refuses to use a smartphone, establishes contact to Alice by way of typewritten letters, and is "revolted" when she finds out that Alice takes pictures with her phone rather than a 'real' camera (Sudjic 2017a, 99). However, it is also made clear that unlike the novel genre, Silvia *is* a dinosaur with obsolete preferences, and she does die before the novel closes. Her brand of Luddism, it seems, is not a viable option – neither for Alice, who compares Silvia's idea of the media market to "that bit at the end" (Sudjic 2017a, 99) of the film *Titanic* where everybody is drowning, clinging to debris, nor for the novel's author, who has achieved some prominence as "the go-to millennial rent-a-voice for all things social media, tech, and well, millennial" (Murray 2017).

And yet... I was going to end this article by reflecting on Sudjic herself as a living example of the integration rather than opposition of literature and internet culture, discussing her own media identity as a literary author who posts images from her life as a writer on her "babynovelist" Instagram account – skeptical as she is of the label 'millennial' (see e.g. Bausells 2018). Sudjic seemed to me the epitome of that interesting convergence of book and digital culture described by Collins, effortlessly combining a proficient use of digital media with a projection of the idea that book culture is somehow superior. The images on the "babynovelist" feed on Instagram showed all the hallmarks of the new internet book culture (see Birke and Fehrle, 2018): close-ups of books cosily arranged next to hot drinks, stylish mirror selfies, and shelfies (i.e. photos of her own book shelves). As on many millennial Instagram accounts, the color pink featured prominently. But as of September 2018 (possibly even a little earlier), this digitally crafted author persona is no longer accessible. When I tried to revisit the Instagram feed, the page was unavailable.[7] It seems that Sudjic has at least to some extent opted out of social media culture. Who knows where the media habits of the 'millennials' are tending next and how they will shape future selves and societies? The claim implicit in *Sympathy* is that for the fullest answer to this question we need to keep reading novels.

---

[7] Some of the images can still be found as illustrations to Murray's (2017) article on Sudjic in the online edition of ELLE.

References

Bausells, Marta. *The First Great Instagram Novel? Olivia Sudjic Isn't Interested in Being a 'Millennial Voice'.* https://lithub.com/the-first-great-instagram-novel/. Literary Hub, 21 May 2018 (15 August 2018).

Benzon, Paul. "Bootleg Paratextuality and Digital Temporality: Towards an Alternate Present of the DVD." *Narrative* 21.1 (2013): 88–104.

Birke, Dorothee. *Writing the Reader: Configurations of a Cultural Practice in the English Novel.* Berlin/Boston: de Gruyter, 2016.

Birke, Dorothee, and Johannes Fehrle. "#booklove: How Reading Culture is Adapted on the Internet." *Komparatistik Online*, 2018: 60–86.

Black Mirror. Dir. Charlie Brooker. Channel 4, 2011–.

Brantlinger, Patrick. *The Reading Lesson: The Threat of Mass Literacy in Nineteenth-Century British Fiction.* Bloomington, IN: Indiana University Press, 1998.

Collins, Jim. *Bring on the Books for Everybody: How Literary Culture Became Popular Culture.* Durham, NC: Duke University Press, 2010.

Fielding, Henry. *An Apology for the Life of Mrs. Shamela Andrews.* London: Penguin Books, 1999 [1741].

Gebauer, Carolin. *Making Time: World-Construction in the Present-Tense Novel* [dissertation project in progress].

Hoskins, Andrew. "The Mediatiziation of Memory." *Mediatization of Communication.* Ed. Knut Lundby. Berlin/Boston: de Gruyter Mouton, 2014. 661–680.

Livingstone, Josephine. *Against Instagram.* https://newrepublic.com/article/144350/instagram. The New Republic, 16 August 2017a (15 August 2018).

Livingstone, Josephine. *The First Great Instagram Novel.* https://newrepublic.com/article/141399/first-great-instagram-novel. The New Republic, 17 March 2017b (15 August 2018).

Lloyd, Scott. *The Future of Literature.* https://www.amazon.com/Sympathy-Olivia-Sudjic/product-reviews/0544836596/ref=cm_cr_arp_d_hist_2?pageNumber=1&filterByStar=two_star. Amazon Customer Reviews of *Sympathy*, 12 March 2017 (15 August 2018).

Murray, Daisy. *Olivia Sudjic Talks to ELLE About Her First Novel 'Sympathy', Navigating Social Media and Being A Millennial Rent-A-Voice.* https://www.elle.com/uk/life-and-culture/culture/interviews/a35986/olivia-sudjic-talks-to-elle-about-novel-sympathy/. ELLE, 2 June 2017 (5 October 2018).

Nünning, Ansgar. "Narrativist Approaches and Narratological Concepts for the Study of Culture." *Travelling Concepts for the Study of Culture.* Eds. Birgit Neumann and Ansgar Nünning. Berlin/Boston: de Gruyter, 2012. 145–183.

Nünning, Ansgar (ed.). *Unreliable Narration: Studien zur Theorie und Praxis unglaubwürdigen Erzählens in der englischsprachigen Erzählliteratur.* Trier: WVT, 1998.

Nünning, Ansgar, and Jan Rupp (eds.). *Medialisierung des Erzählens im englischsprachigen Roman der Gegenwart: Theoretischer Bezugsrahmen, Genres und Modellinterpretationen.* Trier: WVT, 2011.

Nünning, Vera, and Ansgar Nünning (eds.). *Multiperspektivisches Erzählen: Zur Theorie und Geschichte der Perspektivenstruktur im englischen Roman des 18. bis 20. Jahrhunderts.* Trier: WVT, 2000.

O'Brien, Kate Loftus. *'Sympathy' Is the Debut Novel From Olivia Sudjic About Instagram and Intimacy.* https://www.vice.com/en_uk/article/d7b5az/sympathy-is-the-debut-novel-from-olivia-sudjic-about-instagram-and-intimacy. Vice, 28 April 2017 (15 August 2018).

Parikka, Jussi. *What is Media Archeology?* Cambridge: Polity, 2012.

Preston, Alex. *Fiction to Look out for in 2017.* https://www.theguardian.com/books/2017/jan/01/fiction-to-look-out-for-in-2017-arundhati-roy-paul-auster. The Guardian, 1 January 2017 (15 August 2018).

Richardson, Samuel. *Pamela: or, Virtue Rewarded.* Ed. by Peter Sabor. Harmondsworth: Penguin, 1980 [1740].

Ronson, Jon. *So You've Been Publicly Shamed.* London: Picador, 2015.

Ryan, Marie-Laure, and Jan-Noël Thon (eds.). *Story-Worlds Across Media: Toward a Media-Conscious Narratology.* Lincoln/London: University of Nebraska Press, 2014.

Smiles, Samuel. *Self-Help: With Illustrations of Character, Conduct, and Perseverance.* London: Murray, 1878 [1871].

Spitzer, Manfred. *Digitale Demenz: Wie wir uns und unsere Kinder um den Verstand bringen.* München: Droemer Knaur, 2012.

Sudjic, Olivia. *Sympathy.* London: ONE, 2017a.

Sudjic, Olivia. *Author Olivia Sudjic On How Social Media Breeds 'Sympathy-On-Steroids'.* https://graziadaily.co.uk/life/books/internet-millennial-comfort-zone-cost-inner-lives. Grazia, 7 May 2017b (15 August 2018).

Turkle, Sherry. *Alone Together: Why We Expect More from Technology and Less from Each Other.* New York: Basic, 2011.

Twenge, Jean M. *iGen: Why Today's Super-Connected Kids Are Growing Up Less Rebellious, More Tolerant, Less Happy – and Completely Unprepared for Adulthood.* New York et al.: Atria, 2017.

van Dijck, José. *The Culture of Connectivity. A Critical History of Social Media.* Oxford: Oxford University Press, 2013.

Wright, Abbe. *A Conversation with Olivia Sudjic.* https://www.readitforward.com/author-interview/a-conversation-with-olivia-sudjic. Read it Forward, 2017 (15 August 2018).

Bruno Zerweck

The 'Death' of the Unreliable Narrator: Toward a Functional History of Narrative Unreliability

Abstract: Two decades ago, the discussion about the concept of the "unreliable narrator" has been a major driver of a cultural and historical readjustment of narratology allowing for a cognitive, cultural-narratological, and historical theory of unreliable narration. This essay revisits such a call for a historicizing of the phenomenon, promoted foremost by Ansgar Nünning, but claims another fundamental paradigm shift, one towards a functional-historical approach to narrative unreliability that in the end calls into question the relevance of the concept for contemporary fictional literature itself. It shows that unreliable narration, at its core, was a literary phenomenon of Modernism and Postmodernism, based on the creation of fundamental ambiguity within the narrated world and the reading process. The realization that, in the post-truth age we are living in, such a semantic disruption can no longer be a function of 'unreliable' narrative literature, leads me to pronouncing the 'death' of the unreliable narrator. This observation, however, does not render the concept superfluous as a whole – on the contrary it leads us to a rebirth of the phenomenon in many other guises and genres, paradoxically calling again for more complex answers to the problem of unreliability.

1 The significance of unreliability for narratology

When Ansgar Nünning asked me to present his Giessen studies on unreliable narration at the 1999 Conference of the *Society for the Study of Narrative Literature* in Dartmouth, NH, (see Zerweck 2001) I never imagined how this topic would continue to haunt me (and many others) in the future. Now, twenty years later, the discussion around unreliability continues unabated. Indeed, D'hoker and Martens (2008, 2) emphasize its "almost uncanny centrality and importance" within narrative studies, and their judgment is echoed by Tom Kindt and Tilmann Köppe (2011, 1): "Few concepts have attracted the interest of the narratological community as insistently as that of the unreliable narrator."

Within the narratological community – and especially in the context of this essay – the work of Ansgar Nünning is a case in point, for it was he who in the late 1990s played a major role in bringing unreliability into the focus of narratology. In fact, not only is the concept in this instance roughly the same age as its exponent, but it can serve as a diachronic yardstick of his thought: Nünning's 'take' on unreliable narration in many ways encapsulates the changes in his narratological world picture over the last decades. Starting from a structuralist paradigm (Nünning 1989), he went on to call for a cultural and historical narratology (e.g. Nünning 1997, 1998, 1999), before shifting more recently back toward a combination of (neo-)structuralist and rhetorical positions (Nünning 2005, 2008).

However, Wayne Booth's at first glance – but only at first glance – self-explanatory term must bear a burden larger than any (unreliable) narrator's life, inasmuch as to follow the contours of Ansgar Nünning's development will lead us to a better understanding of narratology itself. In the first place, the concept of the unreliable narrator – and the multitude of neologisms and terms that describe it – show how narratological categories develop a life of their own, distancing themselves from what they originally meant and outgrowing their original scope.[1] In this context, I would like to revisit our Giessen call of some twenty years ago for a historicizing of unreliable narration (A. Nünning 1997, V. Nünning 2004, Zerweck 2001). Then, drilling down beyond this twenty-year stratum, I will point up another fundamental paradigm shift, one toward a functional-historical approach to narrative unreliability that in the end questions the very relevance of the concept for contemporary fictional literature. Pronouncing the 'death' of the unreliable narrator in narrative literature will, however, lead me in my concluding section to a rebirth of the phenomenon in many other guises and genres, paradoxically calling again for more complex answers to the problem of unreliability. Before putting these thoughts on the functional history of unreliability into four theses, however, I want to briefly revisit the recent history of the theory of unreliable narration, with a view to developing a narratological paradigm on which to base those later reflections.

---

[1] What James Phelan (2017, xii) asks of narratology in general, to concentrate in the first place on "concepts" because they "are more important than terms", is, I believe, especially important for the study of the complex of unreliable narration.

2 A narratological paradigm of narrative unreliability

From its beginnings in Wayne C. Booth's *The Rhetoric of Fiction* (1961), the phenomenon of narrative unreliability has not been restricted to narratology; on the contrary, as Monika Fludernik (2005, 57) points out, it has been closely entwined with questions of textual semantics, interpretation, and ambiguity. In addition, the effect of unreliability within such a complex can be related to a diversity of real-life referential systems – ethical, cognitive, logical, behaviorist, and linguistic.[2] The concept of unreliability is of its nature, in Mieke Bal's words (2002, 24), a 'traveling concept' that has journeyed "between disciplines, between individual scholars, between historical periods, and between geographically dispersed academic communities." Moreover, it is one borrowed from real-life communication and thereby colliding in its different uses, because "confusion tends to increase with those concepts that are close to ordinary language." (Bal 2002, 26) Given the hugely complex nature of the concept, it comes as no surprise that a multitude of competing approaches to narrative unreliability can be detected within the literary theory of the past sixty years.

A number of scholars have traced the history of research on unreliable narration in greater or lesser detail, shedding light on different concepts of unreliability that are "difficult – even for literary critics – to keep track of" (Vogt 2015, 131). Especially more recent attempts (e.g. A. Nünning 2005, 2008, V. Nünning 2015b, Vogt 2018) sketch how, from 1961 until Ansgar Nünning's cognitive reconceptualization in the late 1990s (e.g. 1997, 1999), the concept of the unreliable narrator was long of only minor importance within structuralist narrative theory. For about ten years, this was followed by a theoretical debate between cognitive and rhetorical narratologists. Those subscribing to Nünning's cognitive-narratological approach (like myself in Zerweck 2001) considered unreliability the (historically variable) product of the process of naturalization realized within the reading process. Rhetorical narratologists in the tradition of Wayne Booth – most prominently James Phelan (e.g. 2005) – focused on the (implied) author-reader communication foregrounded by an unreliable narrator, who is exposed as such through dramatic irony (see A. Nünning and V. Nünning 2007).

---

[2] Unreliable narration is, then, closely linked to real-world cognitive frames and does not constitute a form of 'unnatural' narrative that cannot be naturalized on the basis of such frames (see Heinze 2018, 418).

With the benefit of hindsight it seems that these competing approaches always had much in common. Attacking radical cognitivist approaches, James Phelan (2005, 49) nevertheless acknowledges that readers and authors alike "need conceptual schemata to construct interpretations" or "structural wholes." And Ansgar Nünning, in his revised cognitive-rhetorical theory of unreliable narration (2005, 2008), combines cognitive-narratological premises with Phelan's (2005, 45) reconceptualization of the implied author as "a streamlined version of the real author, an actual or purported subset of the real author's capacities, traits, attitudes, beliefs, values, and other properties that can play an active role in the construction of the particular text."[3] In his synthesis, which has recourse to both Booth and Phelan, Nünning (2008, 31) concluded that "ascriptions of unreliability involve a tripartite structure that consists of an authorial agency, textual phenomena (including a personalized narrator and signals of unreliability), and reader response."[4] And he agreed with Phelan that within this structure the real or implied author "is not a product or structure of the text but rather the agent responsible for bringing the text into existence," fashioning a text "in a particular way in order to communicate sharable meanings, beliefs, attitudes, and values and norms" (Nünning 2008, 50).

Despite their divergences, then, both cognitive and rhetorical approaches agree that unreliability cannot be explained solely within textual parameters. More recently, the controversy has somewhat subsided, with each approach coming to appreciate insights of the other: "Phelan and Nünning concluded that their approaches were largely compatible" (Martens 2015, 157), with rhetorical (e.g. Booth 1961, Phelan and Martin 1999, Phelan 2008), phenomenological (e.g. Riggan 1981), and (cognitive-)narratological (e.g. Hansen 2007, Nünning 2008, Vogt 2018) typologies of unreliable narration being seen as equally grounded in contextual frames of reference. Indeed nowadays, as Liesbeth Korthals Altes (2015, 65) has pointed out, different approaches to unreliable narration "appear complementary, with their respective focus on the text, on the author's communicative intentions, on readers' interpretive activity, and on socially defined communication codes."

---

[3] Booth (2005, 75–76) himself embraced the idea of an implied author being removed to the outside of the text.

[4] While Nünning, largely for logical reasons, concedes the importance of an authorial subject (where there is decoding there must be encoding), I would rather emphasize a premise that lies at the core of Booth's and Phelan's insistence on the role of the (implied) author: the importance of the ethical dimension of fiction (see Booth 2005, 76). This dimension is particularly relevant for a concept like narrative unreliability, which often derives from ethical discrepancies.

Recent studies have set out to broaden and further differentiate the concept of narrative unreliability, most notably Robert Vogt's monograph (2018) on narrative unreliability, which combines possible-worlds theory and cognitive narratology, and the articles in Vera Nünning's (2015a) cross-disciplinary collection, which extends the discussion of unreliability to non-fictional narrative. From a theoretical perspective, Uri Margolin's contribution is particularly appealing.

Margolin (2015, 55) identifies "the main issues involved in theorising (un)reliability in written narrative – be it actuality-oriented or fiction – by proceeding from product (what) to production or performance (how), and ending with the narrator (who)."[5] The product (the narrated) belongs to the *semantic* dimension, the production (the narration) to the *pragmatic* dimension, and the narrator to the *mental/cognitive* dimension of narrative unreliability. In his overview of the different criteria at work in each dimension and of the different elements of the three areas Margolin then integrates the three axes of communication which Phelan and Martin (1999, 94) introduced into the discussion of unreliability: reporting, interpreting and evaluating.[6] Accordingly, he (Margolin 2015, 39–40) distinguishes between the *alethic* (what there is), comprising "claims of what is the case in the domain"; the *epistemic*, concerning "inferences drawn from these facts, putative explanations for them, and, in the human sphere, also [...] the ascription of semiotic, socio-cultural significance to human doings"; and thirdly the *axiological* "consisting of evaluations of any element or action of the domain."

Margolin's integrated model of three domains of unreliability, the respective dimensions involved in each domain and the mechanisms of how unreliability is gradably realized in each of these domains is outstanding in its logical coherence and scope, and therefore an especially valuable theoretical tool in extending the concept of unreliability to non-fiction. It is equally valuable for the analysis of different types of narrative unreliability, drawing our attention to the real-life origins of the concept of unreliable narration on which it strongly relies, and highlighting the opposition of reliable and unreliable narration. Margolin (2015, 35) notes that unreliability depends on reliability as "unmarked, backgrounded or default case."[7]

---

[5] The narrator in this model denotes "the originator, inner-textual or actual, of the narration at hand" (Margolin 2015, 56) and is therefore not necessarily a purely textual function.
[6] Corresponding with these three axes, James Phelan (2005, 2017) has distinguished on the scale of unreliability between six types of unreliable narration: misreporting, underreporting, misevaluating, underevaluating, misinterpreting, and underinterpreting.
[7] Focusing on an interdisciplinary approach to (un)reliability, Margolin (2015, 35) doubts whether literary studies should consider unreliability "the salient case" as opposed to reliability as the "backgrounded case," and points out Andreas Solbach's (2005) defense of "the primacy of reliability" (Margolin 2015, 34). Nevertheless, on the whole, *the interdependency of the reliable and unreliable* is not questioned.

This ties in with Ansgar Nünning's (2008, 41) observation that the idea of unreliability itself rests on "realist and by now doubtful notions of objectivity and truth." Embedded in a mimetic understanding of literature that makes the unreliable narrator a "quasi-human model of a narrator" (Yacobi 1981, 119), these notions include the ideas "that an objective view of the world, of others, and of oneself can be attained," and "that human beings are principally [sic] taken to be capable of providing veracious accounts of events" (Yacobi 1981, 119).

This idea holds for the whole concept of narrative unreliability in fictional texts, whose dissonances are naturalizable with recourse to cognitive frames. Such naturalization only makes sense in contrast to reliability as a cognitive default value violated in the course of unreliable narration (see Nünning 2008, 42; Martinez-Bonati 1981). Hence Kathleen Wall's (1994, 21) observation that an unreliable narrator rests on the idea of "a reliable counterpart who is the 'rational, self-present subject of humanism,' who occupies a world in which language is a transparent medium that is capable of reflecting a 'real' world," is still valid. Similarly, James Phelan (2017, 234) proposes a spectrum of reliable and unreliable narration that depends on the "degree of alignment between author and narrator." If historically and culturally variable norms serve as measure of narrative unreliability, the manifestation of such unreliability must deviate in some form or another from an understanding of reliability – no matter how both are defined and which of Margolin's three fields are targeted by them.

However, one layer of paramount importance for the specifics of fictional unreliability is not addressed in Margolin's narratological paradigm: the *functions* of unreliability. After all, the whole debate around implied/real author, discrepant awareness and unreliable narration as a narrative strategy centers on the problem whether an intention or a functionalizing of intentional design can – or even should – be discerned. For rhetorical theorists the functions of unreliable narration are of their very nature of fundamental importance. Until his late years, Wayne Booth was a strong advocate of the "ethical effect" (2005, 86) of narrative, and James Phelan defines narrative as "action, a teller using resources of narrative to achieve a purpose in relation to an audience" (2017, x).[8] Similarly, cognitive narratologists also highlight the functions of narrative unreliability. Reflecting my own attempt at historicizing the phenomenon (Zerweck 2001), Ansgar Nünning (2008, 56–62) focuses on the functions of unreliable narrators in

---

8 Consequently, Phelan (2017, 100), in addition to his typology along the axes of reporting, evaluating, and interpreting, has proposed another functional "spectrum of readerly effects of unreliable narration that extends from estranging unreliability at one end to bonding unreliability at the other."

specific cultural and historical contexts, and Vera Nünning discusses the "epistemological, cognitive and ethical functions that unreliability can fulfil in fiction" (2015c, 99).

This brief glance at some developments in the recent history of the theory of unreliable narration shows that despite differences and conflicts in approaches to the issue, the fundamental debates seem to belong to the past. More recently, reconceptualizations have sought to integrate different perspectives on unreliable narration by including formerly conflicting premises (e.g. Nünning 2005, 2008), or by developing holistic systems that open up the concept to all discourses – narrative or not, even non-fictional (see e.g. Margolin 2015).[9] These approaches allow us to combine some of the fundamental insights into the phenomenon of narrative unreliability outlined above into a narratological paradigm:

1. Narrative unreliability is a phenomenon situated at the crossroads of different fields and disciplines, including narratology, ethics, epistemology, linguistics, psychology, and cognitive theory. The dominant focus of any given study depends on individual preferences, theoretical expertise, and specific research interests.
2. All current models of unreliable literary narration rely on three core elements: an authorial agency (implied or real), the narrator's utterances as manifested in the text, and a reader. Hence, the study of unreliable narration cannot be restricted to the textual analysis of the narrator's discourse.
3. Unreliability derives from divergent awareness, or dramatic irony, allowing readers to interpret the textual information given by the narrator in accordance with the (real or implied) author's agenda, as distinct from the narrator's stance.
4. Both the cognitive encoding (author) and decoding (reader) of unreliable narration depend on culturally and historically variable frames of references. What is considered true, right or good today may appear false, wrong or bad tomorrow. Author and reader may, therefore – but need not necessarily – share similar premises.

---

9 At the same time, however, Liesbeth Korthals Altes (2015, 65–66) has pointed out the heuristic problem that "such ecumenical practices risk obliterating differences in theoretical presuppositions from which different methodologies may be expected to follow," and observed that "there still seems to be some confusion about the kind of scholarly enterprise one is engaging in." Seizing on this observation I will depart here, up to a point, from these "ecumenical practices" by concentrating on a functional-narratological approach toward a history of narrative unreliability.

5. Unreliable narration concerns the narrated, the narrative act, and the narrator, and touches on the semantic, pragmatic, and mental/cognitive dimensions of narrative. Within each dimension, three aspects can furthermore be considered relevant for establishing unreliability, and can be analyzed as such: the *alethic* (what is), the *epistemic* (what is concluded), and the *axiological* (how it is evaluated).
6. Narrative unreliability is always gauged against the (real or hypothesized) counterpart of narrative reliability. If an unreliable narrative can be detected, a reliable narrative must in principle be considered as a default value.
7. As a literary phenomenon, unreliable narration cannot be analyzed without having recourse to its functions and effects. Both rhetorical and cognitive-narratological studies have emphasized the wide range of cognitive, philosophical, and ethical implications of unreliable narration – hence its particular relevance for the study of narrative fiction.

These seven presuppositions combine cognitive, rhetorical, pragmatic, and cultural insights from different approaches and form a theoretical paradigm framing the following four theses concerning a functional (or rather metafunctional) history of unreliable narration.

3 Toward a (meta-)functional history of unreliable narration: four theses

Unreliable narration, like all narrative techniques, is subject to historical transformation: as a fictive act mediating between the 'real' and the 'imaginary',[10] it has developed along historical lines depending on changing cultural contexts. The cultural discourses mainly reflected by unreliable narration, e.g. subjectivity, epistemological doubt, or fundamental ontological questions, were not prominent in medieval or early modern times. In contrast we find a vast

---

10 Wolfgang Iser's (1993) triadic model of literature as a *fictive* act mediating between elements of the extratextual *real* world and the *imaginary* world evoked by a text has helped to overcome an ontologically questionable notion of fiction as a mirror of reality. See also Zerweck (2001, 167–171) where I have attempted to contextualize unreliable narration within such a triadic understanding.

number of different forms of unreliable narration in late nineteenth-century, twentieth-century, and especially post-war literature.[11]

Such historical observations are mainly based on the functions narrative unreliability fulfills as a fictive act. The functional basis for the historicizing of unreliable narration becomes clear in many instances, e.g. when Nünning (2008, 59) includes Emily Brontë's *Wuthering Heights* (1847) in the history of unreliable narration because it "seriously undermines the assumption that an objective or authoritative version of events can in principle be established." The mechanisms behind – and the results of – such functional transformational processes of narrative have been explored by Monika Fludernik in *Toward a 'Natural' Narratology* (1996). As Fludernik observes, the transitions between different ways of expressing experience in narrative form – or 'experientiality' to use Fludernik's term – are to be found in periods when readers have become used to narrative techniques and have been able to naturalize them with recourse to their frames of reference (see Erll and Roggendorf 2002, 95). The analysis of historical change in narrative forms is thus dependent on the interplay of textual manifestations on the one hand and hypothesized cognitive frames in the reception process on the other.

Fludernik's observations help us to understand the fundamental historical transformation which the phenomenon of unreliable narration as 'fictive' has undergone. By mediating between 'real' contextual frames (on both sides, author as well as reader) and the 'imaginary' world, narrative unreliability functions in a given period as a means to foreground cultural discourses – e.g. epistemological criticism – or to question ethical norms, a process which (like that of narrative as a whole) is as historically variable as its contextual premises and textual manifestations. Basing transitional processes on changes in the functionality and effects of narrative unreliability allows us to come more readily to terms with the complex development of that strategy.[12]

However, the many theories of unreliability have also shown that for a history of unreliable narration we must take into account how these transitional processes depend on our understanding of the nature of unreliability itself. Where do we as theorists and readers stand within this history? At what point

---

11 For historical sketches of unreliable narration see e.g. V. Nünning (1998), Nünning (1999), Zerweck (2001), Nünning (2008), V. Nünning (2015c).

12 See also Erll and Roggendorf (2002, 105) who, with reference to Winfried Fluck's functional history of the American novel (1997), have pointed out how important functional historical approaches are in order to understand the relation between the semantics of literary forms and their social effect – a relation, I would add, which lies in particular at the center of unreliable narration.

did the concept of narrative unreliability come into focus as the projection of narratologists and readers? What functions result from such projections? What does narrative unreliability mean to twenty-first-century readers? Expanding on my approach of 2001, the four theses below seek to answer these questions. They deal with the nature of unreliable narration as a cognitively disruptive metafunctional narrative strategy and will, in the concluding section, move on to develop an idea of the new challenges posed by such a (meta-)functional history of narrative unreliability.

Thesis 1: Narrative unreliability is ultimately based on the metafunction of cognitive disruption, which is a heritage of the concept's real-life roots

Narrative unreliability is one of the few narratological topics which non-narratologists are more than willing to engage in when asking us what we are currently working on. This interest in narrative unreliability can partly be attributed to its political relevance in post-truth times. A second and equally important reason for the accessibility of unreliability beyond literary theory is that it has its roots in real-life concepts. For most people, when talking about literature, unreliability is above all an intuitive category which they project onto narrative, fictional or not. The concept, as Margolin (2015, 31) points out, is indeed "an integral part of our everyday life activities": Unlike many other literary categories, "issues of reliability apply equally to all major kinds of discourses consisting of claims."

The real-life roots of unreliable narration are prominent in the paradigm of unreliability developed above: the authorial agency it depends on, the naturalization processes that constitute it, the mechanism of discrepant awareness constituting some form of 'unsaid message'. That unreliability depends on real-life frames becomes most obvious when we realize that it only makes sense as a deviation from a default value: unreliability is always based on some, in all probability unspoken, understanding of reliability. In real life communication, a departure from such a default value or benchmark will be regarded as a sign of ambiguity and/or cognitive instability, undermining notions of reliability. No matter what areas are affected by it (the narrated, the narration, or the narrator), some sort of ambiguity in the assessment of unreliability needs to be resolved whenever reliability cannot be presumed.

When Wayne Booth introduced the concept of the unreliable narrator to the study of narrative, he also burdened literary theory with the complexity and real-life cognitive roots of the phenomenon. Using Monika Fludernik's (1996, 221) cognitive terminology, one could also say that he projected a 'natural' category based on a real-life macro-frame onto narrative fiction. Accordingly, his projection, the unreliable narrator, includes the basic characteristics ascribed to the macro-frame. And as this projection – in contrast to more technical terminology, like focalization, perspectival structure, or the story/discourse dichotomy – is already multilayered in its real-life context, the literary concept retains that complexity.

Expanding on this idea we can ask: What or who do we take to be an unreliable narrator in 'natural' real-world contexts? The answer is here as difficult as in narratology. Most 'real-life' people would probably settle for 'It depends' – on what is told, on personal factors, on the communicative context, on the different fields touched by the unreliability and so on, all of which are the same areas narratology also embraces. However, since narratologists do not accept the answer 'It depends', they have come up with more systematic accounts. And yet there is no denying that it *does* depend on a whole lot of things; it is therefore no surprise that so many different roads have had to be tried before competing schools and approaches have buried the hatchet and agreed on a few fundamentals such as the necessity of a tripartite model like the one outlined above.

Maybe we can also agree that unreliable narration in narrative fiction inevitably violates some code that signals reliability. Just as in real-life contexts, this violation creates cognitive disruption in the process of reception. With its tripartite design, such narrative transports the cognitive dissonance of ambiguity, which therefore calls for naturalization within the frame of unreliability. Despite all differences in theories of unreliable narration – themselves projections of a real-life macro-frame – all agree that through the mechanism of discrepant awareness unreliable narratives trigger (or even display) disharmony on a cognitive level, creating ambiguity in the narrative process and ultimately causing a cognitive disruption that is resolved in terms of projecting unreliability.

Cognitive dissonance is thus an integral part of the concept of unreliable narration as a projection of 'natural' macro-frames onto literary theory. Without the creation of such dissonance in the first place, we can as little speak of unreliable narration in a novel as we would in a real-life communicative situation. Let us remember that, as Monika Fludernik (2005, 57) has observed, narrative unreliability is so complex because it combines questions of the semantics of texts, of interpretation, and of ambiguity ("*Sinndoppelung*" – i.e. the 'doubling of meaning' – in the original German). This ambiguity can be considered a metafunction of narrative unreliability, because it is fundamental for the creation (by an authorial agent) and reading (by a receptive agent) of narratives as unreliable.[13] All other potential functions of unreliable narrators depend on unreliability's metafunction of ambiguity, because without fulfilling this metafunction they would not, as in real-life communication, be naturalized with recourse to the frame of '(un)reliability'. In the words of Wolfgang Iser, unreliable narration 'ambiguates' the real, and with this specific (indeed unique) metafunction mediates between the real and the imaginary.

Thesis 2: Unreliable narration culminates in twentieth-century literature because of its functional dependency on cognitive disruption
In his brief history of unreliable narration Nünning (2008) holds that the phenomenon reached its peak in the late twentieth century. Before that, unreliability ostensibly played no (or only a small) part in narrative fiction. Until the end of the eighteenth century authors like Richardson, Smollett or Defoe "sought to establish, rather than undermine, their narrator's reliability" (Nünning 2008, 57).

---

[13] Vera Nünning's (2015c, 99–102) account of the functions of unreliable narration illustrates the metafunctional ambiguity in unreliability as a whole. The manifold "cognitive functions of unreliable narrations" (V. Nünning 2015c, 99) force readers to (re)evaluate ambiguities in a narrative and thus strongly rely on cognitive dissonance. The same is clearly true for unreliability "[w]ith regard to epistemology", where "unreliable narrations function as a means of presenting deviating viewpoints" (V. Nünning 2015c, 100) and, as such, epistemological vagueness. A lack of cognitive coherence also underlies the "most visible function of homodiegetic or human-like unreliable narrators," which is to provide "insight into their strange minds, their values, delusions, emotions, and, finally, into their (sometimes twisted) ways of thinking" (V. Nünning 2015c, 100). This is especially true for unreliable narrators like "madmen, paedophiles or murderers" who by way of their normative deviations require the naturalization of normative dissonance and thereby "enrich and refine readers' implicit personality theories" (V. Nünning 2015c, 100). Unreliable narratives whose function "lies in questioning truisms and prevailing cultural norms and values" (V. Nünning 2015c, 101) also rely on the staging of conflicting and thus ambiguous notions in a given historical and cultural context. The fundamental cognitively disruptive function of unreliable narratives comes even more to light in the function of a "de-automisation and de-familiarization of perception and interpretation" (V. Nünning 2015c, 101). Here, unreliable narratives, by disrupting the 'easy' reading process, exactly fulfill, as Vera Nünning emphasizes (V. Nünning 2015c, 101), Viktor Shklovsky's modernist claim as to the true function of fiction: to make what we have gotten to know "'unfamiliar', to make forms difficult, to increase the difficulty and length of perception" (1965 [1917]: 12, quoted in V. Nünning 2015c, 101). Similarly, the ethical function of texts that immerse readers "in the thoughts and world-views of unreliable narrators" is based on moral divergence and deviation faced with which readers are forced to "experience alterity" (V. Nünning 2015c, 102) by naturalizing (ethically) highly ambiguous narratives.

As early as 1800, however, Maria Edgeworth's *Castle Rackrent* (1800) confronts the audience with a fundamentally ambiguous narrative voice and "sets out to destroy the reader's expectations of narrative reliability" (Nünning 2008, 58); then, in the course of the nineteenth century, a series of novels can be said to trigger the cognitive dissonance in readers that we have defined as constitutive of unreliable narration, for example James Hogg's *The Private Memoirs and Confessions of a Justified Sinner* (1824) and Emily Brontë's *Wuthering Heights* (1847). Toward the end of the century, some of Henry James's novels continue this development, anticipating/marking the turn to the epistemological crises of the twentieth century (see Nünning 2008, 59–60; see also V. Nünning 2015c, 100).

The staging and mediation of growing epistemological skepticism is prominent in some examples of unreliable narration in modernist novels, e.g. Ford Madox Ford's *The Good Soldier* (1915), or some of Joseph Conrad's work, e.g. *Lord Jim* (1899) and *Under Western Eyes* (1910). Later in the twentieth century, after World War II, narrative unreliability in literature matured. It became a widespread literary technique, with the number of unreliable narratives increasing exponentially. It is surely no coincidence that Wayne Booth introduced the concept of unreliable narration just in time to give a name to a phenomenon now to be found everywhere, from Vladimir Nabokov's *Lolita* (1955) and William Golding's *Free Fall* (1959) to Ian McEwan's "Dead as They Come" (1979) or *Enduring Love* (1997), Martin Amis's *Money* (1984) and *London Fields* (1989), Kazuo Ishiguro's *The Remains of the Day* (1989), Bret Easton Ellis's *American Psycho* (1991), or Chuck Palahniuk's *Fight Club* (1996).

The observation that most unreliable narrators are to be found in mid and late twentieth-century literature reflects Brian McHale's (1987, 9–10) dictum of the modern epistemological dominant and the postmodern ontological dominant. It seems plausible that in an age of epistemological and ontological doubt, of Modernism and Postmodernism, a phenomenon like unreliable narration, whose metafunction is creating ambiguity and discoherence, must have its heyday. While examples of unreliable narration in twentieth-century literature differ in many ways, they all create dissonant, 'broken' narratives, narratives that destabilize rather than create stability. In this respect they stand in sharp contrast to the panoramic novels of the nineteenth century, whose authors, like Tolstoy or Thackeray, seem more interested in creating the reliable points of view commonly associated with omniscience.

The dominant role of unreliable narration in late twentieth-century fiction can be explained – and this is my second thesis – in terms of its metafunction: creating cognitive disruption and ambiguity. Such dissonances ipso facto put a focus on subjectivity, on questionable ethical norms, the problematic nature of mimesis, and the crisis of representation; doing so, they open up more complex interpretive spaces. In an earlier age of reason and Enlightenment, when epistemological stability was not yet widely questioned, incoherence, dissonance and ambiguity could only be rare exceptions to the rule. The same holds for narratives operating within the unified, homogeneous and progress-oriented mindset of the Victorian world.

This makes the rare exceptions of earlier periods than our own look even more clairvoyant and admirable – their anticipation of the future of both epistemological reasoning and narrative design has an almost uncanny, prophetic quality. But it is only in the age of fully-fledged epistemological and ontological skepticism that narrative instability and ambiguity have become the norm rather than the exception. In the course of the twentieth century, unreliable narration can be said to have become a default mode. After all, how can you tell a fictional story in a reliable way at a time when such a mode of representation is considered impossible to begin with?

This observation, however, forces another – frequently noted (see e.g. Wall 1994, Zerweck 2001, Nünning 2008) – problem on us: the question how long unreliable narration can continue to exist after the belief in epistemological, ontological and ethical unity, and in the possibility of reliable, coherent and unambiguous representation has been destroyed. Where ambiguity and dissonance are the foundations of a prevalent world view, it will be increasingly difficult, if not impossible, to undermine that view by creating ambiguity. Against the background of such a historical and cultural context, would unreliable narration not merely seem an oxymoronic duty?

Thesis 3: In the late twentieth century, unreliability as a fictional literary strategy is running out of steam
Changes in epistemological and ontological world views fundamentally influence the ways we write and read fiction. In my analysis of unreliability in post-war fiction (Zerweck 2001, 162–167), I argued that we can observe three major developments: First (as has been pointed out in thesis two), a large number of realist novels use unreliable narrators to undermine conventional notions of (un)reliability, e.g. Kazuo Ishiguro's *The Remains of the Day* (1989) or Ian McEwan's *Enduring Love* (1997). Second, we find texts like Vladimir Nabokov's *Lolita* (1955) which can, like the first group, be read as unreliable narratives but can equally well be naturalized in other ways, for instance as subtle metafictional games played (whether by implied or real author) with readers' expectations or, indeed, with literary conventions such as unreliable narration itself (see Hof 1984, 24). And, third, in the case of experimental postmodernist texts which "acquire their specificity through concentration and combination, through radicalization of

current anti-illusionist techniques" (Fludernik 1996, 272–273), such as Samuel Beckett's "Ping" (1966) or James Joyce's *Finnegan's Wake* (1939), readings in terms of unreliability are no longer possible. Texts like these are highly ambiguous in a different way: they lack all coherence, creating a language that "exists in and of itself, disjoined from its referential anchorings, free-floating in proper Derridean fashion" (Fludernik 1996, 303). Such writing, I argued, would then mark the 'end' of unreliable narration as a naturalizing strategy. The proclaimed 'end' of unreliability in radical experimental texts is even more evident when one looks at the tripartite paradigm of author (implied or real), text, and reader – the former and latter steered by cognitive schemata –, for unreliability cannot be a way of naturalizing radical inconsistencies whose whole point is to radically undermine realist notions of narration.[14]

However, the concept of unreliability itself, as outlined in the paradigm and theses above, now prompts a more radical conclusion, and against the background of the codependence of narrative reliability and unreliability I would now go further than I did in my 2001 essay in forecasting the end of unreliable narration. Not only highly experimental novels but even the unreliable realist narratives of the late twentieth century already marked the approaching death of the unreliable narrator, at least as we came to know (and love) him/her. While late twentieth-century fiction brought a culmination of unreliability that reflected its metafunction, we can observe how through this very culmination the default value system between reliable and unreliable positions has turned almost diametrically around. Unreliability, it seems, has now become the norm and reliability violates our narrative expectations.

Most novels featuring unreliable narrators undermine mimetic notions of representation and pre-modernist epistemological and ontological certainties and, in doing so, fundamentally attack "problematic notions of truth, objectivity, and reliability" (Nünning 2008, 61). Kathleen Wall (1994, 23) has shown how Kazuo Ishiguro's *The Remains of the Day* (1989) "questions both 'reliable' and 'unreliable' narration and the distinctions we make between them." Similarly, a multitude of late twentieth-century unreliable narratives can no longer be considered in the strict sense unreliable at all anymore, for they either reflect "in a truthful way, the illusions and deceptions of the outer world" (Rabinovitz 1983, 67), or, as Nünning puts it (2008, 61), "the stories they tell may not

---

14 Such radical texts perform what Vera Nünning (2015c, 100) calls the function of "de-automisation and de-familiarization of perception and interpretation" to a point where they can no longer be interpreted as unreliable within a structure consisting of authorial agent, narration and reader.

provide objective renderings of the events but they depict, in a very truthful way, the illusions and self-deceptions of the narrators themselves."

Unreliable narration has always foregrounded the position of the subject (whether narrator, reader or author) and its ways of perceiving, narrating or making unequivocal sense of a (textually encoded) world. Consistently with this insight, Kathleen Wall (1994, 22) claimed "that changes in how subjectivity is viewed will inevitably be reflected" in the deployment of that strategy. And, in fact, from around 1800 until the middle of the last century, we see unreliable narratives undermining essentialist versions of "reality and subjectivity and the moral concerns and unspoken epistemological assumptions" (Nünning 2008, 61) of that era – assumptions that in our post-postmodern era are no longer valid.

In contrast to late nineteenth- and early twentieth-century narratives, contemporary realist unreliable narratives reflect the new understanding of reality, subjectivity, and (un)reliability. They no longer create real cognitive dissonance, the metafunction at the core of unreliable narration. And readers no longer consider unreliability as a deviation from a reliable standard. Instead, contemporary unreliable narrators represent what we have come to accept as normal constraints on human cognition and knowledge. In contemporary literature a completely 'reliable' report claiming objective truth and absolute authority would be highly suspicious, whereas a narrator who voluntarily or involuntarily, consciously or unconsciously exposes his/her cognitive or epistemological limitations is in tune with our notions of 'normality' and the scope of its fictional representations.

In the wake of late twentieth-century unreliable narratives, the change in how we view subjectivity and its representation has reached a point where it is not clear what we expect from either a reliable or an unreliable narrative, or whether we even consider unreliability problematic. At a time when subjectivity (and hence also its representation) are no longer clearly defined, when they are in free fall from the high ground of rationalism and, accordingly, in overt self-denial, how can an authorial agent bring readers, via an ostensibly 'unreliable' narrator, to naturalize ambiguity and cognitive dissonance? How can unreliable – as the reciprocal counterpart to reliable – narration still be an adequate technique of narrative fiction? How can we consider a narrator ethically ambiguous after becoming closely acquainted with Humbert Humbert or Patrick Bateman, the truly gruesome narrator of Bret Easton Ellis's *American Psycho* (1991) – a book I still had to buy under the counter in the 1990s because it was banned from display in the bookshops? Unreliability, to put it bluntly, has become banal and boring. Once it was a literary device that mirrored unreliability in real-life contexts, forcing us to come to terms with ambiguous messages or positions. But this is no longer the case. We may, then, justly proclaim the 'death' of the unreliable narrator.

Thesis 4: Narrative unreliability in literature today only 'stages' unreliable narration as a literary convention

The recognition that narrative unreliability has lost its former impetus and destabilizing potential does not, of course, mean that writers will stop using the technique. A glance at contemporary novels proves that, on a purely formal level, unreliable narrators still exist (although their numbers are significantly diminishing). However, instead of naturalizing such narrators in the terms proposed by classical theories of unreliable narration, twenty-first-century authors and readers will likely activate different frames of reference, for instance aesthetic or dramaturgical ones.

Ansgar Nünning (2008, 58) has acknowledged this same mechanism at work at the inception of the history of unreliable narration. Although the narrator of William Makepeace Thackeray's *The Memoirs of Barry Lyndon, Esq.* (1844) "is a paradigmatic unreliable narrator," Nünning claims that the novel itself should not be considered unreliable because it "does not call into doubt the notion that human beings are principally [sic] taken to be capable of providing veracious accounts of events and of others" (Nünning 2008, 59). This comes down to the realization that, in order to be read (and, indeed, written) on the basis of cognitive frames that lead to the ascription of unreliability in the narrator, the novel needs to create (in this case epistemological) ambiguity. The narrative in *Barry Lyndon*, however, "does not call into doubt" the idea that "veracious accounts of events and of others" are possible; it does not fulfill the metafunction of ambiguity.

This is also true for the use of unreliability in the twenty-first century. The narrators of Jonathan Littell's *The Kindly Ones* (2006) or Martin Amis's *The Zone of Interest* (2014) – novels dealing with the Holocaust – display many typical textual signals of narrative unreliability and aim at typical extratextual frames of reference associated with that strategy. Nevertheless they create no cognitive disruption that calls for naturalization within the parameters of unreliability. Ambiguity and moral conflict are present to a high degree at the core of both novels, yet they are not invoked by the unreliability of the narrative act but by the moral issues the narrative raises: in this case the presence of historical horror, the (implied/real) author's (implied) agenda, and the right of a fictional narrator to present a particular perspective on the Holocaust.

For similar reasons – and unlike Robert Vogt (2018, 292–326) – I would not consider Ian McEwan's *Atonement* (2001) an unreliable narrative despite the fact that it foregrounds the divergent cognitive processing of different focalizers (see Vogt 2018, 325–326). On the surface McEwan's novel might exhibit typical elements of unreliability, but it lacks the classical metafunction of cognitive disruption. What we witness is rather a staging of the limitations and unreliability of various perspectives – something the contemporary understanding of subjectivity and representation has led us to expect.

How can we account for this fundamental change in the nature of unreliability? Tamar Yacobi (1981, 1987, 2005) has provided a cognitive framework that may help us understand how inconsistencies detected within the tripartite structure of authorial agent, narration and reader can be naturalized after the 'death' of the unreliable narrator proper. Yacobi (1981, 114) differentiates five principles governing the naturalization of "referential difficulties, incongruities or (self-)contradictions" within a narrative: "(1) the genetic; (2) the generic; (3) the existential; (4) the functional; (5) the perspectival."[15] The first four principles "have in common that they all resolve the problem at the expense of something other than the mediator, who may remain perfectly reliable" (Yacobi 1987, 336). Only if textual inconsistencies are resolved according to the perspectival principle does unreliability dominate the writing and reading strategy, and dispose authors and readers to hypothesize an unreliable mediator.

What we observe today is that elements of a narrative that would formerly have been both written and naturalized with recourse to the perspectival principle are – depending on individual expectations, presuppositions, literary knowledge, norms, or beliefs of authors and readers – naturalized in accordance with one of Yacobi's other four cognitive principles. If readers apply the generic principle, the oddities of the text can be resolved within the frame of the conventions of the genre in question. A breaking of these conventions – for instance when a fictional Nazi key player is granted interpretational sovereignty of the Holocaust in Littell's *The Kindly Ones* – can then be naturalized as a generic innovation

---

15 Under the *genetic* principle, readers resolve textual contradictions by interpreting them within the authorial or historical context of the work. The *generic* principle allows the naturalization of textual oddities within the framework of particular genres and their conventions. The *existential* principle governs the reader's resolution of textual inconsistencies in terms of real-world models. In the case of the *functional* principle, a work's "aesthetic, thematic and persuasive goals [...] operate as a [...] guideline to making sense of its peculiarities" (Yacobi (1981, 117). Finally, the *perspectival* principle allows the reader to attribute problematic elements of a narrative text to the individual perspective of a fictional reflector.

rather than as an instance of unreliable narration. Alternatively, the functional principle of naturalization would foreground the aesthetic, thematic, or persuasive goals of the work, a case in point being the questioning of knowledge and representation in McEwan's *Atonement*, where, as we have seen, the positing of narrative unreliability is not an adequate strategy of naturalization. In short, the cognitive principles Yacobi develops allow for many kinds of resolution of textual ambiguities involving effects other than that of unreliability. In a world that – against the benchmark of a previous age – can only be perceived unreliably, narrative unreliability can merely be staged. What we have today is in that sense a 'fake' unreliability, which is essentially not unreliable at all, because the authorial agent, via the narrative act, no longer confronts the reader with true ambiguity or irritating cognitive disruption.

4 Conclusion: The importance of unreliability in twenty-first-century culture

The four theses of my functional approach entail a re-evaluation of the history of narrative unreliability. They show that, as a literary phenomenon, unreliable narration lasted some 200 years, from the late eighteenth to the end of the twentieth century. During this time it underwent a fundamental historical transformation, developing, as a projection of the macro-frame of ambiguity and dissonance, parallel to the ideas of the Enlightenment and the rise of modern concepts of subjectivity and epistemology.

The end of unreliable narration in literature began at the moment when readers had become familiar with it as a literary means of framing ambiguity and had begun to naturalize it as a strategy with recourse to other frames of reference than those triggered by cognitive disruption. Postmodern discourses of ontology and the crisis of representation were on the one hand mediated by a multitude of unreliable narratives. On the other hand, these discourses have gradually undermined the original real-life roots of unreliable narration to a point where literary unreliability is no longer a persuasive writing or reading option. The success of unreliable narration in literature has, so to speak, consumed its child, and unreliability, no longer capable of challenging or even surprising readers, is now merely a literary technique staged within western culture.

However, this does not mean that the processes of ambiguation triggered by unreliability are less crucial in present cultural discourse than they used to be. On the contrary: In a culture that has undermined our stability, unmasking the hitherto solid bases of knowledge, epistemology, ontology, and norms as mere phantasmagoria of pre-modern blindness, we need – perhaps more than ever – new ways of mediating ambiguity between the real and the imaginary. And the macro-frame of unreliability is still one of the most effective narrative weapons of choice here – just not in its traditional literary form. We can, in fact, observe a new dawn of narrative unreliability mirroring real-life unreliability in other genres and disciplines. Ansgar and Vera Nünning have both emphasized the need to expand not only "the generic scope of unreliable narration" (A. Nünning 2008, 62) to other fictional genres, but also to "other media and non-fictional text-types, contexts and disciplines beyond literary studies" (V. Nünning 2015a, v). It is in such an expansion that we may grasp how strongly unreliability as a cognitive frame is still pushing us toward dealing with the unexpected and the disruptive.

One area where narrative unreliability still functions very prominently as a strategy of mediating ambiguity is the field of visual media, for instance film. Many forms of unreliable narration, like those analyzed by Eva Laass (2008) in her typology of unreliable film narratives in America, are based on creating fundamental dissonance.[16] This is for instance the case in classical examples of unreliable film narration in which the first version of the narrated story in the end turns out to "have been the visual and auditory representation of a lie" (Bordwell 1985, 61), as in Alfred Hitchcock's *Stage Fright* (1950) or more recently Bryan Singer's *The Usual Suspects* (1995) (see Griem and Voigts-Virchow 2002, 170). As opposed to literary narratives, where we are used to narrators building their narratives on lies, the lies in films cannot be resolved within the tripartite structure of agent, narrator,

---

[16] The question of (un)reliable narration in film is at least as complex as in literature, starting with the discussion whether we can speak of a narrator in film at all, and leading to problems of developing a widely acceptable paradigm of unreliable filmic narration – an academic realm only to be touched on here but of prime importance for a fully-fledged cognitive-functional history of unreliable narration. In his influential cognitive film study *Narration in the Fiction Film* (1985, 62), David Bordwell emphasizes that the cognitive processes of watching film narrative, in contrast to those involved when reading a novel, do not on principle prompt the projection of a teller or even an authorial agent: "To give every film a narrator or implied author is to indulge in an anthropomorphic fiction." Bordwell's approach, and similarly those of Edward Branigan (1992), Noël Carroll (1996), or Celestino Deleyto (1996), are focused on the top-down and bottom-up naturalization processes involved in watching films: "In the fiction film, narration is *the process whereby the film's syuzhet and style interact in the course of cueing and channeling the spectator's construction*" (Bordwell 1985, 53, emphasis in the original). However, other studies on film narration, mainly from literary theorists, disagree with this observation and defend the narrative instance of a filmic narrator, e.g. Chatman (1990), Lothe (2000), or more recently Brössel (2014, 38–42) and Eva Laass (2008, 20–21.), whose cultural-narratological book-length study on unreliability in film is a standard work on the subject.

and reader/viewer. After all, the narration is "not just *reporting* what the liar said but *showing* it as if it were indeed objectively true" (Bordwell 1985, 61, emphasis mine). Hence viewers' cognitive frames include the fundamental expectation – to refer to the title of Jörg Helbig's (2006) collection on unreliability in film – that the "camera doesn't lie".

Another staging of narrative unreliability like that of Hitchcock and Singer is evidenced by the long-running contemporary TV series *How I Met Your Mother* (2005–2014).[17] Here the story is presented retrospectively by the main character, Ted, who regularly interrupts himself, admitting that what was shown was just his wishful thinking and that it was all different – the different version then being presented.[18] As in *Stage Fright* and *The Usual Suspect*, we follow a story put on screen involving a large enterprise with a large number of people – from actors, writers and director to sound, light and editing personnel. And suddenly, with a single twist, their whole product is invalidated, leading viewers to wonder how much of Ted's 'true story' will eventually be reversed in subsequent episodes. We are thus confronted with a radical undermining of the expected, leaving us confused and searching for cognitive strategies that will allow naturalization of this confusion. The effect is extremely unsettling for the viewer, whose naturalization is accordingly based on what we have seen to be the classical metafunction of unreliability: strong ambiguity and radical cognitive dissonance. Such instances of unreliability in film and TV series show that on the screen unreliability still has the unsettling effect it once had on the page: questioning and overturning accepted frames of reference and, in doing so, mediating deep ambiguity between the real and the imaginary.

A further area equally important for future cultural-narratological analysis is non-fictional discourse. Although narratologists have traditionally restricted the concept of unreliability to fiction (e.g. Fludernik 2001), it plays such a prominent – even dangerous – role in non-fictional discourse that an analysis of its subversive metafunction seems highly relevant. Thanks to Vera Nünning's interdisciplinary collection of essays on the subject, narratology has, in fact, begun to take into account that "issues of (un)reliability and (un)trustworthiness play a crucial role in many areas of human life as well as a wide spectrum of academic fields ranging from law to history, and from psychology to the study of culture" (2015a: v). In all these fields non-fictional narrative remains persistently gauged against the default

---

17 Also for Robert Vogt (2018, 338), *How I Met Your Mother* is a prime candidate for an analysis of unreliability.
18 The most prominent examples of this technique can be found in S(eason) 5, E(psiode) 19, S6 E11, S6 E15, S6 E17, S7 E03, S7 E09 and S8 E17, to name but a few episodes from a serial narration that ran for nine years.

value of reliability, and is hence more closely connected to the real-life roots of unreliability than is its fictional counterpart.

However, the observation that a clear resolution of non-fictional unreliability is often undermined by the ambiguity of the phenomenon itself seems far more problematic in non-fictional contexts than on the playground of fictional narrative, especially as "to some extent, unreliability has become a new norm in several formats" (Vera Nünning 2015b, 19). Vera Nünning (2015b, 19) and some other contributors to her 2015 collection have in this respect detected a straddling of the "fact/fiction divide" (2015b, 19) in hybrid formats through the very ambiguity projected by unreliability.

Four years later we have witnessed a multitude of such 'straddling of the fact/fiction divide' in many highly relevant political instances: the propaganda leading to the Brexit vote, Russian trolls' influence on Western media, political supremacy over the truth in Turkish courts, the (right-wing) German AfD's claim to know the new *Volkswillen* ('popular will'), to which the *Lügenpresse* ('lying press') denies the people access, or Donald Trump's brutish attacks on the free press, turning reliable truths into 'fake news' and lies into truth. All of these examples are based on non-fiction narratives which succeed in creating deep ambiguity and radical dissonance on the basis of the cognitive processes that govern our daily judgments of unreliability and reliability.

Unreliable narration might be a literary technique of the past. The phenomenon of unreliability and its exploitation, however, is more central to today's culture, with its struggles between authoritarianism and liberalism, than we would have dreamt in our worst nightmares in the late twentieth century. For the ethics of narrative, unreliability still plays a fundamental role. Things have come full circle, back to Wayne Booth's original coinage of the term in the context of a rhetorical approach to narrative that aimed at the ethical connection between authorial agent and recipient. The unreliable narrator in literature may be dead, but hopefully he/she has taught us how to be vigilant and active in unmasking the exploitation of narrative unreliability around us.

References

Bal, Mieke. *Travelling Concepts in the Humanities. A Rough Guide*. Toronto: University of Toronto Press, 2002.
Booth, Wayne C. *The Rhetoric of Fiction*. Chicago: University of Chicago Press, 1983 [1961].
Booth, Wayne C. "Resurrection of the Implied Author: Why Bother?" *A Companion to Narrative Theory*. Eds. James Phelan and Peter J. Rabinowitz. Oxford: Blackwell, 2005. 75–88.
Bordwell, David. *Narration in the Fiction Film*. Madison: University of Wisconsin Press, 1985.

Branigan, Edward. *Narrative Comprehension and Film*. London: Routledge, 1992.
Brössel, Stephan. *Filmisches Erzählen. Typologie und Geschichte*. Berlin: de Gruyter, 2014.
Carroll, Noël. "Prospects for Film Theory: A Personal Assessment." *Post-Theory: Reconstructing Film Studies*. Eds. David Bordwell and Noël Carroll. Madison: University of Wisconsin Press, 1996. 36–68.
Chatman, Seymour. *Coming to Terms: The Rhetoric of Narrative in Fiction and Film*. Ithaca: Cornell University Press, 1990.
Deleyto, Celestino. "Focalization in Film Narrative." *Narratology: An Introduction*. Eds. Susana Onega and José Angel García Landa. London: Longman, 1996. 217–233.
D'hoker, Elke, and Gunther Martens. "Introduction." *Narrative Unreliability in the Twentieth-Century First-Person Novel*. Eds. Elke D'hoker and Gunther Martens. Berlin: de Gruyter, 2008. 1–6.
Erll, Astrid, and Simone Roggendorf. "Kulturgeschichtliche Narratologie. Die Historisierung und Kontextualisierung kultureller Narrative." *Neue Ansätze in der Erzähltheorie*. Eds. Ansgar Nünning and Vera Nünning. Trier: WVT, 2002. 73–113.
Fluck, Winfried. *Inszenierte Wirklichkeit: Der amerikanische Realismus 1865–1900*. München: Fink, 1997.
Fludernik, Monika. *Toward a 'Natural' Narratology*. London: Routledge, 1996.
Fludernik, Monika. "Fiction vs. Non-Fiction: Narratological Differentiations." *Erzählen und Erzähltheorie im 20. Jahrhundert. Festschrift für Wilhelm Füger*. Ed. Jörg Helbig. Heidelberg: Winter, 2001. 85–103.
Fludernik, Monika. "Unreliability vs. Discordance. Kritische Betrachtungen zum literaturwissenschaftlichen Konzept der erzählerischen Unzuverlässigkeit". *Was stimmt denn jetzt? Unzuverlässiges Erzählen in Literatur und Film*. Eds. Fabienne Liptay and Yvonne Wolf. München: Text + Kritik, 2005. 39–59.
Griem, Julika, and Eckart Voigts-Virchow. "Filmnarratologie: Grundlagen, Tendenzen und Beispielanalysen. *Erzähltheorie transgenerisch, intermedial, interdisziplinär*." Eds. Vera Nünning and Ansgar Nünning. Trier: WVT, 2002. 155–183.
Hansen, Per Krogh. "Reconsidering the Unreliable Narrator." *Semiotica* 165 (2007): 227–246.
Heinze, Rüdiger. "Unnatürliches Erzählen." *Grundthemen der Literaturwissenschaft: Erzählen*. Eds. Martin Huber and Wolf Schmid. Berlin: de Gruyter, 2018. 418–427.
Helbig, Jörg (ed.). *"Camera doesn't lie." Spielarten erzählerischer Unzuverlässigkeit im Film*. Trier: WVT, 2006.
Hof, Renate. *Das Spiel des 'unreliable narrator': Aspekte unglaubwürdigen Erzählens im Werk von Vladimir Nabokov*. München: Fink, 1984.
Iser, Wolfgang. *The Fictive and the Imaginary: Charting Literary Anthropology*. Baltimore: The Johns Hopkins University Press, 1993.
Kindt, Tom, and Tilmann Köppe. "Preface." *Unreliable Narration, Special Issue. Journal of Literary Theory* 5.1 (2011): 1–2.
Korthals Altes, Liesbeth. "What about the Default, or Interpretive Diversity? Some Reflections on Narrative (Un)reliability." *Unreliable Narration and Trustworthiness. Intermedial and Interdisciplinary Perspectives*. Ed. Vera Nünning. Berlin: de Gruyter, 2015. 59–82.
Laass, Eva. *Broken Taboos, Subjective Truths. Forms and Functions of Unreliable Narration in Contemporary American Cinema*. Trier: WVT, 2008.
Lothe, Jakob. *Narrative in Fiction and Film*. Oxford: Oxford University Press, 2000.

Margolin, Uri. "Theorising Narrative (Un)reliability: A Tentative Roadmap." *Unreliable Narration and Trustworthiness. Intermedial and Interdisciplinary Perspectives*. Ed. Vera Nünning. Berlin: de Gruyter, 2015. 31–58.

Martens, Gunther. "Unreliability in Non-Fiction: The Case of the Unreliable Addressee." *Unreliable Narration and Trustworthiness. Intermedial and Interdisciplinary Perspectives*. Ed. Vera Nünning. Berlin: de Gruyter, 2015. 155–170.

Martinez-Bonati, Félix. *Fictive Discourse and the Structures of Literature: A Phenomenological Approach*. Ithaca: Cornell University Press, 1981.

McHale, Brian. *Postmodernist Fiction*. New York: Methuen, 1987.

Nünning, Ansgar. *Grundzüge eines kommunikationstheoretischen Modells der erzählerischen Vermittlung. Die Funktionen der Erzählinstanz in den Romanen George Eliots*. Trier: WVT, 1989.

Nünning, Ansgar. "'But why will you say that I am mad?' On the Theory, History, and Signals of Unreliable Narration in British Fiction." *Arbeiten aus Anglistik und Amerikanistik* 22.1 (1997): 83–105.

Nünning, Ansgar. "Unreliable Narration zur Einführung: Grundzüge einer kognitiv-narratologischen Theorie und Analyse unglaubwürdigen Erzählens." *Unreliable Narration. Studien zur Theorie und Praxis unglaubwürdigen Erzählens in der englischsprachigen Erzählliteratur*. Eds. Ansgar Nünning, Carola Surkamp, and Bruno Zerweck. Trier: WVT, 1998. 3–29.

Nünning, Ansgar. "Unreliable, Compared to What? Toward a Cognitive Theory of Unreliable Narration: Prolegomena and Hypotheses." *Grenzüberschreitungen: Narratologie im Kontext*. Eds. Walter Grünzweig and Andreas Solbach. Tübingen: Narr, 1999. 53–73.

Nünning, Ansgar. "Reconceptualizing Unreliable Narration: Synthesizing Cognitive and Rhetorical Approaches." *A Companion to Narrative Theory*. Eds. James Phelan and Peter J. Rabinowitz. Oxford: Blackwell, 2005. 89–107.

Nünning, Ansgar. "Reconceptualizing the Theory, History and Generic Scope of Unreliable Narration: Toward a Synthesis of Cognitive and Rhetorical Approaches." *Narrative Unreliability in the Twentieth-Century First-Person Novel*. Eds. Elke D'hoker und Gunther Martens. Berlin: de Gruyter, 2008. 29–76.

Nünning, Ansgar, and Vera Nünning. "Dramatische Ironie als Strukturprinzip von *unreliable narration*, *unreliable focalization* und *dramatic monologue*: Ein kommunikations- und erzähltheoretischer Beitrag zur Rhetorik der Ironie im literarischen Erzähltext." *Irony Revisited. Spurensuche in der englischsprachigen Literatur. Festschrift für Wolfgang G. Müller*. Ed. Thomas Honegger, Eva-Maria Orth, and Sandra Schwabe. Würzburg: Königshausen und Neumann, 2007. 51–82.

Nünning, Vera. "Unreliable Narration and the Historical Variability of Values and Norms: The Vicar of Wakefield as a Test Case of a Cultural-Historical Narratology." *Style* 38 (2004): 236–252.

Nünning, Vera (ed.). *Unreliable Narration and Trustworthiness. Intermedial and Interdisciplinary Perspectives*. Berlin: de Gruyter, 2015a.

Nünning, Vera. "Conceptualising (Un)reliable Narration and (Un)trustworthiness." *Unreliable Narration and Trustworthiness. Intermedial and Interdisciplinary Perspectives*. Ed. Vera Nünning. Berlin: de Gruyter, 2015b. 1–38.

Nünning, Vera. "Reconceptualising Fictional (Un)reliability and (Un)trustworthiness from a Multidisciplinary Perspective: Categories, Typology and Functions." *Unreliable Narration* and Trustworthiness. Intermedial and Interdisciplinary Perspectives. Ed. Vera Nünning. Berlin: de Gruyter, 2015c. 83–108.

Phelan, James. Living to Tell about It. A Rhetoric and Ethics of Character Narration. Ithaca: Cornell University Press, 2005.

Phelan, James. "Estranging Unreliability, Bonding Unreliability, and the Ethics of Lolita." Narrative Unreliability in the Twentieth-Century First-Person Novel. Eds. Elke D'hoker and Gunther Martens. Berlin: de Gruyter, 2008. 7–28.

Phelan, James. Somebody Telling Somebody Else: A Rhetorical Poetics of Narrative. Columbus: Ohio State University Press, 2017.

Phelan, James, and Mary Patricia Martin. "The Lessons of 'Weymouth': Homodiegesis, Unreliability, Ethics and The Remains of the Day." Narratologies: New Perspectives on Narrative Analysis. Ed. David Herman. Columbus: Ohio State University Press, 1999. 88–109.

Rabinovitz, Rubin. "Unreliable Narration in Murphy." Samuel Beckett: Humanistic Perspectives. Eds. Morris Béja, Stanley E. Gontarski, and Pierre Astier. Columbus: Ohio State University Press, 1983. 58–70.

Riggan, William. Picaros, Madmen, Naïfs, and Clowns. The Unreliable First-Person Narrator. Norman: University of Oklahoma Press, 1981.

Shklovsky, Viktor. "Art as Technique." Russian Formalist Criticism: Four Essays. Translated and with an introduction by Lee T. Lemon and Marion J. Reis. Lincoln: University of Nebraska Press, 1965 [1917]. 3–24.

Solbach, Andreas. "Die Unzuverlässigkeit der Unzuverlässigkeit." Was stimmt denn jetzt? Unzuverlässiges Erzählen in Literatur und Film. Eds. Fabienne Liptay and Yvonne Wolf. München: Text + Kritik, 2005. 60–71.

Vogt, Robert. "Combining Possible-Worlds Theory and Cognitive Theory: Toward an Explanatory Model for Ironic-Unreliable Narration, Ironic-Unreliable Focalization, Ambiguous-Unreliable Narration and Alterated-Unreliable Narration in Literary Fiction." Unreliable Narration and Trustworthiness. Intermedial and Interdisciplinary Perspectives. Ed. Vera Nünning. Berlin: de Gruyter, 2015. 131–153.

Vogt, Robert. Theorie und Typologie narrativer Unzuverlässigkeit am Beispiel englischsprachiger Erzählliteratur. Berlin: de Gruyter, 2018.

Wall, Kathleen. "The Remains of the Day and its Challenges to Theories of Unreliable Narration." Journal of Narrative Technique 24 (1994): 18–42.

Yacobi, Tamar. "Fictional Reliability as a Communicative Problem." Poetics Today 2 (1981): 113–126.

Yacobi, Tamar. "Narrative Structure and Fictional Mediation." Poetics Today 8 (1987): 335–372.

Yacobi, Tamar. "Authorial Rhetoric, Narratorial (Un)Reliability, Divergent Readings: Tolstoy's 'Kreutzer Sonata'." A Companion to Narrative Theory. Eds. James Phelan and Peter J. Rabinowitz. Oxford: Blackwell, 2005. 108–123.

Zerweck, Bruno. "Historicizing Unreliable Narration: Unreliability and Cultural Discourse in Narrative Fiction." Style 35.1 (2001): 151–178.

Astrid Erll
Odyssean Travels: The Migration of Narrative Form (Homer – Lamb – Joyce)

Abstract: This essay brings cultural and historical narratology into dialogue with classical reception studies. It addresses the reception of Homer's *Odyssey* and its narrative forms across time, focusing on Charles Lamb's children's version *The Adventures of Ulysses* (1808) and James Joyce's modernist novel *Ulysses* (1922) as two landmarks in the epic's modern memory. The essay traces how the *Odyssey*'s *in medias res* beginning initiated the epic's elaborate play with temporal order, which enabled an early exploration of narrative perspective. After a discussion of unreliable narration, multiperspectivity, and narrative coping in the *Odyssey*, the essay shows how these narrative forms and functions travelled and were taken up, reformatted and transformed in Lamb's and Joyce's literary remediations of the Homeric text. These examples show that in the process of classical reception, the migration of narrative form emerges not as a steady and straightforward development, but more as a kind of 'Odyssean travel' – a complex, and often seemingly errant, temporal and cultural dynamic.

1 A tale of two fields, or: Where classical reception studies and cultural and historical narratology meet

No storytelling without the Odyssey – from Dante to Hollywood, from travel writing to adventure games. As one of the oldest extant stories of Greco-Roman antiquity, and with a narrative complexity that far exceeds the already complex *Iliad*, the *Odyssey* has emerged as *the* fundament of storytelling in Europe and beyond, past and present.[1] Its forms have migrated across narrative media genres as diverse

---

1 'Homer' is, of course, not one identifiable author, but an oral tradition that was transcoded into writing during the seventh century BCE. The Homeric epics are often cast as the origin of literature and as a 'European heritage' (see Erll 2018). However, as de Jong (2014, 119) maintains, a "caveat here is that for us, Homer's texts are the first in ancient Greek literature, but

---

Note: I gratefully acknowledge the funding of my research for this essay by the Volkswagen Foundation with an "Opus Magnum" grant.

https://doi.org/10.1515/9783110654370-014

as epic poetry, dramatic monologue, novel, or feature film (see Hall 2008). Irene de Jong, classicist and narratologist, points out that "Greek literature starts with a 'big bang', namely the Homeric epics with their incredibly rich and subtle exploitation of the potential of narrative." A true treasure trove, the Homeric epics "developed most of the classical narrative toolkit: the Muses, the *in medias res* technique, prolepsis and analepsis, embedded focalization, or the tale within the tale." The *Odyssey* in particular thus emerges as the "fountainhead of all ancient (and much later European) narrative" (de Jong 2014, 119).

Since the 1990s, Homer research in Classics departments has embraced narratology. De Jong has provided the massive, 600-page strong *Narratological Commentary on the Odyssey* (2001) and, more recently, Jonas Grethlein (2017) has taken up the challenge with an introduction to the *Odyssey* featuring the programmatic subtitle 'Homer and the Art of Narration' (my translation). Considering its preoccupation with the cultural functions of narrative, it is safe to locate Grethlein's work within the field of 'cultural and historical narratology' in Ansgar Nünning's sense.[2] This recent narratological turn in classical philology opens up new possibilities for a sustained dialogue with cultural narratologists who, for their part, have so far focused largely on modern literature, and specifically on the development of the novel from the eighteenth century onward.

Since the early 2000s, another formidable new field has emerged, that of classical reception studies.[3] This multidisciplinary project, which brings together classical, medieval and modern philology, as well as archeology, art history and media studies, makes it possible to study the afterlives of the *Odyssey* – various forms 'remediation'[4] – in an interdisciplinary dialogue. 'Reception' may to modern philologists sound too one-dimensional, as if a text like James Joyce's

---

that they were in fact preceded by innumerable oral predecessors whose texts have not come down to us, so that Homer was not really the first. There is also the intriguing issue of the indebtedness of early Greek literature to Near Eastern literature."

2 Grethlein (2017, 38) reads the *Odyssey* "as a reflection on the forms and functions of narrative" (my translation). See also Grethlein and Rengakos (2009).

3 On Homer, see for example Greenwood and Graziosi (2010).

4 In memory studies, the term 'remediation' (originally developed as a concept of new media theory by Bolter and Grusin, 1999) is used to describe the repeated mediation of memory matter, across time and space. This is how cultural memories come into existence. Remediation understood in this sense comprises rewriting, translation, adaptation and all other possible forms of 'mediating again'. (For a discussion of remediation and premediation from a memory studies perspective, see Erll 2017.)

Ulysses was just at the 'receiving end' of a classical tradition.⁵ But in fact, this field has given the term 'reception' a new richness and complexity and turned it into a concept that enables the study of some of the most intriguing dynamics in the lives and afterlives of stories. Beyond the older approaches of 'classical tradition' and 'influence-studies', classical reception studies is, as Lorna Hardwick (2009, 1) points out, interested in "all aspects of the reception of the texts and material culture of ancient Greece and Rome, both within antiquity and subsequently." It "investigates the interactions between transmission, interpretation, recontextualisation, translation, rewriting and rethinking in the construction of relationships between past and present and between different locations in the geographies and histories of cultures."

Importantly, reception is not seen as a one-way road. One of the strongest claims of classical reception studies is that whatever is taken as a literary 'original' is continuously transformed in chains of remediation – translations, commentaries, rewritings, performances, adaptations etc. – which, conversely, it may itself have preformed.⁶ Classical reception is thus essentially a form of 'travelling memory' (Erll 2011) as currently addressed in memory studies: the migration, repetition and actualization of cultural contents, forms, and practices across time and space.⁷

With the toolkit of reception studies, the *Odyssey* can be addressed in its various transmedial afterlives: from vase painting to Virgil, from Horace to Shakespeare, from Chapman to Pope, from Keats to Tennyson and to the Pre-Raphaelites, from Joyce to Walcott, from Hollywood to Atwood. In fact, there is a rich body of research that has been preoccupied with precisely such travels of the *Odyssey* – within literary studies most notably William B. Stanford's *The Ulysses Theme* (1963) and Pierro Boitani's *The Shadow of Ulysses* (1994). But the problem is that these works tend to limit the focus, as Stanford's title implies, to the Ulysses *theme*, the afterlives of the *Odyssey*'s thematics or topoi. What has not been studied is how the *Odyssey*'s particular narrative *forms* have migrated to modern literature along with the reception of its story. Not only 'themes'

---

5 The concept should also not be conflated with the idea of 'reception in mind' as addressed in 'reception aesthetics' (Hans-Robert Jauss, Wolfgang Iser). Interestingly, classical reception studies is only interested in the dimension of 'reception in media', i.e. in the remediation of classical texts. It could arguably profit from an extension of its concerns to 'reception in mind' as now studied, for example in cognitive narratology.

6 See, for example, Martindale (2013, 181): "no work of art has its meaning wholly determined by its point of origin."

7 In a recent article (Erll 2018), I have sought to bring these two fields together: literary reception can also be seen as a case of what Ansgar Nünning and I have termed 'the memory of literature' (Erll and Nünning 2005).

travel, but with them also the forms of their narrative mediation. What happens to the forms and functions of an old story in its afterlives? This crucial question about the dynamic of 'narrative in culture' can only be answered through a combination of the two fields, narratology and classical reception studies.

This essay is a first attempt at such a fusion. It sets out to examine the reception of the *Odyssey* as a *narrative*, and it will do so by focusing on two landmarks of its modern memory in the English-speaking world: Charles Lamb's rewriting of the epic into a children's version in the early nineteenth century (*The Adventures of Ulysses*, 1808), and James Joyce's modernist novel *Ulysses* (1922), which uses the *Odyssey* as its 'continuous parallel' (to use a term of T.S. Eliot's).

My aim is to bring 'cultural and historical narratology'[8] as envisioned by Ansgar Nünning to classical reception studies. My focus is on the reception of one particular classical story – that of the *Odyssey*. Taking my cue from cultural and historical narratology, I will analyze the travels and transformations of the *Odyssey*'s narrative forms and functions. Proceeding from Nünning's idea of the 'semantization of form', I argue that changes in the forms of travelling stories are meaningful: they emerge from the cultural contexts in which an act of reception takes place, and they shape the story's future travels.

2 From order to perspective: Unreliability, multiperspectivity, and narrative coping in Homer's *Odyssey*

Unreliability, multiperspectivity, and narrative coping are decidedly modern concepts, developed for the analysis of modern literature at the intersections of narratology and cultural studies – and substantially so by Ansgar Nünning.[9] To different degrees these three categories mingle formal and semantic dimensions, and all three are manifestations of the broader phenomenon of 'narrative perspective', a term Nünning (2000b, 207) understands as a "character's or a

---

[8] This is an approach informed by cultural history and cultural analysis. The focus is on the historical dynamics of narrative forms and their changing functions. See Nünning (2012, 61): "Cultural and historical narratology can [...] be defined as a context-sensitive and diachronic theory of narrative." See also Nünning (2000a); for the 'diachronization of narrative' see Fludernik (2003).
[9] For some examples of Nünning's research on unreliability, see Nünning (1997, 2005); on multiperspectivity see Nünning and Nünning (2000); on narrative coping see Nünning and Nünning (2017); on resilience, narrative and coping, see also Basseler (2019).

narrator's subjective worldview," and which he accordingly sees as "applicable not only to the rhetorical structure of narrative transmission, but, in a more literal manner, to the description of the semantic content of narratives."

This section of my essay will argue that the 'seeds' of modern, perspective-related concepts such as unreliability, multiperspectivity, and narrative coping can already be found in the ancient epic of the *Odyssey*, where they emerged from Homer's daring conceptualization of temporal order. Despite the differences between epic and other narrative genres such as the novel (Bakhtin 1981), and between epic poetry and prose, there is no reason to lose sight of the fact that both are narrative media. A study of the travels and transformations of the *Odyssey*'s narrative forms and functions across time can yield interesting insights into narrative dynamics – not only of modern novels, but also of Hollywood films, graphic novels, and video games, as well as non-fictional genres such as new journalism. After all, *new* narrative always bears a relation to *old* narrative. Through canonization, institutionalization, editing, commenting, rewriting and other forms of remediation, the *Odyssey*'s narrative properties have become cultural memory, and moved through time and space to find expression in modern literature. In this subsection I will, then, discuss quite extensively different forms of unreliability in the *Odyssey*, comment briefly on narrative coping both within the storyworld and in ancient Greece, before turning to the multiperspectivity which emerges in the *Odyssey* in an exchange between Helen and Menelaus.

'Unreliability' is in fact a reproach brought on Odysseus (and by extension on the *Odyssey* and on Homer) by a number of ancient critics, from Plato to Pindar to Dio Chrysostom and Lucian of Samosata, who all suspected that he was a 'liar'. In the introduction to his *True History*, Lucian (second century AD) states that Odysseus "fooled" his listeners "to the top of their bent." Following his example, Lucian sets out to tell a story about his travels to the moon, and asserts that "for I now make the only true statement you are to expect – that I am a liar [...] My subject is, then, what I have neither seen, experienced, nor been told, what neither exists nor could conceivably do so. I humbly solicit my readers' incredulity" (Lucian 1905, 137).

Of course, there is ample evidence in the epic for such a charge of lying: Odysseus calls himself a liar, he is called a liar by other characters, and even the epic narrator describes him as a liar, when Odysseus sets out to tell the long story of his adventures, which form the central part of the *Odyssey*. 'Cunning' (*polymetis*) is one of Homer's recurring epithets for Odysseus. It is a key component of the Odysseus-character. Yet, on the other hand, ancient readers tended to think that the *Odyssey* conveyed a true story, and for modern critics the epic is *per definitionem* told by a reliable and in Bakhtin's (1981) sense 'monological' narrator.¹⁰ To understand this conundrum of truth and lying, reliability and unreliability in the *Odyssey*, a few comments on order, narration and perspective in the *Odyssey* are in place.¹¹

The Homeric epics are famous for their *in medias res* beginnings and elaborate structuring of time, features that Gérard Genette in his *Narrative Discourse* (1983) assigned to the temporal 'order' of the narrative. Thus the main story of the *Iliad* centers on fifty-one days toward the end of the ten-year-long Trojan War. Events that lie outside the main narrative are incorporated into the epic poem by analepses (the rape of Helen) and prolepses (Achilles' death). These terms, by the way, are not Genette's whimsical neologisms, but have their root in ancient Homeric scholarship, in the so-called *scholia*.¹²

The *Odyssey*, too, starts *in medias res* – and does so programmatically.¹³ Its main story covers the last forty-one days of two decades of events connected with the Trojan-Greek War and its aftermath. In a complex narrative ordering of 'middle – beginning – end', the epic poem starts with the hopeless situation at the court of Ithaca just before Odysseus' return, where the suitors have been pressing his wife Penelope to remarry. They have seen through her trick of weaving (by day) and unweaving (by night) old King Laertes' shroud, and she will not much longer be able to withstand them. With the help of Athena (disguised as Mentes), Odysseus' now-mature son Telemachus leaves Ithaca in search of news of his father, sailing to the palaces of Nestor and Menelaus, who had fought with Odysseus before Troy. He hears stories about his father, told by his former comrades-in-arms as well as by Helen. This first part of the epic is the "Telemachy" (Books 1–4). The narrative then switches to events simultaneously

---

10 This traditional view has recently been challenged by Richardson (2006, 337), who casts even the epic narrator as unreliable: "The narrator of the *Odyssey*, who appears objective and perfectly reliable, frequently misleads his listeners/readers by raising false expectations, making prising shifts, concealing facts, leading them to believe inaccurate representations and leaving them in ambiguity."

11 This is also an answer to Vera Nünnning's call (2015, 103) for more attention to be paid in this context to earlier periods, for "[t]he device of embedded unreliable narrators can be found in a host of earlier works [...], and it would be interesting to look at the stories told in earlier texts – for instance by the heroes in Homer's *Ulysses* – from the point of view of unreliable narration, and determine their commonalities as well as differences with modern unreliable narrators."

12 See Nünlist (2009, 65): "Ancient scholars described prolepsis sometimes with the verb *prolambano* (to anticipate) and the cognate noun *prolepsis*. One wonders whether Genette was aware of the fact that, in a way, he *re*introduced a centuries-old term in his *Discours du récit* of (1972) 1980" (my transcriptions).

13 In the proem, the narrator asks the Muse to "start from anywhere" in the story (*Odyssey* 1.10).

experienced by Odysseus on the island of Calypso, from where (after Athena's intervention with Zeus) he is set free after seven years. He sails on a self-made raft to Scheria, the island of the Phaeacians. At King Alcinous' court he is treated with great hospitality, tells the story of his adventures ("Apologue", Books 9–12), and is conducted home in one of the Phaeacians' famous magical ships. Back in Ithaca ("Nostos", Books 13–24) he disguises himself as a beggar, meets his son, and in a veritable orgy of bloodshed the two defeat the suitors. Odysseus reveals himself to Penelope. Their marriage – and with it peace on Ithaca – is restored.

The most striking formal feature of the *Odyssey* is its combination of heterodiegetic and homodiegetic narration. Embedded into the main narrative, which is mediated by an omniscient, 'epic' narrator, are several first-person narratives. Odysseus' 'Apologue'[14] is by far the longest of these, covering Books 9 to 12. It consists of the stories told by the protagonist himself at the court of the Phaiacians about his Mediterranean errancy. This embedded first-person narrative contains the best-known parts of the *Odyssey*, Odysseus' 'adventures': the Ciconians, the Lotus Eaters, the Cyclops, Aeolus, the Laestrygonians, Circe, The Underworld (Nekyia), Sirens, Scylla, Thrinacia, Charybdis, and Calypso.

In Genette's terms, the Apologue is a very long external and completive analepsis, taking up almost a fifth of the entire epic poem and covering the events of a whole decade. Analepses in the Homeric epics are, as de Jong remarks, "the necessary corollary to the *in medias res* device." What "is new in the *Odyssey* is the scale on which this technique is employed" (de Jong 2001, 221). What is also new in Homer's second epic is that important analepses are consistently delegated to embedded first person narrators, not only to Odysseus in the Apologue, but also to Nestor, Menelaus and Helen (in the "Telemachy"). Moreover, there is a sizeable body of what might be called 'false analepses'. These are Odysseus' 'lying tales', which he serves up to various interlocutors when he is back in his homeland of Ithaca but still disguised as a beggar.[15]

My argument in this essay is that Homer's elaborate play with temporal order in the *Odyssey* carved out a new space for an equally elaborate play with perspective, and with related phenomena such as un/reliability of character-

---

14 *Apologos* is a Greek term for a story.
15 In many of the 'lying' (or 'Cretan') tales that Odysseus tells (to Athena, Eumaeus, Antinous, Penelope, and Laertes) while operating undercover on Ithaca, he fashions himself as a Cretan (notorious in the ancient world as liars), who has fought in the Trojan war and then erred across the sea, in ways reminiscent of, but also departing from, Odysseus' real experiences.

narrators, multiperspectivity, and narrative coping – narrative forms and functions, that is, which would come to blossom in modern literary history, particularly in the modern and postmodern novel.[16]

In stark contrast to the overall anachronic design of the *Odyssey*, the Apologue (like the other embedded tales) is told in strict chronological order. In the terminology of ancient critics, the *Odyssey* proceeds *anastrophe* ("out of chronological sequence"), while the Apologue proceeds *dienekeos*, "continuously from beginning to end" (Hunter 2018, 130).[17] The *Odyssey* thus features two models of narrative order, which are connected to two forms of narrative mediation: anachrony is the form used by the heterodiegetic epic (or 'authoritative') narrator, and chronology that of diverse embedded homodiegetic, or 'personal', voices.[18]

Odysseus' Apologue adheres mostly to what modern narratology has identified as the typical features of homodiegetic narration: restrictions of place, of access to other characters' minds, and of understanding (de Jong 2001, 223). There is also the typical interplay between the 'narrating I' and the 'experiencing I' that characterizes retrospective autodiegetic narratives, and makes them narratives of memory. Odysseus-the-narrator adds retrospective explanations and evaluations to his narrative, Odysseus-the-experiencer sometimes does not know what trials lie ahead of him. As de Jong (2001, 225) has shown, Odysseus' tale displays a strikingly subjective style. There are many examples of his particular character-language, words such as "unfortunate", "eating our hearts out", "most pitiful", which in fact occur only in Odysseus' speech and never in the epic narrator's language. Odysseus' own words, it seems, are the building-blocks of 'his own worlds' – the very stuff that Nünning's 'narrative perspective' is made of. In the Apologue there emerges an early form of what Susan Lanser (1992) has called a 'personal voice'.[19]

---

[16] Importantly, these three narrative features are possible both in fictional and non-fictional texts. My discussion therefore remains unaffected by the vexed question whether Odysseus' Apologue, or the entire *Odyssey*, could be seen as a fictional narrative (see Grethlein 2017, 203).

[17] See also Hunter (2009, 52): "*Anastrophe* denoted any mode of narration in which the order (*taxis*) of events and the order of the telling were not coincident (the issue, in other words, from which all modern narratology takes off)" (my transcription). Chronological narration was also called 'natural narrative' (*kata physin*) (see Hunter 2009, 53), which provides an interesting link to Fludernik's (1996) 'natural narratology'.

[18] Lanser's (1992) categories of feminist narratology (authoritative and personal voice) fit here very well.

[19] See Lanser (1992, 18–19) "I use the term *personal voice* to refer to narrators who are selfconsciously telling their own histories." But note that "the authority of the representation is dependent in turn on the successful construction of a credible voice."

But is Odysseus a reliable narrator? First of all, the mediation of the events in the Apologue remains monoperspectival: Odysseus is the sole survivor.[20] All his crew are dead. No other character could qualify the way in which he narrates his adventures. His memory, his perspective is all we (and his listeners at the Phaiacian court) have. Worse still, many of his stories are simply incredible: one-eyed giants, witches that turn men into swine, conversations with the dead. No wonder that in antiquity several prominent commentators deemed Odysseus' tales outright lies. Given this kind of reception, the Apologue, in the words of modern narratology, seems a pre-eminent case of unreliable (or untrustworthy) narration. But while there is strong evidence of an ancient reception of the Apologue as unreliable, there are no textual signals in the poem itself that would support this point.[21] On the contrary, not only are the Phaeacians appreciative of Odysseus' stories and seem to believe every word of them – his tales are also authenticated by the fact that some episodes of his travels are mentioned by the epic narrator in the main narrative: the proem mentions the crew's sacrilege on Thrinakia; Polyphemus the Cyclops is mentioned by both the narrator and Zeus; and Odysseus' encounter with Circe is 'verified' by a knot he has learned from her (see Grethlein 2017, 109; de Jong 2001, 221–222). What is more, the epic's proem sums up the *Odyssey* in a way that refers wholly to the stories of the Apologue (and *not* to the parts told by the epic narrator, which after all make up four fifths of the poem). In doing so, it "sets up Odysseus as a privileged source of knowledge, the one who was there" (Bakker 2009, 134).

Yet readers, ancient and modern, still seem to carry away from the Apologue the impression that something might be wrong with Odysseus' tale.[22] The reasons for this suspicion may also lie in the setting of his storytelling: its performativity (he tells his adventures orally at a banquet at King Alincous' court) and its concomitant *addressivity*.[23] It is important to keep in mind the twofold embeddedness of the Apologue: it is structurally embedded in the main narrative, and it is socially embedded (in the sense used in linguistic and conversational storytelling

---

20 "His story is an instance of the 'sole survivor' motif: one person survives a disaster so as to be able to recount it" (de Jong 2001, 223).
21 On the relevance of textual signals for unreliable narration, see Nünning (1997).
22 Ancient criticism had its own catalogue of terms for what we now call unreliable narration. "In the rhetorical exercise of *anaskeue* (my transcription), in which mythical narratives and other stories were proved to be obvious falsehoods" speakers had, according to Aelius Theon (ca. first century AD), a range of arguments at their disposal: unclarity, improbability, inappropriateness, defectiveness, excessiveness, unusualness, inconsistency, ordering, inopportuneness, unevenness, falsehood (Hunter 2009, 54; see also Theon, *Progymnasmata* 76.20–25).
23 I use the term in Bakhtin's sense: "An essential (constitutive) marker of the utterance is its quality of being directed to someone, its *addressivity*" (Bakhtin 1986, 95).

research) in a particular context of oral storytelling.[24] Odysseus has gone down in history as a captivating, even enchanting storyteller (see Grethlein 2017, 53–54 on *thelkteria*), arguably also because he is able to 'gear' his stories to his audience. As a guest at Alcinous' court, showered with presents and promised a safe passage home, he is careful to make a good impression with his autobiographical narration. More specifically, certain passages seem addressed to particular members of the audience. The women's catalogue (*Odyssey* 11.225–332) in Odysseus' Nekyia, his visit to the Underworld, appears directed to Queen Arete, not only in subject matter (heroines instead of heroes), but also, as Skempis and Ziogas (2009) have shown, in terms of the genre-conventions that the speaker draws on.[25]

If Odysseus as narrator in the Apologue is interpreted as unreliable, then this judgment cannot be grounded in textual evidence. And it is certainly not the perception of his intradiegetic audience. Odysseus' unreliability in the Apologue can, I would argue, be seen to reside only in the selections, combinations, and accentuations he makes of his memories with the intention of 'tuning' his audience – in short, in his tale's addressivity.[26] While ancient and medieval scholars (like the influential Byzantine Homer-scholar Eustathius) tended to naturalize the Apologue's fantastical events as either 'lies' or 'allegories', and eighteenth-century writers did so according to the anthropological knowledge of their day,[27] modern readers may resort to concepts of 'memory-related' and 'addressivity-related' unreliability.[28] Odysseus' tendency – and sheer talent – for audience tuning becomes even more obvious when he recounts his adventures a second time, to Penelope at the end of the story (this

---

24 In the epic poem, Odysseus is often compared with a bard – one reason why ancient readers tended to equate him with Homer – but the poem makes clear that he does not 'sing' his adventures but rather 'speaks' them.
25 Arete reacts accordingly and exhorts her husband not to be stingy with gifts (*Odyssey* 11.339). See also Doherty's early feminist narratological work on implied audiences in the *Odyssey* (1996).
26 On 'audience tuning', a psychological concept of addressivity, see Echterhoff et al. (2008).
27 See, for example, Henry Fielding, who explains in the introduction to the eighth book of his novel *Tom Jones* (1985 [1749], 361–362) that the *Odyssey* contains "miracles", but "not, as Mr. Pope would have it, because Ulysses told a set of foolish lies to the Phaeacians, who were a very dull nation; but because the poet himself wrote to heathens, to whom poetical fables were articles of faith."
28 Ansgar Nünning (2005, 93) has emphasized the different actualizations of potentially unreliable narrations across history: "I regard unreliable narration as not only a structural or semantic aspect of the text but also a phenomenon that involves the conceptual frameworks readers bring to it." See also Zerweck (2001) and V. Nünning (2004).

time, however, mediated by indirect speech). When addressing his wife, he prudently leaves out his affair with Calypso and downplays his relation with Circe (*Odyssey* 23.310–343).

An entirely different type of embedded story is to be found in the 'lying tales' Odysseus disseminates after his return to Ithaca. Here, too, he carefully shapes his stories to his addressees.[29] That these stories are glaring examples of counterfactual narrative is something only the reader knows. The primary addressees of the lying tales, the characters in the storyworld, are misled and, for the most part, seem to take everything Odysseus says at face value. Ironically, the only thing the swineherd Eumaeus refuses to believe about Odysseus' tall tale is the one true thing he says when he predicts the imminent return of the King of Ithaca (*Odyssey* 14.362–365). The lying tales are, then, a way of staging unreliable narration at the level of character and story.

However, in the lying tales, textual evidence does not point to the ethical dimension of unreliable narration, which has been at the core of narratological concerns ever since Booth's (1961) conceptualization of the term. In the *Odyssey* "untrue narratives that offer pleasure are celebrated for their own sake" (Hall 2008, 46). The art of storytelling is more important than the moral value of truth. In the lying tales, unreliability emerges not as a moral category, but as an aesthetic one.

Odysseus' embedded stories point to the phenomenon of unreliable narration in various ways, and different routes can be taken to actualize this textual potential. From the perspective of modern narratology, the Apologue could be seen as the lying tales' "counterpart of narrative reliability," a category developed by Bruno Zerweck in this volume as a conceptual foundation of unreliable narration. Conversely, a reception history approach to unreliability would have to take into consideration that the lying tales have often been seen in a very different light as an indication of Odysseus' general propensity for untruth and hence of the dubiousness also of the Apologue.[30] One thing is clear, however:

---

29 "Each time Odysseus carefully chooses his fictional identity, with an eye to his addressee: speaking to (i) the young, armed shepherd, he takes on the role of a father with children of his own and a military man; (ii) Eumaeus, of the son of a slave woman; (iii) Antinous, of a rich man fallen on hard times; (iv) Penelope, of an aristocrat and grandson of Minos." (de Jong 2001, 327)

30 A reception history approach to unreliability would also have to take into account the *Odyssey*'s 'situatedness', in David Herman's (2008) sense. Originally an oral epic, the *Odyssey* was not read silently in ancient Greece, but recited by a bard, usually at banquets or festivals. Even after it had been written down, it remained a performative genre. Hence the classical scholar Egbert J. Bakker (2009, 118) argues that the *Odyssey* calls for "a narratology of performance" and points out that what "is fictional in narratology and in the novel (i.e., the narrator that the unresolved question of Odysseus' reliability is an effect of the epic's movement 'from order to perspective'. It is the *Odyssey*'s elaborate play with temporal order and the delegation of analepses to the protagonist that engendered the textual potential of unreliability.

But – apart from filling temporal gaps – what are the functions of Odysseus' Apologue, that insert which takes so long in both story and discourse time: a whole night in the storyworld and 2140 lines in the epic? Since antiquity, this question has been raised again and again. A recent, truly cultural-narratological answer is offered by Grethlein when he claims that it is Odysseus' way of coping. Odysseus narrates his difficult experiences "in order to cope with them. Retrospection gives him sovereignty over events in which he no longer had agency, but was merely a victim. As a narrator, Odysseus gives form to these experiences and thus makes them graspable, intelligible" (Grethlein 2017, 118; my translation). The Apologue is Odysseus' way of regaining (narrative) sovereignty. Thus equipped, he can return to Ithaca, face the suitors and reclaim his wife and kingdom after twenty years.

This argument is much in line with recent research on narrative coping. In *Emotion and Narrative* (2019), psychoanalyst Tilmann Habermas asserts that narrating emotional experiences may help the narrator to master the narrated situation and its emotional impact.[31] In Ansgar and Vera Nünning's words, "storytelling and the acquisition of narrative authority is an effective way not only of coming to terms with one's conflicting emotions and experiences; it is also a way of coping with crises and problems, enhancing one's sense of manageability" (Nünning and Nünning 2017, 167).

---

and the narratee), becomes embodied in epic". In a bard's recital, the series of Odysseus' (more or less unreliable) embedded narratives turns into a series of embodied personal histories. In the epic's ancient situatedness, Odysseus' tales thus emerge as examples of what Ansgar Nünning and Christine Schwanecke have called "dramatic unreliability", which tends to come with a "heightened degree of indeterminacy" (Nünning/Schwanecke 2015, 95). But in its reception history, the *Odyssey*'s situatedness has seen many transformations. Ancient and medieval scholars would approach the question of Odysseus' unreliability on the basis of silent reading and close textual and linguistic analysis (see Nünlist 2009).

[31] Habermas (2019, 220) emphasizes the "necessity to study narrative coping as a process over an extended period of time". He has analyzed how frequent re-narrating of self-experienced events may enhance coping. In this light, it is interesting to note that the lying tales, false as they are, all contain key experiences of Odysseus' adventures. It seems that Odysseus continues his work of narrative coping on Ithaca. Moreover, by taking on different roles, he also probes different perspectives. Habermas maintains that "integrating diverse narrative perspectives of self and others, present, past, and hypothetical is central for coping with experiences" (2019, ix-x).

Coping is not only a narrative function that concerns the *Odyssey*'s storyworld. It also defines the poem's relation to the extratextual world of archaic Greece. The eighth century BCE, the time when the *Odyssey* must have taken shape as an oral poem, marks the beginning of the 'great Greek colonization', when various Greek tribes founded settlements, new *poleis*, across the Mediterranean, from Southern Italy to North Africa and the Black Sea. The adventures of the *Odyssey* may have served in archaic Greek society as a way of narrative coping with the then-recent experience of colonization. Plot elements that point to this function are recurring instances of in/hospitality and encounters with strangers, who are frequently cast as nonhumans (e.g. the Cyclops or the Laestrygonians) – a strategy of representing the Other and a form of exculpating oneself from colonial violence, which would reemerge in modern European empires (see Malkin 1998 and Dougherty 2001).

If a consideration of the Apologue yields insights into questions of unreliability and narrative coping in the *Odyssey*, for palpable instances of multiperspectivity, we have to turn to the Telemachy and its embedded first-person narratives – to an exchange of stories at Menelaus' court (*Odyssey*, 4.240–289). When Telemachus arrives in search of his father, all that Menelaus and Helen can offer are old tales about Odysseus in the Trojan War. Wife and husband each narrate a story which is testimony to Odysseus' courage and cunning. Helen begins with a tale about how Odysseus entered Troy disguised as a beggar and how she recognized and secretly helped him. Menelaus reciprocates with a tale about how the Greek warriors entered Troy. His anecdote describes how Helen imitated the voices of their wives in order to lure them out of the wooden horse, while Odysseus saw through the pretense and exhorted his men not to reveal themselves.

While the two tales are quite similar in their characterization of Odysseus as a *trickster*, they display a diametrically opposite perspective on Helen. In Helen's narrative, her former self showed solidarity with the Greeks; but in Menelaus' narrative, she was clearly on the Trojan side. This is an instance of (embedded) multiperspectival narration, and one whose conflict of perspectives remains unresolved by the epic narrator. Interestingly, before she begins with her narrative, Helen mixes a drug into the wine that makes her listeners forget all anger and sorrow (*Odyssey*, 4.220–221). This provision raises the question of how much multiperspectivity is tolerable, both in a marriage and when it comes to the foundational myths of a national culture. The multiperspectival rendition of Helen's role in the Trojan War constitutes a perennial conundrum. It engendered a narrative tension that would preoccupy historians, dramatists and poets for generations to come, from Herodotus to Euripides and to H.D.'s *Helen in Egypt* (1961).

To sum up, the *Odyssey*'s elaborate play with time is not just an aspect of its 'epic machinery'. It emerges as a means to carve out a space for exploring narrative perspective. The *in medias res* technique requires analepses and enables the insertion of embedded first-person narratives (such as Odysseus' long Apologue, his 'lying tales', Helen's and Menelaus' tales). And with these emerge in the epic poem, of all places – that allegedly most monological and monoperspectival of all genres – early instances of narrative unreliability and multiperspectivity as well as a sense of the interrelatedness of autobiographical narration and coping.

3 Charles Lamb's *The Adventures of Ulysses*: Reformatting the *Odyssey*

Cultural memory never works in straightforward ways, but comes in fits and transformations. While the combination of homodiegetic narration (embedded, framed or not) with stories of errancy and adventure has travelled extremely well and reappears in texts by John Bunyan, Aphra Behn, Daniel Defoe, and Joseph Conrad (the latter with clear instances of unreliability), and while these classics of early-modern and modern English literature can thus be argued to have an 'Odyssean grounding', this is an effect of implicit cultural memory, of the unacknowledged and often unconscious travels of narrative schemata (see Erll 2019). Here, however, I will stick to overt, explicit rewritings of the *Odyssey*, which state their debt to the Homeric epic, making it new in several ways. Interestingly, some of the most transformative work in this history of explicit reception has taken place on the level of form.

A key moment of the *Odyssey*'s incursion into modern English literature and media culture is Charles Lamb's children's version *The Adventures of Ulysses* (1808). This small book, with its simplified prose retelling of the *Odyssey*, was frequently reprinted in the nineteenth and early twentieth centuries. The story entered wide reading circles, impressing generations of schoolchildren, for whom Lamb's *Ulysses* was a set text – among them the young James Joyce.

In his preface, Lamb states that he tried to avoid "the prolixity" of Homer and give "a rapidity to the narration, which I hope will make it more attractive, and give it more the air of a romance to young readers." Eschewing 'prolixity' (note the implied antagonism between the slow, complicated epic and the fast and simple romance) means in Lamb's *Adventures* first and foremost formal simplification.[32] Lamb completely does away with the epic's *in medias res*

---

[32] See Perl (1984, 145–146) for a discussion of Lamb's rewriting of the *Odyssey* into a romance.

structure and embedded narratives. He dissolves the *Odyssey*'s complex anachronic structure and narrates the adventures in strict chronological order. He omits the Telemachy, arguing that it was already well done for young readers by François Fénelon's didactic novel *Les aventures de Télémaque* (1699), and renders the Nostos very briefly at the end of the book, whereas in the *Odyssey* it takes up half the epic. What remains is the Apologue as the best-remembered kernel of the *Odyssey* – a passage that represents no more than a fifth of the Homeric poem.

As a major catalyst in the modern memory of the *Odyssey*, Lamb's version can be credited with firmly establishing the mnemonic bias of remembering the Homeric narrative as a series of chronologically presented 'adventures' – a tendency, which has its roots in ancient rewritings (see, for example, Lucian's chronological, adventure-focused *True History* or Apuleius' *The Golden Ass*), but which this popular children's version propelled into the nineteenth and twentieth centuries. Expressions of this modern memory of the *Odyssey* range from James Joyce's *Ulysses* to Hollywood road movies.[33]

In Lamb's rewriting, the events related in the Apologue are no longer told by Odysseus himself, but by an authorial narrator. *The Adventures of Ulysses* is thus not only a resequencing, but a thorough reformatting of the *Odyssey*, in which originally complex narrative forms (anachrony, hetero- and homodiegetic narration, different levels of embedding) are streamlined into a strictly chronological plot, monoperspectivally told by only one authoritative, always knowing, openly evaluative, and utterly reliable voice – an eminent example of the narrator's role in nineteenth-century 'fictions of authority' (see Lanser 1992). The Apologue as Odysseus' performance of a personal voice is condensed into a few lines: "Then at the king's request he gave them a brief relation of all the adventures that had befallen him since he launched forth from Troy" (Lamb 1811 [1808], 21). And while the preface, which introduces Odysseus as "a brave man struggling with adversity," touches on the issue of coping, Lamb's *Adventures* clearly no longer feature the representation of the *act of narrative coping* that the *Odyssey* explored.

Nevertheless, Lamb's structural changes do not go against the grain of the ancient epic, but rather single out and reinforce certain tendencies implicit in the *Odyssey*. Lamb's "swiftly moving, plot-driven episodes" (James 2009, 108) are an actualization of the episodic structure of the

---

[33] See Hall (2008, 49), who stresses the role of *The Golden Ass* as a link to picaresque 'road novels' (such as *Don Quixote* and *Tom Jones*) and to road movies. Mackey-Kallis (2001) even argues that the Odyssey is an archetype manifesting itself in most Hollywood movies.

Apologue,[34] and of the *Odyssey*'s general emphasis on plot (rather than on character development, see Grethlein 2017, 81). Cultural memory is always selective and a matter of actualization. In his chronological reformatting, Lamb actualized the plot-drivenness and episodic properties of Homer' *Odyssey*; Joyce (as we will see below) would remember Lamb's temporal reformatting, but at the same time actualize Homer's preoccupation with perspective.

The Adventures of Ulysses displays many characteristic dynamics of 'classical reception' as a form of cultural memory. Charles Lamb belonged to a group of Romantics (among them Hazlitt and Keats) who revaluated Homer in the Elizabethan translation by George Chapman (1614). The decision to draw on Chapman's translation of Homer for *The Adventures of Ulysses* (Lamb explicitly acknowledges this "obsolete version" in his preface) rather than on Pope's (1725) was, as Felicity James (2009, 107) emphasizes, part of this Romantic circle's aim, namely

> to celebrate the achievements of the Elizabethan poets, and to open them up to a wider readership. One of the most important aspects of *The Adventures of Ulysses* is its distinctive, strongly-flavoured prose, which comes – sometimes directly – from George Chapman's 1614 translation of the *Odyssey*. Like Keats looking into Chapman's Homer, the book registers the Romantic thrill at re-encountering the Elizabethan versions of the classics, and the new worlds opened up by these 'bold' translations.

Remembering Chapman's translation rather than Pope's by then far more current one implies a turn against the elitist classicism of the eighteenth century. This is an important insight for the project of an historical narratology, which operates in dialogue with memory studies and classical reception studies. Acts of cultural memory do not usually refer to a single 'original', but draw on (often long) series of intermediaries. What Homer reformattings such as Lamb's *Adventures* (often contentiously) remember is not such much 'Homer' as the history of Homer-reception. And here Lamb's contention also concerns social class: his "desire to adapt his *Odyssey* for child readers may be seen as one more step in that sociable conversation, a gradual broadening and democratising of the classics" (James 2009, 111). Part of his democratizing impulse is Lamb's choice of the more widely known Latin rendition of Odysseus' name – 'Ulysses' – derived from Virgil's *Aeneid* and other rewritings. And it is exactly this title that Joyce would also choose for his modernist novel.

---

[34] The Apologue is a catalogue narrative, and its episodes follow the schema of 'presentation of enemy – confrontation – flight', with the recurring formulae of refrain composition, such as 'from there we sailed on with a grieving heart', a formula that occurs five times in the Apologue (see de Jong 2001, 222).

4 James Joyce's *Ulysses*: Modernist transformations

James Joyce was always ready to acknowledge his debts. He quoted Édouard Dujardin more than once for the invention of the interior monologue, and he was never ashamed to remember that his first and most profound impression of Homer's *Odyssey* was mediated to him by Charles Lamb's *The Adventures of Ulysses*. Famously, in a letter to his Aunt Josephine, Joyce recommended that she "buy at once the *Adventures of Ulysses* (which is Homer's story told in simple English much abbreviated) by Charles Lamb [...] Then have a try at *Ulysses* again" (10. November 1922; Ellmann 1992, 293).

Joyce first encountered Homer at the age of twelve, when he studied *The Adventures of Ulysses* for the Intermediate Examination in English.[35] It was one of the prescribed books at Clongowes College, where Lamb's already quite concise rewriting was further cut down: "The class read only seven of the ten chapters, which take the story of Odysseus up to the meeting with Telemachus at the hut of Eumaeus [...] so that the emphasis [...] falls on the wanderings of the hero rather than on his return to Ithaca" (Wykes 1968, 302). There is a debate in Joyce research about what exactly he may have remembered from Lamb, commentators struggling with the author's opaque comment that at twelve he liked the "mysticism in Ulysses" (qtd. in Wykes 1968, 302), possibly referring to the allegorizing readings of his Jesuit teachers. According to James (2009, 144), "the humanity and sympathy highlighted in Lamb's version of *Ulysses*, as well as the linear, chronological progression of the narrative, and the 'pleasure of language' which shines through from its use of Chapman may all have had a powerful effect on Joyce as a young reader."

Joyce's most original and persisting contribution to the memory of the *Odyssey* is that he found in its protagonist the "complete all-round character." In a conversation recorded by Frank Budgen, Joyce explains that his Odysseus is not only "a complete man," but also "a good man. At any rate, that is what I intend that he shall be" (Budgen 1973 [1934], 18). With his Leopold Bloom, an unheroic Jewish-Irish Dubliner, an advertisement canvasser with an unfaithful wife, the image Joyce offers of a modern Odysseus is one of a profoundly human character.

---

[35] "The version Joyce used was John Cooke's revised school-text version in 1893–4," a slightly censored version of Lamb's already expurgated rewriting. In this version "the lapping of the blood remained, but mild sexual allusions were removed" (James 2009, 114; see also Stanford 1951 and McCleery and Gunn 1992).

In terms of narrative form, what, then, are Joyce's debts to Lamb and Homer? The clearest indication of *Ulysses*' debt to Lamb's *Adventures* is, next to the novel's title, its chronological rendering of a series of 'adventures' or 'episodes' taking place in modern Dublin.[36] On closer inspection, it becomes clear that Joyce achieves an interesting merger of Lamb's and Homer's temporal structuring: while he retains Lamb's *conventional* model of strict chronology, he also draws on Homer's device of reducing the main narrative to a minimum of time. Joyce pushes this strategy to the *experimental* extreme: where Homer concentrates on 41 days, Joyce tells the story of a single day in Dublin, June 16, 1904. In strict temporal order, each episode is assigned a particular hour of the day.

Where Lamb had done away with the Telemachy, Joyce reintroduces it (the relation between Stephen/Telemachus and Bloom/Odysseus is a major topic in the novel). But this creates a problem for the narrative's chronology, for, as in Homer's *Odyssey*, the Telemachy and the beginning of the Odyssey proper (Odysseus' release from Calypso's island) occur more or less simultaneously. Where the *Odyssey*'s anachronic narrative enables an elegant mediation of simultaneity by means of switching between storylines (Homer's 'interlace technique', see de Jong 2001, 589), Joyce, who adheres to Lamb's chronology, solves the problem with comic primness and starts the day all over again. As the Linati-schema (produced by Joyce in 1920) shows, the first three chapters, focusing on Stephen Dedalus/Telemachus, take place at 8am, 10am, and 11am respectively, and chapters 4 and 5, which introduce Leopold Bloom/Odysseus, are again set at 8am and 9am. What this indicates is that the formal feature of chronological narration, which in Lamb carries the function of simplification and conventionalization, works in Joyce as a means of 'prolixity', of intensified complexity and experimentation.

What, then, has happened to unreliability, multiperspectivity, and narrative coping – features that were made possible in Homer's *Odyssey* above all by the epic's anachronic structure and its embedded first-person narratives? Lamb had discarded the latter and straightened out the former. While Joyce's *Ulysses* partly follows Lamb's *Adventures* in its formal choices (strict chronology in the main narrative, no lengthy embedded Apologue), this modernist novel is also strongly interested in the questions of narrative perspective elicited by Homer's *Odyssey*. But it is detective work to figure out where exactly

---

36 But these episodes do not follow the order of the adventures in the Apologue any longer. For a comparison see Wkyes' (1968, 306) table and his cogent observation that Joyce "uses the episodes where he needs them in order to tell his tale of modern Dublin."

in Joyce's veritable 'Odyssey of style' (Lawrence 1981) these key features of the Homeric epic have gone ashore.

Two things are of paramount importance when looking at Joyce's *Ulysses* as an instance of Homer-reception. First of all, Homeric references do not sit neatly where we would expect them – in the respective 'episodes' – but are often distributed across the text. Secondly, while *Ulysses* brings to blossom the seeds of narrative perspective found in the *Odyssey*, perspective tends not to be expressed in embedded first person *narration*, but by means of high-modernist forms of interior *focalization* such as free indirect discourse and interior monologue.[37]

Where, then, is the Apologue to be found in *Ulysses*, and where connected phenomena, such as unreliable narration and narrative coping? If we proceed according to the 'logic of episodes', then we should look for the Apologue in the "Nausicaa" episode. (In Homer's epic, Nausicaa is King Alcinous' daughter, who finds Odysseus at the beach of Scheria, falls in love with him, and brings him to her parents' court, where he recounts his travels.) In Joyce's "Nausiccaa" episode, there is, in fact, a small scene where Bloom recapitulates his day so far. Typically, this recapitulation is not mediated by first person narration, but in an interior monologue:

> Long day I've had. Martha, the bath, funeral, house of Keyes, museum with those goddesses, Dedalus' song. Then that bawler in Barney Kiernan's. Got my own back there. Drunken ranters what I said about his God made him wince. Mistake to hit back. Or? No. (*Ulysses* 13.1214–1217)

Bloom's résumé happens rapidly and in the matter-of-fact way typical of his mind-style. This is not an Apologue, but a mental self-narration. But it is a means of coping. Bloom further dwells on the anti-Semitism he encountered in Barney Kiernan's pub and concludes with "Three cheers for Israel" (*Ulysses* 13.1220).

As to unreliable narration – *Ulysses* actualizes Odysseus' performance in this respect in diverse ways. In a scene reminiscent of Odysseus' transformed

---

[37] These are narrative forms that Homer did not have at his disposal, arguably because they do not work in orally performed texts. The *Odyssey* does feature, however, what de Jong (2001, xiii) has called 'embedded focalization', which Bakker describes as "the use of an emotionally charged term that usually occurs in the speech of characters but that occasionally can be used in the narrator text to convey a character's point of view." According to Bakker, oral performance is not "conducive to what comes so easily to the authors of the modern novel. In performance, the narrator does not so much enter the mind of the character, as in modern fiction; rather, the perspective of the character can intrude in the discourse of the narrator" (Bakker 2009, 120–121). It is Ansgar Nünning's decoupling of purely rhetorical forms (narration and focalization) from the concept of 'perspective' and its semantic definition as a character's or narrator's worldview that first enables the kind of comparison made here.

tale to Penelope, Bloom tells Molly at night about the events of his day, providing her with a heavily edited version that omits his various erotic adventures and adds some invented aspects that he feels must please his listener. As in the *Odyssey*, the tale addressed to the wife is presented as reported speech – not by an epic narrator (of course), but by the particular voice of the "Ithaca" episode, which Joyce has called 'catechism-impersonal':

> With what modifications did the narrator reply to this interrogation?
>
> Negative: he omitted to mention the clandestine correspondence between Martha Clifford and Henry Flower, the public altercation at, in and in the vicinity of the licensed premises of Bernard Kiernan and Co, Limited, 8, 9 and 10 Little Britain street, the erotic provocation and response thereto caused by the exhibitionism of Gertrude (Gerty), surname unknown. Positive: he included mention of a performance by Mrs Bandmann Palmer of Leah at the Gaiety Theatre [...].
>
> Was the narration otherwise unaltered by modifications?
>
> Absolutely. (*Ulysses* 17.2250–2268)

This is an example of editing out, recombination and most importantly, addressivity in a personal narrative, and in this respect the episode is very close to the Homeric original and its variant of addressee-related unreliability.

Odysseus' lying tales, however, are no longer directly connected to the protagonist of *Ulysses*. They have migrated to characters other than Bloom, to 'Noman' in the "Cyclops" episode and to the sailor Murphy in the "Eumaeus" episode. "Cyclops" is the only chapter in *Ulysses* that is mediated by a first-person narrative situation. Its homodiegetic narrator, the prejudiced 'Noman', is the epitome of unreliability and its diverse 'sins': untrustworthiness, misreporting, misinterpreting and misevaluation (see Phelan 2005). The narrator's name is of course a reference to Homer's epic, where Odysseus (as he recounts in the Apologue) cunningly introduces himself to the Cyclops as 'Noman', disguising his name and identity. Thus, in one sense, it is an Odysseus-figure who does the unreliable narration in Joyce's "Cyclops" chapter, too. Yet, at the same time, this narrator is clearly on the 'wrong' side, applauding the anti-Semitic invectives lashed against Bloom by 'the citizen' ("the Cyclops" in Joyce's schema) and relishing Bloom's eventual flight from the pub ("the cave" in Joyce's schema).

A similar instance of an unreliable narrator being and not being an Odysseus-figure (but clearly not Bloom) and telling stories that seem to be associated with Odysseus' adventures can be encountered in the "Eumaeus" episode – and aptly so, for in Homer's epic it is in Eumaeus' hut that Odysseus tells his tallest lying tales. Late at night in the cabman's shelter, Bloom and Stephen encounter the sailor D.B. Murphy (in Joyce's schema "Ulysses Pseudangelos", i.e.

the false messenger), who tells them his highly untrustworthy stories – which, however, all resonate with what everyone knows about Homer's Odysseus. Murphy speaks about his many travels and 'queer sights'[38]; he hasn't seen his wife in seven years, and he has a son who is now eighteen.

This strategy of splitting the Odysseus-figure into three (Bloom, Noman, Murphy) and distributing Odysseus' embedded narratives across diverse narrators, brings to light some aspects of unreliability hidden in the *Odyssey*. Noman's aggressive tone points to what Odysseus' Apologue may have covered up: his own guilt of aggression, of entering the Cyclops' cave without invitation. Murphy's tall tales performatively re-actualize the suspicion about Odysseus' adventure-tales that has been articulated again and again in reception history – that they are just that: pretty tall tales. Interestingly, such criticism of Odysseus and his narrative self-representation is steered away from the main Odysseus-figure, Leopold Bloom, and staged instead through two comparatively minor voices. Perhaps this is because such criticism is not 'tellable' if you are (as Eustathios' wrote about Homer) *philodysseus*[39] – or in today's language 'camp Odysseus' – as James Joyce, with his vision of Odysseus as a deeply human 'allroundman', arguably is. Be that as it may, Noman's and Murphy's tales convey a strong sense of perspectivity, and – with their performativity and embeddedness in a concrete social context, as well as with their tangible, shrewd first-person narrators deftly addressing and tuning their audiences – actualize some of the Homeric modes of generating narrative perspective.

The seed of Homer's multiperspectival narration bears rich fruit in *Ulysses'* final episode, "Penelope." Molly's monologue is an overt actualization of the multiperspectical constellation of Menelaus' and Helen's narrative. The first seventeen chapters of *Ulysses* are focalized mainly by the male characters Stephen and Bloom, and the two have their own particular perspectives on Molly (who is both a 'Penelope', to whom Bloom/Odysseus returns, and a 'Helen', who shamelessly cheats on him). Counterbalancing this male perspectival bias, the novel's eighteenth and final chapter represents for the first time the female protagonist's perspective. And as in Homer, some striking differences emerge – most famously, about the actual number of Molly's lovers, but also about many other aspects, such as her different accentuation of the intimate memories she shares with Bloom of their first kiss at Howth Head. Like Bloom's recapitulation

---

38 "Why, the sailor said, shifting his partially chewed plug. I seen queer things too, ups and downs. I seen a crocodile bite the fluke of an anchor same as I chew that quid." (*Ulysses* 16.465–468)
39 See Strauss Clay (1983, 9–53).

of his day in "Nausicaa", Molly's perspective is rendered by means of interior monologue. It is a stream of consciousness, the representation of a flow of thoughts. It is *not* speech, and therefore it lacks the addressivity of Homer's embedded multiperspectival narration. But Molly's monologue seems its functional equivalent: it introduces a female standpoint via juxtaposition, and it engenders ambivalence about earlier monoperspectivally male renditions. Most of all, Joyce's modern Odyssey gives this female perspective far more space – and it has the last word.

The problem of narrative coping, too, has travelled from Homer to Joyce's *Ulysses*, where it remains tied to the Bloom/Odysseus figure. But in contrast to the *Odyssey*, the problem is not solved in *Ulysses*. Distributed across the novel are instances of Bloom's failed attempts at storytelling and hence failed attempts at narrative coping. While the Homeric Odysseus is depicted as a gifted narrator, on equal footing with professional bards, this clearly cannot be said of Bloom. As early as in the "Hades" episode, when he tries to tell an anecdote about the Jew Reuben J. Dodd, Bloom falters and fails, and the anecdote must be completed by the more competent narrator Martin Cunningham. In the "Eumaeus" episode, Bloom tries to tell Stephen about his ambiguous position as a Jew in Ireland and the anti-Semitism he experienced in Kiernan's pub earlier that day, but the young man is not interested and only comments "Count me out" – "meaning work" (*Ulysses* 16.1148), but by implication also including himself as an appreciative audience (which Odysseus certainly did have in the Phaeacians). It seems that none of the Dubliners whom Bloom encounters during his day is much interested in his story – in stark contrast to Homer' Odysseus, whom Alcinous both exhorts and enables to tell his tale.

Bloom's narrative coping, then, does not take place in social settings of conversational exchange. The significance of narrative for coping shines elsewhere: in Bloom's imagination, which is frequently guided by narrative schemata derived from popular literature and culture, such as pantomimes, Victorian novels, or travel books. After he has recapitulated his day for Molly and as he is just about to fall asleep, Bloom casts his experience of June 16, 1904 as 'travelling' with 'Sinbad the Sailor':

He rests. He has travelled.

With?

Sinbad the Sailor and Tinbad the Tailor and Jinbad the Jailer and Whinbad the Whaler and Ninbad the Nailer and Finbad the Failer and Binbad the Bailer and Pinbad the Pailer and Minbad the Mailer and Hinbad the Hailer and Rinbad the Railer and Dinbad the Kailer and Vinbad the Quailer and Linbad the Yailer and Xinbad the Phthailer. (*Ulysses* 17.2320–2326)

These lines at the end of the "Ithaca" episode mediate Bloom's thoughts just before falling asleep and before the "Penelope" chapter turns to Molly. They highlight the significance of age-old narrative schemata derived from travel literature for the framing of and coping with experience. While Joyce is careful never once to mention the *Odyssey* in his novel, the Sinbad-stories are clearly a remediation of Odyssean adventures – and perhaps the phonetic variants of 'Sinbad the Sailor' point not only to Bloom's gradual dozing off, but also to the unending chain of Odyssean remembering, reception, and remediation, into which Joyce inserts his novel.

The reference to Sinbad is a hint at the power of narrative schemata for the articulation of Bloom's experience, memory, and self-image (see Erll 2019). Casting himself as an Odysseus-like traveler enables Bloom to frame his day in terms of errancy and encounters with the foreign and dangerous, as well as to highlight his own endurance and cunning. This is not a mode of narrative coping based on *narrating one's experience* to someone else (the Apologue-model), but it is a way of coping by *using narrative resources as schemata* to frame situations, to make sense of and eventually cope with life experience.[40] The nexus of narrative and coping is thus transformed from social activity in the ancient *Odyssey* into mental activity in the modern *Ulysses* – into the protagonist's recourse to schemata derived from a narrative tradition of which the *Odyssey* is a major, foundational, and possibly 'salutogenetic' part.

5 Conclusion

The road of narrative forms from the *Odyssey* to *Ulysses* cannot be travelled in just three steps. With its comparison of Homer, Lamb, and Joyce, this essay has clearly taken a short-cut. Hugh Kenner has pointed to the problem in Joyce research that "we talk on about Joyce and his use of Homer without feeling obliged to specify *which* Homer, as though 'Homer' were an immutable constant" (Kenner 1989, 286). And James Ramey (2007, 98) has drawn attention to the fact that rather "than simply knowing and using the *Odyssey* as a template, Joyce became a Homerist," studying Homer reception from Virgil and Ovid to Dante and Fénelon, to Tennyson and Hauptmann, to Samuel Butler and Victor Bérard. The *Odyssey* (in *Ulysses* and elsewhere) is not an immutable reference point, but a 'moving target', which changes with each act of reception.

---

40 This shift is in line with Herman's (2004, 167–168) description of the shift of Actors' roles from that of Agents (in the epic) to Experiencers (in the modernist novel).

This credo of classical reception studies has important implications for a cultural and historical narratology. 'Reading formally backwards'[41] from Joyce to Lamb to Homer generates a strong sense of the episodic kernel and the chronological properties of the *Odyssey* (which were brought out in Lamb's reception) as well as of its preoccupation with perspective (which Joyce's reception emphasizes). Narrative forms and functions do not develop neatly step by step, year by year; their development is often contingent on acts of reception, on the culturally and historically situated remediation and reactualization of past stories and their narrative properties, some of which may have been lying dormant.

Conversely, classical reception studies (and by extension memory studies) can only profit from formal approaches such as narratology, from not only directing their attention to the content of travelling stories but also to the reception of form. For if form does indeed carry content, if, as Ansgar Nünning maintains, it is 'semanticized', then the formal dynamic of a story across time and space – evidenced, for example, in the change from anachrony to chronology or between different forms of narration and focalization – will also transform the meanings and functions of the story. And such transformations can be generative in shaping the future memory of the 'original' narrative. The *Odyssey* was never the same after Lamb's *Adventures*, and Lamb's *Adventures* and the *Odyssey* were never the same after Joyce's *Ulysses*.

---

[41] On "reading backwards from *Ulysses*" to Homer, see Perl (1984, 144).

References

Bakhtin, Mikhail Mikhailovich. "Epic and Novel." *The Dialogic Imagination: Four Essays*. Ed. Michael Holquist. Transl. Caryl Emerson and Michael Holquist. Austin: University of Texas Press, 2011 [1981]. 4–40.
Bakhtin, Mikhail Mikhailovich. *Speech Genres and Other Late Essays*. Transl. Vern W. McGee. Austin: University of Texas Press, 1986.
Bakker, Egbert J. "Homer, Odysseus, and the Narratology of Performance." *Narratology and Interpretation: The Content of Narrative Form in Ancient Literature*. Eds. Jonas Grethlein and Antonios Rengakos. Berlin: de Gruyter, 2009. 117–136.
Basseler, Michael. "Fictions of Resilience: Narrating (Environmental) Crisis and Catastrophe in Cormac McCarthy's *The Road* and Jesmyn Ward's *Salvage the Bones*." *The American Novel in the 21st Century: Cultural Contexts – Literary Developments – Critical Analysis*. Eds. Michael Basseler and Ansgar Nünning. Trier: WVT, 2019 (forthcoming).
Boitani, Piero. *The Shadow of Ulysses: Figures of a Myth*. Oxford: Oxford University Press, 1994.
Bolter, Jay David and Richard Grusin (eds.). *Remediation: Understanding New Media*. Cambridge, MA: MIT Press, 1999.
Booth, Wayne C. *The Rhetoric of Fiction*. Chicago: University of Chicago Press, 1983 [1961].
Budgen, Frank. *James Joyce and the Making of Ulysses*. Bloomington: Indiana University Press, 1973 [1934].
de Jong, Irene J. F. *A Narratological Commentary on the* Odyssey. Cambridge: Cambridge University Press, 2001.
de Jong, Irene J. F. "Diachronic Narratology (The Example of Ancient Greek Narrative)." *Handbook of Narratology*. Ed. Peter Hühn. Berlin: de Gruyter, 2014. 115–121.
Doherty, Lilian Eileen. *Siren Songs: Gender, Audiences, and Narrators in the Odyssey*. Ann Arbor: University of Michigan Press, 1996.
Dougherty, Carol. *The Raft of Odysseus: The Ethnographic Imagination of Homer's Odyssey*. Oxford: Oxford University Press, 2001.
Echterhoff, Gerald, E. Tory Higgins, René Kopietz, and Stephan Groll. "How Communication Goals Determine When Audience Tuning Biases Memory." *Journal of Experimental Psychology: General*, 137.1 (2008): 3–21.
Ellmann, Richard (ed.). *Selected Letters of James Joyce*. London: Faber and Faber, 1992.
Erll, Astrid. "Travelling Memory." *Parallax*. Special Issue *Transcultural Memory*. Ed. Rick Crownshaw. 17.4 (2011): 4–18.
Erll, Astrid. "Media and the Dynamics of Memory: From Cultural Paradigms to Transcultural Premediation." *The Oxford Handbook of Culture and Memory*. Ed. Brady Wagoner. Oxford: Oxford University Press, 2017. 305–324.
Erll, Astrid. "'Homer' – A Relational Mnemohistory." *Memory Studies* 11.3 (2018): 274–286.
Erll, Astrid. "Homer, Turko, Little Harry: Cultural Memory and the Ethics of Premediation in James Joyce's *Ulysses*." *Partial Answers* (2019, in press).
Erll, Astrid, and Ansgar Nünning. "Where Literature and Memory Meet: Towards a Systematic Approach to the Concepts of Memory in Literary Studies." *Literature, Literary History, and Cultural Memory*. Special issue of *REAL – Yearbook of Research in English and American Literature 21*. Ed. Herbert Grabes. Tübingen: Narr, 2005. 265–298.

Fielding, Henry. *The History of Tom Jones*. London: Penguin Books, 1985 [1749].
Fludernik, Monika. *Towards a 'Natural' Narratology*. London: Routledge, 1996.
Fludernik, Monika. "The Diachronization of Narratology." *Narrative* 11.3 (2003): 331–348.
Genette, Gérard. *Narrative Discourse: An Essay in Method*. Ed. Jonathan Culler. Ithaca: Cornell University Press, 2006 [1983].
Graziosi, Barbara, and Emily Greenwood (eds.). *Homer in the Twentieth Century: Between World Literature and the Western Canon*. Oxford: Oxford University Press, 2010.
Grethlein, Jonas, and Antonios Rengakos (eds.). *Narratology and Interpretation: The Content of Narrative Form in Ancient Literature*. Berlin: de Gruyter, 2009.
Grethlein, Jonas. *Die Odyssee: Homer und die Kunst des Erzählens*. München: Beck, 2017.
Habermas, Tilmann. *Emotion and Narrative. Perspectives in Autobiographical Storytelling*. New York: Cambridge University Press, 2019.
Hall, Edith. *The Return of Ulysses: A Cultural History of Homer's* Odyssey. Baltimore: Johns Hopkins University Press, 2008.
Hardwick, Lorna. "Editorial." *Classical Receptions Journal* 1.1 (2009): 1–3.
Herman, David. *Story Logic: Problems and Possibilities of Narrative*. Lincoln, NE: University of Nebraska Press, 2004.
Herman, David. *Basic Elements of Narrative*. Oxford: Blackwell, 2008.
Hunter, Richard. "The Trojan Oration of Dio Chrysostom and Ancient Homeric Criticism." *Narratology and Interpretation: The Content of Narrative Form in Ancient Literature*. Eds. Jonas Grethlein and Antonios Rengakos. Berlin: de Gruyter, 2009. 43–61.
Hunter, Richard. *The Measure of Homer. The Ancient Reception of the Iliad and the Odyssey*. Cambridge: Cambridge University Press, 2018.
James, Felicity. "Lamb and *The Adventures of Ulysses*." *The Charles Lamb Bulletin* 147 (2009): 107–115.
Joyce, James. *Ulysses. The Corrected Text*. Ed. Hans Walter Gabler. London: Penguin, 1986.
Kenner, Hugh. *Ulysses: Revised Edition*. Baltimore: Johns Hopkins University Press, 1987.
Lamb, Charles. *The Adventures of Ulysses*. London: Edward Moxon, 1811 [1808].
Lanser, Susan Sniader. *Fictions of Authority: Women Writers and Narrative Voice*. Ithaca: Cornell University Press, 1992.
Lawrence, Karen. *The Odyssey of Style in* Ulysses. Princeton, NJ: Princeton University Press, 1981.
Lucian. *The Works of Lucian of Samosata*. Vol. II. Transl. H.W. Fowler and F.G. Fowler. Oxford: The Clarendon Press, 1905.
Mackey-Kallis, Susan. *The Hero and the Perennial Journey Home in American Film*. Philadelphia: University of Pennsylvania Press, 2001.
Malkin, Irad. *The Returns of Odysseus: Colonization and Ethnicity*. Berkeley: University of California Press, 1998.
Martindale, Charles. "Reception – a New Humanism? Receptivity, Pedagogy, the Transhistorical." *Classical Receptions Journal* 5.2 (2013): 169–183.
McCleery, Alistair, and Ian Gunn: "Afterword: On Looking Into Joyce's First Homer." *Adventures of Ulysses, John cooke's Edition*. Eds. Alistair Mecleery and Ian Gunn. Edinburgh: Split Pea Press, 1992. 159–165.
Nünlist, René. "Narratological Concepts in Greek Scholia." *Narratology and Interpretation: The Content of Narrative Form in Ancient Literature*. Eds. Jonas Grethlein and Antonios Rengakos. Berlin: de Gruyter, 2009. 63–83.

Nünning, Ansgar. "'But why *will* you say that I am mad?' On the Theory, History, and Signals of Unreliable Narration in British Fiction." *Arbeiten aus Anglistik und Amerikanistik* 22.1 (1997): 83–106.
Nünning, Ansgar. "Towards a Cultural and Historical Narratology. A Survey of Diachronic Approaches, Concepts, and Research Projects." *Anglistentag 1999 Mainz*. Eds. Bernhard Reitz and Sigrid Rieuwerts. Trier: WVT, 2000a. 345–373.
Nünning, Ansgar. "On the Perspective Structure of Narrative Texts: Steps toward a Constructivist Narratology." *New Perspectives on Narrative Perspective. Papers presented at the Symposium on 'Narrative Perspective: Cognition and Emotion' held in Utrecht in June 1995*. Eds. Seymour Chatman and Willie van Peer. Albany: State University of New York Press, 2000b. 207–223.
Nünning, Ansgar. "Reconceptualizing Unreliable Narration: Synthesizing Cognitive and Rhetorical Approaches." *A Companion to Narrative Theory*. Eds. James Phelan and Peter J. Rabinowitz. Oxford: Blackwell 2005. 89–107.
Nünning, Ansgar. "Narrativist Approaches and Narratological Concepts for the Study of Culture." *Travelling Concepts for the Study of Culture*. Eds. Birgit Neumann and Ansgar Nünning. Berlin: de Gruyter, 2012. 145–183.
Nünning, Ansgar, and Vera Nünning (eds.). *Multiperspektivisches Erzählen: Zur Theorie und Geschichte der Perspektivenstruktur im englischen Roman des 18. bis 20. Jahrhunderts*. Trier: WVT, 2000.
Nünning, Ansgar, and Vera Nünning. "How to Stay Healthy and Foster Well-Being with Narratives, or: Where Narratology and Salutogenesis Could Meet." *How to Do Things with Narrative: Political and Narratological Perspectives on Anglophone Texts*. Eds. Jan Alber and Greta Olson. Berlin: de Gruyter, 2017. 157–186.
Nünning, Ansgar, and Christine Schwanecke. "The Performative Power of Unreliable Narration and Focalization in Drama and Theatre: Conceptualizing the Specificity of Dramatic Unreliability." *Unreliable Narration and Trustworthiness: Intermedial and Interdisciplinary Perspectives*. Ed. Vera Nünning. Berlin and Boston: de Gruyter, 2015. 189–219.
Nünning, Vera. "Unreliable Narration and the Historical Variability of Values and Norms: The Vicar of Wakefield as a Test Case of a Cultural-Historical Narratology." *Style* 38 (2004): 236–252.
Perl, Jeffrey M. *The Tradition of Return: The Implicit History of Modern Literature*. Princeton: Princeton University Press, 1984.
Phelan, James. *Living to Tell about It. A Rhetoric and Ethics of Character Narration*. Ithaca: Cornell University Press, 2005.
Ramey, James. "Intertextual Metempsychosis in *Ulysses*: Murphy, Sinbad, and the 'U.P.: up' Postcard." *James Joyce Quarterly* 45.1 (2007): 97–114.
Richardson, Scott. "The Devious Narrator of the *Odyssey*." *The Classical Journal* 101.4 (2006): 337–359.
Skempis, Marios, and Ioannis Ziogas. "Arete's Words: Etymology, Ehoie-Poetry and Gendered Narrative in the *Odyssey*." *Narratology and Interpretation: The Content of Narrative Form in Ancient Literature*. Eds. Jonas Grethlein and Antonios Rengakos. Berlin: de Gruyter, 2009. 213–240.
Stanford, William B. "Joyce's First Meeting with Ulysses." *The Listener* XLVI (July 19, 1951).
Stanford, William B. *The Ulysses Theme. A Study in the Adaptability of a Traditional Hero*. Second ed. Oxford: Blackwell, 1963.

Strauss Clay, Jenny. *The Wrath of Athena: Gods and Men in the* Odyssey. Princeton: Princeton University Press, 1983.
Wykes, David. "The *Odyssey* in *Ulysses*." *Texas Studies in Literature and Language*. 10.2 (1968): 301–316.
Zerweck, Bruno. "Historicizing Unreliable Narration: Unreliability and Cultural Discourse in Narrative Fiction." *Style* 35.1 (2001): 151–178.

Janine Hauthal
A European Storyteller? Collective Narration in John Berger's *Into Their Labours*

Abstract: Based on the understanding of cultures as narrative communities, this article explores the aesthetic figurations of Europe in John Berger's *Into Their Labours* (1979–1990) and demonstrates how the trilogy's generic hybridity, multiperspectivity, and collective narration support Berger's creation of a communal voice. Adopting a cultural narratological approach, the case study first shows how interconnecting centripetal and diverging centrifugal narrative forces create a tentative sense of coherence akin to the short story cycle, while the trilogy's macrostructural pattern transforms the individual stories into a master narrative of crisis. Secondly, an analysis of perspective structure and narrative voice in the three parts reveals that, in the trilogy as a whole, peasant culture emerges as a narrative community. Thirdly, in scrutinizing spatial markers as a means to connect the modernization processes depicted by Berger with Europe and European mobilities, the article draws attention to the trilogy's previously neglected European dimension. Narrating Europe from a transnational perspective, Berger clearly counters the longstanding traditions of British Euroskepticism and insularity and, indeed, can be seen a 'European storyteller'.

1 John Berger's we-narrators

When John Berger received the Petrarch award in 1991, jury member Peter Handke expressed his ambivalent stance toward the writing of the British author in his laudatory speech, which the German weekly *DIE ZEIT* published on 15 November 1991.

> Since his novel *G.* or so, Berger presents himself as a 'we-narrator'. He always acts as a speaker, a spokesman: not of a group emerging episodically from the text but of one that is predetermined. John Berger passionately understands himself as a speaker, in synchrony with others, the women, the lonely villagers in the Savoy area, the country-(wo)men who ended up in ('immigrated to', he says) the metropolises. And yet, as a speaker for the many – or should I remain fair and say: 'of the many'? –, Berger does not perceive himself as a chronicler but as somebody who explicitly differs from the

---

Note: The research for this article was financed by the Research Foundation – Flanders (FWO).

https://doi.org/10.1515/9783110654370-015

latter and as somebody he esteems: namely as a storyteller, a storyteller of the 'we', up into the dreams playing along and conspiring with his heroes, as the European equivalent of García Márquez [...]. (Handke 1991; my translation)[1]

Handke's statement echoes the widespread opinion that, after *G.*, innovative and experimental features of Berger's fiction have been replaced by a 'painstaking realism' (cf. Lippincott 1991, 137–138), tragedy (cf. Levy 2004, 311–318), and narrative orality (cf. Merrifield 2012, 88–105; Hertel and Malcolm 2016, 15–17). Moreover, the Austrian writer aptly draws attention to how the expatriate British author, by way of 'we-narrators' who speak both for and of others, tends to fashion himself as a "spokesman" in order to distinguish himself from a distant chronicler. However, from a narratological point of view, Handke's use of the term 'we-narrator' is misleading since, in his writing, Berger rarely makes use of the first-person plural outside of direct speech. Hence, a narratological analysis of narrative voice and collective narration aiming to clarify how exactly Berger emerges as 'a storyteller of the we' in his works after *G.* is clearly overdue.

Taking its cue from Handke, the present article seeks a new approach to John Berger's *Into Their Labours*. In contrast to Berger's much-quoted critique of Western visual culture in *Ways of Seeing* (1972), his trilogy – or indeed his literary work in general – has attracted curiously little critical response, and the few exceptions tended to dispense with a theoretical and methodological framework in favor of traditional literary criticism (see Dyer 1986; Engelberg 1998; Merrifield 2012).[2] Recently, however, scholars have started to fill this lacuna (see Welz 1996, 186–200; Schmitt-Kilb 2012; Aleksandrowicz-Wojtyna 2016; Wojtyna 2016), even though some concentrate on just one – generally the same – story from *Pig Earth* (see Bowen 2016;

---

1 See the German original: "Berger [tritt] [...] etwa seit seinem Roman *G.*, als ein Wir-Erzähler auf [...]. [...] [E]r ist immer der Sprecher, der *spokesman*: einer Gruppe, die sich nicht erst episodisch fügt aus dem Text, sondern von vornherein feststand [...]. John Berger versteht sich mit Leidenschaft als Sprecher, Mitgeher für die anderen, die Frauen, die einsamen Dörfler in Savoyen, die in die Metropolen verschlagenen (‚immigrierten', sagt er) Landmenschen [...]. [...] Dabei, als Sprecher für die vielen – oder sollte ich gerecht bleiben und sagen: ‚von den vielen'? –, sieht sich John Berger freilich nicht als einen Chronisten, sondern als jemand, den er von diesem ausdrücklich unterscheidet, den er auch höher schätzt: eben als Erzähler, als Erzähler vom ‚Wir', bis in die Träume mitspielend und verschworen mit seinen Helden, als die europäische Entsprechung zu García Márquez [...]."
2 As Ralf Hertel and David Malcolm note, scholarship on Berger and Berger's work is "hagiographic" and full of "uncritical adulation" (2016, 18; see also Bowen 2016, 64).

Lutostański 2016). A notable exception in this respect is a chapter by Ansgar Nünning (1995, 16–33), in which he discusses *Into Their Labours* as a revisionist-historical novel that broadens the thematic scope of traditional historical fiction by unlocking "Alltagsgeschichte" (Nünning 1995, 6–15) – i.e. the 'history of everyday life' or 'people's history' – a field of historical study (social history) that emerged in the 1980s under the influence of such new approaches at the time as 'oral history', 'popular culture', 'microhistory', and 'history from below'. Highlighting not only the fragmented and episodic structure and the predominance of iterative narration in Parts I and II, but also the trilogy's representation of time and semanticizing of space, as well as Berger's use of magical realism and multiperspectivity, Nünning demonstrates how thematic and formal innovation coincide in the "critical counterhistories" ("kritische Gegengeschichten"; 1995, 17) recounted in *Into Their Labours*.

Building on Nünning's findings, I aim to explore the aesthetic figurations of Europe in Berger's trilogy and to investigate whether, and to what extent, its generic hybridity and narrative strategies contribute to narrating Europe from an expatriate British and/or transnational perspective. Analyzing "formal narrative techniques [...] not just [...] as structural features of a text, but as highly semanticized narrative modes engaged in the processes of cultural construction and worldmaking" (Nünning 1995, 62), my methodological approach will conform to the premises of a context-sensitive cultural narratology, delineated elsewhere by Nünning as an understanding of "culture not as 'text' but as [...] 'narrating communities'" (2009b, 61).[3] The article will, then, be particularly interested in the semanticizing of narrative forms (see Nünning 2009b, 62–64), the construction of coherence, and identity formation (see Nünning 2013, 31–46). Concretely, it will examine how, in Berger's portrayal of the local peasantry and migrant workers as a narrative community, specific formal choices concerning literary genre, narrative voice, and models of space serve to translate a context-specific local experience into narrative, and in doing so contribute to the cultural construction of 'Europe'.

---

[3] The understanding of cultures as "Erzählgemeinschaften" – narrating communities that differ "not only with regard to the subjects and themes they are particularly interested in, but also with regard to their favoured modes of storytelling, their ways of constructing narratives" (Nünning 2009b, 61) – was first theorized by Wolfgang Müller-Funk (2008) and later conceptually enriched with a melding of cultural history, memory studies and narratology (see Nünning 2010, 2012a, 2013).

Accordingly, the focus of my case study will be threefold. To begin with, I shall proceed from the claim that previous research has not sufficiently accounted for the trilogy's generic hybridity. By focusing on individual stories, or by approaching all three parts as novels in their own right, existing scholarship has not done justice to the trilogy's characteristic tension between interconnecting "centripetal" and diverging "centrifugal narrative forces" (Lundén 2014, 55): it is from this, I would argue, that a tentative sense of coherence emerges. In pursuit of this argument the article will first trace thematic connections across the trilogy's three parts in order to show how notions of modernity resonate in Berger's depiction of modernization as industrialization, and how – throughout the trilogy – he balances openness with closure and distance with involvement, creating an authenticity that resonates powerfully with nostalgia.

Secondly, even though Nünning, Lutostański, Welz, and Wojtyna have already scrutinized the trilogy's organization of multiperspectivity, focalization, and diegetic levels, and have made valuable observations concerning metanarrative passages and informative lacunae, I believe that an analysis of the trilogy's perspective structure and narrative voice can benefit from the insights of narratological studies of multiperspectivity (cf. Nünning and Nünning 2000) and recent research on collective narration (cf. Bekhta 2017). A narratological analysis of Berger's creation of a 'communal voice' (*sensu* Lanser 1992) will also help to explain how, in *Into Their Labours*, peasant culture emerges as a 'narrative community', i.e. a community "forged and held together by the stories [its] members tell about themselves and their culture as well as by conventionalized forms of storytelling and cultural plots" (Nünning 2009b, 61).

Thirdly, the aim of this article is to draw attention to the trilogy's European dimension – an important aspect largely ignored in earlier studies – by examining the extent to which the trilogy's representation of space can be linked to Europe. Arguably, investigating what kind of 'fictions of Europe'[4] emerge from the trilogy's three parts is particularly pertinent in view of the author's expatriate experience and his long concern with Europe. In 1962, Berger relocated to the European continent, moving first to Geneva and then to the Haute-Savoie in

---

[4] The term 'fictions of Europe' was first used (but not defined) in an eponymous article by sociologist Jan Nederveen Pieterse (1991). My use of the expression 'fictions of...' is also indebted to Vera and Ansgar Nünning's phrase "fictions of Empire" in their 1996 article on the making of British imperialist mentalities. The generative nature of this expression has become evident in numerous publications – see, for instance, "fictions of authority" (Lanser 1992), "fictions of loss" (Arata 1996), "fictions of migration" (Sommer 2001; Freitag 2010), "fictions of (generational) memory" (Nünning 2003; Neumann 2005; Erll 2017), "fictions of cognition" (Freissmann 2011), "fictions of spirituality" (Bingel 2013), and "fictions of time" (Lange 2017).

France, where he lived from 1974 (see Dyer 1986, 116) until his death in 2017. Like the novels of Julian Barnes (also a professed Francophile) and those of expatriate British writer Tim Parks, who lives in Italy, many of Berger's stories are set on the European continent or feature continental European characters[5] – a fact that has prompted critics and scholars to attribute a 'European' quality to all three writers (see, for Barnes: Guignery and Roberts 2009, 29 and 64; for Parks: Fenwick 2003, 104–137), with Achim Engelberg (1998) in particular claiming that the European dimension of the trilogy makes Berger a 'European storyteller' (see also White 2011). Addressing this issue, it will be argued here that, throughout the trilogy, spatial markers serve as a means to connect the modernization processes depicted by Berger with Europe and European mobilities. At the same time the article will demonstrate how Berger's 'ways of telling' (Dyer 1986) counter the longstanding history of British Euroscepticism (Spiering 2015) and insular mentality (Kamm and Sedlmayr 2007).

2 Industrialization and the decline of peasant culture: *Into Their Labours* as a 'narrative of crisis'

Published between 1979 and 1990, *Into Their Labours*[6] traces the decline of peasant culture and the resultant migration into the cities. The trilogy is predominantly set in the French Alps where Berger lived since 1974, after having left Britain. With its rustic local focus, the trilogy attests the "remarkable increase in interest in the rural and the regional" that Liesbeth Korthals Altes and Manet van Montfrans have observed in contemporary

---

5 In addition to *Into Their Labours*, see Berger's novels *A Painter of Our Time* (1958), *G.* (1972), and *To the Wedding* (1995). For Barnes, see his novels *Metroland* (1980), *Flaubert's Parrot* (1984), *Talking it Over* (1991), *The Porcupine* (1992), and *The Noise of Time* (2016), as well as the short story cycle *Cross Channel* (1996) and his essay collection *The Lemon Table* (2004). According to Parks, *Dreams of Rivers and Seas* (2008) is "[his] only novel set outside Europe" (Parks, n.p.), and he has also authored numerous non-fiction works concerned with life in Italy, ranging from *Italian Neighbours* (1992), and his bestseller *Italian Ways* (2003), to *A Literary Tour of Italy* (2015).
6 The title of the trilogy is based on a biblical quote by St John which features as a motto in all three parts: "'Others have laboured and ye are entered into their labours.' ST JOHN 4–38" (see e.g. *PE* ix). Here and in what follows, quotes from the three parts of the trilogy are annotated as follows: *Pig Earth* will be abbreviated as *PE*, *Once in Europa* will be referred to as *OE*, and *Lilac and Flag* as *LF*.

European fiction since the 1960s (2002, 9). The first two parts of the trilogy, *Pig Earth* and *Once in Europa*, consist of short stories interspersed with drawings and poems, while the trilogy's final part, *Lilac and Flag: An Old Wives' Tale of a City*, is best described as a novel.

Pig Earth consists of ten short stories that alternate with seven poems. Each story focuses on different characters, creating a multiperspective narration that will be analyzed in Section 3 below. The stories cover various aspects of rural life, both one-off and recurrent, such as the slaughter of a cow, the selling of a calf, the mating of goats, the repair of a water pipe, or the kidnapping of two tax inspectors. Some of the stories revel in the harmonious unity between man and animal, palpable in the following passage: "He sat on a milking stool in the dark. With his head in his hands, his breathing was indistinguishable from that of the cows. The stable itself was like the inside of an animal. Breath, water, cud were entering it; wind, piss, shit were leaving it." (*PE* 13) However, Berger avoids a sentimental idealization of peasant life; after all, agricultural machinery forms part of this unity, and its use or rejection by local farmers provides glimpses of industrialization in Part I of the trilogy which Parts II and III further elaborate. As a result, thematic occurrences relating to the trilogy's portrayal of modernization as progressive industrialization interconnect the individual stories and provide the trilogy with a well-defined narrative development.

Once in Europa, the trilogy's second part, is framed by two poems. In between, five short stories continue the depiction of peasant life, focusing here more on love and family relationships. In many of these stories, an antagonism between rural and urban cultures becomes evident. "Boris Is Buying Horses", for instance, recounts a peasant's fatal attraction for a married 'city woman' (cf. *OE* 44), and the eponymous "Once in Europa" depicts men and women struggling with the transition from agricultural labor to work in factories and shops – the typical transition from a "culture of survival" to a "culture of progress" and migration (*PE* xix).

Finally, *Lilac and Flag* narrates "how the children and grandchildren of rural peasants" struggle to survive in "the mythic city of Troy" (*LF* flap). In contrast to the two previous volumes, Part III of the trilogy does not consist of short stories and includes only one poem, attesting to the overall shift from lyric to narrative mode, which corresponds to the change noted by Nünning (1995, 17) from holistic to fragmented experience in the characters' lives. *Lilac and Flag* features a frame narrative, in which an old woman who has spent her whole life in a mountain village functions as a first-person narrator. The eponymous story of two lovers is embedded in her daily routine. Although parts of the novel exhibit realistic detail, magical elements abound, especially in the dreamlike ending, imagining the afterlife of three dead characters. On the whole, the fact that the trilogy at once records the eclipse of peasant culture and preserves it (transformed into stories) creates strong resonances with nostalgia (see Hitchcock 2000; Nünning 1995, 32).

While, in Part I of the trilogy heterodiegetic narrators prevail, Part II reveals a progressive involvement of (homo- and autodiegetic) narrative instances in the storyworld. At first sight, *Lilac and Flag*'s ambivalent, but overall heterodiegetic first-person narrator steps out of this line of development. Overall, the old woman's presence on the level of the characters and her involvement in the story she tells are ambivalent. On the one hand, her several appearances in the intradiegetic storyworld suggest that she is a homodiegetic narrator. Yet on closer inspection her appearances turn out to be metaleptic transgressions of an otherwise heterodiegetic first-person narrative. For instance, her welcoming of Sucus's father after his death (see *LF* 43) and, on the novel's final pages, of dead Sucus himself (see *LF* 160) indicate that she speaks from the realm of the dead.[7] However, while readers might expect that her speaking position frees her from realist constraints, other scenes clearly show that the narrator's perceptive capacities are subject to restrictions (see *LF* 118–119, 146–157). However, rather than prompting readers to question the reliability of the narrator, such inconsistencies – as well as Berger's use of an omnipresent rather than omniscient narrative agent – tend to elicit reader participation and prepare for the novel's magical realist ending, namely the meeting of the dead characters (Hector, Naisi, Sucus) aboard the 'white ship' at the novel's close.

Berger's mix of short and long narrative forms with drawings and poems continues what Hertel and Malcolm describe as "his commitment to formal openness" (2016, 21). According to these two scholars, much of Berger's work has "an open, unfinished quality, [and is] characterised by a lack of closure" (Hertel and Malcolm 2016, 21), which can be seen as supporting the writer's desire to actively engage the reader (see also Szuba 2016). Loosely interconnected narrative voices and strands, associative narrative progress, and the interplay of various genres and media create ruptures and invite readers to actively establish their own connections, "to fill gaps and lacunae that are exceptionally wide" (Hertel and Malcolm 2016, 20). At the same time, the simplistic, obviously amateurish quality of the drawings further authenticates both stories and acts of storytelling, especially in the first part of the trilogy with its

---

[7] See also the scene in which the female narrator approaches Hector with a story from his childhood and he does not react, which adds a ghostlike quality to this (one-sided) 'encounter' (cf. *LF* 133–134).

predominantly documentary style. Ultimately, the loose, but still recognizable, sense of coherence that results from the trilogy's generic hybridity tasks readers with co-creating coherence, and potentially increases reader participation.

As Wojtyna demonstrates (2016, 83–92), this argument can be extended to the trilogy's language and style. With its description of landscapes, characters and everyday routines, as well as its recurrent use of French words (such as *eau de vie, gnôle, alpage*), which emphasize the strong relation of narrative to locality, *Into Their Labours* offers much detail; at the same time, however, "incomplete characterisation, stylistic discontinuities, and uncertainty about narrative voices" (Wojtyna 2016, 83) defy explication and open possibilities for readers' (interpretative) engagement with the text. Given that the tension between centripetal and centrifugal narrative forces is one of the central dynamics of the short story cycle (see Lundén 2014, 55), the trilogy's first two parts – with their common location and recurrent theme but different narrators and focalizers – clearly qualify as short story cycles. However, the "tension between openness and closure" (D'hoker and Van den Bossche 2014, 9) also extends to the trilogy's third, novelistic part, indicating the limitation of the concept of short story cycle as a generic frame. Alternative macrostructural narrative patterns – in particular the notions of 'broken narratives' and 'narratives of crisis' – might work better as explanatory frames, and it is to a consideration of these that I shall now turn.

In its accounts of the disruption of individual lives, its reflections on cultural and socioeconomic changes, and its questioning of the hegemonic master narrative of industrial progress – and above all, perhaps, in the way it challenges readers to assume an active role – *Into Their Labours* displays salient features of the so-called 'broken narratives' which have figured prominently since the new millennium (and especially since 9/11, see Nünning and Nünning 2016, 37) and have become the subject of ongoing scholarly debate (see Babka et al. 2016). However, the trilogy does not evolve around any defining breach (see Nünning and Nünning 2016, 59–60) nor does it "foreground or even flaunt the impossibility of coherence, order and attempts at sense-making" (Nünning and Nünning 2016, 75). Rather, it traces processes of industrialization and trajectories of increasing alienation and (rural) migration, and, in doing so, imposes its own (alternative) pattern of sense-making. All three parts reflect the common theme of modernization as industrialization. Following Nikos Papastergiadis, who describes exile as "not just the consequence *of* modernity, but also a metaphor for the processes *within* modernity" (1993, 1), it can be argued that *Pig Earth* records modernity as "the experience of estrangement that *precedes* departure" (Papastergiadis 1993, 13), while the trilogy's subsequent two parts depict those already 'on the move', i.e. the migrant workers of the local factory and the erstwhile peasants who now roam the city of Troy.

The centrality of Berger's concern with modernity already shows in the extensive introduction to *Pig Earth*. Here Berger conceives of the peasantry as a transnational, globe-spanning "class of survivors" (*PE* xi) who share "a cyclic view of time" (*PE* xvi). He warns his readers, however, not to confuse the "peasant suspicion of 'progress'" (*PE* xxvi) with right-wing conservatism, defending privilege and trying to preserve the status quo. He argues instead that peasants tend to experience change on a daily basis: the vagaries of the weather, crop failure, sickness of animals or of themselves. And they seek to counter these hardships by repeated acts of survival based on tradition and knowledge passed on from generation to generation.

Characters in the trilogy reflect this attitude rather didactically and reveal that, at the onset of the trilogy, the peasant community is on the brink of change. Pépé, for one, compares tradition to knowledge and indicates that the peasants' cyclical view of time is not opposed to progress as such but allows for a 'slow step-by-step progress'.

> [...] I would like to go back! *To see how the things we know today were first learnt*. Take a chevreton. It's simple. Milk the goat, heat the milk, separate it and press the curds. Well, we saw it all being done before we could walk. But how did they once discover that the best way of separating the milk was to take a kid's stomach, blow it up like a balloon, dry it, soak it in acid, powder it and drop a few grains of this powder into the heated milk? [...] All the mistakes which had to be made! And *step by step, slowly, the progress*! (*PE* 48; my emphasis)

In *Pig Earth*, this slow progress is opposed to the rapid processes of industrialization and modernity, which are framed as the harbingers of crisis and doom, threatening the peasants' survival by destroying their identity – as in the passage where 63-year-old farmer Marcel explains to himself the need to plant new apple trees:

> My sons won't work on the farm. [...] Why work with such effort and care for *something which is doomed*? And to that I reply: Working is a way of preserving *the knowledge my sons are losing*. I [...] plant out these saplings to give an example to my sons if they are interested, and, if not, to show my father and his father that the knowledge they handed down has not yet been abandoned. *Without that knowledge, I am nothing*. (*PE* 66–67; my emphasis)

Throughout the trilogy, the appeal of the city attracts especially the younger generation with the promise of a new life without the burden of hard physical work. Berger illustrates the resultant generation gap in the short story "The Value of Money" in which Marcel refuses to use the machine his son Edouard bought for him and denounces the capitalist logic that informs its distribution: the machine's sole purpose is to "wipe us out" (*PE* 70). At the same time, however, Marcel realizes how futile his opposition is and indicates that more than a mere generation conflict is at stake when he acknowledges the fundamental, irreversible nature of the change brought about by the existence of machines:

> They make sure we know the machines exist. From then onwards working without one is harder. Not having the machine makes the father look old-fashioned to the son, makes the husband look mean to his wife, makes one neighbour look poor to the next. (*PE* 73)

Here and elsewhere in the trilogy, Berger's stories repeatedly narrativize the change brought about by modernization as a 'turning point' (see Nünning and Sicks 2012, 42) – significant, unexpected, impactful, irrevocable, and unrepeatable – in the history of peasant culture and hold it responsible for that culture's decline.

The invariably ill-starred love stories between peasant men and city women are another case in point. Speaking of the men's desire for something other than peasant life, a dream of freedom, and of new levels of choice which come at the (as yet unknown) expense of undermining the certitudes of peasant life, these stories show the destructive impact of such liaisons on the peasants. Their destructive force comes to the fore in the story about the death of Boris, who – freed from having to care for domestic animals – loses his connection to the task-based 'earthly' existence that kept him alive and sane ("Boris is Buying Horses", *OE* 33–63). Similarly, in *Lilac and Flag*, the lovers only reunite and find happiness in a magical afterlife. Thus the failing love stories of *Into Their Labours* highlight both the trilogy's critique of capitalist modernity as an alienating force and, as Papastergiadis puts it with reference to Arnold Gehlen, "the ambivalence of the 'freedom' that is gained" through industrialization (1993, 13).

With modernization providing thematic connections both between the three volumes and between individual stories, and in doing so serving as a marker of change throughout the trilogy, a tentative sense of coherence emerges, centering on the notion of crisis. In this way the trilogy as a macro-structure transforms the individual stories into a master narrative of crisis (see Nünning 2009a, 2012b), imposing structure, generating emotions, reducing complexity, serving normative, political and legitimizing functions, and contributing to the formation and maintenance of collective identities (see Nünning 2009a, 249–253), or what Nünning has also called a "course-of-disease scheme" (2009a, 244). The individual stories and volumes of *Into Their Labours* are interconnected, therefore, not just by a common location and a recurrent theme, but also by a narrative pattern: the pattern of crisis. As the following section will show, this also contributes to the trilogy's construction of a communal voice.

3 *Into Their Labours* as a we-narrative? Multiperspectivity and 'communal voice'

I have already referred to Ansgar Nünning's observation that generalizations, iterative narration, and the accentuation of the habitual in the shape of everyday rituals, shared knowledge, traditions etc. play a central role in shaping Berger's trilogy as a collective narration (see Section 1 above; Nünning 1995, 19–23). The trilogy's perspective structure, however, is equally instrumental in this respect. To begin with, the work includes several different narrators, so that it is possible to speak of a multi-narrator text (cf. Nünning and Nünning 2000, 42). Thus in *Pig Earth* heterodiegetic narrators prevail; but "The Wind Howls Too" and "The Three Lives of Lucie Chabrol" feature homodiegetic narrators.[8] In *Once in Europa*, two of the seven short stories feature a heterodiegetic narrator, while the remaining five are told by overt homo- and autodiegetic narrators respectively. Finally, in *Lilac and Flag*, the old woman acts as the novel's heterodiegetic first-person narrator.

Even if one were to assume that the stories in the first two volumes featuring a heterodiegetic narrator are told by the same voice, the trilogy could still be called multiperspective, as each of these stories centers on a different character, and these characters often function as focalizers. Moreover, the inclusion of poetry and drawings arguably offers multiple perspectives on, and different ways of telling about, peasant culture that are not restricted to narrative or even literary genres. In this sense, the trilogy's multiperspectivity is multidimensional. However, in contrast to works in which multiperspective narration serves to reflect epistemological skepticism, "open[ing] up a broad scope of interpretative possibilities, and requir[ing] the reader to make considerable efforts in order to reach a synthesis" (Neumann and Nünning 2011, 103), Berger's use of this narrative technique is best described as "additive multiperspectivity" (Neumann and Nünning 2011, 102) since the individual perspectives largely converge and complement each other. In other words, by combining diverse perspectives with conjunctive tendencies that indicate a convergence of experience, the overall perspective structure of *Into Their Labours* balances centrifugal and centripetal narrative forces. This balance provides one of the building blocks of the trilogy's collective narration.

---

8 Neither André, who remembers his grandfather Pépé, nor Jean, who narrates the life of Lucie Chabrol, function as protagonists of the stories they tell, even though each of them plays a central role in the protagonist's life. Hence they can be classified as allodiegetic rather than autodiegetic narrators (in the sense of Herman and Vervaeck 2005, 84).

In light of recent narratological research on collective narration, the trilogy's narrative voice can be further defined as a "communal voice" (Lanser 1992, 21). In *Into Their Labours*, this voice is produced neither in "a *singular* form in which one narrator speaks for a collective, [nor] in a *simultaneous* form in which a plural 'we' narrates" but rather "in a *sequential* form in which individual members of a group narrate in turn" (Lanser 1992, 21; emphasis in original). The trilogy includes different types of collective narration, but none of them can be defined as a "we-narrative" proper in the sense of Natalya Bekhta's recent definition, i.e. a narrative in which either "a group is speaking as a whole", or "several [...] group members speak in unison, referring to the group they represent" (2017, 178).[9] Most uses of first-person plural pronouns in the trilogy pertain to the introduction and are best described as an academic or author's 'we' which serves to include the reader (cf. "Paradise, as we now understand it", *PE* xvi; see also *PE* xix–xx, xxiii). In the remainder of the trilogy, the first-person plural is exclusively used in stories told by first-person narrators, whose uses of 'we' usually hinge upon an implicit "I + somebody" equation and do not represent a collective subject (Bekhta 2017, 171). In *Pig Earth*, for instance, the homodiegetic narrator Jean reflects that "the *Life of Voltaire* belonged to that collection of books which we knew existed and which entailed a way of life we could not imagine. At what time of day did people read? we asked ourselves." (*PE* 97) Only a page later, Jean's use of 'we' is explicitly defined as referring to "we children" (*PE* 98). Consequently, in these and other instances, the first-person narrators' use of 'we' is reducible to a group of individuals behind which the narrator masks himself (cf. e.g. *PE* 42, 44, 46, 153, 171; *OE* 6, 31, 33, 92, 94, 97). Only in *Lilac and Flag* does the use of 'we' shift to a slightly more intersubjective, communal stance, as the old woman presents herself as a spokesperson on behalf of women in general. This becomes evident in expressions such as "We women, rivers of pain and relief" (*LF* 30; see also *LF* 117) and in the plural 'women' in the title of Part III.

In view of the overall small number of we-uses, however, *Into Their Labours* cannot, despite Handke's claims, be called a we-narrative proper – i.e. one "in which collective subjectivity defines the dominant mode of narration" (Bekhta 2017, 166). Since, linguistically, the narrators' rare uses of 'we' allow one to infer an individual speaker, the trilogy's communal voice cannot be ascribed to the

---

9 Concerning the relation between we-narrative and communal voice, see Bekhta who points out: "But as is clear from Lanser's definition, 'communal voice' is a qualifier much broader in scope than 'we-voice' and is not necessarily created with the help of the technique of we-narration. In other words, one has to distinguish between rhetorical effects and their means: we-narration is only one technique amongst many that can produce an effect of a communal story." (2017, 169)

technique of we-narration; it must be classified, rather, as a 'rhetorical effect' (Bekhta 2017, 169). Pursuing this point, the following section will, therefore, focus on other narrative techniques – namely Berger's depiction of the peasantry as a 'narrative community' and his creation of reader complicity – in order to demonstrate that (and how) they contribute to the trilogy's construction of a 'communal voice'.

4 Creating complicity: Peasant culture as a 'narrative community' and the trilogy's implied readership

Throughout the trilogy, intratextual allusions disclose the communal character of its narrative voice. Already in *Once in Europa*, cross-references indicate that characters know one another. Odile Blanc, the narrator of the eponymous story "Once in Europa", for instance, refers to Lucie Chabrol, who features in three of the stories included in *Pig Earth* (cf. *OE* 100). And in *Lilac and Flag*, the first-person narrator frequently alludes to characters from the trilogy's first two volumes.[10] Moreover, not only the frame narrative of *Lilac and Flag*, but all the stories in the trilogy are set in the old woman's home village. This creates the impression that they originate in a communal reservoir of tales with which all the inhabitants of the village are familiar. The recovery of a sense of community lends a nostalgic quality to *Lilac and Flag*; more importantly, it indicates that Berger's literary imagining of the peasants as a narrative community is based on an understanding of culture as an "ensemble of narratives" (Nünning 2009b, 61), which the author – so it seems – merely recorded.[11] Fashioning a community of peasants of which he is the spokesperson, he thereby creates their communal voice.

Three further characteristics of the old woman's tale confirm the trilogy to be a kaleidoscopic universe of communal tales and, ultimately, create a

---

10 See, for example, the following references to Marius, who features twice in *Pig Earth* (cf. *PE* 40–44; 163–169) as well as in *Once in Europa* (*OE* 64–91), and to Félix, the accordion player of the homonymous story in *Once in Europa* (cf. *OE* 4–32): "It was in these tanneries that Marius worked long ago, when many men still came back alive from the city." (*LF* 5); "If I'm not mistaken, the third of June was Félix's birthday. Félix had an accordion whom he called Caroline." (*LF* 24) See also Nünning's observations concerning the leitmotifs of 'hay making' and 'survival', and the coherence-creating function of characters' memories (1995, 21; 27; 28).

11 Berger's understanding of culture as a narrative community may also explain why, in his introduction to the trilogy, he refers to the peasantry as a 'culture (of survival)' (*PE* xix) rather than as a 'class'.

tenuous sense of narrative coherence or even closure. First of all, the fact that she, too, is a peasant establishes continuity between the three parts of the trilogy. Like the narrator in the passage from *Pig Earth* quoted above, she 'relates' and 'translates' what the characters undergo in the city (in)to her own peasant frames of reference. It turns out that the old woman lives in the same mountain village from which the male protagonists (Sucus and Hector) of *Lilac and Flag* hail and to which they dream of returning. Significantly, it is these two characters' minds (and theirs alone) that she can access, as the following passage exemplifies:

> He [Sucus] lay down on the grass and looked up at the stars. In the sky he saw a boat. [...] The ship's deck was the flat stomach of the woman he'd met outside St. Joseph's and the bowsprit was her crossed ankles. If you are asking how an old woman like me can know what Sucus dreamt about, remember that dreams are among the oldest things in the world. (*LF* 20–21)[12]

The narrator's metafictional reflection on her (restricted) ability suggests that the shared ancestry of narrator and characters facilitates focalization.

Thirdly, an accumulation of metafictional elements and comments toward the novel's close implies that the intradiegetic storyworld is entirely the narrator's invention and, as such, is literally an 'old wives' tale'. At the beginning of "Selling", the old woman explicitly discloses the (both factual and fictional) sources that inspired her narrative, for she herself has never set foot in the city of Troy:

> I have lived all my long life in the village. What I know of Troy comes from *The Messenger* – the provincial newspaper – from television, from my dreams, from my broken heart, and from what those who come back tell me before they disappear for good. (*LF* 120)

One of her comments even creates a *mise en abyme* structure, implying that the occurrences in Hotel Patrai feature an alter ego of hers:

> To their [Sucus and Zsuzsa's] surprise, at the reception desk at the far end of the hall sat an old woman rather like myself. She wore black, she had worn hands with arthritic knuckles, her forearms, if they could have seen them, were weathered, and the rest of her body, if they could have seen it, was very pale. (*LF* 109)

Metafictional comments by other characters equally point to the narrative's constructed nature. In the final chapter, for example, Naisi starts gambling on

---

12 See also: "From where he [Superintendent Hector] stood between the azaleas, his head full of names, he could distinguish the sea he wanted to cross and the arc lights of the docks." (*LF* 74)

board the white ship, using his place in the story as wager: "Can I bet my place in this story? Can I buy with that? [The croupier] stared at him, his eyes wide open with admiration. If I lose, said Naisi, I'm erased! The boy handed him a hundred chips." (*LF* 165–166) Moreover, based on the likeness of narrator and receptionist, Zsuzsa's conclusion that the latter has invented a grandson in order to fight her loneliness can be read as a metafictional comment: "I knew there was no grandson. [...] She invents him and makes him a waiter, see? There aren't any waiters around the hotel when she arrives. She's by herself. So she invents this grandson for company." (*LF* 113) Together, these metafictional comments strengthen the effect of 'complicity', because the more overt the narrator, the more explicit her reader guidance and her attempts to entice reader involvement become.

The question remains, however, to whom this collective voice is addressed. A preliminary answer can be found in the detailed descriptions of peasant routines. They not only confer a documentary quality on the short stories but also reveal the narrators' profound knowledge of peasant life and thereby authenticate both stories and acts of storytelling. In addition, they hint at the fact that the stories imply readers who are unfamiliar with peasant culture and its intricate forms of knowledge. The following passage from the first short story "A Question of Place" reveals how the detailed description of the actions involved in slaughtering a cow helps to enlist the reader.

> The son pushes a spring through the hole in the skull into the cow's brain. It goes in nearly twenty centimetres. He agitates it to be sure that all the animal's muscles will relax, and pulls it out. The mother holds the uppermost foreleg by the fetlock in her two hands. The son cuts by the throat and the blood floods out on to the floor. For a moment *it takes the form of an enormous velvet skirt, whose tiny waist band is the lip of the wound.* Then it flows on and resembles nothing.
>
> *Life is liquid. The Chinese were wrong to believe that the essential was breath. Perhaps the soul is breath.* The cow's pink nostrils are still quivering. Her eye is staring unseeing, and her tongue is falling out of the side of her mouth. (*PE* 4; my emphasis)

As the highlighted phrases indicate, metaphorical and philosophical observations are often accompanied by the depiction of routine activities, which ground these utterances of authority in experience. While the generic references to characters as "the son" and "the mother" at first seem to indicate a distant narrator-focalizer, the narrator's figurative language, in contrast, suggests a spatial and cognitive proximity to peasant culture. General reflections and the repeated use of sensuous similes and metaphors additionally cast doubt on the narrator's seemingly objective point of view. They indicate involvement, and thus contribute to the creation of what Handke has called Berger's 'complicit voice'. Moreover, they demonstrate that *Into Their Labours*, too, as Ralf Hertel (2016) has convincingly argued for Berger's later fiction, is characterized by a writing style that addresses readers' senses (*aisthesis*) rather than their intellect (*noesis*).

Throughout the trilogy, however, Berger's ways of fostering reader complicity change. In the trilogy's final part, the sensuous writing style and documentary realism of the first two parts is replaced by magical realism and metafictional elements. The predominantly covert narrators of *Pig Earth* make way for the overt narrator in *Lilac and Flag*, who explicitly seeks to guide and involve readers. This change runs parallel (or rather counter) to the increasing alienation and to the broader cultural dynamics of displacement that peasants, migrant workers and city dwellers experience in the trilogy – as if to compensate for characters' separation and to restore a sense of community in the realm of fiction that may elicit readers' sympathies.

Handke's statement therefore needs adjustment: Berger speaks not just *of* (rather than *for*) a collective of peasants (see Lutostański 2016), but also *to* a non-peasant audience. The construction of such an implied readership indirectly points to narrating instances willing to act as mediators to such audiences, balancing distance and involvement, outsiders' and insiders' points of view (see Wojtyna 2016, 80). While the author claims such a position for himself in his extensive introduction to *Pig Earth*, he tends in the trilogy as a whole to delegate it to his many female protagonists and narrators, epitomized by Odile Blanc in "Once in Europa" and the old woman in *Lilac and Flag*, who seem to ideally embody his idea of the peasant culture of survival.

The recurrence of female narrators complicates the often-rehearsed argument in scholarship on Berger's trilogy, namely that the author "invites identification of literary figures and author by placing an author figure in his texts" (Hertel and Malcolm 2016, 12, note 2; see also Turney 2016). However, notwithstanding the validity of this statement with regard to *A Painter of Our Time*, *G.*, and *To the Wedding*, in the trilogy it only applies to the stories "The Three Lives of Lucie Chabrol" from *Pig Earth* and "Boris is Buying Horses" from *Once in Europa*. Most stories in all three parts feature neither explicit author figures nor characters named 'John' or 'Jean' that might invite identification with Berger.

I have argued above that the common location and recurrent theme of Berger's trilogy, as well as his use of additive multiperspectivity and creation of reader complicity, are key factors in his creation of a communal voice throughout the trilogy and in its consequent depiction of the peasantry as a 'narrative community.' The fact that Berger's female narrators refute the simple equation between author and narrators provides a final building block to this argument. Affording the depiction of both commonality and internal divisions in larger communities, the trilogy's loose narrative structure lends itself to the imagination of collectives such as the peasantry and European migrants, and the final section of my article will explore how Berger's collective narration can be linked to Europe and European mobilities.

5 Utopian spaces and the 'other Europe': The trilogy's European dimension

The trilogy's literary representation of space evolves from an opposition of rural and urban areas (see Nünning 1995, 26–32) to the imagination of transnational spaces, and thus lends itself to the imagination of collective agencies. Not just its setting and characters but its transnational spatial markers serve in particular to connect the processes of industrialization and rural migration that it depicts with Europe and European mobilities.

To begin with, a transnational (but not specifically European) dimension in its imagination of space is evidenced by the fact that the trilogy – apart from the incidental fact that the village's name, "Lucky-Horse-With-A-Broken-Leg" (*LF* 166; *LF* 152), indicates an English approximation to a French original – at no point thematizes issues of translation or intercultural misunderstanding between the British author and his French environment. The trilogy is, in fact, characterized by an overall lack of national stereotypes – which is particularly striking in comparison with works by other British writers who have engaged with a foreign European country, as Julian Barnes has with France in his collection of short stories *Cross Channel* (see Hauthal 2018), or Tim Parks, whose campus novel *Europa* abounds with national stereotypes. In contrast to these authors, Berger's account of peasant life clearly seeks to transcend national, racial and ethnic divisions. Many critics have seen the transnationalism of Berger's 'ways of telling' as specifically European; Engelberg (1998), for instance, refers to Berger as a European storyteller ("europäischer Erzähler").

In its representation of space, the trilogy acquires a European dimension whose emphatic nature becomes particularly palpable in "Once in Europa", the eponymous story of Part II. This story is partly set in "the Barracks", the wooden lodgings of the local factory workers who have migrated from different corners of Europe to the French Alps. The sheds they live in are differentiated by letters forming the phrase "IN EUROPA".

> Each shed of the Barracks was designated with a letter. I think that when they were first built the letters of the sheds went regularly from A to H. Then some man lodging there

had an idea to make a joke which consisted of changing the letters. From the time I could first read as a child the eight sheds were marked IN EUROPA. (*OE* 123)

The residents of the Barracks sympathize with the autodiegetic narrator Odile Blanc and demonstrate their solidarity after the father of the child she is expecting has died in the factory's furnaces. Odile describes her own mourning process and the help she receives by switching from first to third person and back to first:

> The nothingness into which he [Stepan] had disappeared filled me. Every hour was the same. Every minute was the same. To piss I went into the plantation just as I did when his boots weren't open mouths screaming. Odile did not scream, she waited. IN EUROPA, shed A. I went on waiting. Every evening some of his comrades came to see me. They came in pairs. They brought me plates of food which I couldn't eat. One brought me a newspaper in a language I couldn't understand. They said I should go home. They said they would come and see me if I went home. One of them gave me a lace shawl in black. I folded it up. Each day which passed brought me more hope. (*OE* 127)

The Barracks provide a utopian space that is explicitly designated as European. With their work-related cross-border movement (as well as their solidarity), the international group of immigrant factory workers are 'doing Europe' at a time largely predating the foundation of the European Union. Similarly, the mythical city of Troy in *Lilac and Flag* acquires a European dimension inasmuch as it invokes Europe's contended Greek origins by alluding to Homer and his *Odyssey*.[13] Moreover, although geographical references to American cities such as "Chicago" (*LF* 106) complicate matters, the names of Troy's different areas – "Budapest" (*LF* 7), "Alexanderplatz" (*LF* 9), "Swansea" (*LF* 24), "Sankt-Pauli" (*LF* 106) – confirm its European dimension. In its depiction of acts of cross-border traveling, working abroad, and (in the case of the unnamed writer) retiring to another European country, Berger's trilogy shows how European mobilities – one of several "everyday ways of being European" in the sense of sociologist Adrian Favell (2005, 1116) – facilitate European integration.[14]

At the same time, however, the utopian space of the Barracks provides only a temporary glimpse of an integrating Europe and, in all three volumes a polar opposition between rural and urban areas prevails – which suggests that Engelberg's (1998) label 'europäischer Erzähler' neglects a division that plays a prominent role in Berger's trilogy, namely that of

---

[13] The *Odyssey* forms, as Astrid Erll's analysis of mnemohistory has recently demonstrated, "a *relational* heritage (not 'of,' but) *in* Europe" (2018, 283; original emphasis).
[14] My forthcoming book on British 'fictions of Europe' – an analysis of how Europe is imagined in contemporary British writing – expands on the idea of 'doing Europe' and on the shift in focus this implies, from 'feeling' to 'being' European.

culture. In analogy to definitions of working-class fiction, one could say that Berger's 'peasant fiction' is both shaped by and presents a 'distinct form of consciousness' (cf. Fordham 2009) that can perhaps best be specified by modifying Engelberg's label with Charity Scribner's notion of an 'Other Europe' (cf. Scribner 2002). In its concern with that 'Other Europe', *Into Their Labours* foregrounds – as Papastergiadis puts it – "the contradiction between the modern rationality that validates progress and achievement in linear metaphors of movement [...] and the multi-dimensional experience of displacement and estrangement inherent in the incessant migrations of modernity" (1993, 12).

6 Conclusion

With its focus on peasants, women, factory workers, and rural migrants into cities, *Into Their Labours* sketches a transnational community that both undermines and rewrites the traditional European master narrative of integration. Emerging in the aftermath of the Second World War, this master narrative is based on an emphatic idea of European civilization, modernity, and peacekeeping at the expense of forgetting Europe's colonial crimes and its long history of gender-, race-, and class-based oppression and (capitalist) exploitation (see Schulze-Engler 2013). *Into Their Labours* tells stories of an 'Other Europe', emerging in the very act of 'doing' and 'living' Europe, and thus diversifies received monolithic ideas of the European myth as idea or belief. This makes it possible to connect Berger's expatriate account of what we might call 'peripheral modernities' to other British 'fictions of Europe' (e.g. by Bernardine Evaristo and Jamal Mahjoub) that are similarly transnational in scope, but more overtly concerned with issues of ethnicity and/or race.

Finally, the European outlook of 'fictions of Europe', both by Berger and other British writers, demonstrates how a transnational idea of Europe has begun to take shape in contemporary British writing. And this idea plays an important role in the formation of 'post-insular identities' – i.e. identities abandoning the rhetoric of nationalist exceptionalism that informs traditional insular constructions of Englishness vis-à-vis Europe and that only recently culminated in the 'Brexit' vote in favor of the UK leaving the European Union. Although not all British writing about Europe is by any means 'transnational' – in many 'fictions of Europe', transnational associations turn out to be only temporary and characters' ways of 'doing Europe' often fall far short of 'feeling European' – and even though narrators may relapse into using national stereotypes, together these texts still point to the increasing significance of networks and connections on a European scale beyond borders and across nations (see Hauthal forthcoming). In the British context, they attest to fiction's capacity for (alternative) worldmaking. It remains to be seen whether British novelists and dramatists will still imaginatively venture across the Channel in a post-Brexit future.

References

Aleksandrowicz-Wojtyna, Marta. "Spatiotemporal Gymnastics in John Berger's *Into Their Labours*." *On John Berger: Telling Stories*. Eds. Ralf Hertel and David Malcolm. Leiden: Brill Rodopi, 2016. 95–109.
Arata, Stephen. *Fictions of Loss in the Victorian Fin de Siècle*. Cambridge: Cambridge University Press, 1996.
Babka, Anna, Marlen Bidwell-Steiner, and Wolfgang Müller-Funk (eds.). *Narrative im Bruch*. Wien: Vienna University Press, 2016.
Bekhta, Natalya. "We-Narratives: The Distinctiveness of Collective Narration." *Narrative* 25.2 (2017): 164–181.
Berger, John. *Pig Earth. Into Their Labours, Part 1*. New York: Vintage, 1992 [1979].
Berger, John. *Once in Europa. Into Their Labours, Part 2*. London: Bloomsbury, 2000 [1983].
Berger, John. *Lilac and Flag: An Old Wives' Tale of a City. Into Their Labours, Part 3*. London: Bloomsbury, 1999 [1990].
Bingel, Hanna. *Fictions of Spirituality: Die narrative Verhandlung von Religiosität und spiritueller Sinnsuche in ausgewählten amerikanischen Gegenwartsromanen*. Trier: WVT, 2013.
Bowen, John. "Economy, Seduction, Transumption: 'Boris' and *G*." *On John Berger: Telling Stories*. Eds. Ralf Hertel and David Malcolm. Leiden: Brill Rodopi, 2016. 63–76.
D'hoker, Elke, and Bart Van den Bossche. "Cycles, Receuils, Macrotexts: The Short Story Collection in a Comparative Perspective". *Cycles, Receuils, Macrotexts*, special issue of *Interférences littéraires/Literaire interferenties* 12 (2014): 7–17.
Dyer, Geoff. *Ways of Telling. The Work of John Berger*. London: Pluto Press, 1986.
Engelberg, Achim. *Über Dörfer und Städte: Der europäische Erzähler John Berger*. Berlin: VanBremen VerlagsBuchhandlung, 1998.
Erll, Astrid. "Fictions of Generational Memory: Caryl Phillips' *In the Falling Snow*." *Memory Unbound. Tracing the Dynamics of Memory Studies*. Eds. Lucy Bond, Stef Craps, and Pieter Vermeulen. New York: Berghahn, 2017. 109–130.
Erll, Astrid. "Homer: A Relational Mnemohistory." *Memory Studies* 11.3 (2018): 274–286.
Favell, Adrian. "Europe's Identity Problem." *West European Politics* 28.5 (2005): 1109–1116.
Fenwick, Gillian. *Understanding Tim Parks*. Columbia: University of South Carolina Press, 2003.
Fordham, John. "Working-Class Fiction Across the Century." *The Cambridge Companion to the Twentieth-Century English Novel*. Ed. Robert L. Caserio. Cambridge: Cambridge University Press, 2009. 131–145.
Freissmann, Stefan. *Fictions of Cognition: Representing (Un)Consciousness and Cognitive Science in Contemporary English and American Fiction*. Trier: WVT, 2011.

Freitag, Britta. *Theorie, Aufgabentypologie und Unterrichtspraxis inter- und transkultureller Literaturdidaktik: British Fictions of Migration im Fremdsprachenunterricht*. Trier: WVT, 2010.
Guignery, Vanessa, and Ryan Roberts (eds.). *Conversations with Julian Barnes*. Jackson: University Press of Mississippi, 2009.
Handke, Peter. *Wir-Erzähler und Ich-Erzähler*. www.zeit.de/1991/47/wir-erzaehler-und-ich-erzaehler. Die Zeit, 15 November 1991 (7 August 2018).
Hauthal, Janine. "Unity in Diversity? Imagining Europe in Julian Barnes' *Cross Channel*." *Constructing Coherence in the British Short Story Cycle*. Eds. Florian Kläger and Patrick Alasdair Gill. New York: Routledge, 2018. 159–180.
Hauthal, Janine. *Britain in Europe: The Emergence of Post-Insular Identities and Transcultural Discourses in Contemporary British Literature* (forthcoming).
Herman, Luc, and Bart Vervaeck. *Handbook of Narrative Analysis*. Lincoln: University of Nebraska Press, 2005.
Hertel, Ralf. "The Body of the Text: *To the Wedding*, *From A to X*, and the Corporeality of John Berger's Later Fiction." *On John Berger: Telling Stories*. Eds. Ralf Hertel and David Malcolm. Leiden: Brill Rodopi, 2016. 143–161.
Hertel, Ralf, and David Malcolm (eds.). *On John Berger: Telling Stories*. Leiden: Brill Rodopi, 2016.
Hitchcock, Peter. "They Must Be Represented? Problems in Theories of Working-Class Representation." *PMLA* 115.1 (2000): 20–32.
Kamm, Jürgen, and Gerold Sedlmayr (eds.). *Insular Mentalities: Mental Maps of Britain*. Passau: Stutz, 2007.
Korthals Altes, Liesbeth, and Manet van Montfrans (eds.). *The New Georgics: Rural and Regional Motifs in the Contemporary European Novel*. Amsterdam: Rodopi, 2002.
Lange, Nina. *Fictions of Time: Zeitvorstellungen, Zeiterfahrungen und Zeitreflexionen in englischen und amerikanischen Romanen der Gegenwart*. Trier: WVT, 2017.
Lanser, Susan Sniader. *Fictions of Authority: Women Writers and Narrative Voice*. Ithaca: Cornell University Press, 1992.
Levy, Eric P. "'Seeing That Eye': Tragedy and the Vision of Vision in John Berger's *Pig Earth*." *Critique* 45 (2004): 311–318.
Lippincott, Robin. "One Big Canvas: The Work of John Berger." *Literary Review* 35 (1991): 134–142.
Lundén, Rolf. "Centrifugal and Centripetal Narrative Strategies in the Short Story Composite and the Episode Film." *Cycles, Recueils, Macrotexts*, special issue of *Interférences littéraires. Literaire interferenties* 12 (2014): 47–60.
Lutostański, Bartosz. "Refuting a Sentence, or: How John Berger Refutes Himself." *On John Berger: Telling Stories*. Eds. Ralf Hertel and David Malcolm. Leiden: Brill Rodopi, 2016. 111–127.
Merrifield, Andy. *John Berger*. London: Reaktion, 2012.
Müller-Funk, Wolfgang. *Die Kultur und ihre Narrative: Eine Einführung*. 2002. Wien: Springer, 2008.
Nederveen Pieterse, Jan. "Fictions of Europe." *Race & Class* 32.3 (1991): 3–10.
Neumann, Birgit. *Erinnerung – Identität – Narration: Gattungstypologie und Funktionen kanadischer Fictions of Memory*. Berlin: de Gruyter, 2005.
Neumann, Birgit, and Ansgar Nünning. *An Introduction to the Study of Narrative Fiction*. Stuttgart: Klett, 2011 [2008].

Nünning, Ansgar. *Von historischer Fiktion zu historiographischer Metafiktion. Band II: Erscheinungsformen und Entwicklungstendenzen des historischen Romans in England seit 1950*. Trier: WVT, 1995.
Nünning, Ansgar (ed.). *Fictions of Memory*. Special issue of *Journal for the Study of British Cultures* 10.1 (2003).
Nünning, Ansgar. "Steps Towards a Metaphorology (and Narratology) of Crises: On the Functions of Metaphors as Figurative Knowledge and Mininarrations." *Metaphors Shaping Culture and Theory*. Eds. Herbert Grabes, Ansgar Nünning and Sibylle Baumbach. Tübingen: Narr, 2009a. 229–262.
Nünning, Ansgar. "Surveying Contextualist and Cultural Narratologies: Towards an Outline of Approaches, Concepts and Potentials." *Narratology in the Age of Cross-Disciplinary Narrative Research*. Eds. Sandra Heinen and Roy Sommer. Berlin: de Gruyter, 2009b. 48–70.
Nünning, Ansgar. "Kulturen als Erinnerungs- und Erzählgemeinschaften: Grundzüge und Perspektiven einer kulturgeschichtlichen Erzählforschung." *Rahmenwechsel Kulturwissenschaften*. Eds. Peter Hanenberg, Isabel Gil, Filomena Viana Guarda, and Fernando Clara. Würzburg: Königshausen & Neumann, 2010. 237–256.
Nünning, Ansgar. "Narrativist Approaches and Narratological Concepts for the Study of Culture." *Travelling Concepts for the Study of Culture*. Eds. Birgit Neumann and Ansgar Nünning. Berlin: de Gruyter, 2012a. 145–184.
Nünning, Ansgar. "Making Crises and Catastrophes – How Metaphors and Narratives Shape Their Cultural Life." *The Cultural Life of Catastrophes and Crises*. Eds. Carsten Meiner and Kristin Veel. Berlin: de Gruyter, 2012b. 59–88.
Nünning, Ansgar. "Wie Erzählungen Kulturen erzeugen: Prämissen, Konzepte und Perspektiven für eine kulturwissenschaftliche Narratologie." *Kultur – Wissen – Narration: Perspektiven transdisziplinärer Erzählforschung für die Kulturwissenschaften*. Ed. Alexandra Strohmaier. Bielefeld: transcript, 2013. 15–53.
Nünning, Ansgar, and Kai Marcel Sicks. "Turning Points as Metaphors and Mininarrations: Analysing Concepts of Change in Literature and Other Media." *Turning Points: Concepts and Narratives of Change in Literature and Other Media*. Eds. Ansgar Nünning and Kai Marcel Sicks. Berlin: de Gruyter, 2012. 1–28.
Nünning, Vera and Ansgar. "Fictions of Empire and the Making of Imperialist Mentalities: Colonial Discourse and Post-Colonial Theory as a Paradigm for Intercultural Studies." *Intercultural Studies: Fictions of Empire*. Eds. Vera and Ansgar Nünning. Special issue of *Anglistik und Englischunterricht* 58. Heidelberg: Winter, 1996. 7–31.
Nünning, Vera and Ansgar. "Multiperspektivität aus narratologischer Sicht: Erzähltheoretische Grundlagen und Kategorien zur Analyse der Perspektivenstruktur narrativer Texte." *Multiperspektivisches Erzählen: Zur Theorie und Geschichte der Perspektivenstruktur im englischen Roman des 18. bis 20. Jahrhunderts*. Eds. Vera and Ansgar Nünning. Trier: WVT, 2000. 39–77.
Nünning, Vera and Ansgar. "Conceptualizing 'Broken Narratives' from a Narratological Perspective: Domains, Concepts, Features, Functions, and Suggestions for Research." *Narrative im Bruch*. Eds. Anna Babka, Marlen Bidwell-Steiner, and Wolfgang Müller-Funk. Wien: Vienna University Press, 2016. 37–86.
Papastergiadis, Nikos. *Modernity as Exile: The Stranger in John Berger's Writing*. Manchester: Manchester University Press, 1993.

Parks, Tim. *Novels*. https://timparks.com/tim-parkss-eighteen-novels. Webpage Tim Parks (7 August 2018).
Schmitt-Kilb, Christian. "A Huge Lacuna vis-à-vis the Peasants: Red and Green in John Berger's Trilogy *Into Their Labours*." *Ecology and the Literature of the British Left: The Red and the Green*. Eds. John Rignall and H. Gustav Klaus. Farnham: Ashgate, 2012. 207–220.
Schulze-Engler, Frank. "Irritating Europe." *The Oxford Handbook of Postcolonial Studies*. Ed. Graham Huggan. Oxford: Oxford University Press, 2013. 669–691.
Scribner, Charity. "John Berger, Leslie Kaplan, and the Western Fixation on the 'Other Europe'." *Inszenierungen des kollektiven Gedächtnisses: Eigenbilder, Fremdbilder*. Eds. Moritz Csáky and Klaus Zeyringer. Innsbruck: StudienVerlag, 2002. 236–246.
Sommer, Roy. *Fictions of Migration: Ein Betrag zur Theorie und Gattungstypologie des zeitgenössischen interkulturellen Romans in Grossbritannien*. Trier: WVT, 2001.
Spiering, Menno. *A Cultural History of British Euroscepticism*. London: Palgrave Macmillan, 2015.
Szuba, Monika. "John Berger's Endless Text: Aesthetics of the Fragment, the Nouveau Roman, and Storytelling." *On John Berger: Telling Stories*. Eds. Ralf Hertel and David Malcolm. Leiden: Brill Rodopi, 2016. 129–142.
Turney, Richard. "'Naturally, I have changed most of the names': The Johns of *A Painter of Our Time*." *On John Berger: Telling Stories*. Eds. Ralf Hertel and David Malcolm. Leiden: Brill Rodopi, 2016. 31–48.
Welz, Stefan. *Ways of Seeing – Limits of Telling: Sehen und Erzählen in den Romanen John Bergers*. Eggingen: Edition Isele, 1996.
White, Jerry. *Revisioning Europe: The Films of John Berger and Alain Tanner*. Calgary: University of Calgary Press, 2011.
Wojtyna, Milosz. "Prominent Absences: John Berger's Benjaminian Storytelling." *On John Berger: Telling Stories*. Eds. Ralf Hertel and David Malcolm. Leiden: Brill Rodopi, 2016. 77–93.

Roy Sommer
Brexit as Cultural Performance: Towards a Narratology of Social Drama

Abstract: Brexit is not only the most important, but also the most confusing challenge to European integration. While political scientists, historians, and economists are struggling to come to terms with current events, literary and cultural theory has remained so far conspicuously silent, although one might argue that Brexit is first and foremost a cultural phenomenon, a contest of stories and worldviews that transcends rational argument. Redefining Victor Turner's anthropological notion of social drama as narratives in conflict and engaging with Ansgar Nünning's work on events, turning points and narratives of crises, this essay shows how retrospective and prospective worldmaking interact and how leading playwrights explore anger, frustration, and envy in an attempt to understand, and maybe heal, the current divisions in British society. It makes the case for a narratological approach to current events, opening up the horizons of cultural narratology both as a critique of politics and as a dialogue with political science.

1 Introduction

Brexit has been called a tragedy, a farce and, most recently, a democratic travesty. Resignations and promotions (exit, enter, exit, enter...), intrigue and betrayal, secrets and lies, promises and threats, twists and turns, plans and manifestos, bargaining and gambling, cunning and scheming, ancient rituals and new proceedings, winners and losers (both at the mercy of the wheel of Fortune), two brothers in opposite camps (not Edgar and Edmund, but Boris and Jo), young vs. old, the city and the country, two houses (London and Brussels), turning points and points of no return: Shakespeare would have loved it.

Most people, regardless of their own political stance, hate it. Anyone who has even the slightest sense of responsibility will be worried about endless gridlock, a waste of time and energy needed to fight more important battles. No one can seriously welcome political turmoil, the ending of so many Renaissance tragedies. We're not watching a theater play, after all, but have become actors

---
Note: I would like to thank Carolin Gebauer for her insightful comments on an earlier draft of this essay.

https://doi.org/10.1515/9783110654370-016

or extras ourselves in what the anthropologist Victor Turner (1974) has called 'social drama'. A deep crisis shakes the foundation of British society, frustrates London, further alienates Northern Ireland and Scotland, and undermines the very values on which community depends: truth and trust. These are deeper concerns than the economic scenarios of a good deal, a bad deal, or no deal. When social cohesion is at risk, everything is at stake, as Zadie Smith (2018) reminds us. Recalling her feelings on the day after the referendum, she holds that Brexit is not just about Britain's relationship with the European Union, but also *not* about England's union with Northern Ireland and Scotland:

> That two supposedly well-educated men [Nigel Farage and Boris Johnson], who have presumably read their British history, could with such utter recklessness throw into hazard a hard-won union of three hundred years' standing – in order to satisfy their own professional ambitions – appeared that morning a larger crime, to me, than the severing of the decades-long European pact that actually prompted it all. (Smith 2018, 23)

Utter recklessness, ambitions and pacts – reading Brexit as social drama seems not too far-fetched, given that its dramaturgy freely borrows from the staples of Shakespearean tragedy. How cultures stage and perform their social dramas is a key concern of cultural narratology, a confluence of structuralist, cognitivist, and culturalist approaches to worldmaking and world disruption.

More specifically, my analyses of current events will draw on, and make a contribution to, the narratology of drama and the narratology of crises proposed by Ansgar Nünning. Nünning's pioneering work on events, metaphors of crisis, and turning points has encouraged and enabled me to read the social drama of Brexit as a multi-actor cultural performance, a contest of stories and worldviews over ethical and moral issues that reflects a society's search for core values and a new collective imaginary. Political crisis and social drama are two sides of the same coin, a fight over the alleged will of the people, a cultural construct claimed by all parties involved. Proceeding from this assumption, I will show how narrative worldmaking works both in retrospect, by appropriating and reinterpreting past events for specific purposes, and in a prospective manner in an attempt to shape the future.

If crises defy rationalization (the "will of the people", an ideological construct that gives unity to a bottomless pit of irreconcilable opinions, emotions and beliefs inaccessible to reason), they call for dramatization, both metaphorically and as a cultural practice. Staging plays is a tried and tested method of coming to terms with social drama that worked well for Shakespeare and can work for us too: the aesthetics of performance, the creative license enjoyed by playwrights and the potential of dramatic narratives to access hidden emotions like anger, envy or shame can initiate new debates and help to reestablish common ground. By commissioning nine leading British playwrights to produce a series of short dramatic monologues that represent and juxtapose highly idiosyncratic views on Brexit, *The Guardian* has made an important contribution to the cultural work that may eventually help to overcome the current gridlock. Possibly, hopefully, eventually: Britain's social drama, if we follow Turner, is only in its second act.

2 Re-reading Victor Turner: The four acts of social drama

In the essay "Social dramas and ritual metaphors," the opening chapter of *Drama, Fields, and Metaphors: Symbolic Action in Human Society* (1974), Victor Turner charts his own intellectual journey and development as a cultural anthropologist, creating a network of "root metaphors" or "conceptual archetypes" that form the foundations of an anthropological theory of society.[1] Having acknowledged his debt to thinkers like Karl Marx, Emile Durkheim, and Henri Bergson, Turner holds that theories "become relevant only if and when they illuminate social reality" (1974, 23), and that any theory of society and community should beware static concepts and consider instead "the dynamic quality of social relations," as well as "the actual flux and changefulness of the human social scene" (1974, 24). The foundational idea, present throughout his work, is "that human social life is the producer and product of time, which becomes its measure" (Turner 1974, 23–24).

Dynamics and flux, changefulness and time, human life and scene – these key features of social life and lived experience are core concepts of what Turner calls "the processual view of society" (1974, 23), an approach that refrains from juxtaposing social statics and social dynamics but always insists on "the dynamic quality of social relations" (1974, 24). Turner further holds that in what he calls "the process of social time" a form can be observed that is "essentially *dramatic*," a "product of *culture* and not of nature" (1974, 32, original emphases). This view, it should be pointed out, is fully compatible with more recent

---

[1] Turner (1974, 26) adopts the term "conceptual archetype" from Max Black: "Black prefers the term 'conceptual archetype' to 'root metaphor', and defines it as a 'systematic repertoire of ideas by means of which a given thinker describes, by analogical extension, some domain to which those ideas do not immediately and literally apply."

constructivist and semiotic definitions of culture. From an observer's retrospective vantage point, sequences of events – Turner also uses the terms "processual units" (1974, 34) or "phases in social processes" (1974, 37) – can be either "social enterprises" or "social dramas" (Turner 1974, 35).

Social enterprises include, but are not restricted to, economic activities such as improvements to shared infrastructure (see Turner 1974, 34), as well as rituals that reconcile conflicting views and foster political integration (see Turner 1974, 41)[2]; both kinds of social enterprise serve to bring about and uphold social cohesion (see Turner 1974, 46).[3] While social enterprises are thus fundamentally harmonic, "'conflict' is the other side of the coin of 'cohesion'" (Turner 1974, 46). Social dramas – i.e. "units of aharmonic or disharmonic process, arising in conflict situations" (Turner 1974, 37) – act out cultural conflicts, bringing "fundamental aspects of society, normally overlayed by the customs and habits of daily intercourse, into frightening prominence" (Turner 1974, 35).

What makes drama as a 'traveling' concept (Bal 2002) so attractive for an anthropological conception of society? On the one hand, the temporal structure of drama, its "diachronic profile" (Turner 1974, 37), emphasizes once again the processual nature of human social behavior. On the other hand, drama serves as a root metaphor, because it best expresses the feeling that something significant or even vital is at stake: "People have to take sides in terms of deeply entrenched moral imperatives and constraints, often against their own personal preferences. Choice is overborne by duty" (Turner 1974, 35).

Turner's description uncannily anticipates the Brexit conundrum forty-two years prior to the referendum: A prime minister who was against Brexit during the referendum campaign has taken on the task of implementing what she claims is the 'will' of the British people – an empty phrase given the undecidedness of the electorate and the wide range of conflicting and irreconcilable views on the issues involved.[4] Zadie Smith (2018, 30) has recently emphasized that

---

[2] For a survey of current definitions of ritual, see Vera Nünning and Jan Rupp's (2013) survey article. On the confluences in narrative research and ritual studies see Sommer (2013, 79–87).

[3] As I have shown elsewhere (see Sommer 2017), social cohesion is grounded in cultural models. By this I mean commonly held assumptions, beliefs and worldviews that may be contested, but are too deeply anchored in the cultural imaginary to be overthrown by such criticism, and consistently inform the shared narratives from which "narrative communities" (Müller-Funk 2008) emerge. How social cohesion and collective bonding can be studied from the joint perspective of narrative research and ritual studies remains a fascinating question (see Nünning and Rupp 2013).

[4] Theresa May has repeatedly defended her politics with reference to the 'will' of the people. Most recently, she attacked the Shadow Chancellor, John McDonald, who announced that Labour would back a second referendum if her Brexit deal was defeated in the House of

there is, however, compelling evidence to question the idea that a referendum based on misinformation and widespread ignorance is the pinnacle of democracy: "As painful as it is to write it, when Google records large numbers of Britons googling 'What is the EU?' in the hours after the vote, it becomes very difficult to deny that a significant proportion of our people were shamefully negligent in their democratic duty on 23 June 2016."

In addition to the emphasis on the temporal nature and cultural significance of social conflict, the metaphor of drama puts emphasis on individual and collective agency:

> The organizational foci of temporal structures are 'goals', the objects of action or effort, not 'nodes', mere points of diagrammatic intersection or lines of rest. Temporal structure, until at rest and therefore atemporal, is always tentative; there are always alternative goals and alternative means of attaining them. (Turner 1974, 37)

Thus, psychological factors, e.g. "volition, motivation, span of attention, level of aspiration" (37), become the focus of analysis. Finally, the structure of drama with its generic subdivision of acts allows Turner to distinguish four main phases that structure the social drama internally: breach, crisis, redressive action, and reintegration. As his definitions are important for my following observations, I will quote them at length.

1. *Breach* of regular, norm-governed social relations occurs between persons or groups within the same system of social relations, be it a village, chiefdom, office, factory, political party or ward, church, university department, or any other perduring system or set or field of social interaction. Such a breach is signalized by the public, overt breach or deliberate nonfulfillment of some crucial norm regulating the intercourse of the parties. To flout such a norm is one obvious symbol of dissidence. [...] A dramatic breach may be made by an individual, certainly, but he always acts, or believes he acts, on behalf of other parties, whether they are aware of it or not. He sees himself as a representative, not as a lone hand.

2. Following breach of regular, norm-governed social relations, a phase of mounting *crisis* supervenes, during which, unless the breach can be sealed off quickly within a limited area of social interaction, there is a tendency for the breach to widen and extend until it becomes coextensive with some

---

Commons: "His comments about the second referendum today show that what the Labour Party want to do is frustrate Brexit. They want to overturn the will of the British people. Parliament overwhelmingly gave the British people a vote. They voted to Leave. I think it's a matter of trust in politicians that they actually deliver on Brexit for the British people." See Sparrow (2018).

dominant cleavage in the widest set of relevant social relations to which the conflicting or antagonistic parties belong. [...] This second stage, crisis, is always one of those turning points or moments of danger and suspense, when a true state of affairs is revealed, when it is least easy to don masks or pretend that there is nothing rotten in the village. [...]
3. This brings us to the third phase, *redressive action*. In order to limit the spread of crisis, certain adjustive und redressive 'mechanisms', [...] informal or formal, institutionalized or ad-hoc, are swiftly brought into operation by leading or structurally representative members of the disturbed social system. [...] When one is studying social change, at whatever social level, I would give one piece of advice: study carefully what happens in phase three, the would-be redressive phase of social dramas, and ask whether the redressive machinery is capable of handling crises so as to restore, more or less, the status quo ante, or at least to restore peace among the contending groups. Then ask, if so, how precisely? And if not, why not? It is in the redressive phase that both pragmatic techniques and symbolic action reach their fullest expression. [...]
4. The final phase I distinguished consists either of the *reintegration* of the disturbed social group or of the social recognition and legitimization of irreparable schisms between the contesting parties [...].

(Turner 1974, 38–41; original emphases)

"Study carefully what happens in phase three": that's where Brexit is currently heading,[5] caught between the pragmatic pressures of a tight schedule, as the roadmap agreed between London and Brussels demands a final decision on the when and how, and the growing dissent among members of parliament after the resignation of several members of the cabinet and growing dissatisfaction with the prime minister's Brexit deal. But the "true state of affairs" (see phase 2) has, at the time of writing, not yet been revealed: Will a majority eventually approve the terms and conditions that are still a well-kept secret? Or will May lose the vote and with it her job? What will happen if she sees it through? Will May's main antagonist, Boris Johnson, consent to support the decision of a majority that will almost certainly come with a tight margin?

---

[5] The last draft of this essay was finalized on 8 December 2018, three days before (what was to be) the crucial vote in the House of Commons on Theresa May's agreement with the European Union.

Also, as Turner points out, "though choices of means and ends and social affiliation are made, stress is dominantly laid upon loyalty and obligation, as much as interest, and the course of events may then have a tragic quality" (1974, 35). Tragedy, however, rarely ends in triumph, at least not for the protagonists and antagonists, but in silence and conquest, chaos and death, if we think of *Hamlet* and *King Lear*. Who will be lucky Fortinbras, taking over after the dust has settled? Will the Union of England and Scotland survive the unavoidable impact of harsh realities? Given the small margin of the Leave victory in the referendum and the wide range of motivations behind it, a miraculous restoration of social cohesion, switching back from drama to ritual, appears the least likely outcome. Macbeth saw it coming: "blood will have blood" (III.iv.121). Luckily, social drama is only an analogy.

Turner also warns us to beware the implications of conceptualizing the social world as a world in flux or a world in becoming: "Becoming suggests genetic continuity, telic growth, cumulative development, progress, etc. But many social events do not have this 'directional' character" (1974, 30). The challenge for a doubly metaphorical view of "liquid modernity" (Bauman 2000) as social drama, then, lies in avoiding both retrospective sense-making and a view of society that is colored, implicitly or explicitly, by the observer's perspective. Both may, to a certain degree, be unavoidable, but need to be reflected critically. With the benefit of hindsight, contingency is easily dissolved in a sequence of events that appears natural or even logical, as we know that other, alternative options were not realized; and it is always easy for the observer to view circumstances and judge decisions taken by others in a more detached, abstract manner than for participants on stage, as it were, acting in a play whose script has not yet been finalized.

Such problems are a key concern in ethnographic methodologies that distinguish between the "emic" perspective of insiders to the group whose behavior is the object of fieldwork, and the "etic" perspective of the outside observer (see V. Nünning and Rupp 2013, 3–4). Like the ethnographer or participating observer, the narratologist has to negotiate both roles. Ours is the double perspective, emic *and* etic, of the 'affected' observer who finds it difficult to understand what all the fuss (and fuzz) is about – on this side of the Channel, relentless Euroskepticism is the territory of political extremism – yet knows that if Britain suffers, we will suffer too.

Coming to terms with current events is a collective task for the humanities and the social sciences, a serious challenge to our premises, research paradigms, and methodologies. When the Leave campaign triumphed in Britain, commentators were surprised; when Donald Trump came to power, few had predicted his victory. Now, after a hectic period of collective rationalization, we not only know that we were wrong, we have come up with all sorts of convincing explanations of our failure to anticipate what we now see – or think we see – was inevitable. We're beginning to believe we *know* why, when in truth we have only become used to the thought and have accepted our fate. Our faith in scholarship and science, briefly shattered, has been restored. This is natural and logical (what else should we do?), but the true challenge for scholars of Brexit – and for a narratology of social drama – is to remember and theorize Turner's dictum, revitalized by the lessons learnt in 2016, that if past events appear to have a directional character, it's because we tend to rationalize history within a neat paradigm of causality. With some modifications (see below), social drama is a far more helpful concept for narrative research and the study of culture, because it allows us to theorize the anti-causality, irrationality and contingency of narrative in performance. Social drama is not a causal but a nodal paradigm; it is not concerned with retrospective, but with prospective worldmaking, with possibilities and eventualities.

3 Stories in conflict: The narrativity of social drama

Before we discuss the narrativity of social drama in detail, paving the way for a narratological reading of Brexit stories, some clarifications are needed. Why should literary scholars take the cumbersome detour through anthropology to recover a borrowed term, a concept that is part of our own disciplinary heritage? The advantage of a theoretical re-import of drama is that it loses some of the conceptual baggage acquired over more than twenty-three centuries of theorizing. This concerns two related issues, generic typologies separating the study of narrative from the study of drama, and the fiction/non-fiction divide. Let's begin with genre.

Ever since Aristotle introduced the distinction between tragedy and epic writing in his *Poetics* (ca. 335 B.C.), a short text that still offers valuable thoughts and observations on the nature of writing and on dramaturgy, genre theory has categorically separated the study of drama from the study of narrative. Despite many convergences, scholars have tended to study the dramatic and epic modes (theater play vs. novel) in isolation (see Nünning and Sommer 2002, 105–109). While drama theory has focused on the dramaturgical and performative aspects of storytelling, narrative theory or narratology has put more emphasis on the ways narrative content is mediated rhetorically in writing.

This generic bias has been addressed in what Ansgar Nünning and I, following Manfred Jahn (2001), have termed the 'narratology of drama' (see

Nünning and Sommer 2002, 2006, 2008 and 2011; Sommer 2008 [2005]).[6] However, although the generic boundary between drama and narrative may have been successfully redrawn, the tradition of restricting literary drama theory to theatrical performances has been steadfastly upheld. While narrative research has long developed into a truly cross-disciplinary field, investigating the forms, functions and uses of narrative fiction and everyday storytelling alike, the occasional foray into non-literary forms of drama have remained exceptions to the rule. Literary and cultural theory is thus obliged to cultural anthropology for returning the borrowed term in such an enriched form, with considerable value added in its suggestion of a new research paradigm. To continue the economic metaphor, Turner's work, vastly increasing the usefulness and reach of drama as a conceptual tool, without changing it beyond recognition, is the intellectual equivalent of a high interest rate.

There are, however, three theoretical shortcomings that a narratology of social drama must address – thereby itself, of course, undergoing development. First, Turner's startlingly far-sighted four-phase model neglects the framing of social conflict. Every drama needs an exposition or backstory, and likewise every social breach has its own history of misinterpreted warning signs and failed diplomacy. The roots of Euroskepticism can be traced back on one side of the Channel to de Gaulle's anti-British policy in the aftermath of World War II, on the other side to Daniel Defoe's poem "A True-Born Englishman" (1701), a biting satire on Anglocentric xenophobia in the Restoration period two-and-a-half centuries earlier. Sadly, such an endeavor is beyond the scope of this essay. Secondly, Turner's model rejects on principle the concept of nodality, which for him is still strongly tinged by contemporary notions of society as a static system. I will return to this issue below. Thirdly, Turner fails to account for multi-actor conflicts and chaotic disruptions of the status quo.

Let's begin with this third criticism. Turner's notions of breach and crisis focus on 'orderly' conflict, for instance when he discusses possible consequences of a breach: "If it is a social drama involving two nations in one geographical region, escalation could imply a stepwise movement toward antagonism across the dominant global cleavage between communist and capitalist camps" (Turner 1974, 38). His binary view of conflict, clearly influenced by Cold War realities, also informs his view of the fourth phase, redressive action, which leads to temporary climax, solution, or outcome: "Oppositions may be found to

---

[6] More recently, Muny (2008) has explored narrative perspective in drama; Weber's (2017) study explores epic tendencies in drama; and Jan Horstmann (2018) has proposed a "narratology of the theater"; Christiane Schwanecke's book, to date the most comprehensive contribution to the field in English, is forthcoming (2019).

have become alliances, and vice versa. Asymmetric relations may have become egalitarian ones. High status will have become low status and vice versa" (Turner 1974, 42).

This is more reminiscent of the ending of a Shakespearean tragedy than the proxy wars, asymmetrical conflicts, insurgencies and counter-insurgencies that have haunted the Middle East since the millennium; or – less horribly but equally frustrating – tribalism and partisan policies under Trump and the parliamentary deadlock in a kingdom that is currently united only in name. Social drama in our time is characterized by fuzziness and messiness, often seemingly more farcical than tragic, until violence erupts and reminds us that Britain's "post-democracy" (Crouch 2004) may well be on the brink of system failure.

Liquid modernity requires conceptual tools that allow us to chart, interpret and maybe even predict the constant flow of ideas, worldviews, and beliefs that are staged in social drama. Coming to terms with the narrative dynamics of a world in flux is not an easy task. Such fluid world dynamics are the domain of a yet to be developed narratology of social drama that views drama as narratives in conflict. Investigating the dramatic uses of narrative in culture thus means analyzing a market of ideas and stories competing for what one might call the sovereignty of interpretation over highly sensitive issues. This competition is never fair, once a breach has occurred: lies compete with truths, conspiracy theories clash with narratives of rationality, narrative promises seek to distort realities beyond recognition.

Beneath the surface of actions a storytelling machine is at work: stories told to oneself, to one's affiliates, to one's colleagues in parliament (the term originates in the French verb *parler*, and signifies speech and talk), stories told to the press (which will create their own stories from original soundbites), stories told to potential voters during election campaigns, and stories told in biographies and autobiographies once the dust has settled.[7] When individuals appear as narrators of their own stories, they adopt a specific teller persona. Like social roles in interaction, this persona is tailored to suit the audience and is never fully and truly identical with the teller's inner self. His or her stories may even be designed to conceal the true motivations behind his or her actions, an effect that narratologists of drama call unreliable narration (see Nünning and Schwanecke 2015).

To add to the confusion, it is obvious that everyone has their own stories, and in truly controversial matters that form the core of social drama we need to multiply this chain of stories not only by the number of seats in Parliament but

---

[7] There is also a growing body of Brexit fiction (see Eaglestone 2018).

really by the number of people that hold an opinion on the issues involved and may tell a story of their own. A narratology of social drama can account for such story-driven multi-actor dynamics in a world designed by narratives in conflict by theorizing the nature, forms, and uses of stories and storytelling. In a series of essays that explore the wide-ranging implications of narrative's "performative power" (Nünning 2010, 191), Nünning has paved the way for such a theory, reflecting systematically on metaphors of crisis (Nünning 2009), as well as on the nature of events (Nünning 2010) and their turning-points (Nünning 2012).

Stories are, first and foremost, configurations and sequences of events. As elementary units of stories, events function as the "building blocks of narrative worldmaking" (Nünning 2010, 191). Nünning reminds us that only through storytelling is a mere happening transformed into an event, i.e. into a happening to which we ascribe more relevance than to other happenings: "Lots of things happen every day but only very few of them become events, let alone what posterity will regard as 'great historical events'" (2010, 193). As storytellers, we are all experts in this process: we know intuitively how through processes of selection, abstraction, prioritization, and weighting we can and do sieve through "the totality of all situations, occurrences, and actions" (Nünning 2010, 201) to filter out those happenings we deem worth telling. Once that has been decided, we apply strategies of emplotment to arrange events into sequences, giving priority to some happenings over others and assigning meaning and significance to what we deem most important. In the process we tend to resort to "cultural hierarchies of norms and values" (Nünning 2010, 198), usually subconsciously, i.e. we are not fully aware of the criteria, at least partly supplied by culture-specific models, beliefs and worldviews, that color the ways in which we turn lived experience into storied experience. These stories need not be articulated, they can also be virtual narratives that structure the way we think about ourselves and others, about how we remember the past, how we relate to the world. But they exist in our minds, and we can either share them or not (which is one of the reasons why pollsters were surprised by the outcome of the referendum).

Not all events are equal, of course; in the terminology of narrative theory they possess varying degrees of "eventfulness" (Hühn 2014). Among the most significant events are turning points, i.e. "occurrences which are accredited with a high degree of relevance, importance and the potential to change the plot" (Nünning 2012, 40), that are "not understood as something given or natural, but rather as something that is made or constructed by an observer or storyteller" (Nünning 2012, 39). One might even think of them as "non-events", for "the very moment that marks the turning point does not constitute a particularly eventful incident in itself, but it has usually been preceded by one or several important events" (Nünning 2012, 44). While Nünning's analysis is based on an interpretation of Kazuo Ishiguro's novel *The Remains of the Day* (1989), turning points in real life share a similar feature set: significance, breach of canonicity (i.e., the deviation from what is expected and considered to be the norm), effect (far-reaching implications and consequences for the person, institution, or phenomenon concerned), irrevocability, and unrepeatability (Nünning 2012, 42).

This does not mean, however, that we experience turning points in fiction exactly as in life. Novels and dramatic genres such as the memory play or the dramatic monologue often play with the specific limitations of retrospective narration in order to create a specific effect, a discrepancy between the narrator's and the reader's interpretation of fictional events. When fictional narrators reflect on life, the subjective and selective nature of memory is often emphasized in subtle ways, allowing us to conclude that they may be deluding themselves. Sometimes they may appear unreliable or even untrustworthy, as their retrospective evaluation of significant events as turning points differs from our understanding of what 'really' happened in the fictional world. The following examples show how scripted Brexit dramas can make use of this discrepancy between a character's self-fashioning and the viewer's judgment.

4 Retrospective worldmaking: How *The Guardian* puts the referendum on stage (and screen)

In the aftermath of the British referendum *The Guardian*, the leading newspaper featuring the Remain campaign (see Buckledee 2018, 4), commissioned nine British playwrights to produce short dramatic monologues that engage with the individual worldviews of voters. The short scripts were filmed and made available online.[8] *The Guardian*, renowned for its in-depth journalism, thus became actively engaged in the cultural work which, in Turner's model, follows the initial breach and crisis. By "giving voice to a divided Britain through new dramas" (the aim of the project as stated on the website), *The Guardian* can be said to initiate redressive action. Below I will focus on four of the nine "Brexit shorts" that portray an English upper-middle-class woman, a working-class

---

[8] See https://www.theguardian.com/stage/series/brexit-shorts (8 December 2018).

internet 'troll', a second-generation immigrant and a Welsh farmer, all of whom, as is made clear implicitly or explicitly, voted Leave. Tellingly, these plays make use of unreliable narration, albeit in different ways.

David Hare's *Time to Leave* (2017) tells the story of Eleanor Shaw ("in her 50s, well-spoken, Home Counties") from Winchester, who voted leave "like everyone else she knows." We follow her through her well-maintained garden and listen to her wondering "why it hasn't worked": "I don't understand why I don't feel better. Of course I didn't believe them – nobody did – when they said people would take back control. We're not that stupid." She goes on to mention how the local community was deceived on two different occasions, when waste collection was reduced to a two-weekly service, and when the local hospital closed against the (apparent) will of the majority. In the classical fashion of an unreliable narrator she keeps contradicting herself, complaining first that the Common Market "was bound to fail once the Mediterraneans flocked in," before distancing herself from racism: "I don't mind the BBC calling people who voted like me racist, because I know it isn't true."

As such lip-service is typical of right-wing conservatives, such statements also serve as an instruction on how to 'read' her character. Hare portrays a person whose worldview is best expressed in clichés: "If you can, find a gardener who doesn't want to be paid in cash, I can't. And don't even try to get a man up a ladder without stuffing his mouth with gold", and stereotypes: "Good fences make good neighbours". In a final epiphany, she realizes that venting her anger in the referendum – "It's about the anger. It used to be the young who were angry. Now – funny – it's the old" – hasn't solved the problem. "But the other day I was in the garden, tying in the roses and suddenly I understood. From nowhere. I realised. 'Oh that's why it hasn't worked. That's why we're all so unhappy. We voted to leave Europe. But that's not what we wanted. We wanted to leave England.'"

Burn by James Graham (2017) has the longest stage directions of the four monodramas discussed here. It serves to characterize its character Carol from Mansfield (Nottinghamshire), an internet troll who enjoys spreading rumors online that set Remainers against Leavers:

> *A cluttered front room in Mansfield, Nottinghamshire. The curtains are mostly drawn so it feels like evening. Carol, early 40s, is at her computer at a table, surrounded by notepads and post-it notes, tapping away furiously. She uses a desktop computer and an Android phone interchangeably (rhythm is key here). Carol talks at a hyperactive, stream-of-consciousness pace. She sips from various cups and eats crisps.*

Talking to herself, mainly, she relaxes after work by surfing social networks and Brexit-related forums. Her self-characterization, at times unintentionally comic ("I do wish that 'troll' didn't conjure – you know, fat, ugly, festering under a bridge in the dark. I know it's dark in here, but I'm on nights this week if you must know."), revolves around a family history of 'resistance':

> My mum, she stood for the seat, round here, yonks ago, after the strike, '84. That other little "civil war". Proper mobilised her; dad a total waste o' space but she ... she was there, soup kitchens, picket lines, speeches, started reading "lit-e-ra-ture". Gran were the same, during the war, saw an opening, an opportunity, got stuck in. I'm like that ... well, I'm a warrior who's been waiting for a war. This is it. This is my time.

Of course, there is a big difference between supporting the miners' strike in 1984–1985 that eventually diminished the power of the unions, i.e. 'analog' political engagement for the common cause, and being stuck in front of a screen. Tied to her screens with a malicious grin, Carol is not motivated by a political agenda but seeks – and finds – excitement and distraction from her desolate neighborhood (shown in the establishing shot). Poetic justice calls when one of her posts makes a man assault a woman – in real life. The final stage direction shows how reality sets in:

> Carol panics, moving from window to window on screen...
> Carol starts to disconnect everything she can find – her computer, yanking the internet cable out, turning off her iPad, even turning off the lights...
> She sits there, quietly for a moment, catching her breath in the semi-darkness...
> Cut to black.

In a similarly didactic vein, Meera Syal, acting her own character Priti in the play *Just a T-shirt* (2017), portrays a second-generation immigrant who is being interviewed at a police station. She introduces herself, talking about politics and her Sikh father first:

> How did I vote? I don't see what that's got to... (*Beat*) If I have to ... well I voted leave, like everyone else I know. Except for Pavel next door, obviously ... I mean he calls himself Paul but we all knew he was Polish ... like my dad telling everyone to call him Bob when he first arrived ... cos who's going to hire a bloke called Balwinder? I said dad, wasn't your turban a bit of a giveaway?

She then recalls how she was spat at by a Nazi on the street, and when Pavel stepped in to help her he was assaulted and hurt so badly that he was taken into intensive care. The assailant's T-shirt had a slogan on it: "Yes we won! Now send them all back!" At this point – long after the viewer – she realizes that people like her have contributed to the rise of racism and xenophobia.

The final play I am going to discuss here is *The Pines* (2017), the straightforward narrative of a Welsh farmer. The language (Welsh, with subtitles) emphasizes the pluralism inherent in British society. Gary Owen's unnamed dairy farmer "is sick of being ridiculed for voting leave when he is subsidising everyone, including the Londoner who has gentrified the local café." We first encounter him doing paperwork in the small office space in his farmhouse (an allusion to EU bureaucracy). The ambient sounds (cows, a machine) emphasize farm life. He faces the camera, gets up, buttons his overall, steps out and starts talking to an invisible interviewer, complaining about the fact that low milk prices are an indirect subsidy for consumers, while the producers are not compensated fittingly:

> I was thinking a lot about subsidy before the vote. The supermarkets pay 24p a litre for milk. But it costs 32p to produce a litre of milk. So if I work a 10-hour day – and I do, at least – for the last two and a half hours of the day, I'm working for free. So the supermarkets, the little shops, the restaurants and every person in this country who drinks milk – they all get subsidised. By me.

His next issue is the way an English middle-class woman, who after selling her flat in Clapham buys "Cefn Hirgoed," a cottage that his grandmother used to live in, and opens a café, now renamed "The Pines" ("Cos it's easier to say, I suppose."). Instead of making a meaningful contribution to the local community (symbolized by the fact that she doesn't buy his milk, which she finds too expensive, despite driving a "massive car"), she turns out to be an environmentalist who – he admits – buys eggs, but nothing else: "And they say – you've got to diversify! Try selling directly, keep more of the money for yourself. Well, we do. Sell fruit in the summer, we sell eggs. The little café down the road, the Pines, buys a lot of eggs from us, to be fair."

In his monologue he acknowledges three times that he might be treating the woman unfairly – i.e. the reference to the eggs, "to be fair" – and when he insinuates that she buys her milk at the local supermarket: "I like to think she went straight to Tesco to buy a job lot of cheap milk just to spite me. But probably not." But where else would she buy it, if local produce is too expensive for her, despite the fact that "she's done pretty well, the place is always full"? Despite his admission that "she's not a spiteful woman" (the third qualification of his otherwise rather negative characterization), his speech implies envy beneath the frustration. After all, if an outsider can turn his grandmother's cottage into a thriving café, why didn't he (or someone else from the community) try this before? This reading is supported by his final comment, which hardly hides his satisfaction after the referendum, when he enjoys the sensation of revenge: "Went into the Pines the day after the vote, to deliver my eggs. She was staring at her iPad saying – it just doesn't feel like my country any more. And I couldn't help but think – now you know how we feel."

What Owen shows us, then, is the archetypal conflict between city and country, newcomers and locals, outsiders and insiders, but with a twist: While at first we may sympathize with a farmer who has reasons to complain (milk prices are really low and encourage agricultural industrialization over traditional farming), the way he contradicts himself (she buys his eggs, after all, and lots of them) and his somewhat aggressive attitude, which suggests that he's not the most welcoming person to talk to, let us question his trustworthiness: has he really tried – and failed – to talk to her? Isn't a busy café good for the local community (the woman might actually employ somebody from the village)? Is a cottage-turned-café the kind of business that will make you rich? While one can certainly understand his frustration with low prices and bureaucracy, the farmer's final statement also reveals a xenophobic, chauvinist tendency: the Welsh countryside belongs to his close-knit community and outsiders are not welcome. Through this final twist, Owen's farmer joins the ranks of unreliable Brexiteers.

Despite the fact that these four playwrights have created very different characters with very different stories and reasons for voting 'Leave', their dramatic monologues all make use of unreliable narration. The unreliability of these storytellers reveals different character traits, namely anger (Eleanor), malice (Carol), naïvety (Priti), and envy (the Welsh farmer), and thus calls for different viewer responses: Empathy with someone who has realized that she has made a mistake (Carol and Priti), the confirmation of the old wisdom that income and social status alone won't save you from unhappiness (Eleanor) and, finally, the feeling that the unnamed Welsh farmer revels in his new neighbor's distress while he is deeply embittered himself – the script's open ending and Steffan Rhodri's brilliantly ambivalent performance allow for different readings. Yet all these characters share one common trait: the leave vote they seek to justify is motivated by psychological factors beyond their conscious control; speaking to the camera, the three female characters start reflecting on their behavior, beliefs and attitudes and gain new, sobering insights in a final twist or epiphany: "I wanted to leave England" (whatever this means) (Eleanor), "I am not a warrior but a fool" (Carol) and "I am Pavel" (Priti). Only the Welsh farmer has no regrets: "serves you right" he seems to think, complacent in his attitude – his grudges are deeper and older.

What are the intended effects of these monologues? Which audiences did *The Guardian* and the playwrights seek to address? One viewer comments on *Time to Leave*: "The point of the play is to upsmug guardian readers. Not something they actually need, imo." He or she might indeed be right. Real Brexiteers won't be persuaded to change their minds but might even feel misrepresented, belittled or patronized. These Brexit shorts appear to be, first and foremost, a Remain attempt to understand Leave. But that is no mean feat, considering that in order to bridge a gap someone has to start building bridges.

5 Prospective worldmaking: Turning points, tipping points, and points of no return in social drama

In real life we tend to mark not only past events, but also future happenings as turning points, anticipating an event's significance and discussing its possible consequence(s) before things actually happen. In retrospect, such events may appear less eventful and be seen as non-events, as one begins to realize the greater significance of events leading up to the assumed turning point. Future events, in contrast, are often so eagerly anticipated that we imagine them as 'hyper-events' that will change everything. This prospective quality of turning points is foregrounded in social drama, where a lot depends on decisions whose outcome is completely open. The vote in the House of Commons on 11 December 2018 is a prime example of such a 'nodal' event (i.e. an event that has the potential to generate at least two further events): everyone agrees that it will mark a turning point, but no one knows whether it will lead to Brexit, a second referendum, or Prime Minister May's resignation. There is also a possibility that 11 December will turn out to be a non-event, if the vote is delayed or has to be repeated for some reason. With the benefit of hindsight, we may also decide to reconsider its significance – after all, the next turning point is coming.

In addition to turning points, I would like to focus here on two other types of event that characterize the course of social drama: tipping points and points of no return. The former happen when a development gathers momentum so that changes no longer occur incrementally, but exponentially: the unexpected takes control.[9] We speak of the latter when we have moved too far to return safely, so the only way is forward (a famous example is the plane running out of fuel). To this technological dimension, however, a psychological dimension is added: When fighting escalates, it is often because all parties involved are afraid of losing face. Stepping back, even though it may be the reasonable

---

9 Climate change is a current example, but tipping points also have a psychological dimension.

thing to do, is no longer an option. The point of no return thus marks the phase in the escalation of a conflict when it's too late – or one *feels* it's too late – to walk away, de-escalate, disengage.

Hyper-events, i.e. eagerly awaited nodes like future turning points, tipping points and points of no return, link the formal analysis of narrative to aspects of dramatization (increasing the tellability of events) and performance. Storytellers introduce all sorts of twists, turns, and exaggerations designed to make things more interesting, meaningful, suspenseful, amazing, unbelievable, or horrifying. Some people are better at dramatizing life than others, creating gripping stories out of the most trivial occurrences through narrative performance. The ways we achieve dramatization – through pondering and careful consideration or in an improvised manner – also depend on a large number of factors, ranging from individual competence, through emotional involvement, to the discursive contexts of telling that Herman (2009) calls "situatedness".

By telling and sharing stories we not only make sense of our lives, but also join, remain part of, or distance ourselves from a 'narrative community'. This concept, first introduced by Wolfgang Müller-Funk (2008), plays a vital role in Nünning's (2010) approach: "Narrative ways of worldmaking arguably not only reflect but also partake in and shape the narrative communities and the hierarchies of norms and values that distinguish cultures from one another" (208). Shared narratives can of course also serve institution-building on a much larger scale. While Benedict Anderson (1991) has pointed out that nations are 'imagined communities', we're only beginning to understand the crucial role of stories in developing – and disrupting – such mental images and worlds.

Brexit is a rare example of an emergent super-event, a seemingly endless sequence of events that combine all the qualities of turning points, tipping points and points of no return that allow narratologists to study social drama as a clash of narrative perspectives. On the one hand, competing stories 'from below' struggle for attention and demand recognition of individual experiences, reminding us that Brexit is also the result of millions of one-issue voters venting their anger and other emotions. On the other hand, leading politicians exploit the power of narrative propaganda to redefine Britain's imagined identity 'from above,' conjuring up images of a Shakespearean "vassal state" (Boris Johnson, Jacob Rees-Mogg).[10] In this process, the unexpected looms large: Brexit was, as Paul J. J. Welfen (2017) has argued, an unforeseen accident; now, hardline Brexiteers find themselves united with Remainers over their rejection of May's deal.

---

[10] See Poole (2018) and The Telegraph (2018).

If the rhetoric of social drama involves narratives as ways of worldmaking (Nünning 2010), and if narrative in performance means stories about the future in conflict with other stories about alternative futures, a narratology of social drama needs to abandon an old premise of narrative theory, namely the assumption that storytelling is always a retrospective activity. This is, for instance, the rhetorical definition proposed by James Phelan (2005, 18): "narrative itself can be fruitfully understood as a rhetorical act: somebody telling somebody else on some occasion and for some purpose(s) that something happened." While it seems plausible to claim that you can only tell stories about events that have already happened, social drama is at least as much about the future as it is about the past. Narrative is not only retrospection, but also promise, prophecy, prediction: somebody telling somebody else on some occasion and for some purpose(s) that something *will* happen.[11]

Stories have the capacity to link not only past events, but also future ones in appealing ways: If you vote 'Leave', there will be an additional £350 million a week for the National Health Service (NHS), money formerly transferred to Brussels.[12] Polish immigrants will be held at bay. And Britain will be great again, a sovereign nation, not a vassal state run from Brussels. After his resignation, Jo Johnson recently criticized his brother's false promises in the months leading up to the referendum: "In the campaign there were undoubtedly promises made that have shown to be undeliverable. No-one can dispute that. It was a false prospectus. It was a fantasy set of promises that have been shown up for what they were."[13] In the right narrative, false promises create worlds that seem so much more appealing than reality that people forget we're not living in fiction.

Stories also have the potential to construct future turning points, tipping points and points of no return: "[E]very 'now' contains a multitude of possible continuations" (Bode and Dietrich 2013, 1). This is obvious when we're observing social drama as it is still unfolding, because we, the affected observers, cannot possibly know the eventual outcome. With the benefit, or rather, the

---

11 These purposes are not necessarily noble: narrative is a valuable propaganda tool, as Nünning (2010) points out.
12 As James Forsyth and Fraser Nelson point out in an article in *The Spectator*, this promise may be kept and broken at the same time: "Theresa May plans to give the NHS a present, ahead of its 70th birthday in July – a settlement of 3 percent extra a year, which would mean that by the next election NHS spending would be £350 million a week more than it is today. This means [...] that the famous Brexit bus pledge is to be honoured – though not of course with money saved by leaving the EU." (Forsyth and Nelson 2018).
13 See BBC News (2018).

obstacle of hindsight, however, we're facing the historian's dilemma: Although we can tell many different stories about the past, we can't add different happenings to the list of actual historical events. In retrospect, the speculative nature of alternative futures is revealed. In the heat of social drama, however, speculative stories and suggestive metaphors are often preferred to laborious fact-checking and dry accounting: "When a story or a metaphor comes to be regarded as a political argument, what an irresistible argument it always seems!" (Nünning 2010, 195). People are people, especially in times of crisis.

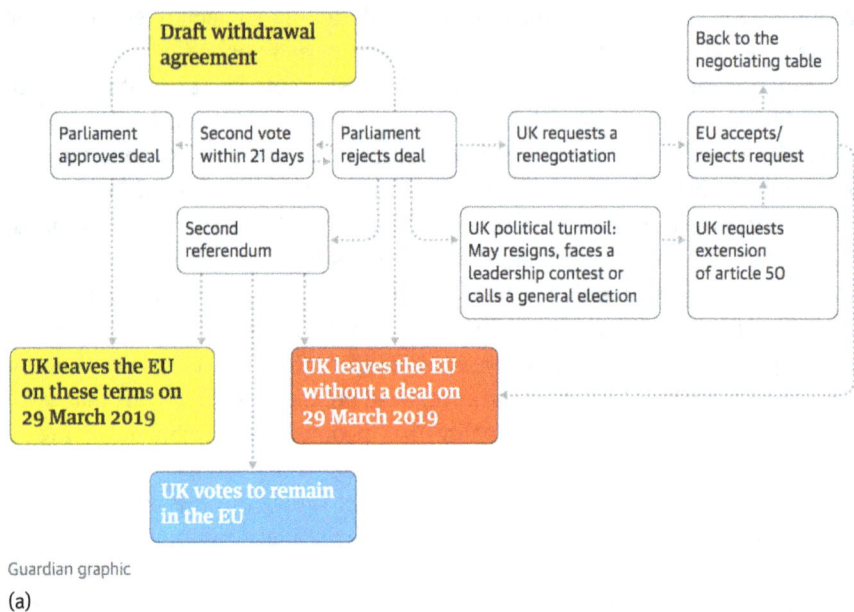

(a)

Fig. 1: Brexit nodes (a) Prospective view of events (b) Retrospective view with forking end.

Figure 1 juxtaposes two visual representations of the Brexit process. The left-hand table, published by *The Guardian*,[14] is fully prospective, illustrating the nodal nature of the draft withdrawal agreement. The right-hand one, from the BBC,[15] is a combination of simplified prospecting (the forking path) and

---

14 See https://www.theguardian.com/politics/2018/nov/16/amber-rudd-appointed-work-and-pensions-secretary.
15 See https://www.bbc.com/news/uk-politics-32810887.

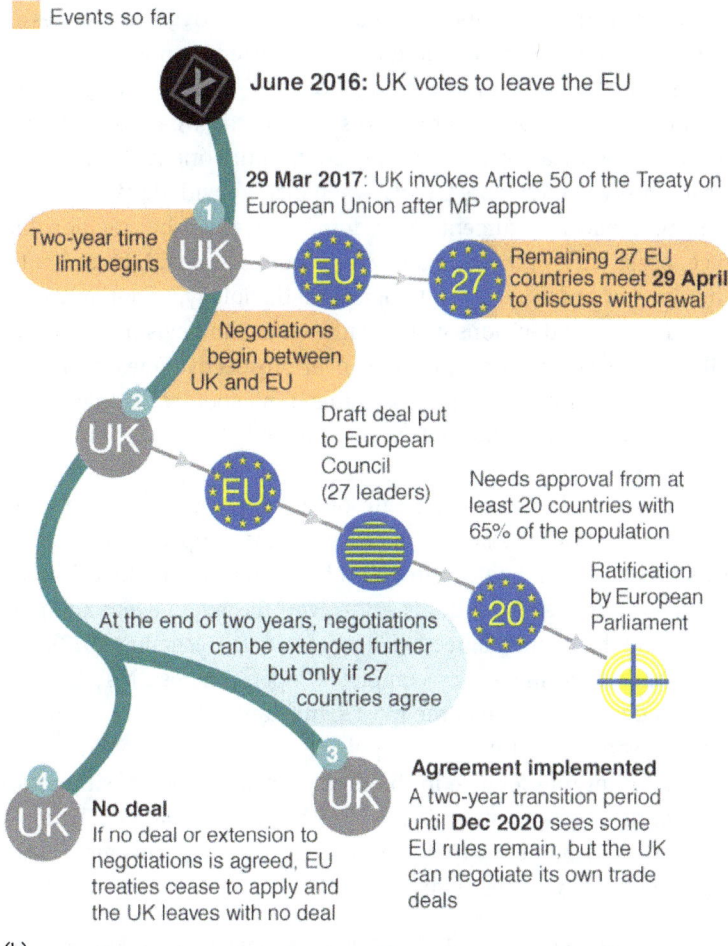

(b)

Fig. 1 (continued)

retrospective closure, as unrealized nodal options in the sequence of events leading up to the final decision have been eliminated.[16]

---

[16] The official briefing paper issued by the House of Commons library, "Brexit timeline: events leading to the UK's exit from the European Union," has no visual timeline but offers a comprehensive list of past events as well as a "future timetable." Interestingly, the crucial December vote is missing here – apparently by the time of publication, on

By the time this book goes on sale, both diagrams will have been superseded and can be historicized accordingly. After a heated debate, Parliament will (probably) have made a decision that may then have triggered a series of subsequent decisions and events. Should one really waste ink considering such developments that are the stuff of newspapers but will appear strangely outdated even before this text goes to press? Yes and no, as what concerns me here is not the actual political events, but the nodal, future-oriented worldmaking that one can observe much more clearly when dealing with developing stories. My final theoretical argument, therefore, concerns the relationship between choice, possibility, and contingency in narrative drama. Like generally accepted definitions of narrative, narratological methodology, commonly concerned with the analysis of decisions made, paths taken, and closure achieved, tends to privilege retrospective theory designs over prospective ones. Bode and Dietrich's (2013, 1) pioneering work addresses this blind spot by distinguishing between (retrospective) events and nodes, i.e. situations "that allow for more than one continuation".

The draft withdrawal agreement, a result of lengthy negotiations between London and Brussels is a prime example of nodality. It is a super-node in that it not only allows for more than one continuation but also prompts rhetorical action from all sides, intended to influence the way the super-event unfolds. While place and time have been agreed (Westminster, 11 December 2018), the outcome at the time of writing seems completely open. Theresa May has described the upcoming vote as "one of the most significant votes that parliament has held for many years" – a future turning point.

Trump, in his recent interference in the Brexit debate, dabbles with possible futures in a more enigmatic manner. A report by *The Guardian* on Trump's reaction to the Brussels agreement that was reached on 25 November 2018 shows how possible futures are implied:

> Trump was speaking to reporters outside the White House when he was asked about the deal May struck with the EU's other 27 heads of state and government on Sunday. "Sounds like a great deal for the EU," the president said. "I think *we have to take a look at, seriously, whether or not the UK is allowed to trade*. Because, you know, right now, if you look at the deal, *they may not be able to trade with us* . . . I don't think that the prime minister meant that. And, *hopefully, she'll be able to do something about that*. (Emphases mine)[17]

November 7, 2018, this upcoming hyper-event had not yet been considered a significant turning point. See https://researchbriefings.parliament.uk/ResearchBriefing/Summary/CBP-7960#fullreport.

17 See Borger et al. (2018).

The first two sentences are a simple story linking three events (a press conference, a question and an answer) in a chronological manner. But then, in the remaining sentences, the seemingly boring story takes an interesting turn. We have two references to the future (italicized – the first two instances refer to the same issue), both of which have the potential to constitute turning points – possibly even tipping points or, as far as trade with the US is concerned, points of no return – in the Brexit process. Either the UK will not be allowed to trade with the US (which may or may not deter MPs from approving May's deal with the EU, or, beyond this, have a negative influence on Britain's economic future), or May will be able to prevent such a scenario.

Considering what is at stake, we are still, in Turner's terminology, in the phase of initial crisis. More promises will have to be made (and broken), threats exchanged, and dystopian scenarios developed, before Britain is ready for redressive action – if Parliament approves May's deal, this will possibly be the beginning of phase three. On Wednesday, November 28, 2018, leading economists of the Bank of England published a new, sobering Brexit impact assessment: "Economic forecasts strike blow to Theresa May's Brexit deal: Bank and Treasury predictions showing UK would be better off within EU undermine PM's position."[18] The shadow cabinet remains split on whether Labour should back a second referendum.[19] Others will wait and see, or get ready for the next round of storytelling: "The BBC has already begun its own preliminary work on potential general election night coverage, checking the availability of a studio for either a new vote or a second referendum."[20]

While Bode and Dietrich's notion of nodality provides a narratology of social drama with an important tool that allows us to speak of events in a prospective as well as a retrospective manner, their proposal is not fully convincing. By establishing a new corpus of "future narratives," which they distinguish from "past narratives," they give weight to their claim that nodality is a structural feature of certain stories: "The node is what future narratives *have* – and other kinds of narrative do not have" (Bode and Dietrich 2013, 2; emphasis mine). Nodality as a functional hypothesis, as a *perceived* quality of narrative progression, is more context-dependent than Bode and Dietrich seem willing to admit. While reading a novel, listening to a story in everyday conversation, or watching a theater play,

---

18 See Sabbagh and Partington (2018).
19 *The Guardian*, offering "rolling coverage of the day's political developments as they happen," is set to become the main chronicler of Brexit, creating an archive of nodal events that will be an important resource for future historians (see Sparrow 2018).
20 See Stewart and Waterson (2018).

all events can function as nodes, and all nodes as events. It's simply a matter of perspective.

The nodal nature of turning points, tipping points and points of no return (which one might even describe as three distinct kinds of node, using Bode and Dietrich's advanced mathematical modeling) can be demonstrated by looking at how audiences view theater performances. The events presented on stage may have a retrospective quality in the sense that the playwright has scripted the play so that no surprise is possible. But we, the audience, may either not know the outcome (if we haven't read the play) or (if we have read the play too often) may choose to watch with the innocent curiosity of the seasoned connoisseur: like classical music enthusiasts wanting to be *surprised* by the conductor's interpretation of the score, we want to see how Hamlet's indecision causes his downfall *this time*. The events we interpret as turning points in the theater – a look, a gesture, an aside – will not coincide in every staging of *Hamlet*. Each performance tells a unique story, a new *Hamlet*, even though the script, Shakespeare's narrative, remains the same. Nodality, one might say, is created in and through performance as an act of interpretation. In this respect, a script works like a score.

Nodality is equally vital for theatrical and social drama, albeit for different reasons. On the stage it creates narrative interest, in real life it is the driving force behind narrative worldmaking: the future depends on decisions made today, and these in turn are informed by the ways we imagine the future. Theatrical performance is a genuinely nodal activity in that it seeks to suspend time and to achieve effects of transportation, i.e. make audiences forget they are watching a play. This works best when events (a kiss, a pledge, a dead body) are viewed as potential nodes, allowing the plot to develop in different directions. While playwrights, screenwriters and novelists create this illusion through careful narrative design, the real-world equivalent is the urgency with which we await hyper-events like a vote, a referendum, or an election, eager to learn whether or not nodality will have worked in our favor.

6 Conclusion

If we compare the developing story of political Brexit with the Brexit shorts, a significant difference becomes obvious: the nodal structure of daily drama leading up to the vote in the House of Commons is juxtaposed with the closure of the plays. Of course, scripted, i.e. fictional, dramatic monologues follow a different logic than the utterances, speeches and stories by politicians trying to win a majority for or against an agreement with the European Union. One might therefore object that juxtaposing literary and political discourses is methodologically flawed and somewhat misleading. Using Turner's acts of social drama, however, a different explanation is also possible. Political discourse is still in crisis mode: three days prior to the crucial vote, several alternative scenarios remain a realistic possibility – and none of them will predictably make a significant majority of 'the people' whose 'will' has set all this in motion happier than the status quo ante.

The Brexit shorts, however, try to cope with crisis by exploring the minds of political others. Resorting to the dramaturgical staple of unreliable narration, the playwrights may indeed reveal a political bias, but their works, and *The Guardian*'s initiative, are an attempt to address the knowledge gaps and false expectations exposed by the referendum results. After the Brexit shorts, *The Guardian* has continued its efforts to reunite a divided nation by launching another project, this time in the realm of non-fiction: *Stoke-on-Trent* is a series of documentaries portraying life in the "Brexit capital" in an objective, unbiased manner.

One can only hope that such redressive action will eventually lead to reintegration and thus a happy ending in this social drama, regardless of the outcome of the specifically political theater it entails. Until then, my already partly outdated and – by the time of publication, in June 2018 – fully superseded discussion of the nodal nature of upcoming events should serve as a reminder that one needs to beware the vortex of retrospective sense-making. For the record: right now, we still don't know what 'Brexit means Brexit' means – Brexit seems as incomprehensible today as on 23 June 2016, more like Beckett than Shakespeare, in fact. If that's true, we're in for a long wait.

References

Anderson, Benedict. *Imagined Communities. Reflections on the Origins and Spread of Nationalism*. London: Verso, 2006 1983.
Bal, Mieke. *Travelling Concepts in the Humanities: A Rough Guide*. Toronto: University of Toronto Press, 2002.
Bauman, Zygmunt. *Liquid Modernity*. Malden, MA: Blackwell, 2000.
BBC News. *Jo Jonson: 'Democratic Travesty' Not to have Another Brexit Vote*. https://www.bbc.com/news/uk-politics-46162114. BBC News, 10 November 2018 (8 December 2018).
Bode, Christoph, and Rainer Dietrich. *Future Narratives: Theory, Poetics, and Media-Historical Moment*. Berlin: de Gruyter, 2013.
Borger, Julian, Daniel Boffey, and Dan Sabbagh. *May's Brexit Deal Sounds Like a 'Great Deal for the EU', Says Donald Trump*. https://www.theguardian.com/us-news/2018/

nov/26/trump-brexit-deal-theresa-may-great-deal-for-eu. The Guardian, 27 November 2018 (8 December 2018).

Buckledee, Steve. *The Language of Brexit: How Britain Talked Its Way Out of the European Union*. London: Bloomsbury, 2018.

Crouch, Colin. *Post-Democracy*. Cambridge: Polity Press, 2004.

Eaglestone, Robert (ed.). *Brexit and Literature: Critical and Cultural Responses*. London: Routledge, 2018.

Forsyth, James, and Fraser Nelson. *£350 Million for the NHS: How the Brexit Bus Pledge is Coming True*. https://www.spectator.co.uk/2018/05/350-million-for-the-nhs-how-the-brexit-bus-pledge-is-coming-true. The Spectator, 26 May 2018 (8 December 2018).

Graham, James. *Burn*. https://www.theguardian.com/stage/2017/jun/26/burn-a-new-play-by-james-graham-brexit-shorts. 26 June 2017 (8 December 2018).

Hare, David. *Time to Leave*. https://www.theguardian.com/stage/2017/jun/19/time-to-leave-a-new-play-by-david-hare-brexit-shorts. 19 June 2017 (8 December 2018).

Herman, David. *Basic Elements of Narrative*. Malden, MA: Wiley-Blackwell, 2009.

Horstmann, Jan. *Theaternarratologie: Ein erzähltheoretisches Analyseverfahren für Theaterinszenierungen*. Berlin: de Gruyter, 2018.

Hühn, Peter. "Event and Eventfulness." *Handbook of Narratology: Vol. 1*. Eds. Peter Hühn, Jan Christoph Meister, John Pier, and Wolf Schmid. Berlin De Gruyter 2014. 419–434.

Hunt, Alex, and Brian Wheeler. *Brexit: All You Need to Know about the UK Leaving the EU*. https://www.bbc.com/news/uk-politics-32810887. BBC News (8 December 2018).

Jahn, Manfred. "Narrative Voice and Agency in Drama: Aspects of a Narratology of Drama." *New Literary History* 32.3 (2001): 659–679.

Müller-Funk, Wolfgang. *Die Kultur und ihre Narrative: Eine Einführung*. Second ed. Wien: Springer, 2008.

Muny, Eike. *Erzählperspektive im Drama: Ein Beitrag zur transgenerischen Narratologie*. München: iudicium, 2008.

Nünning, Ansgar. "Steps Towards a Metaphorology (and Narratology) of Crises: On the Functions of Metaphors as Figurative Knowledge and Mininarrations." *Metaphors Shaping Culture and Theory*. Eds. Herbert Grabes, Ansgar Nünning, and Sibylle Baumbach. Tübingen: Narr, 2009. 229–262.

Nünning, Ansgar. "Making Events – Making Stories – Making Worlds: Ways of Worldmaking from a Narratological Point of View." *Cultural Ways of Worldmaking: Media and Narratives*. Eds. Vera Nünning, Ansgar Nünning, and Birgit Neumann. Berlin: de Gruyter, 2010. 191–214.

Nünning, Ansgar. "'With the Benefit of Hindsight': Features and Functions of Turning Points as a Narratological Concept and as a Way of Self-Making." *Turning Points: Concepts and Narratives of Change in Literature and Other Media*. Eds. Ansgar Nünning and Kai Sicks. Berlin: de Gruyter, 2012. 31–58.

Nünning, Ansgar, and Christine Schwanecke. "The Performative Power of Unreliable Narration and Focalization in Drama and Theatre: Conceptualizing the Specificity of Dramatic Unreliability." *Unreliable Narration and Trustworthiness: Intermedial and Interdisciplinary Perspectives*. Ed. Vera Nünning. Berlin: de Gruyter, 2015. 189–219.

Nünning, Ansgar, and Roy Sommer. "Drama und Narratologie: Die Entwicklung erzähltheoretischer Modelle und Kategorien für die Dramenanalyse." *Erzähltheorie transgenerisch, intermedial, interdisziplinär*. Eds. Vera Nünning and Ansgar Nünning. Trier: WVT, 2002. 105–128.

Nünning, Ansgar, and Roy Sommer. "Die performative Kraft des Erzählens: Formen und Funktionen des Erzählens in Shakespeares Dramen." *Shakespeare Jahrbuch* 142 (2006): 124–141.
Nünning, Ansgar, and Roy Sommer. "Diegetic and Mimetic Narrativity: Some further Steps towards a Narratology of Drama." *Theorizing Narrativity*. Eds. John Pier and José Angel García Landa. Berlin: de Gruyter, 2008. 331–354.
Nünning, Ansgar, and Roy Sommer. "The Performative Power of Narrative in Drama: On the Forms and Functions of Dramatic Storytelling in Shakespeare's Plays." *Current Trends in Narratology*. Ed. Greta Olson. Berlin: de Gruyter, 2011. 200–231.
Nünning, Vera, and Jan Rupp. "Ritual and Narrative: An Introduction." *Ritual and Narrative: Theoretical Explorations and Historical Case Studies*. Eds. Vera Nünning, Jan Rupp, and Gregor Ahn. Bielefeld: transcript, 2013. 1–24.
Owen, Gary. *The Pines*. https://www.theguardian.com/stage/2017/jun/26/the-pines-a-new-play-by-gary-owen-brexit-shorts. The Guardian, 26 June 2017 (8 December 2018).
Phelan, James. *Living to Tell About it. A Rhetoric and Ethics of Character Narration*. New York, NY: Cornell University Press, 2005.
Poole, Steven. *What Is A 'Vassal State'? Jacob Rees-Mogg's Mid-Brexit Vision Explained*. https://www.theguardian.com/books/2018/feb/02/word-of-the-week-steven-poole-vassal. The Guardian, 2 February 2018 (8 December 2018).
Sabbagh, Dan, and Richard Partington. *Economic Forecasts Strike Blow to Theresa May's Brexit Deal*. https://www.theguardian.com/politics/2018/nov/28/economic-forecasts-strike-blow-to-theresa-mays-brexit-deal. The Guardian, 28 November 2018 (8 December 2018).
Schwanecke, Christine. *A Narratology and Transgeneric History of Drama: The Cultural Dynamics and Performative Power of Dramatic Narration and Narrative in British Plays from the Renaissance to the Twenty-First Century*. 2019, forthcoming.
Shakespeare, William. *Macbeth*. Ed. Sandra Clark. London: Bloomsbury Arden Shakespeare, 2015.
Smith, Zadie. *Feel Free: Essays*. London: Hamish Hamilton, 2018.
Sommer, Roy. "Drama and Narrative." *The Routledge Encyclopedia of Narrative Theory*. Eds. David Herman, Manfred Jahn, and Marie-Laure Ryan. London: Routledge, 2008 [2005]. 119–124.
Sommer, Roy. "Obama's American Narrative: A Narratological Approach to Complex Rituals." *Ritual and Narrative. Theoretical Explorations and Historical Case Studies*. Eds. Vera Nünning, Jan Rupp, and Gregor Ahn. Bielefeld: transcript, 2013. 77–99.
Sommer, Roy. "Kollektiverzählungen: Wie narrative Wirklichkeitsentwürfe gesellschaftlich wirksam werden." *Liechtenstein erzählen 1: Demokratische Momente*. Eds. Roman Banzer, Hansjörg Quaderer, and Roy Sommer. Zürich: Limmat Verlag, 2017. 213–235.
Sparrow, Andrew. *Brexit: Theresa May Says McDonnell Wants to Overturn Will of British People – As It Happened*. https://www.theguardian.com/politics/live/2018/nov/28/brexit-pmqs-may-corbyn-hammond-economic-analysis-confirms-that-leaving-eu-will-make-uk-poorer-politics-live. The Guardian, 28 November 2018 (8 December 2018).
Stewart, Heather, and Peter Walker. *Amber Rudd Returns to Theresa May's Cabinet as Work and Pensions Secretary*. https://www.theguardian.com/politics/2018/nov/16/amber-rudd-appointed-work-and-pensions-secretary. The Guardian, 16 November 2018 (8 December 2018).

Stewart, Heather, and Jim Waterson. *Brexit: Corbyn Wants TV Debate with May Before* I'm a Celebrity *Finale*. https://www.theguardian.com/politics/2018/nov/27/corbyn-wants-brexit-tv-debate-with-may-before-im-a-celebrity-finale. The Guardian, 28 November 2018 (8 December 2018).

Syal, Meera. *Just a T-shirt*. https://www.theguardian.com/stage/2017/jun/19/just-a-t-shirt-a-new-play-by-meera-syal-brexit-shorts. The Guardian, 19 June 2017 (8 December 2018).

The Telegraph. *Boris Johnson Warns UK Cannot Become 'Vassal State' of EU*. https://www.telegraph.co.uk/news/2017/12/17/boris-johnson-warns-uk-cannot-become-vassal-state-eu. The Telegraph, 17 December 2017 (8 December 2018).

Turner, Victor. *Dramas, Fields, and Metaphors: Symbolic Action in Human Society*. Ithaca: Cornell University Press, 1974.

Walker, Nigel. *Brexit Timeline: Events Leading to the UK's Exit from the European Union*. https://researchbriefings.parliament.uk/ResearchBriefing/Summary/CBP-7960#fullreport. House of Commons Library, 7 November 2018 (8 December 2018).

Weber, Alexander. *Episierung im Drama: Ein Beitrag zur transgenerischen Narratologie*. Berlin: de Gruyter, 2017.

Welfen, Paul J. J. *The Accidental Brexit: New EU and Transatlantic Perspectives*. London: Palgrave Macmillan, 2017.

Contributors

Michael Basseler is Academic Manager at the International Graduate Centre for the Study of Culture, Justus Liebig University of Giessen. His doctoral dissertation on cultural memory and trauma in the contemporary African American novel won the JLU dissertation prize in 2008. Among his research interests are narrative theories, the intersection of literary and cultural studies, and transdisciplinary perspectives in the study of culture. His second book (Habilitation) deals with the American short story from the perspective of 'literature and knowledge' (*An Organon of Life Knowledge*, Bielefeld 2019). His current project focuses on the literary and cultural dimensions of resilience-thinking.

Sibylle Baumbach is Professor of English Literatures at the University of Stuttgart. Her research interests include Early Modern English literature and culture, the aesthetics of fascination, and literary attention. She was a member of the German Young Academy and taught at the universities of Warwick, Giessen, Stanford, Mainz, and Innsbruck. Her publications include monographs on *Literature and Fascination* (2015) and *Shakespeare and the Art of Physiognomy* (2008) and (co-)edited volumes on *Regions of Culture – Regions of Identity* (2010), *A History of British Poetry* (with Birgit Neumann and Ansgar Nünning, 2015), and *Literature and Values* (with Herbert Grabes and Ansgar Nünning, 2009).

Hanne Birk is postdoc at the Department of English, American, and Celtic Studies at the University of Bonn. She studied English and German Literatures and Cultures as well as Philosophy in Germany and Canada. She wrote her dissertation on Indigenous literatures (*AlterNative Memories: Kulturspezifische Inszenierungen von Erinnerung in zeitgenössischen Romanen indigener Autor/inn/en Australiens, Kanadas und Aotearoas/Neuseelands*, 2008). Her interests led to extensive research stays in London (UK), Heraklion (Crete), Sydney (Australia) as well as in Auckland and Wellington (Aotearoa New Zealand). Both her research and teaching focus on South Pacific Literatures and Cultures, Indigenous Studies and Narratologies.

Dorothee Birke is currently Visiting Professor at the English Department at the University of Innsbruck. She wrote her dissertation at the University of Giessen (*Memory's Fragile Power*, publ. 2008), and completed her post-doctoral thesis at the University of Freiburg (*Writing the Reader*, publ. 2016). Her work has appeared in journals such as *Style, Studies in Eighteenth-Century Culture* and *Narrative* (2013: ISSN award for best contribution, together with Birte Christ). She has held fellowships at the Freiburg Institute of Advanced Studies and the Aarhus Institute for Advanced Studies. Her current research interests include chrononarratology, media-ecological perspectives on literature and political drama.

Stella Butter is Professor of English and American Literature at the University of Koblenz-Landau. She received her PhD from the University of Gießen for a study on literature as a medium of cultural self-reflexivity (*Literatur als Medium kultureller Selbstreflexion*, 2007). Her post-doctoral thesis, awarded by the University of Mannheim in 2012, concentrated on literary representations of contingency and the cultural functions that these literary scenarios fulfil (*Kontingenz und Literatur im Prozess der Modernisierung*, 2013). An overarching interest in the way processes of modernization are depicted and shaped by literature and the media also informs her current research projects on constructions of home in contemporary British and American literature as well as on biopolitics and literature.

Astrid Erll is Professor of Anglophone Literatures and Cultures at Goethe-University Frankfurt. Her research interests include memory studies, media theory, cultural narratology and transcultural studies. She wrote her dissertation on memories of World War I in German and English novels (*Gedächtnisromane*, 2003). Her introduction to memory studies (*Kollektives Gedächtnis und Erinnerungskulturen* 2005, third ed. 2017) has been translated into English (*Memory in Culture*, 2011), Chinese, Spanish, and Polish. With Ansgar Nünning, she is general editor of the series *Media and Cultural Memory* (de Gruyter, since 2004) and co-editor of *A Companion to Cultural Memory Studies* (2010).

Marion Gymnich is Professor of English Literature and Culture at the University of Bonn. She wrote her PhD thesis on notions of female identity in novels by twentieth-century women writers and completed her post-doctoral thesis (*Habilitation*) in the field of postcolonial literature at the University of Giessen. She is a principal investigator in the Cluster of Excellence "Beyond Slavery and Freedom" (funded by the German Research Foundation/DFG) and in the research project "La phraséologie du roman" (funded by the DFG and the *Agence Nationale de la Recherche*). Her research interests include feminist and postcolonial narratology, the interface between literature and linguistics, and genre theory.

Janine Hauthal is Postdoctoral Fellow of the Research Foundation – Flanders (FWO) at the Vrije Universiteit Brussel (2014–2021). Her dissertation (*Metadrama und Theatralität*, 2009) received the bi-annual award of the German Society for Contemporary Theatre and Drama in English. Her research focusses on metareference across media and genres, postdramatic theatre (texts), British 'fictions of Europe', and cultural and transgeneric narratology. Her work has been published in *Modern Drama, Journal for Postcolonial Writing,* and *English Text Construction* as well as with Brill, de Gruyter, and Routledge. Her most recent FWO-funded project is entitled "Europe in the Anglophone Settler Imagination since 1989".

Sandra Heinen is Professor of English Literature and Media Studies at the University of Wuppertal. She received her PhD at the University of Giessen with a dissertation on authorial self-fashioning during the Romantic period (*Literarische Inszenierung von Autorschaft*, 2006) and completed her post-doctoral thesis (*Habilitation*) at Goethe-University Frankfurt with a thesis on contemporary Indian English Fiction. Her other research interests include gender studies, transmedial narrative research, and adaptation studies.

Guido Isekenmeier is Assistant Professor of English Literatures at the University of Stuttgart. His dissertation dealt with television news coverage of the 2003 Iraq War ('*The Medium is the Witness*', 2009). He coordinated the research network 'Literary Visuality Studies' funded by the German Research Foundation (*Literary Visualities*, 2017, co-edited with Ronja Bodola) and is a founding member of the German John Fowles Society (*Recollecting John Fowles*, 2018, co-edited with Gerd Bayer). His research focuses on literary description, visual culture, and intertextuality/intermediality (*Interpiktorialität*, 2013, edited volume; *Intertextualität und Intermedialität*, forthcoming, co-authored with Andreas Böhn and Dominik Schrey).

Birgit Neumann is Professor of English Literature and Anglophone Studies at Heinrich-Heine-University Düsseldorf (Germany). Her research focuses on Anglophone world literatures, postcolonial studies, memory studies, ekphrasis, and ecocriticism. She has published monographs on memory in Canadian novels (2005) and on nationalist xenophobia in eighteenth-century British literature (2009). She has co-edited special issues and volumes on *Anglophone World Literatures* (with Gabriele Rippl, 2017), *Ecocriticism – Environments in Anglophone Literatures* (with Sonja

Frenzel, 2017), *Global Perspectives on European Literary Histories* (with César Dominguez, 2018) and on *New Approaches to the Anglophone Novel* (with Sibylle Baumbach, 2019). A monograph (co-authored with Gabriele Rippl) on ekphrasis in postcolonial literatures is forthcoming in 2019 from Routledge.

Jan Rupp completed his postdoctoral qualification at the University of Heidelberg and has served as an interim professor at the University of Frankfurt and the University of Giessen respectively. He is the author of *Genre and Cultural Memory in Black British Literature* (2010) and a second monograph on representations ritual in modernist *Pageant Fictions* (2016). Among his edited volumes, he has published, with Ansgar Nünning, a collection of essays on the medialization of storytelling in the contemporary novel (2011). His research interests include cultural memory studies, narrative and new media, (neo-)Victorian studies, and postcolonial literatures.

Roy Sommer is Professor of English and Director of the Center for Graduate Studies at the University of Wuppertal. He was awarded the prize for the best PhD dissertation submitted in 2001 at the University of Giessen (*Fictions of Migration*, 2001) and completed his post-doctoral thesis (*Habilitation*) there in 2005. Sommer has received scholarships and research grants from the German Science Foundation, the Federal Ministry of Education and Research, and the Volkswagen Foundation. His research interests include fictional and factual storytelling, narrative theory, and the study of reading.

Carola Surkamp is Professor of TEFL (Teaching English as a Foreign Language) at the University of Goettingen. Her main research interests include literature and film in the EFL classroom, drama in education and (inter)cultural learning. She is the co-author of various books on the use of literature and films in the foreign language classroom, among them *Englische Literatur unterrichten 1: Grundlagen und Methoden* (fourth ed. 2016; with Ansgar Nünning) and *Filme im Englischunterricht: Grundlagen, Methoden, Genres* (2011; with Roswitha Henseler and Stefan Möller). She also edited the encyclopedia *Metzler Lexikon Fremdsprachendidaktik* (second ed. 2017) and is co-editor of the journal *Der fremdsprachliche Unterricht Englisch*.

Bruno Zerweck is headmaster of the Elisabeth-von-Thüringen Gymnasium in Köln-Sülz. His research interests include cognitive and cultural narratology, TV and film theory, and the didactics of teaching English literature and culture. He wrote his dissertation (*Die Synthese aus Realismus und Experiment*, 2001) on the forms and cultural functions of the English novel of the 1980s and 1990s. With Ansgar Nünning, he has intensely worked on the theory of unreliable narration, co-editing the collection *Unreliable Narration* (1998). His essay "Historicizing Unreliable Narration" (2001), published in *Style*, represented a major contribution to a historical and cultural understanding of narrative unreliability.

www.ingramcontent.com/pod-product-compliance
Lightning Source LLC
Chambersburg PA
CBHW061932220426
43662CB00012B/1884